PUHA

J. Bradley Van Tighem

*"If you talk to the animals they will talk with you…
and you will know each other."*

—*Chief Dan George*

Dedicated to:

Kenneth "Walking Free" Bunker
Eternal Friend and Consummate Wild Man

Acknowledgments

This story has been a six-year endeavor with numerous contributions from friends and family. Any contribution, however large or small, was invaluable in helping me to complete this work. My heartfelt thanks go out especially to these individuals:

My friend and coworker Clint Thurman for many useful discussions on plot and character development early in the writing process.

My Adult School instructor Ana Manwaring for jumpstarting my writing career, providing me with many useful references on how to be a writer, and for introducing me to the rest of my writing group.

My falconry teachers, Seda Hale and Dave Vegher, for their endless patience.

My friend and coworker Robert Thunelius for reading through the story in its infancy and providing many useful insights, despite the poor formatting on his portable reading device.

My good friend Richard Antaki for lending a generous ear to my early story ideas in between our frequent dissertations on fantasy baseball.

My illustrator Zak Hennessey for his excellent portrait of Laughing Crow and his enduring patience throughout the whole cover art design process.

My editors, Lisa Christie and Naomi Long, for many painstaking hours spent pulling the knots and tangles out of my writing to make the words and story comprehensible.

My writing group: Amber-Rose Reed, Kerry Granshaw, Nathan Jackson, and Brandan Merrick. The story, the characters, and the words are infinitely more interesting thanks to your invaluable contributions.

My oldest son Jason for allowing me to read the whole story aloud to him as part of his bedtime ritual and for participating in NaNoWriMo with me.

And finally, special thanks to my wife Lyn and my sons, Jason and Aaron, for their unending love and support of this gargantuan effort.

The late 1700s. Unsettled Texas.

Part I

Hunters

Dusk was closing in on a late summer day on the Southern Plains. A small herd of painted horses stirred nervously, grunting and snorting the dusty air to clear their breathing, preparing themselves for the command to sprint. It could come at any moment. Their noses smelled not only the wooly scent of buffalo in the air but also the distant aroma of other, unfamiliar horses and the pungent, human odors of their riders. These painted war beasts were the prized possessions of the black-faced commanders who sat on their backs, stroking them with great affection and whispering calming words in their attentive ears. These hidden predators watched and waited with the patience of a snake—not driven by hunger like the prey they were hunting.

Meanwhile, a light, cool breeze blew from the northeast, delivering the thick, overpowering musk of a large buffalo herd to another small group of mounted hunters waiting nearby. The Lipan hunters had set up camp the previous night in hopes of bringing down one of the great beasts of the plains. The leader of these men was Storm Feather, one of the most skilled hunters and warriors of the Lipan band that he called family.

"We must make a quick kill before night falls upon us," said Storm Feather. "These are Nokoni lands, and we must be sure to leave quickly before they know of our presence."

As he surveyed the outlying rolling plains of tall grass, he scouted the buffalo that grazed there, and also, with great patience and care, the surrounding canyon areas for any signs of the Nokonis. His people called them "Northerners" because they came to the Southern Plains from the north. Storm Feather knew they were a hostile people, drawn to settling their disputes with violence rather than peace talk.

On previous occasions, when Storm Feather's band had many more hunters and horses, they would slay as many as ten or more of the buffalo at one time. But with fewer numbers and the presence of Northerners, he felt it best to make a single, safe kill and leave the area as quickly as possible. Storm Feather weighed the risks of hunting in the Two Rock area against what looked like an easy kill for his skilled party. Scouting the grazing land further south the previous day had not led them to the buffalo herds that they normally pursued. Storm Feather did not want to return to his people without a kill, for they sorely needed the food.

"Hopping Bird, watch closely and learn, but stay out of sight," said Storm Feather to the youngest member of the hunting party.

"Let us begin." With a nod from Storm Feather, the hunt commenced with the dispatch of two of the Lipan riders. It was their plan to stir up the herd and identify a straggling bull or cow that could easily be separated from the rest. Each of the hunters wore deerskin shirts and either deerskin leggings or loincloths, and all wore the traditional headband of the Lipans. Also, each was armed with a bow, a quiver filled with arrows, and a hunting knife. Storm Feather also carried a large spear adorned with three eagle feathers.

The two riders closed the distance between them and the buffalo herd in a few heartbeats. Soon, pandemonium broke out as the once peaceful herd of grazing buffalo exploded into a thundering stampede. The riders positioned themselves alongside the moving swell of beasts, trying to spot an old or weak member who was falling behind.

Dust sprayed in their eyes, forcing them to squint in search of targets. The perceptive riders quickly spotted an older cow that was struggling to keep up. They moved their horses between it and the rest of the herd, and swiftly separated it from the rumbling masses.

Seeing this, Storm Feather, and the two hunters waiting with him, launched into a full gallop towards the selected quarry. While the first two riders remained flanked to the left side of the cow, Storm Feather quickly approached from the right side, bow drawn.

"Move away from the herd! Keep it moving to me!" he shouted above the deafening sound of the stampeding buffalo.

Storm Feather was the most accurate with his bow and one of the only men in his band who could shoot well from the back of a horse, so it was his job to kill the buffalo. The first of his arrows struck the cow in the chest, puncturing its right lung. Wasting no time and knowing that the tired, angry animal could easily turn on him, Storm Feather delivered a second arrow to the midsection of the slowing buffalo. The bewildered cow cried out in pain as Storm Feather thrust his spear into the animal's flank, knocking it down and killing it instantly.

Storm Feather dismounted and kneeled down next to the dead beast, then thanked the Great Spirit for allowing him to take its life. His men were cheering and raising their bows victoriously.

"Carve this animal quickly. We must leave this place," commanded Storm Feather, exhilarated yet fearful that the booming noise of the herd might alert unwelcome attention. The other riders hastily dismounted and began to dress the fresh kill and prepare it for travel.

Hidden in a sheltering canyon, Hopping Bird watched the hunt intently through the cloudy dust and reacted with jubilant pride as the members of his band gathered around the fallen buffalo. He was not yet old enough to participate in the hunt and was brought along to help out with the preparations and learn from the experiences of the men. After observing many hunts like this, he hoped that Storm Feather would someday invite him to join the hunting party.

Amidst the pounding hooves and thickening dust clouds, the Lipan hunters had not noticed the group of Nokoni riders approaching them rapidly from the south. Hopping Bird was the first to see them and his jubilance quickly turned to terror.

"There are riders! Storm Feather! Riders!" He yelled as loudly as he could to alert the men of his village. But they were too busy cleaning and skinning the buffalo carcass to hear his warnings and to notice the incoming raid.

Most of the Northerners wore animal headdresses and rode horses with colorful, spotted patterns of brown, black, and reddish-brown on white. All of the men were shirtless and wore breechcloths. Each man carried a bow and either a lance or tomahawk. Each of them also carried a round shield made from thick buffalo hide—they were not hunters of buffalo on this day, but hunters of men. Their faces were painted almost entirely in black—a trademark of the militant Nokoni band. They moved towards the Lipan hunters at a tremendous pace with effortless skill. Their confidence was heightened by the two great advantages of warfare: speed and surprise.

Their leader was the largest of the attacking men and he wore a buffalo horn headdress and rode with greater swiftness than the others. His large shield was adorned with many black feathers, as was his headdress. In one fluid motion, he loaded his bow and unleashed an arrow that struck one of the buffalo hunters in the chest, knocking him off his feet.

The Lipans were disoriented by the swiftness of the attack, veiled by the onset of darkness, and they were caught in a vulnerable position away from their horses. Before the remaining four hunters could react, the Nokoni leader took down another one of them with an arrow to the shoulder. Two other Northerners launched arrows, hitting one Lipan in the leg, while the rest of the black-faced riders closed in with their lances and tomahawks at the ready.

Storm Feather wiped the buffalo blood from his hands and retaliated with a shot from his bow, which struck one of the Nokoni riders, knocking him off his horse. The other uninjured Lipan fired an arrow at the Nokoni leader, who blocked it with his shield and began to close in on him with his large battle-axe raised to the sky. Now, within a few horse strides, the undaunted leader swung his weapon violently at his attacker's head, knocking him unconscious.

Storm Feather shot at one of the raiders, but he was able to duck in time to avoid the whistling arrow. The Nokoni headman reversed his direction, rearmed his bow, and took aim at the Lipan leader, who was still facing the other marauders. In a flurry of arrow crossfire, Storm Feather was hit twice in the chest and fell to the ground, barely able to move.

The leader of the Northerners dismounted and walked over to his maimed enemy. He grabbed Storm Feather's spear and ripped off the three eagle feathers, clenching them in the palm of his hand. He lifted the large Lipan's limp body off the ground and cradled him with one powerful arm as the two men locked eyes. Then, he dipped three of his fingers into Storm Feather's bloody chest and painted lines across his blackened face. The Nokoni leader leaned in close and whispered, "The pain you feel now will be much greater in the next world." With that, he crumpled the feathers and drove his enemy's spear into the Lipan's chest.

Hopping Bird witnessed the grisly scene from his hidden spot. He watched in horror as the Northerners finished off his people with their lances and tomahawks. He felt his whole body shake and was powerless to stop it.

When the killing was over, the Nokonis dismounted to collect their scalps and mutilate the bodies of the lives they took, knowing that these disfigurements would be carried into the afterlife.

The Nokoni leader ordered some of his men to finish butchering and skinning the buffalo and to divide it into portions for each to carry back. The mixed blood of men and buffalo stained the prairie grass and soaked into the dry earth. Time was crawling closer and closer to nightfall.

The leader approached the one fallen Nokoni and directed the other men to load the lifeless body onto the man's horse for the return home, and a proper burial. Once the horses were loaded with the choice parts of the buffalo and the Lipans' weapons, the leader commanded his riders to gather up the Lipan horses and attach them by a lead to his horse.

Amidst a chorus of primal war-whoops, the Nokoni leader raised his arms to the darkening sky and yelled with a loud, booming voice: "I am Laughing Crow and this is my land!"

The Buffalo People

The line of red ants marched along the hot desert floor with a purpose that was unknown to the boy watching them. In his mind, he imagined they were embarking on an adventure into unexplored lands. He wondered what these twenty or so ants were thinking. *Are they looking for a new home? Are they hunting for insects or other ants?*

Hollow Leg was fascinated by ants because they reminded him of the people in his Lipan village: they lived in groups, they seemed to talk to each other, they guarded their homes, and they fought with other ants.

It was the fights that he loved the most, especially the great battles between the red and black ants. To him, the red ants were the Lipans and the black ants, the Spanish soldiers. It was usually the Lipan ants who won because they were better fighters and could sting the black ants. The soldiers only won if they had significantly greater numbers to overcome the powerful red warriors.

As he watched the ants march in single formation on this sunny afternoon, he envisioned the men of his village riding on horseback, in search of soldiers. Suddenly, from the opposite direction came two more Lipan ants. *Scouts!* The larger group surrounded the two scouts and examined them, like dogs sniffing each other's scent. The scouts were passing information to the leader of the Lipan ants; perhaps there was something of interest on the trail ahead.

The Lipan ants headed straight for a black anthill. "Spanish soldiers, I hope you're ready!" he said to himself, anticipating the battle that was about to ensue. Without hesitation, the Lipan ants attacked the first Spanish sentinel, pulling at its legs and mouth claws from every direction. The guard was quickly dismembered and left to die on the battlefield, as the raiding Lipans moved to the next combatant. Sensing the intrusion, black ants poured out from their hole and rushed into the fray, all of them except for one, the smallest of the black ants. This one ran away from the frenzied fighting and climbed up the stalk of a nearby plant. Hollow Leg watched with this tiny soldier as the red and black ants fought for their lives.

Suddenly, unexpectedly, *they* came. The thundering hooves of their horses and the piercing war cries of the men announced their arrival. They were clad in buffalo head-dresses—*buffalo people*—their faces painted black, the color of death. The red ants fled, vanishing into the dust. The black ants were all dead. Their bodies decayed into the earth, leaving no trace of their presence. Only the buffalo people and the people they were attacking remained.

From his hidden spot between two large boulders, he watched in horror as the buffalo people shot one arrow after another into the bodies of his white-skinned parents. The picture in his head was blurred and slow-moving. His family was helpless against the relentless charge of men on swift horses. The agonized screams of his mother were silenced by the stroke of a war club.

In the final moments, only his father was still alive. Two buffalo people dismounted. One of them pulled his father up from the ground and held him facing the other. His father was bloody, pierced by two arrows, but he did not cry out or beg for mercy. His father stared defiantly at his captor and shouted strange, muffled words. Then there was blackness, silence.

Sweaty and shaken, Hollow Leg broke free of the nightmare's grip. It always ended this way. For a few moments he didn't know where he was, until he saw the ants. The black ants were dead. The red ants lifted their lifeless bodies and carried them away. The smallest black ant was nowhere to be seen.

Hollow Leg didn't feel like watching the ants anymore. He ran back to his village as fast as his legs could take him.

"Hollow Leg, are you all right?" asked Painted Wings, his Lipan mother. "You look like you just saw a rattlesnake."

He ran to the safety of his mother's arms. She gently wiped the sweat from his face. "The buffalo people! They came in my dream again!" he said, trembling.

"Last night?" she said.

Oftentimes, he woke up in the middle of the night screaming after seeing the buffalo people. She would comfort him, staying with him if he couldn't go back to sleep. This dream, and a shadowy memory of his real mother's voice, was all he remembered of his white-skinned parents.

"No, just now, while I was watching the ants," he said, breathing hard. "I was just watching the red and black ants fight and then suddenly I was dreaming about the buffalo people. It was so real." *Now the buffalo people come to me during the day, not just at night.*

Yellow Feather, his grandfather, overheard the conversation. "Hollow Leg, it's only shadows of the past telling of things long ago. The shadows can't hurt you."

"But I've dreamed it for so long now. Will it ever go away?"

"It might stay with you for a long time. You'll outgrow the dream when you become a man." His grandfather's words soothed him.

"We'll always be here to comfort you, little one. Always know that," said his mother with another hug.

Painted Wings and Red Arrow had been loving parents for as long as Hollow Leg could remember. They didn't have any children of their own, which left him at the center of their world. They taught him the village ways and cared for him as if he were Lipan. They told him that he was very lucky to have survived the raid that killed his white-skinned parents seven winters ago, but he felt even luckier to have them as his adopted parents.

"Do you have enough dried deer meat for the trip? We have extra if you need it," said Desert Flower, looking at her older sister, Painted Wings. "Is he all right?"

"Just another bad dream. I think we have plenty, though it never seems like enough for Hollow Leg," laughed Painted Wings.

They named him Hollow Leg because he could eat more than any two children his age, despite being the skinniest child in the village. The two sisters gave him portions of their meals because he was always hungry. They said they wanted him to grow some meat on his scrawny bones and he was more than happy to oblige.

"We better pack an extra bag of food for my leg!" said the boy, joining in with his family. He was feeling better now that the excitement of the trip occupied his mind.

"Don't forget your warm leggings and shirt," his mother reminded him with a smile. "It might get cool at night."

The people of his village were preparing to go to the summer gathering of the Lipan people who lived in the desert wastelands east of the Rio Pecos—the Llano Estacado. Every year, the many Lipan villages came together and visited family and friends for a couple of days. They played games, held contests of strength and skill, danced, and performed special ceremonies for naming or rites of adulthood.

His village consisted of forty men, women, and children. Each family had its own tipi, which was framed with cottonwood, oak, or willow poles and covered with the hides from buffalo, elk, or deer. At the center of the roof was a hole to let out the smoke from the fire pit.

Painted Wings finished packing the clothes, food, cooking pots, and utensils for the trip when Red Arrow and a few of the other men arrived back home.

"How did the hunt go?" asked Painted Wings.

"We got a few rabbits and nothing else," said Hollow Leg's father, tossing his weapons to the ground, disappointed. His long, black hair clung tightly to his dirty, wet back.

"Well, we have a good supply of pinion nuts and prickly pears for the trip and can gather more on the way," she added. "We'll be fine with what we have. And we have plenty of dried buffalo meat from the summer hunt."

"Hollow Leg, you must be excited about the gathering. You'll have a new name given to you by the elders, just like the other boys in our village," said Red Arrow, as he packed his arrows for trading with the other men at the gathering. Usually the boys in their village were named before they could walk.

Hollow Leg looked wide-eyed at his father. "What do you think it will be, Father?"

Red Arrow smiled. "I don't know. I won't be part of the ceremony. Walking Free or one of the other elders will give you your name."

"Hollow Leg suits you so well. It will take me some time to get used to a new name," his mother added, smiling.

His father was a quiet man. He only spoke when he needed to, although he was always generous with his words when he talked to his son. Most of the time he was off hunting with the other men, so his family didn't see much of him. When he was home, he was usually preoccupied with making weapons: bows, arrows, and spears. There was great demand for his finely crafted weapons.

"How will they know what to name me?" Hollow Leg asked.

"Well, one of the elders will want to meet you and learn some things about you. Then, the one who is chosen to perform the ceremony will smoke a special pipe and pray to the Great Spirit asking for wisdom and guidance. There will be a giant bonfire, and he will sing and dance around it. Then the Great Spirit will create a vision of your future in his mind. From this dream, he will choose a new name for you and present it to the rest of the elders. Many believe that the strength and power of the name will predict a man's future."

"So, when you were named, the medicine man saw a red arrow in his dream?"

"Yes, that's what he told me. My name carries with it a powerful spirit and it has given me inner strength and courage at times when I've needed it most," answered Red Arrow, looking directly into the young man's eyes.

Red Arrow gently grabbed his son by the shoulder and squeezed it. Hollow Leg smelled the musky scent of rabbits on his father's hands. "I need to get the horse ready for the trip," his father added.

"Hollow Leg, can you fetch some water before your father gets back?" asked Painted Wings.

He grabbed the buffalo paunch and ran down to the creek to collect water. There were several creeks that supplied his village with clean water for drinking and bathing. Without the life-giving waters of the Rio Pecos, they could not live in this desolate, unforgiving land.

As the day was ending, Hollow Leg climbed up to his favorite rock to watch the sunset and feel closer to the Great Spirit. He loved the beautiful landscapes around his village: the large, twisted rock formations, the endless mesquite, and the winding creeks. He especially loved the sunsets. He believed that the Great Spirit painted a new one each day just for his village. For now, the Great Spirit embraced and protected him, but when the sun left the sky, he feared the buffalo people would return in his sleep. He prayed that his new name would protect him and give him courage to fight the demons in his head.

The Village
Medicine Man

Just after sunrise, the people of Hollow Leg's village began their journey southwest for the gathering. It was a nice day for travel, a little cooler than most summer days, which were usually sunny, very hot, and humid.

A string of men on horses, and women and children on foot, moved single file along a dusty path that sliced through the scattered sagebrush and mesquite. Rocky buttes encased the valley around them. The horses kicked up clouds of smoky dust as they walked. Now and then, a rabbit bolted from their path or a coyote watched them from a distance, blending in perfectly with the mottled earth. Buzzards and hawks circled above their heads as they passed through the valley.

The horses pulled pole-drags filled with supplies: mainly clothes, food, cooking implements, and hides to line their tipis. The pole-drag frames were made from cedar or oak and also served as tipi poles. There were not enough horses to carry all the supplies, so some of the village dogs were enlisted to pull loads of supplies. The remaining dogs roamed freely among the people, fulfilling valuable roles as village sentries. With their keen sense of hearing and smell, they were always first to alert the village when strangers approached, especially at night.

Walking Free, the village medicine man, traveled with Hollow Leg and his family. He spent much of his time with them since his wife died many years ago of the Spanish fever. As he stared into the vast desert landscape, his mind drifted back to times long ago when his people used to raid Pueblo villages, capturing horses and people that could be sold or traded to the Spanish as slaves to work in their silver mines. They stole horses from the Spanish too, and on occasion, the Northerners who competed with them in the horse trade. Back then, the Lipan villages were larger and more active and could supply the raiding parties with many fighting men. Walking Free often led the raids and Yellow Feather served as one of his best scouts; it was then that their lifetime friendship was forged. Now, many of the Lipan people had divided into smaller bands and only saw each other at the summer gatherings. The lust for raiding and the acquisition of more horses was much stronger in the Northerners.

"Desert Flower, keep your eye open for sotol flower stalks," reminded the old medicine man, riding his horse beside Painted Wings's sister as she walked. The flower stalks from this spiny succulent plant made some of his most potent medicines. Parts of the sotol plant were especially useful for soothing sore bones and it could also be distilled into a potent spiritual drink.

Desert Flower laughed. "Yes, I'm sure you and Yellow Feather need plenty of sotol for your aching bones!" He could fool the rest of the village into believing that sotol was used purely for medicinal purposes, but not Desert Flower. She was learning as much as she could from him about remedies, as his understudy, and as his friend. She was always willing to help him locate and gather some of the rarer plants and herbs he needed for his concoctions.

"The spirit drink of the sotol plant and the smoke of my tobacco pipe keep my mind sharp, Desert Flower," proclaimed the venerable medicine man, a statement he had made many times before. He was convinced this was the reason he and Yellow Feather had lived so long.

Walking Free always enjoyed attending the annual gatherings. It gave him a chance to visit with old friends. He also enjoyed watching the boys and men compete in the many contests of strength and skill. His aging body no longer permitted him to compete, so he watched and wagered on the outcomes with the other elders. Long ago, his wife used to tease him about gambling so much.

As he rode, Walking Free felt the pangs of hunger bite at his body. He had begun to fast in preparation for the ceremonies he would perform, one of which would be Hollow Leg's naming ceremony. Fasting cleansed the body and freed the mind, clearing a path for the Great Spirit to walk. Along with hallucinogens like the peyote plant, his mind could journey to places unseen to him before. He looked forward to Hollow Leg's ceremony with great anticipation, though with some trepidation. He hoped that the name he would give to his friend's grandson would be a strong, protective name, but he had no control over it. He was just a vessel for the Great Spirit.

The Elders Assemble

Hollow Leg's village arrived at the gathering just around dusk of the following day. From a nearly endless cluster of tipis spread out across the chaparral, the women and children emerged to welcome them and offer help in setting up their lodges.

An elder man who Walking Free recognized as Big Sky, one of the village leaders, approached him. Big Sky was a short man with a hunched posture who walked with a slight limp. Walking Free and Yellow Feather dismounted to greet their friend.

"It's good to see you again, friends," offered Big Sky looking at both Walking Free and Yellow Feather, then grasping Walking Free's shoulder with his crumpled right hand.

"Your warm greeting always makes the trip worthwhile, Big Sky," returned Walking Free, placing his right hand on the old man's shoulder too. This was a longstanding friendship that had lasted at least thirty winters. It was good to see his friend's smiling face again.

"Walking Free and Yellow Feather, we need to assemble the elders in the Spirit Lodge to discuss some recent events," implored Big Sky. "One of the boys can show you where the lodge is when you are ready."

"We will be there shortly," responded Walking Free.

The Spirit Lodge was the largest tipi at the gathering. It could easily hold twenty men, but for now, seven elders sat on the ground at the back of the lodge, facing the entrance, in a half circle. Also, Silent Thunder, a well-respected warrior from Walking Free's village, joined the council elders. The fire pit at the center of the lodge was flaming at a low level in front of them.

A thin young man entered the lodge and stood before them. Walking Free guessed that he was about fourteen, but his eyes seemed older, and troubled, as if his innocence had been poured into the earth. He was dressed only in a breechcloth.

Big Sky stood up and introduced him as Hopping Bird and told the gathering of men that he had seen the killing at Two Rock. He invited Hopping Bird to sit in front of the council as he returned to his seated position with the other elders.

"Hopping Bird, how many Northerners were there and what did they look like?" asked Big Sky.

"There were ten of them and their faces were covered in black and they wore buffalo skins on their heads. One of the men was much larger than the others. He carried a big shield with many dark feathers hanging from it and a large symbol of a flying black bird in the center. He and his men were very swift riders. They seemed to come from out of the dust. Their arrows kept firing. There was no time to warn them! I tried!" Hopping Bird was sweating as he spoke and his crossed legs began to shake. Walking Free and Yellow Feather exchanged knowing glances.

Walking Free pondered his statement for a moment as he watched the dancing shadows cast by the fire. He then spoke to the boy and the other men.

"It was Laughing Crow, the large man you described, Hopping Bird. His shield bears the symbol of the Thunder-Bird, the spirit of war. He is a fierce warrior and leader, and yes, from what you said about the black face paint, they were Nokonis. This all happened at Two Rock?"

22

"Yes," answered the young man.

"Did Our Brother not know the risks of hunting so close to Nokoni territory?" asked Walking Free. The medicine man knew not to speak the name of the leader, Storm Feather, for it was considered bad luck to use the name of the dead. As was the Lipan custom, Walking Free referred to the deceased man as "Our Brother."

"We were unable to find a buffalo herd in our normal hunting areas. We had hunted buffalo in the Two Rock area before and had scouted the area for Northerners carefully before the hunt began." The young man seemed calmer now.

"I see," replied Walking Free.

"Please return to your family now. Thank you," added Big Sky.

After Hopping Bird left, one of the elders added wood to the fire. Then, Walking Free addressed the council.

"The Nokonis have been moving further and further south, hunting the buffalo on lands that were once our lands. They have taken horses and other goods from Our Brother's people, but never bloodshed like this. And I fear that they will continue to move south and threaten the rest of our villages. This Laughing Crow is young and very bold."

Silent Thunder stood up and angrily addressed the men.

"What should we do? Are we to sit back and let the Nokonis spill Lipan blood whenever they please? They have already been sucking the life out of Our Brother's band like hungry leeches. Will my band be next? Or yours, Big Sky?"

"Our people and the Northerners have shared the Llano peaceably for many winters," said Walking Free.

"You call this peaceable?" interrupted Silent Thunder. His eyes were wild with passion and his fist was raised high into the air.

"Let him speak, Silent Thunder," insisted Big Sky, sternly. As the unspoken leader of the elders, his voice, and his wishes, rose above them all.

Walking Free stood up and began speaking with more force in his words.

"What would you do, Silent Thunder? Declare war against the Nokonis and sentence our men to certain death? While the Nokonis don't outnumber us, they are skillful warriors and have many more horses than we do. And if they were to get help from the Penatekas, we would lose many good men." The Penatekas were another band of Northerners located further east of the Nokonis.

Walking Free sat down. He felt weak and light-headed from his fast, but knew he had to remain calm and focused for his fellow elders. Pausing for a brief moment, he took a deep breath, and continued in a softer tone.

"I see that we have one of two choices. Either we do nothing and hope that this was a single killing, or we move south and concede the Two Rock area to the Northerners. In either case, with the loss sustained by Our Brother's band and the increased pressure on them by the Nokonis, it would be wise if they moved further south. They could join with another band. Also, our people should no longer hunt buffalo near the Two Rock area. It is too dangerous, and from what I know of this Laughing Crow, he will not hesitate to attack our people again if we wander near his lands."

Silence fell upon the council. Big Sky looked around to see if any others wanted to speak and then slowly rose to his feet, aided by his walking staff.

"There is much wisdom in your words, Walking Free," declared Big Sky. "Over the next couple of sleeps we should contemplate these choices carefully and pray to the Great Spirit to show us the way. It is not a decision to be taken lightly.

Let us leave now, discuss this privately, and bring it to a vote tomorrow after the sun has rested."

The men of the council nodded in agreement and returned to their families for the night. Big Sky, the last to leave along with Walking Free, limped to the center of the tipi and kicked dirt on the fire pit.

Strength and Skill

The following day, the people at the gathering awoke with a dark cloud over them, even though it was a clear and sunny morning. The news of the meeting had spread to all the people and the loss of Storm Feather and his men felt like a hard blow to the pit of their stomachs. Though the mood was somber, the elders wanted the events of the day to continue as planned in hopes that everyone's spirits would be lifted.

Hollow Leg, who was awake since sunrise, arrived back at the temporary lodge of his parents. Yellow Feather and Desert Flower were there also.

"Grandfather, I walked up to the top of that ridge and watched a crow and a red-tailed hawk chasing each other." Hollow Leg pointed to a mesa to the west of their camp. "I didn't realize that crows were so fast! The hawk kept diving to avoid the crow's attacks, but the crow stayed right on its tail. Then they flew back up into the sky and dove again into the valley below." Hollow Leg's eyes lit up with excitement as he spoke.

"Hollow Leg, let me tell you a story about the crows and the hunting birds," his grandfather began. "The Great Spirit blessed the hunting birds like the hawk, the eagle, and the owl with keen eyesight and knife-like claws. The crow was not given these gifts and complained to the Great Spirit, 'You gave the hawk powerful talons and the owl night eyes, what have you given me?' The Great Spirit answered him, 'I HAVE given you gifts! I have bestowed upon you the gift of intelligence and a loud voice that can be heard above all other birds.' The crow responded, 'But what do I do with these gifts? I cannot use them to hunt…' Again, the Great Spirit answered, 'You must learn how to use your talents.' So, armed with his wit and his loud voice, the crow became the scourge of all the hunting birds and vowed to harass and torture them relentlessly whenever he crossed paths with them."

Hollow Leg had heard the story before, but he never tired of hearing his grandfather tell stories. Desert Flower offered him some pinion nuts and dried buffalo meat, which he ate enthusiastically.

While he was relaxing with Yellow Feather, one of the boys from his village ran up to him, "Hollow Leg! Come! The running race is about to start!"

Hollow Leg sighed. "Do I have to go, Grandfather? I'll never win. I'm not a good runner."

"It doesn't matter that you win, but you should go and do your best. It's important to be involved with the other boys, so you can make new friends," said Yellow Feather. "You might not be fast and powerful like the hawk, but have cleverness and the gift of many friends like the crow."

Hollow Leg reluctantly followed his grandfather's advice and left with the boy to join the others in the race.

He hated the contests of strength and skill because he wasn't very big or very fast, but he didn't want to disappoint his family. He knew that he was different than the other boys in his village and he felt embarrassed when he wasn't good at their physical games. *Why do they make me do this? Can't they see that I'm different!*

Boys of different ages were allowed to compete. One's age determined where one started in the race. The youngest boys started at the front and the oldest at the very end, and those with in-between ages were bunched in the middle. There were twelve boys in this race.

Hollow Leg nervously took his starting spot next to six other boys who were twelve winters old. They were barefooted and shirtless and dressed in loincloths made of deerskin. There was no laughing or talking as the contestants were focused on the race. It was a contest for respect.

To his left stood Kicking Bull from his village. He was tall and slender and had large shoulders like his father, Silent Thunder, who was one of the strongest men in the village. With all these physical gifts, Kicking Bull felt he was better than the others, especially Hollow Leg who he taunted relentlessly.

Yellow Feather was given the honor of starting the race as he had done every year as long as Hollow Leg could remember. "Let's have a fair race. No bumping or tripping or else you'll sit out the rest of the contest and all contests that follow," he said.

Kicking Bull turned briefly to Hollow Leg and gave him a sneering wink, then smiled that mocking smile which Hollow Leg had seen many times before. *I just want this to be over.*

With a drop of Yellow Feather's hand, the race began. Hollow Leg started well, but soon was passed by the older boys who were more athletic than him. Before long, Kicking Bull sprinted far ahead of him too. The racers ran straight through the middle of the camp. After running halfway, Hollow Leg began to tire as it became difficult for him to breathe. His body tensed up as his chest heaved from the fatigue and soon he was barely running at all, allowing the rest of the runners to pass him easily. Despite giving it his best effort, he finished last.

Kicking Bull won the race followed by one of the oldest boys. He raised his hands in victory after he crossed the finish line and whooped and hollered in celebration. The other boys congratulated him with warm praise and by hitting him on the arm lightly with their fist.

"Good race," congratulated Hollow Leg in sincerity, struggling hard to catch his breath.

Kicking Bull reacted with his usual arrogance. "You could never keep up with me, Broken Leg! I think a tortoise could beat you in a footrace!" He laughed and abruptly walked away with his friends.

Hollow Leg felt the sting of hot tears. He turned his head to hide his shame. *I am weak, like the smallest of black ants.*

A short time later, the arrow-shooting contest began. The contestants were expected to fire four arrows at a marked area on the trunk of an old oak tree and then four more at a moving target from a closer distance. The moving target was a piece of soft pine mounted with sinew to a large willow hoop. Two of the men would roll the hoop back and forth to each other as the contestants fired their arrows at it. One stone was awarded each time a participant hit the oak tree, while two stones were awarded for hitting the moving hoop target. Right before the contest, Yellow Feather instructed the older boys to stand further away from both targets to make it more difficult.

Most of the boys hit the still target one or two times, except for Kicking Bull who hit it three times. Hollow Leg was amazed by how effortless and steady he was with his bow. His arms barely quivered and his hands hardly shook. Kicking Bull also hit the moving target twice, while most of the other boys completely missed it.

Hollow Leg was one of the last contestants. He was much more confident in his ability to shoot a bow than he had been in any of the other contests.

"Go ahead, Hollow Leg, it's your turn." His grandfather motioned for him to begin shooting at the oak tree target. A large crowd gathered around him.

He loaded up one of the blunt-tipped arrows in the dog-wood bow that Red Arrow made for him and retracted the bow carefully, using all his strength, while maintaining a steady aim. He felt like his whole body was shaking like a sapling in a windstorm, but he took a deep breath and tried to hold his body still as he focused. *Whoosh... Thwack!* The first arrow struck the target, chipping off pieces of loosened bark. Pleased with his effort and empowered by the cheers of the crowd, he couldn't contain the smile that forced its way up from his heart to his mouth. He loaded another arrow and carefully took aim. *Whoosh!* He missed, just barely. He hit the target with his last two arrows and everyone cheered and shouted his name as Yellow Feather handed him three stones. He quickly scanned the crowd for Kicking Bull, but he was nowhere to be found.

Yellow Feather led him to a flat, open area as the group of spectators followed them closely. Many of them cheered him enthusiastically for his impressive performance in the still-shooting event, and they encouraged him to do well in the next part of the contest.

Yellow Feather stopped him and smiled. "Are you ready, Hollow Leg?"

Hollow Leg nodded nervously. Two of the men stood at a distance to either side of him. One of them held the hoop target, and when Yellow Feather signaled, he rolled it to the other man, from left to right. Hollow Leg quickly loaded an arrow and tracked the target with it. *Whoosh!* His arrow missed the target on the left, kicking up a cloud of dust where it landed on the ground. *Breathe. Just remember to breathe.* The hoop was then rolled in the opposite direction. *Thwack!* His arrow thumped off the side of the target, knocking the hoop off balance so it wobbled to the ground. The spectators whooped with excitement. His next shot sailed over the target…too high.

Yellow Feather leaned in from behind Hollow Leg's back and whispered, "Just one more hit, Hollow Leg, and you'll be tied with the leader." The hoop was sent rolling from his right. He loaded and aimed carefully. This time, he held his breath the whole time as he followed the hoop. His mind was locked on the target while the sounds and movements around him faded into the background. *Whoosh... Thwack!* His arrow ripped through the left side of the target, knocking the hoop into a spin and forcing it down. The crowd cheered and slapped him on the back or shoulder as he stood staring at the fallen ring of wood. He looked back at his grandfather, who nodded and smiled with pride. Hollow Leg raised his arms to the sky, the bow still in his right hand, and yelled triumphantly to the sky so the Great Spirit and all around him could hear.

Though it was still a tie with Kicking Bull, it was a great victory for the white-skinned boy who had done so poorly in the other contests. He could not remember winning a contest like this before. It was a strange feeling for him. He wanted to freeze the moment and hold it in his palm for as long as possible. He wanted to paint his memory with every detail so he would never forget. His shiny moment was soon smudged by reality.

"The wrestling contest is next. Let us gather behind my tipi so we can begin the choosing of sticks," said Silent Thunder. As he passed Yellow Feather and Hollow Leg, he nodded to the elder and ignored the boy.

Hollow Leg shook out of his reverie. He remembered that the wrestling contest was the final event for the boys and it was his least favorite. The boys who were quick and strong dominated the wrestling matches, and his fragile, thin body was neither of these. To start, boys of similar ages selected sticks from one of the elder men, and the boys who chose sticks of the same size were opponents in the first round of contests. The object was simple: either put your opponent in an inescapable hold or force him to yell out your name as a sign of surrender.

Hollow Leg drew his stick and waited as the other six boys his age selected theirs. To his right, he saw Walking Free placing bets with the other elders. *I hope he isn't betting on me.* After all the sticks were picked, the boys walked around comparing sticks to find who their first opponent would be. His stick matched Kicking Bull's, who glared at him after they both realized they would be opponents. Hollow Leg was petrified. He was afraid to look up, knowing that Kicking Bull's stare would cover him.

Hollow Leg kept his eyes glued on the first two matches. He didn't want to look at the crowd, Yellow Feather's proud face, or Kicking Bull's hateful eyes. He wished he could run away and be alone in the wilderness, but he promised himself and his family that he would not quit.

Then the dreadful moment came.

"Hollow Leg and Kicking Bull are next!" shouted Silent Thunder.

The crowd, who had gathered around a circle of dirt to watch the previous matches, parted to let the next two contestants into the ring. Hollow Leg entered the circle reluctantly, with eyes still averting contact with his opponent. Kicking Bull walked right in, stretched his muscles, and smiled confidently at the onlookers. He once again stared down his opponent. Hollow Leg could feel the warmth of his fiery gaze. Worse, he could feel the echo of his pounding heart in his ears.

"Go!" yelled Yellow Feather.

The two wrestlers circled each other. Hollow Leg did not know how to attack, so he waited and circled, preparing to react defensively. Then, Kicking Bull lunged, grabbed his arm and leg, and slammed him down into the dirt. The dust flew into his eyes, making it difficult to keep them open. Hollow Leg was on his side as Kicking Bull pulled his arm behind his back, then dropped the full weight of his muscular body on top of him. Hollow Leg could not resist. He felt powerless and couldn't move. The pain in his arm was sudden and sharp, but he clenched his teeth to hold in a scream. All he could see were the feet of the crowd, jumping with excitement.

Kicking Bull leaned his head towards Hollow Leg's ear and snarled at him. "Say my name and I will stop the pain! Say it!"

The pain surged as Kicking Bull twisted and pulled his arm higher up his back.

"Kicking…Bull," Hollow Leg mumbled through his strained breath.

"Louder, Broken Leg!" Kicking Bull commanded. "I want everyone to hear who is the best!"

"Kicking Bull!" he yelled as loud as he could, though most of the wind had been knocked out of his chest.

"Kicking Bull is the winner!" declared Yellow Feather. Hollow Leg lifted his throbbing head and saw Silent Thunder smiling and laughing, as Walking Free and the other elders paid him for winning the bet.

Kicking Bull loosened his hold and leaned even closer to Hollow Leg's ear. "You'll never be Lipan! Never!" He grabbed the stick that Hollow Leg had chosen, snapped it in half, and threw it in the dirt.

Hollow Leg was relieved the contests were finally over, for he longed to spend some time alone. Although he spent a lot of time with his family and Walking Free, he rarely played with the other Lipan boys. When he wasn't with family, he was usually off by himself watching and studying insects or birds or animals—a passion he shared with his grandfather.

Yellow Feather was also a keen observer of nature, especially birds. Since he was too old to go hunting with the other men, he was always available to answer Hollow Leg's questions about birds and nature and to teach him skills like archery and tracking. Hollow Leg cherished his relationship with his grandfather and learned many things from him. He hoped he had not shamed him with his many failures that day.

He looked down at the dirt and saw his chosen stick from wrestling, snapped in half. This was the most difficult day of the year for Hollow Leg.

Lifted by the Spirits

Now that the contests were over, the people got together for a hearty feast of rabbit and deer stew, wild berries, prickly pears, and corn. After some music, dancing, and storytelling, which followed the meal, the women and children retired for the night. Hollow Leg said he was too excited to sleep, but while his mother rubbed his back, he fell into a deep slumber.

Once they were asleep and the darkness had set in, the men built a huge bonfire in preparation for their traditional events. They seated themselves around the fire, with the elders around the innermost circle. Big Sky stood up and addressed them.

"The council has decided that the remaining survivors of Our Brother's band will join my band. It is too dangerous living near Laughing Crow's village. Our people will stay away from the Two Rock area from this day forward. Let us relax now and enjoy our traditions."

Many of the men began smoking tobacco in their pipes, including Yellow Feather and Walking Free, as a form of relaxation and preparation for meditation and prayer. Some of the men drank mescal, an alcoholic drink made from the agave plant. Still others played drum music. It was a relaxing time of bonding for the men.

Walking Free and Yellow Feather left the others after a while to prepare for the naming ceremony. Walking Free had finished preparing his body by fasting the past two days, only drinking water. He had agreed to give Hollow Leg a proper Lipan name. He felt a name should have been given long ago when he first joined the band, but without an invitation from his father, it was not allowed. Once the request was made, Walking Free chided Red Arrow about it, jokingly, but understood his hesitation, knowing Hollow Leg's ancestry.

Yellow Feather and Walking Free stood together in a nearby tipi. Walking Free felt honored to be chosen as the seer for this ceremony. He was also glad that his friend Yellow Feather was helping him prepare, as he had done many times before. Yellow Feather painted his face in bright colors: red, yellow, and white, fitted him in a custom-tailored deerskin outfit with deerskin moccasins, and adorned him with a large bear-claw necklace. On his head, he wore a colorful headdress garnished with many eagle feathers. In his left hand was a buffalo-tooth necklace that was given to Hollow Leg as a gift from his father—one of his most treasured possessions. In most other naming ceremonies, the seer would hold the child, but on this occasion, Hollow Leg's necklace would suffice since he was older. Yellow Feather also dressed festively, yet modestly, so as not to take attention away from the seer.

Properly attired, both the men sat cross-legged in the tipi, and lit up their pipes. This time, the seer's pipe was filled not only with tobacco but with special vision medicine, prepared in advance by Walking Free. The other elders closed their eyes and began to slowly chant songs to the Great Spirit, as Walking Free inhaled the mind-altering fumes. The seer's prayers for Hollow Leg's future health and prosperity were symbolically lifted up by the smoke in the four directions: Northeast, Northwest, Southeast, and Southwest. Once under the light grasp of the medicine, the seer put his pipe down and signaled for Yellow Feather to help him to his feet.

The two men traversed slowly back to the rousing fire, where the other men were seated in silence. The only sounds were the slow, quiet beat of a solitary drum, the crackling of the fire, and the soft chants of the seer. Yellow Feather seated himself as the seer began to dance around the fire, chanting more emphatically with the rising percussion. It seemed as if Hollow Leg's necklace was dancing with him as he raised it high above his head. As the moment slowly intensified, visions of Hollow Leg's future appeared to Walking Free in brief, fleeting images, reflected by his vocal incantations.

"Desert Sunset…"

"Resting Lizard…"

"Chased Jackrabbit…"

"Brown Hawk…Two Hawks…Three Hawks!"

After a brief pause, the ritual continued:

"Snowy mountains…"

"Large pines…"

"Wolf stalking…"

"Two wolves running…"

"Many wolves!"

He slowly raised the buffalo-tooth necklace to the sky:

"Many Wolves!"

"Many Wolves!"

And in a loud, booming climax:

"MANY WOLVES!"

Strength Unseen

Just before sunrise the next morning, Walking Free approached the tipi where Hollow Leg was sleeping in search of the boy.

"Hollow Leg, wake up! Wake up and come with me!" whispered Walking Free, being careful not to wake the others. Stepping into his moccasins and rawhide leggings, a sleepy Hollow Leg pulled himself to his feet and left with the elder.

"Let's go to higher ground to talk."

Hollow Leg nodded, still drowsy. "Is this about the naming ceremony?"

"Yes," responded the medicine man.

"Is it a strong name, Walking Free?" Hollow Leg perked to attention, dowsed by his curiosity.

"Let's climb up to that ledge and I'll tell you all about it." Walking Free pointed to a rocky ledge atop a steep hillside.

Hollow Leg withheld any further questioning while the two hiked up to the ledge. A sudden fear crept into his mind. *Walking Free did not say it was a good name. Would he have told me if it was? He saw how I lost many of the contests yesterday. He saw me lose to Kicking Bull. Kicking Bull and the others will taunt me even more now. What will I do?*

They arrived at the ledge moments later.

"Sit down, Hollow Leg."

Both of them sat cross-legged, surrounded by a panoramic view of the Rio Pecos valley and facing the sun rising in the east. The darkness of the night was slowly giving way to the sun's golden radiance. A running bird was canvassing the area for waking lizards or snakes, looking over each rock carefully before moving onto the next. It was a fairly large, dark bird with a tail that flicked up and down constantly. It rarely flew, because it was such a fast runner. The running bird was one of Hollow Leg's favorite birds and he hoped seeing one here was a lucky sign.

Walking Free began to speak to him in earnest.

"Hollow Leg, I was watching you in the contests yesterday and I saw what you did not see. I know that you saw yourself losing in many of the contests and you saw others like Kicking Bull winning. It must have been very discouraging for you." Walking Free looked out over the land, not speaking for several moments, and then returned his gaze to the young boy. "But I saw a boy growing into a man. The boy wasn't Kicking Bull; it was you, Many Wolves."

"Many Wolves?" asked Hollow Leg, bewildered.

"Yes. From this day forward, your Lipan name will be Many Wolves. The name Hollow Leg has been released to the spirit world and will never be used again."

"But I don't understand. It's a very strong name…wolves are sacred to our people." *I'm not strong and I'm not brave.*

"The strength of a man is not in his arms and legs. The strength of a man is in his mind and in his heart. Courage is found not only in battle but in providing for your family and protecting those who cannot protect themselves. When we choose a leader for our village, do we choose the fastest man or the best hunter? No. We look for a man who will take care of us and make good decisions that will benefit us all. That man does not put himself above the others. He does not rule his people with force, but serves them with wisdom and kindness."

"Silent Thunder does not seem to be wise or kind."

Walking Free laughed. "Many times he appears to be hot-headed, but his intentions are good and he is very passionate about the safety of our village. Perhaps I haven't given you the best example."

Walking Free breathed deeply, pondering his thoughts.

"Let me use the wolf—an animal that is deeply revered by all Lipans—as another example. Our ancestors believed that the wolf's spirit is a kindred spirit. Wolves share a similar life to us, much closer than any other animal. They live within a social structure, a pack, much like the way we live in our village. They choose a leader to make decisions for the pack. This wolf is not necessarily the strongest, but the most confident and dependable, the one who will always put the needs of the pack ahead of his own. He's not prone to make hasty, misguided decisions or to mistreat other members of the pack, otherwise he would endanger them all. There is much to admire in our brothers, the wolves."

Many Wolves had never realized the intense similarities between wolves and man. Still, he had burning questions.

"Walking Free, what did you see in the vision? Can you tell me?"

"Yes, Many Wolves. I saw many places: deserts sprinkled with mesquite and cacti, green meadows surrounded by snow-covered mountains, and rolling hills of grassy plains. For most visions, I see just one distinct landscape, but with you, I saw many. This makes me believe that you will travel to many different places in your lifetime and feel at home in each. I saw rabbits, deer, and elk as if through the eyes of a stalking hunter. I also saw various birds on the wing, like crows and owls. But the one bird I remember most was a brown hawk with a black-and-white tail that we call the wolf hawk."

"That sounds familiar. I think I've seen them before. Why are they called that?"

Many Wolves recalled seeing a nest with a pair of birds that looked like that near the village. He never knew they were called wolf hawks.

"We call them wolf hawks because, like wolves, they live in social groups and hunt in packs. They mostly live in the desert areas, but we have seen them on the plains during their breeding season."

Walking Free paused, and then entered his mind as if in a trance, closing his eyes.

"Finally, the vision ended with the most powerful image of all. I was moving rapidly, as if darting like a running bird or riding a swift horse. I could not tell which it was. Though the landscape was blurred all around me, I could clearly see wolves running on either side of me. We were moving together as members of one pack. Every so often one of the wolves would turn his head to look at me, as if he knew me, as if I was his brother."

Walking Free stopped and opened his wise eyes. For a few moments, there was silence as the two friends sat together. The moment was frozen in time for Many Wolves, who felt dazed by the force of it. Walking Free's visionary words and the radiant beauty of the morning sun, fully raised now and warm on his face, was overwhelming. *What does it all mean?*

Walking Free looked directly at him and continued.

"Many Wolves, you have a good heart and patience and intelligence. You treat your family and friends with great respect. You control your anger when others insult you, while Kicking Bull does not. These are all traits of a strong man, a leader. You also have many great talents and gifts. You study the birds of the air, the lizards and snakes, the insects to learn their ways. Your bond with animals is very, very strong. This bond will serve you well in life. Embrace this gift and nurture it."

Many Wolves was amazed that this wise man could see all this in him. Humbled by the praise, he averted his teary eyes from the revered medicine man.

"I also believe you have a future outside of our village, outside of the Lipan world. But it's your journey to make and your future to uncover. The fact that your skin is white, and not dark like the Lipans, might allow you to make friends with those who are enemies of our people."

Many Wolves did not understand how being white-skinned would help him. He always thought of it as a curse. For now, he just wanted to try to remember Walking Free's words, even if he didn't know their true meaning.

"Continue to learn from the people around you. Learn about medicines from Desert Flower. Learn to track animals from your grandfather, who is one of the greatest trackers I know. Learn to use bows and spears and to ride horses well. Honing these skills will make you a successful hunter and a great protector of your village. Don't be concerned with your body strength, you are still young. Your body will grow into your spirit. And remember, Many Wolves, true strength is in the heart and in the mind."

Soul Stealer

With its giant mouth, the Rio Pecos consumed the rainfall and snowmelt from the mountains in the north and deposited it as salty, clouded excrement to the Rio Bravo in the south. Winding its way through miles and miles of desolate, unforgiving wilderness, its thick, muscular body created a treacherous obstacle for man and beast alike. Most who dared to cross were swallowed whole by a massive force of slippery muscle only to be regurgitated as bony refuse downstream—a haunting reminder to the living.

The river divided the Mexicans, Pueblos, and Spaniards in the west from the plains people and their buffalo in the east. Its bending, free-formed shape defined the western boundary of the Nokoni and Penateka lands. The protection it provided was more secure than the strongest walls of any white man's fort.

Unlike manmade barriers, the river breathed and lived, which created a small weakness in its otherwise impenetrable defense. Every year when the leaves began to fall, its huge body receded in preparation for its winter sleep, exposing its underbelly for a brief time, until the winter rains and snowfall would rouse it once again, filling its girth. The Rio Pecos was most narrow at Horsehead Crossing. It was from here that the Nokonis launched their raids on the Mexican haciendas to the south and the Spanish and Pueblo settlements to the northwest. Like bees driven to nourish the hive, the Nokonis rode out each fall from Horsehead Crossing in search of their precious nectar, the horse.

At a camp west of this well-traveled passage, Laughing Crow's war party of forty Nokoni riders received word from their scouts that a small group of Mexican vaqueros had stolen as many as thirty horses from a Spanish village the day before. The vaqueros had ridden south through the desert wasteland with the horses and were setting up camp near an offshoot of the Rio Bravo.

"How many men do they have and what weapons?" asked Laughing Crow, surrounded by his band's best warriors.

"About twenty men. Most have French long guns and others have lances," said the Nokoni scout, who had just returned from a closer look at the vaquero camp. "Right now they are singing and laughing and drinking the Mexican firewater."

Laughing Crow calculated that this would be an easy victory if his tactics were properly executed. The Mexicans with lances could not touch the swift Nokoni riders, and the ones with long guns could fire off a single shot at most, before his men would close in on them and finish them off. His mind continued to race forward. Forty of us and twenty of them, slowed by the firewater, he thought. Thirty horses and easy scalps to take from these weak thieves!

"Crooked Twig, should we attack now or wait until nightfall?" asked Laughing Crow, directing his question to the elderly man. Crooked Twig, the leader of the Nokoni band, had been listening in on the conversation. He wore a long gray braid, and the deep lines on his leathery face seemed to mark the many battles of his life. He had chosen Laughing Crow to lead the war party because of the young warrior's proven skill and aggressive tactics on the battlefield. He once told Laughing Crow that he reminded him of himself when he was young and his skin was smooth.

"We will attack now," responded Crooked Twig. "With the firewater in their bellies they will be easier to kill."

Laughing Crow would have preferred to attack with the moon on his shoulder, not the autumn sun. One dead Nokoni warrior was one too many and the safety of nightfall was only a short time away. But, he did not want to oppose Crooked Twig's decision in front of the men and risk losing their respect.

"Riders of the Nokonis, attack them from all directions. Weave and duck to make yourselves hard to hit with their gunfire and close quickly on them when they reload. Kill the men with the long guns first and make sure no one escapes," Laughing Crow commanded. He then spun his horse around to face the enemy and raised his large shield high above his head. The men loaded arrows in their shield-bearing hands and prepared their bows, awaiting their war leader's signal.

"Let them crawl and bleed in the afterlife!" shouted Laughing Crow, leading the charge on the Mexican encampment.

Incited by the yells of their riders, the Nokoni horses sprinted towards the camp from the north, the northeast, and the northwest, reaching a full gallop in a heartbeat. Sensing the incoming danger, a few of the vaqueros, who were away from the camp, raced to their horses and rode off to the south.

Ignoring these runners, the Nokonis focused their attention on the larger group of men at the camp. The steady rumble of hooves was divided by booming explosions of sporadic gunfire. The few vaqueros who were able to discharge their guns could not hit the fast-moving Nokoni riders, who weaved skillfully between the patches of mesquite. From the cover of horse-risen dust and gunpowder smoke came a barrage of deadly arrows from the Nokoni warriors. Laughing Crow saw one vaquero drop the lead ball for his long gun and then stumble to pick it up from the dusty ground. The Mexican looked up at the rider with glassy eyes full of fear and tried to load his weapon. Amused by this weakness, Laughing Crow launched three lethal arrows at close range into the Mexican's chest. The force of his arrows was so great that the points passed completely through the man's body.

One by one, each vaquero was punctured with arrows. The screams of those who survived the ranged assault were silenced by the thrust of a lance or the crushing blow of a tomahawk. The agonizing cry of the last vaquero triggered the jubilant war-whoops of the victorious Nokonis, who dismounted and began slicing off the scalps of the men they claimed as their kills.

Laughing Crow saw that the horses that were grazing near the camp had scattered wildly in every direction, driven away by the screams and gun blasts. He quickly turned to his left and saw Crooked Twig. He had arrived at the camp just as the Nokoni riders were regrouping. The elder headman's hands were relaxed on his reins. No arrow had been fired. No lance had been removed from his saddle. *This man is no warrior! He is a coward, not a leader!*

"What shall we do now?" one of the warriors asked, looking at both Laughing Crow and Crooked Twig.

Crooked Twig looked at Laughing Crow and slowly nodded for him to respond.

"Take ten men and track down the vaqueros who ran away. The rest of you find the horses and bring them back to camp," said Laughing Crow. "I will stay here with Crooked Twig and await your return."

The exuberant men rode off, leaving Crooked Twig and Laughing Crow alone at the camp. This was exactly what Laughing Crow had wanted, what he had planned.

"I will search around the camp to see if there are any vaqueros hiding," said Laughing Crow. He had learned from experience that some men would hide when threatened by violence. Though the land around the camp was barren, there were a few clumps of mesquite that were large enough to conceal a man's presence.

His hunch was correct. As he was checking the northern area of the camp, he saw a small cloud of dust in the distance, uncovering a vaquero on foot who had hidden during the attack and was trying to escape. Laughing Crow leaned forward and dug his knees into his horse. With an arrow nocked, he approached the man swiftly. The vaquero, hearing the drumming hooves of a horse, stopped, turned, and aimed his long gun at the Nokoni attacker. Laughing Crow launched the arrow into the Mexican's chest, knocking him to the ground before his fumbling hands could pull the trigger. He dismounted and thrust his lance into the man's heart, finishing him off.

Laughing Crow tore the Mexican's shirt off his chest and spread it on his horse. Then, he lifted the dead vaquero and laid him on the shirt, the scent of firewater still oozing through his dead skin. He hoped the shirt would keep the blood off his horse. He checked to make sure the gun was loaded and then tied it to his saddle. He felt exhilarated as he rode back to camp.

When Laughing Crow arrived, Crooked Twig was waiting for him, alone, patiently sitting on his horse. Laughing Crow pulled up his horse next to his leader.

"I see you found a runner, Laughing Crow. Nothing escapes you." Crooked Twig smiled at the young warrior.

"This *coward* was hiding in the bushes," said Laughing Crow, implying that the Mexican was not the only coward. His tone was serious and hateful.

Crooked Twig stared into Laughing Crow's eyes, ringed in black war paint. It seemed as if stillness settled in the air between them, too still, as if the moment was holding its breath. Time seemed to slow down too. When Crooked Twig finally spoke, his voice was soft. "Why did you bring him back here?"

Pulling the loaded gun from his saddle, Laughing Crow snapped, "I wanted you to see the man who killed you."

"What?" Crooked Twig whispered, his face terror-stricken when he saw that the French-made weapon was pointing at him.

Laughing Crow fired the booming gun into the headman's chest, knocking him off his startled horse. Through a mist of rising smoke, he watched as the old man toiled in pain, and then Laughing Crow rode a short distance away and dumped the vaquero's body on the ground, tossing the long gun next to him. He buried the bloody shirt in a shallow hole between two mesquite bushes. *They'll never find this.* Then he rode back to where Crooked Twig lay.

He knelt beside his victim, who was spitting out blood as he gasped desperately for air. Laughing Crow moved in close to the old leader's face so he could feel the man's breath, and he began to speak in a calm voice.

"I have dreamed of this moment many times, Crooked Twig. Lately, I dream of it almost every night. While other men dream of beautiful women or heroic battles, I dream of you…and this. It's my favorite dream. I see you dying in my dream. I see your blood soak into my skin like it does now. I see your body tremble from pain like it does now. The dream always ends with me stealing your last breath, stealing your soul." Laughing Crow paused for a moment before continuing, his large black eyes penetrating the old leader's helpless stare like a thousand steel knives. "Do you know what I like most about this dream? It's knowing that I'll have the exact same dream again and again, night after night. The only sad part about killing you is that I won't have this wonderful dream again."

Laughing Crow cracked a smile as he reached for his knife and plunged it into Crooked Twig's side. The young warrior's calm expression gave way to a vengeful snarl and the grinding of teeth. The old man's body convulsed as the deliberate strokes of Laughing Crow's blade tore his insides apart. He did not want death to come too quickly; he wanted this moment to last. With a final heave, Crooked Twig breathed his last breath, releasing his soul to the new leader. For a brief instant, the wind stirred and then there was only silence as Laughing Crow stood above the lifeless body, savoring the timeless moment. He felt invigorated by the fresh air of his new world, his new life. *He was the leader of the Nokonis.*

Laughing Crow believed that the spirit of a man, his soul, left him in his last breath. If he could steal the souls of great men, he would be rewarded with *puha*, power beyond what he could get from any ritual or ceremony performed by the greatest medicine man.

While Laughing Crow was scraping off the scalp of a vaquero, mixing the blood of the enemies he killed, the rest of the Nokoni riders returned to the camp and found their slain leader. Laughing Crow showed them the dead vaquero and described how the Mexican had hidden in the brush nearby and had shot Crooked Twig with his long gun. He also explained how he had ended the leader's life to release him from his pain.

"Crooked Twig has died in battle. He will be remembered as a great leader and warrior who will be rewarded with many gifts in the afterlife," said Laughing Crow solemnly. "Let us take him home so we can honor his life and bury him near his people."

As Laughing Crow gazed in his mirror, admiring his clean, smooth face, freshly plucked of all facial hair, he recalled the events of that unforgettable day eight winters ago with great clarity. He savored the memory of that one moment when he became the undisputed leader of the Nokonis. He visited it often in his mind, and he knew he would lead the Nokoni people until the day he died gloriously in battle.

A Dark Heart
on the Plains

"**M**alone, look at those crazy lizards! It's even too hot for *them* in the shade!"

Laughing Crow could not believe that the midsummer heat arrived in early fall. A web of sweat encased his entire body. It smeared the red and white paint on his face of thirty-three winters and was dripping off his dangling earrings, adding a glisten to the beads and shells. It was forging new waterways along the scar and tattoo lines of his large, sturdy chest. It drenched the deerskin material of his dangling breechcloth.

Most of the people of his Nokoni village took care of their chores in the cool, early morning hours and were now enduring the heat as best they could. Some rested or played games in their tipis, while others waded in the brisk, refreshing water of the Rio Brazos offshoot, following the lead set by the large herd of horses that belonged to the village. In a few hours, the rocky canyon to the west would gradually throw a blanket of cooling shade over the village so the people could return to their normal work routines.

Malone laughed and teased his leader. "The great warrior Laughing Crow can kill a hundred men and survive brutal injuries, yet he can't take a little heat! Maybe you need to live with the fish in the streams!"

Malone was Laughing Crow's second-in-command and his closest and most trusted friend. He didn't like his Nokoni-given name, so he took the name of a brave white man that Laughing Crow had once tortured and killed. From shared hunts and battles, the two men had forged an unbreakable bond of friendship. Malone was a lean, muscular man with a handsome, sharp-lined face that was cut like stone. Despite his rugged looks, he had an easy way about him.

Laughing Crow smiled and returned to his spacious tipi and his beloved shade to resume his task of cleaning the Lipan scalps he had taken the day before. The flesh on the scalp was shaved away from the skin and was then stretched across a willow twig, bent into a ring, and then secured with fine sinew. Finally, the hair on the scalp was cleaned and oiled.

Shortly after, Malone stuck his head into the leader's tipi. "Laughing Crow, one of the widows of the village wishes to speak with you."

"Tell her to wait," said Laughing Crow, sighing.

He inspected one of the scalps for a while, and then finally came out into the heat.

"What do you want?" he asked, with a bothered expression. It was the widow of Prowling Coyote, the warrior who died in the *Navoonah* raid at Two Rocks a day earlier.

"Laughing Crow, you have left us nothing! My husband's horses, his weapons, and his other possessions should be our property!" accused the widow.

"You know our traditions. A warrior's favorite horse dies with him and his weapons are buried with him. He must be ready to face the afterlife."

"My husband has served as your Blood Rider for over three winters and this is how you repay his family?" The widow's voice was shaking from anger.

"What was taken by the Blood Riders belongs to the Blood Riders," said Laughing Crow, growing more impatient. The

Blood Riders were an elite group of ten of the Nokonis' finest warriors, including Malone and Laughing Crow, who was the leader. Becoming a Blood Rider was the highest rank a warrior could attain and it was the dream of every young boy in the village. The Blood Riders led the raids and received the most glory and spoils of war. They were the most prosperous men in the band, and were treated with the utmost respect. When a Blood Rider died, the possessions that weren't buried with him were distributed among the surviving members.

"If Prowling Coyote was here, you would not get away with this treachery!" yelled the widow. Her eyes darted from side to side as if to see what attention she had drawn.

"Do not dishonor us again by speaking his name!" Laughing Crow was losing his temper, nourished by the scorching heat. He wasn't sure how much more of her insolence he could tolerate. Using the name of a dead person was taboo in his village and he didn't want this widow bringing bad luck to his people. A few of the villagers were already drifting closer to see what all the shouting was about. He wanted to end this nonsense and return to his work.

"Malone, take this woman to Rosa, so that she might learn how to speak to me with respect," commanded Laughing Crow.

Rosa was a stout, Mexican woman who was captured in a raid nineteen winters ago. She was Laughing Crow's slave and the mother of his oldest son. She was the most physically intimidating of the band's women and she cherished the opportunity to use her whips on others.

"Have Rosa move this widow's camp away from the Blood Riders. I don't want her family near us any longer," added Laughing Crow.

"You can't do this to us! The elders will hear of this and they will honor my wishes!" The widow screamed as Malone led her away, kicking dirt.

The threats of the widow did not concern Laughing Crow in the least. They were quickly forgotten, like a wisp of smoke.

Laughing Crow added the cleaned scalp of Storm Feather, the *Navoonah* leader he killed, to a string of scalps that draped his tipi, the largest in the village. These were his most prized scalps, stripped from the heads of leaders he killed. He also had four poles full of scalps he had collected, spanning many raids. Each pole was set up around his tipi, in each of the four directions. His gaudy display of scalps served both as a protective talisman to ward off evil spirits and as a symbol of his elevated status.

"Water!" commanded Laughing Crow after finishing with his scalps. He was glad to be done with this tedious job. The merciless, unyielding flow of sweat clouded his vision and had made his tools much harder to handle. The heat molded the unpleasant aroma of decaying flesh into a sickening stench, much to the delight of several horseflies that were buzzing around him.

Fetching his own water was a task below him, so he ordered Sun Sparrow, who was napping in the tipi, to get it for him. She was the favorite of his five wives. She was average in height, and her body was healthy-looking, not too thin like many of the other women of the village. Her skin was smooth and unblemished, and her long black hair was always clean and oiled. Laughing Crow loved her soft-spoken nature and her bright smile. She was a prize among women. With a subservient look on her face, she roused and rushed off to get his water. She did not delay, fearing her husband's impatient temper.

"Laughing Crow, were you too harsh with the widow? She is mourning for her husband and her mind is fragile," said Malone, who had just returned.

"She should know to control her emotions," said Laughing Crow. "If she were a man, I would have whipped her myself, until her back was raw."

"Do you think she will take her grievance to the elder council?"

"Let her do as she pleases. What can they say? The elder council knows who provides the security and prosperity that they enjoy. Those crazy old buzzards feed off the scraps of power I choose to feed them!" Laughing Crow marked his words with intended disrespect. "You worry like an old woman, Malone!" he added at last, laughing loudly.

Despite his brash behavior, Laughing Crow's band thrived under his leadership. They owned a large herd of horses, with at least forty of them owned by him personally. From their strategic location on the plains, they controlled a vast spread of prime buffalo lands and could harvest buffalo whenever they needed it. Time was not wasted on hunting; his men were well-trained, efficient hunters who could be depended on to bring home surplus amounts of buffalo for their conclave of over four hundred people. It was a greater challenge finding grazing lands for the *remuda*, which forced them to find new village locations often.

"We should hunt down the rest of Storm Feather's people," said Malone, as Laughing Crow hung his scalps. "They will not have enough men to protect their village and they're only a day's ride away."

"There's not much left to take," responded the burly leader in a low, gravelly voice. "We've already taken most of their horses and we don't need any more *Navoonah* slaves in our camp. Our time would be better spent protecting our territory to the north and east where the Pawnees and Wichitas are pushing us."

Sun Sparrow returned with a tortoise shell filled with water that was fetched by one of the other wives. Laughing Crow snatched it from her and gulped down the cool water. It soothed his parched throat. Because of her status, Sun Sparrow had authority over the other wives and the family's slaves. Any task that she considered laborious, like cleaning hides or fetching creek water, was given to the "lesser" wives or to their slaves. It was the practice of Laughing Crow's band to enslave the women and children of the people they raided. For this reason, there were a large number of children with mixed blood in his band—*Navoonah*, Mexican, and Pueblo—people he considered to be inferior to the *Noomah, the people*. He took three Mexican women as wives after killing their husbands in raids, to serve him, and Sun Sparrow.

"Another!" he barked. Though Sun Sparrow ranked high among women, she was still far below the men. She poured more water from a water bag into the shell. This time he poured the water over his hair and face, feeling refreshed.

"Malone, have our scouts located any more villages south of here?"

"Not that I know of, but they're still looking," answered Malone.

Laughing Crow signaled for even more water to pour over his long, straight black hair.

"Laughing Crow, we will need to initiate a new Blood Rider. We have lost a warrior who was one of the most skilled with the bow," said Malone, deliberately avoiding the use of Prowling Coyote's name.

"I'll make arrangements for some of the younger warriors to ride with the Blood Riders, so we can evaluate their skills and courage. They will lead the charge with me when we ride on the Pawnees and Wichitas, so we can see which of them has a taste for war. And we'll see which of them survive… that is the true test." After he spoke, he glanced over at Sun Sparrow. She was just lying down to resume her nap.

"Make me some deer meat!" the leader ordered. Sun Sparrow stood quickly and hurried off to gather the food and get the fire started. A short distance away he heard her repeat his instructions to one of his other wives. He ate only freshly cooked meat—no dried meat, nuts, or berries—and he was very particular about how it was prepared. The heat didn't deter his appetite.

While the Nokoni headman waited, he pulled out his mirror and continued to groom his hair and repair his thick side braids. Most *Noomah* wore their hair long and parted in the middle. They believed that hair was an extension of the soul. The mirror was a rare item Laughing Crow had received from a French trader, in exchange for two healthy mares. It reflected his wealth and vanity.

"Malone, I hope this cursed heat doesn't last much longer. The men don't want to hunt or raid in this weather. I can't say that I blame them. Either the heat or the boredom will suck the life out of me."

The Wind Wolf

In the weeks that followed the gathering, the stagnant, humid heat of summer relented to uncharacteristically calm and cloudy weather. Brief late-afternoon thunderstorms were frequent on the Southern Plains, but this strange weather was a precursor to more animated weather heading towards Many Wolves's village.

"Many Wolves, I expect the Wind Spirit will blow through our village tonight," predicted Yellow Feather, with a raspy, smoke-infested voice. Imitating a great wind, he blew air in his grandson's face and mussed his long dark brown hair with his hand. Then he laughed.

The sound of his grandfather's scratchy laugh was sweeter to Many Wolves than any bird's song. The wheezy tones of his laugh echoed the beats of his warm, generous heart. It was the kind of unique sound that rose above all other sounds, like the howl of a wolf or the scream of a red-tailed hawk.

"Many Wolves, can you gather up the clothes and tools outside and put them in the hut? Desert Flower and I will secure the lodge so the wind doesn't blow it away," said Painted Wings.

As the cool, northern wind began to slowly build up strength, Painted Wings and Desert Flower reinforced their hut by driving the frames deeper into the ground. Using buffalo sinew, they tied extra hides tightly around the huts to hold the thatched walls and roofs in place, covering the doors as well. Once their family was safely inside, they secured the door as tight as a drum. Without a fire to keep them warm and provide light, Many Wolves's family braced themselves in the cold for the worst of the storm. The distant moon illuminated silhouettes in the darkness.

"Grandfather, why can't we start a fire?" asked Many Wolves.

Yellow Feather spoke deliberately.

"When the Wind Wolf howls, he calls to his brother, the Fire Wolf, to join him in the hunt. If the Fire Wolf is awake, he joins his brother and they attack and kill many animals, but do not eat their blackened flesh. The charred bodies from the mighty grizzly to the tiny tick are left in their path. This is why we put the Fire Wolf to sleep when his brother calls."

Yellow Feather lit his tobacco-filled pipe to share with Red Arrow, as the rest of the family, Desert Flower, Painted Wings, and Many Wolves, huddled together in the shelter. Many Wolves felt as secure as a caterpillar in its cocoon. He had experienced storms like this before, without fear. He cherished times like this when his family was free from their daily routines and he could stay up late and listen to his grandfather's stories.

"Grandfather, did you know those red and brown hawks are called wolf hawks?" asked Many Wolves, remembering the wolf hawks from the dream that Walking Free described.

"Yes, Long Drink," addressing Many Wolves by a name he had once given him after watching Many Wolves gulp down a man's share of water. "They drive the rabbits and squirrels crazy because they live and hunt in groups, like we do, and like wolves. Most winged predators hunt alone. Imagine if you were a rabbit running away from a hawk that was chasing you and—WHOOSH—out of nowhere, another hawk attacks you…and another! I think a shell-less, three-legged turtle has a better chance of surviving!" Yellow Feather chuckled. Taking another puff from his pipe, he launched into one of his stories.

"Once I saw four or five of these birds chasing the same jackrabbit across the desert floor. The first one lunged at the rabbit with his big claws, but the rabbit darted to the side and left the hawk rolling in the dirt." As he said this, Yellow Feather twisted his fingers up like claws and pounded his hand in the dirt. "Then another hawk tried to impale the rabbit with his needle-sharp talons, but it failed to land a single claw on the illusive animal. At last, the third hawk, approaching from a different angle, caught the rabbit by its powerful back legs and was dragged in the dirt like a man being dragged by a horse. But, it slowed down the rabbit just enough for the first hawk, on its second try, to grab it by the head and stake it to the ground. The rest of the birds piled on like a swarm of buzzards on a fresh carcass." His grandfather's eyes focused intently on him as he told the story.

"Sometimes I think they should be called coyote hawks because they appear clumsy and playful at times when they hunt, though they are cunning and smart. They don't appear to have the grace and power of wolves," said Yellow Feather, catching his breath after so much talking, and taking a few moments to smoke his pipe.

"There's a nest of them on the other side of the canyon that I've been watching, but I only see two adult birds," said Many Wolves. "I think there are four young hawks in the nest. I see the adult birds bring snakes and lizards and rabbits for the babies."

"It's late in the year for birds to be nesting, Long Drink. Some birds will lay more eggs later in the breeding season when the hunting is good. When those babies grow up, they'll stay with their parents to form a family group, unlike any other winged hunters I know. Like wolves and people, their chances to survive improve as a pack."

The wind picked up considerably as it whistled through the village. Many Wolves heard the sand and loose mesquite branches pelt against the walls of his shelter. He heard untied pieces of buffalo hide flap around wildly at the mercy of the howling wind. *The Wind Wolf is angrily calling to his brother.*

"Grandfather, what animal is your favorite?"

Yellow Feather laughed. "I'm not sure I have one favorite. Crows and coyotes are two that I like because they are tricksters; they use their wits to survive. Long ago I watched a crow try to crack open a nut for the longest time. It flew high up in the air with the nut in its beak and then dropped it down on a large boulder far below, trying to crack it open." Yellow Feather picked up a small rock, held up his hand, and dropped it on the ground. "The crow seemed to grow more and more frustrated with the nut, but it didn't give up until the shell finally broke. That crazy crow just wouldn't quit!" His grandfather paused to catch his breath.

"How about you, Long Drink?" Yellow Feather asked. "What is the animal that brings a smile to your heart?"

Many Wolves had to think for a moment. He had loved to watch all kinds of birds, animals, and insects.

"I haven't seen some of the animals that you have, but one of my favorites is the big-headed lizard. It's green with black-and-white stripes around its neck, and it has a HUGE head!" Many Wolves stretched his arms wide to exaggerate the head size.

"We call that one the necklace lizard because those stripes look like a necklace," added Yellow Feather, painting imaginary stripes on either side of his grandson's neck. "What do you like best about the necklace lizard?"

"I love its gigantic head! If I were a grasshopper or a beetle and I saw that big head coming after me, I'd be scared! I also love to watch them run on two legs from rock to rock. They look like little men when they run like that. I once saw one catch a lizard almost as big as itself! It grabbed the lizard by the head and shook it around like a dog when it plays with a stick. Eventually, when the lizard was dead, it swallowed it whole, starting with the head."

"Don't spare us any details!" added Painted Wings, rolling her eyes.

Many Wolves and Yellow Feather looked at each other, grinning from ear to ear.

"Painted Wings, you can't appreciate a good story! My grandson is becoming quite the storyteller," Yellow Feather squeezed Many Wolves's arm affectionately. "Good storytellers are never without friends!"

"Do you have any more good stories about animals or birds, Grandfather?"

Yellow Feather paused to think of another story, as he emptied his pipe ashes into a crevice between two rocks.

"Have I told you about Half Leg?" asked Yellow Feather.

"I don't think so," answered Many Wolves, though he had heard it many times before.

"Half Leg was a blue jay I got to know quite well. He'd love to visit us while we ate, squawking away with his loud, annoying voice: SQUAWK! SQUAWK! SQUAWK!" Yellow Feather flapped his arms when he made the bird sounds.

Many Wolves loved this part of the story, and he loved the way his grandfather used funny sounds to bring life to his stories. Yellow Feather had many crooked arrows in his quiver of tricks.

"Once I started giving him a nut or two, he always came back the following day looking for his handout," continued Yellow Feather. "Now the crazy thing about Half Leg was that he had only one leg, the other one was just a rotted old stump. But that didn't stop the little trickster from hopping around looking for scraps. He'd look at me cock-eyed, thinking I had nothing better to do than serve him a treat. One day I decided I wouldn't feed him by the fire pit where we usually ate, but see if he would come into my lodge for his treat. So, each day at about the same time, I would wait in my hut, blow a whistle, and call out his name. Half Leg! Half Leg! When he flew down and started hopping around on his one leg outside the lodge, I'd toss him a nut or two."

Many Wolves yawned. It was getting late and his grandfather's voice was very soothing.

"Day after day I did this, making him come closer and closer to me to get his nut. Finally, he was taking it straight from my hand! Imagine that! When the leaves started to fall each year, he would fly south for warmer weather, but he would always show up again when the green grass returned, until finally after about five winters, he never returned."

Though the fury of the Wind Wolf was at its climax, Many Wolves was asleep, safely nestled in his mother's loving arms.

Crows!

After two days, the wind subsided and the people of Many Wolves's village returned to their normal routines. There was much work to do. Some of the women repaired the thatching on huts that had torn free of their supports, while others gathered roots and prickly pears to replenish the food supplies. The men rode out to hunt, hoping to find buffalo grazing in the grasslands north of the village.

"Grandfather, I'm heading out to hunt some rabbits for us," Many Wolves said as he packed his hunting bow, which his father had helped him to make, and arrows into his deerskin bag, hoping to do his part to try to help his family with their food supplies.

"Any meat you can get will help, Many Wolves. The men might not be back for a few sleeps," explained his grandfather. "I expect the animals will be hungry like we are, so they shouldn't be hard to find."

With his bag slung over his shoulder, Many Wolves set out in search of rabbits towards the direction of the southern mesas, one of his favorite spots to hunt and explore. The strong winds had erased all animal tracks from the previous day; only fresh footprints remained on the smooth, sandy desert floor. *Tracking should be easier today.* The air was calm and the swirling dust had settled.

Walking along the windy paths between mesquite and sagebrush, he discovered many new rocks that had been uncovered by the wind. He found several pieces of obsidian and flint that he liked and stashed them in his bag. His father had taught him that these types of rocks could be shaped into sharp, flattened flakes by hammering on them with larger rocks. These flakes could then be fashioned into hard arrow points. He was pleased with his findings and looked forward to breaking them apart when he returned home.

On this warm humid afternoon, the animals were more active than usual. Running birds darted around, looking in bushes for lizards and snakes. Flycatcher birds floated in the air like butterflies chasing after small winged insects. Many Wolves spotted a coyote running and jumping up on all fours to try to catch a leaping rat. He had mostly seen feeding activity like this at sunrise and dusk, but the animals, like the people in his village, had been forced into their shelters by the storm. They were hungry and needed to fill their empty stomachs.

Suddenly, the unusual calm was disturbed by a loud ruckus of crows in the distance, "*Caw! Caw! Caw!*" They were very excited about finding something, Many Wolves thought. He had seen crows chasing hawks or falcons or owls, especially owls that were helpless in the blinding daylight. While other birds chased bigger birds away to protect their own nest or territory, crows seemed to enjoy chasing other birds for sport. Teasing other birds, especially larger predatory birds, was a game they relished and they spent much of their daytime perfecting this renegade pastime. Sometimes it was just one or two crows and other times more than ten, and it didn't seem to matter if their victim was perched in a tree, standing on the ground, or flying in the air.

Distracted from his hunt and his rock collecting, Many Wolves began to walk towards the direction of the sound; he recalled the story his grandfather had told him about crows and how they were blessed with intelligence and a loud voice for harassing the more powerful hunting birds.

The sound sharpened as Many Wolves approached its source and he could tell that it was more than one crow creating the noisy disruption. It was so loud he could no longer hear the sloshing of sand as it flew off his deerskin moccasins. He recognized familiar landmarks and realized that it was the same place he had watched the wolf hawks at their nest. *Where are they?* He began running towards their nest, which was built between two thick arms of a large bear cactus. His grandfather called them "bear cacti" because from a distance they looked like large bears walking on their hind legs.

Arriving at the nest, he watched as five crows frantically took turns diving down at something on the ground near the base of the cactus. Then, he spotted the first of their victims, a small bundle of feathers and down lying lifeless on the ground just a few steps to his left. The dead hawk was spotted with bloody marks all over its body where the crows had pecked at it, and the eye of the young bird had been plucked away.

Many Wolves felt a surge of emotion rush through his body as he studied the corpse of the young hawk. He was overwhelmed with the protective instincts of a parent and he began yelling at the crows. "Look what you've done! Get away from here! Get out!"

He took his bow from his deerskin bag, loaded an arrow, and in his rage fired it at one of the black marauders, but missed.

"Get out!" he yelled over and over again, and then ran towards the spot the crows were attacking. Hidden in the thick clump of sagebrush at the foot of the cactus, he recognized the outlines of two more young hawks. Getting closer, he could see their mouths gaping in fright as the hateful crows continued to launch their attacks.

Without hesitation, he dropped his bow and emptied the contents of his bag, mostly arrows and the rocks he had collected, and walked slowly towards the birds, not wanting to scare them any further. Reaching down, he cautiously grabbed the first flightless hawk securely around the shoulders and placed it in his bag, keeping his hands away from the bird's large talons. Though the bird's feet were large, they had not yet learned to walk or run with them. In the same way, he captured the second bird and carefully put it with its sibling. Meanwhile, the crows had flown to an adjacent mesquite tree a short distance away, still screaming in protest.

Then one of the crows started diving on a bush on the other side of the tree. With his bag carefully strapped around his shoulder, Many Wolves walked over to see if another hawk was there. Sure enough, a third nestling had flattened itself on the ground, just under another patch of sagebrush. The hawk's mouth was wide open and its head swiveled back and forth, tracking its attacker. As he approached, the crow withdrew from its assault and Many Wolves noticed this hawk, which was smaller than the other two, and had blood on its neck and wings. He picked up the injured bird and gently placed it in his bag.

With his free hand, he gathered the arrows he had removed from his bag, leaving the prized rocks behind, and headed back towards his village. The crows followed him for a long time, still screaming over their loss, until eventually they gave up and retreated.

As Many Wolves walked, several thoughts crossed his mind, like raindrops dousing him from all directions. *Where are the parent birds? Why aren't they protecting their babies? Has the wind blown them far away?* The young hawks were safe for now, but Many Wolves realized that if he had not been there, the crows would have torn them apart one at a time. He didn't know why he felt compelled to save the hawks. Perhaps it was because he had spent many afternoons watching them in their nest and he couldn't let them die.

It was as if the hawks were already part of his family.

A Call for Arrows

Dusk was quickly fading into darkness as Laughing Crow stood in front of his tipi with Malone.

"Laughing Crow, we just received word from our scouts. They discovered two Lipan villages to the southwest," said Malone.

"These are new villages? Why hadn't they found them before?" asked the Nokoni leader, who was reinforcing the steel tip of his lance with fresh buffalo sinew.

"These villages are far to the south. It's at least a day's ride from here."

"How many men at each village—men who can fight?" asked Laughing Crow, emphasizing the latter part of his statement.

"They are small bands. About fifteen men at one camp and twenty at the other," said Malone.

"And horses?"

"They have seen twenty or thirty at each."

"We will move on these *Navoonah* villages when the new moon arrives, no sooner," said Laughing Crow. "We have more of a threat from the Wichitas and Pawnees to the north. Each day they kill more of our buffalo and ravish our grazing lands with their horses. They must be confronted immediately; we will not allow them to barter for their actions. Then, we will confront these Lipans with fifty warriors and negotiate with them in a position of strength. As much as I hate these *Navoonah* dogs, I do not wish to shed blood with them knowing we must fight the Wichitas and Pawnees first."

"Why would we offer peace to the *Navoonah*?" asked Malone.

"These Lipans are not raiding our lands like the Wichitas and Pawnees, Malone," said Laughing Crow, pausing to take a break from repairing his weapon. "If we show them the strength of our warriors and our numbers, they will comply with our demands, and we will weaken them by taking their horses in exchange for our peace. If they remain near our lands, we can continue to take food and horses from them as payment for our mercy."

Laughing Crow considered himself a careful planner and great motivator of men. It was the raiding lifestyle that he had chosen for his people and he knew their lives and future were in his hands. The men of his village thirsted for war and it was his responsibility to quench it with a minimal loss of life. Instinctively he knew when he was pushing his men too hard and when they needed a break. He wanted Nokoni casualties to stay at a minimum. To achieve this, his Blood Riders and warriors needed to be rested and prepared for war—and it was of the utmost importance that the advantages of surprise and greater numbers were always in his favor.

"Malone, inform the men that we will ride tonight. There is enough moonlight to feed the eyes of our horses. We will take down the Wichitas before the sun rises. Have the men bring their arrows to me and I will choose who will ride with us," commanded Laughing Crow.

As Malone walked off, Laughing Crow called for one of his wives. "Sun Sparrow, bring me some wet clay and some blackberry juice. I wish to make some war paint." She rushed off to fulfill his request. He entered his tipi to wait for her return.

It was Laughing Crow's tradition to have any man who wanted to join his war party present him with one of his finest, unmarked arrows. The Blood Riders were excluded from this ritual since they were expected to attend all raids. If Laughing Crow wanted the man to join the raid, he would accept the arrow and mark a part of the man's face with war paint.

Soon, the men began to assemble in a line in front of Laughing Crow's blazing fire pit, which crackled loudly with cedar. Each man carried an arrow, and nothing else. The men were silent and respectful as they patiently waited for the Nokoni leader to approach the first one in line. This was an important moment for them. Riding into war with Laughing Crow was a great honor that earned them much respect in their village. The tension was as thick as honey.

Sun Sparrow arrived with a small bowl of blackened clay and brought it to her husband. She handed it to him without a word, and left.

Laughing Crow walked outside and handed the bowl to Malone, who stood at his right side facing the gathering of men with the flames roaring behind them. Halfway encircling the fire pit, the Blood Riders stood behind Laughing Crow and Malone with the fire between them. They were adorned with buffalo headdresses, and every Blood Rider was holding a lance and a shield. Each lance stood twice as high as the man holding it, and each large, round shield covered half the man's body.

Malone motioned for the first man to come forward. He was young, in his early twenties, and his face was familiar to Laughing Crow, though the leader could not recall his name. The young man appeared healthy and fit. He wore only a breechcloth and a buffalo-tooth necklace around his neck, taken from a buffalo he had killed. Laughing Crow looked the man deeply in the eyes, searching for a sign of weakness—weakness that could not be masked by the flame's reflection. After a brief moment, he grasped the man's right forearm with his right hand. The man reciprocated.

"May the Thunder-Bird of War grant you strength and courage," uttered the Nokoni leader, his usual blessing. Then he dipped his right hand in the bowl of blackened clay and marked the man's forehead with a single, broad stroke of war paint. The man handed his arrow to Malone, who set it on the ground to his right.

The man walked away, jubilantly uttering a celebratory war-whoop: "Yee-Yee-Yee!" His acceptance was applauded with thundering approval from the Blood Riders who yelled their war cries, stomped their feet on the dusty ground, and pounded their shields with their lances. The rest of the men in line remained silent and respectful.

In a similar way, the next man was accepted into the war party.

Then an older man approached Laughing Crow, his sagging muscles and wrinkly skin revealed his age.

Laughing Crow looked at the man with disgust.

"Laughing Crow, I know that I'm old, but I can still use a bow and ride well. I just want to hear the rumble of hooves and the cries of our warriors once more before it is my time to leave this world," the old man pleaded, finding it difficult to look into the leader's eyes.

"There is no place for beggars in our war party, old man. Your weakness would endanger us all," said Laughing Crow sternly. "Keep your arrow and do not offer it to me again or you will be beaten," he added, signaling for the man to leave immediately.

As the older man slumped away, he was jeered and laughed at mercilessly by the other men. One younger man, who was waiting his turn in line, charged at the older man, knocked him to the ground, and then kicked him several times, yelling insulting words, "How do you expect to stay on your horse, old man, when you can't even stay on your feet?" The other men laughed even louder.

71

The fourth man approached and was not offered a fore-arm shake by Laughing Crow. "Remain here and protect our families," said Laughing Crow. To some of the men he rejected, he offered encouragement like this, but to most, just silence.

The man walked off, clearly disappointed, and greeted only by silence from his peers.

A younger man now approached dressed only in a breech-cloth. His body was strong and healthy, and he carried himself with confidence.

Laughing Crow studied him and asked, "Do you have buffalo teeth or bear claws to show me that you have hunted and killed?"

"No," the young man answered in a voice that was not yet deep enough to be a man's. "But I am strong and I will prove my skills in war," he added enthusiastically.

Without much thought, Laughing Crow responded, "You must show me that you can kill a great beast before I will let you hunt men."

"Next time, I will bring you this proof," promised the young man. He thrust his chest forward as he spoke.

Laughing Crow grinned subtly as the confident young man walked away, admiring him for his courage and commitment. *You will be a warrior soon.* The other men offered him words of encouragement and slapped him affectionately on the back and arm as he walked by.

This was how the ritual proceeded until Laughing Crow had invited twenty men. From the pile of unmarked arrows, he selected three while Malone refused to take any, favoring his own arrows. The rest of them were left for the Blood Riders to distribute among themselves. Later each of them would paint their own unique mark on the shaft of these arrows, so they could easily claim their kills when the fighting was over.

"Those who have been chosen to join us, step forward," barked Malone.

The Nokoni headman addressed the war party, his low, deep voice resonating through the camp. "Prepare yourselves for war. Do not eat, so you will hunger for the flesh of your enemy. Paint your faces black, the color of death, so they know it will be you sending them to the afterlife. Decorate your horses with paint and feathers to protect them. Sharpen your lance points and shave the shafts of your arrows so that they will fly with force through your enemy's heart." He paused briefly before continuing. "Be ready to ride with the moonlight on your shoulder."

Laughing Crow dismissed them and began marking his Thunder-Bird symbol on the arrows he selected, using what remained of the blackberry extract. Malone stayed with him.

"Laughing Crow, I'm going to use the new shield I've been making since our last raid," said Malone, when they were alone.

"I would like to see it, my friend," he said with sincere warmth. His tone and mood had lightened now that the other men were gone.

Malone walked to his tipi, which was adjacent to Laughing Crow's, and returned with the shield. He showed it to Laughing Crow. "I made it with three thick layers of buffalo hide instead of two." He pounded on the interior of the shield with his fist to demonstrate its strength and then handed it to his leader.

"Very nice craftsmanship, Malone. I see that you have added many eagle feathers and the hair of your slain enemies. They will bring you good *puha*, my friend." Laughing Crow examined both sides of the shield with great interest. "I like the drawing of the painted horse, a powerful spirit, especially for one who is a great rider. I'm sure this shield will serve you well."

Laughing Crow handed the shield back to Malone. "I need to get some rest before we ride," he said and then walked into his tipi. He motioned for Sun Sparrow, and one of his other wives who usually slept with him, to go to one of his other tipis to sleep with his wives and children there.

The Nokoni leader wanted to be alone, to picture in his mind the events of the next day.

The Den

A s Many Wolves walked back towards the village with the three young birds packed in his hunting bag, he felt burdened by his new responsibility. He had three homeless young animals that now depended completely on him. Returning them to their nest was no longer an option because the parent birds had left and the crows would surely return.

His other dilemma was whether or not to tell his village about the birds. His people believed that nature should take care of itself—the delicate balance of all living things should not be tampered with. Knowing this, he expected that Walking Free and the elder council would force him to return the birds to their nest, where the parent birds would eventually return to take care of them. But Many Wolves's instincts were telling him that this would be certain death for them. *The birds will be my secret, at least for a while, until I'm ready to tell the village.*

With this settled in his mind, he had to figure out where to keep the birds. He needed a place that he could access easily and that was safe from predators. Also, he would have to ensure that the young hawks could not escape. *If I build a simple nest in a large tree, will it be safe from foxes and wildcats?* He decided a nest in a tree was not feasible. He remembered seeing hawk and crow nests in large bear cacti, which made them safe from ground predators, but would it be protected from large hawks and eagles?

After weighing many options, he decided that the best choice would be some type of a hole, perhaps an abandoned den. He remembered an old fox den he had found two summers ago, that had not been used since that time. It was a spacious hole located underneath a large rock. It would suffice if there were some way to cover the opening. The den was only a short walk from his village, making it an ideal location.

The birds were motionless and very quiet in his deerskin bag as he walked towards the place he hoped would be their new home. He wondered if the darkness of their enclosure was soothing for them and took care not to jostle the bag around unnecessarily. He was worried about the smallest bird and how serious its injuries were.

Arriving at the den, which was located on a steep hillside, he dropped his bow and arrows, and then placed the bag gently on the ground in a shaded area.

The silence of the calm, late-afternoon weather was shaken by a loud rattling noise, coming from the bowels of the darkened burrow. Many Wolves froze. This was what his grandfather had taught him to do when in the presence of a disturbed rattlesnake. "Freeze until you see the snake and then slowly walk away," were his grandfather's exact words.

Bending down cautiously to peer into the den, his heart pounding in his chest, he examined the dimly lit den space from one side to the other. Beads of sweat rained down on his eyelids and the rest of his face. Then, on the right side, toward the back of the den, he saw the silhouette of a large rattlesnake, coiled tightly with its shaking rattle protruding up from the center of its spiraling body. The vibration of the rattle intensified as he moved towards the snake for a closer look. The coiled reptile was partially illuminated by streaks of sunlight that snuck through cracks in the flat, rocky shelf above it. Many Wolves slowly moved backwards, away from the deadly snake until the rattling halted. He took a deep breath of relief and wiped his wet face.

What do I do now? he asked himself. *Do I look for another den or remove the rattlesnake? If I move the snake, it might return to the shelter. I have to kill it.* He trembled at the thought of having to confront the snake again. He wanted to walk away and leave it, but time was working against him. Soon it would be dark and the birds would need a shelter. Finding another den like this one would take time and daylight and he had very little of each. *I have to kill the rattlesnake. It's too far in a corner to shoot it with an arrow. If I could snare it and pull it out of the den, then I could kill it. I can do this.*

He spotted a small mesquite tree at the base of the hill and ran over to it. Using the edge of his bone knife, he sawed off a piece of mesquite that was fairly straight and about twice as thick as his largest finger. The rough wood was not easy to cut, but eventually he was able to break it free. The branch stood taller than he did as he held it next to him on the ground. It was limber and flexible and not too dry.

Reaching into his food pouch, he took out a large strand of deer sinew, and cut off a piece about as long as his arm. Then he pulled out a small chunk of quartz that was shaped into a long, sharp point, and began to drill a hole near the tip of the branch. He tied one end of the sinew into a loop large enough to push a fist through, and the other end he tied securely through the hole in the branch, just as his grandfather had taught him. He had made many snares like this before to catch lizards, but never one for catching an animal as large and deadly as a rattlesnake.

He returned to the den and was again greeted by the large snake's menacing alarm. He knelt down and began to crawl slowly towards the snake, with the snare-stick extended from his trembling right hand. The snake reacted with louder and more rapid vibrations of its beaded tail. Many Wolves was now close enough to see slitty eyes staring back at him. Its head was large, much larger than other snakes he had seen, and its body was undulating back and forth, a sign of its growing agitation. Despite all the movement of its body, its head remained still, completely focused on him.

Many Wolves moved the snare-stick carefully along the ceiling of the den towards the snake's head. The beads of sweat were dripping into his eyes again, making it hard for him to see clearly. His hands seemed to be shaking even more now as he fought to steady the snare-stick.

Suddenly, like the thrust of a lighting bolt, the rattle-snake lunged at him with a loud hissing sound, fangs bared. Startled, Many Wolves rocked backwards, pulling the snare-stick with him. The snake recoiled, still agitated, and directed its hateful gaze at the young boy. Many Wolves took a deep breath. He was scared and he just wanted to walk away from the dreadful serpent. *I have to do this.*

Many Wolves took a moment to regain his breath and to wait for his fluttering heart to slow down. Again, he moved cautiously closer with the snare-stick outstretched in his quivering hand. The rattler had moved a bit closer to him and he could see more of its detail in the improved light. Its body was thick and muscular and composed of many shades of brown, with a distinct necklace-like pattern of darker brown along the length of its back. Slowly, he moved the snare towards the reptile's over-sized head. The serpent's extended tongue flicked deliberately, reaching a standstill before retracting. With the loop aligned perfectly, Many Wolves slipped the sinew around the snake's motionless head; only its tongue was moving. Breathing hard, Many Wolves continued to move the snare past the snake's wide head towards its narrower neck.

Once the noose was in place, he paused to catch his breath, and then tugged the snare-stick quickly to the left with all his strength, yanking the snake out of its coil. Fearing that the snake might lunge towards him, he dropped the snare-stick and crawled backwards. Regaining its coiled, striking position, the snake faced him again. Many Wolves could see that the noose had tightened around its neck and was holding.

He grabbed the snare-stick again and stood up. Without allowing himself any time to think, he quickly pulled the snare-stick towards him, dragging the squirming reptile out of its hideout. Lifting it off the ground, he slammed its head into the flat stony roof of the den. The snake was heavier than he expected and easily as long as his body. It was hissing loudly. He swung the pole again and heard a loud, crunching sound as the snake's head smashed against the hard rock. It was stunned by the blow as its body struggled to coil back into itself, its rattle still moving, but much less violently. Many Wolves swung it one more time against the rock and the snake's body went limp. The rattling stopped. He plunged his bone knife through the snake's head to make sure it was dead and then tossed the snare-stick, with the snake and knife still attached, away from the den.

He sat down, his trembling body drained of energy and completely encased in sweat. He was amazed at what he had just done.

After a brief rest, he rose to his feet and inspected the new shelter he had fought so hard for. The den was spacious enough for the birds, though the wide opening at the front would need to be covered. A bedding of small sticks on the ground would make them feel more at home, he thought. Looking around the rocky hillside, he spotted many rocks that could be stacked up against the opening to close it off.

The den faced the east—morning exposure to sunlight would be ideal for the birds to warm them after a cool night. It would also provide shade and cool weather in the hot afternoons. First, he gathered as many small sticks as he could find lying on the ground, mostly pieces of mesquite, and laid them across the floor of the den evenly. Then, he set out to gather some large rocks.

Once he had gathered about thirty stones, he began to fill in the opening to the den, fitting the rocks as tightly as possible. A hungry coyote or fox could dig extremely well, so he built a double-thick rocky barrier, with the smaller rocks on the inside, filling the crevice, and the largest rocks, ones he could barely carry, on the outside. He saved the largest rock to serve as a door that he could slide off and on, though not easily.

Now that the den was ready, he reached into the bag and took out the first bird. The frightened bird's beak was wide open, as it was when the crows were attacking, and its big, bulging eyes were fixated on Many Wolves. The bird had many new, dark feathers coming in, but still much of its white down remained. It would be some time before it had a full set of feathers. He placed the fragile nestling in its new home and then reached for the second bird, which was about the same size. Like the first bird, it was scared, but showed no signs of aggression, as if it trusted its new caregiver.

With two of the birds in the den, he reached in for the last bird, the injured one. It was noticeably smaller and had visible wounds on the top of its wing and neck, where the crows had nipped at it. Many Wolves recalled how Desert Flower had used sage on his open wounds, but he was afraid to try any medicine on the bird. He hoped nature would heal it.

The three hawks were reunited for the first time in their new home. He just sat and stared at them for a long while. They were amazing creatures, with their large, intelligent eyes and rugged beaks and talons, each a puffed-up mixture of down and brownish feathers. They were calm and motionless in the den.

With the birds tucked inside the burrow, Many Wolves stood up and walked over to the dead snake. He had heard stories of rattlesnakes still trying to bite long after they were killed, so he was extra careful with it. Pinning the head of the dead reptile down with the butt end of his snare-stick, he carefully extracted his bone knife and then cut off the snake's head just below the neck. Once the head was removed, he flicked it far away from the den and then covered it with sand to mask its scent.

Cutting off a small piece of snake flesh, he stuck it on the end of a small mesquite branch and slowly approached the birds. He offered the meat to the birds, but they seemed too scared to eat. The daunting task of keeping them fed now entered his mind. As he had done with the rattlesnake, he could use a snare to catch lizards and snakes for them. Also, from reading tracks, he could find where rabbits and jumping rats were feeding at night. To trap these, he could place snares along their commonly used trails, attached to sharpened bones that could be buried in the hard soil. As long as the sinew was strong and well-anchored, he felt confident that he could catch some small animals this way.

Sensing their lack of interest, Many Wolves scraped the piece of snake meat off and left it sitting in the nest. *Maybe they'll eat it after I leave.* The rest of the snake's body he would take home to his village, where he would bleed and skin it for his family to eat. He felt good that he wouldn't be returning to his village empty-handed.

He closed up the opening of the den with the large rock and headed back to the village as dusk was closing in all around him.

A Killing Moon

"**M**alone, have you heard anything from the Invisible Ones?" Laughing Crow whispered as he rode up next to Malone. It was nighttime and they were waiting on a hill just within earshot of the Wichita camp. The rest of Laughing Crow's war party of thirty mounted Nokoni warriors, which included all of his Blood Riders, were assembled on the hill with him, awaiting word from the scouts.

Silent Weasel and Little Owl were two long-standing members of the Blood Riders that Laughing Crow considered his two best scouts. He called them the "Invisible Ones" for their ability to sneak into any camp undetected. On this night, they were directed to silence the dogs that were guarding the camp and kill as many Wichitas as possible before the alarm was sounded. On their cue, Laughing Crow would lead the rest of the men into war.

"I haven't heard a sound from them or any dogs barking," said Malone.

Satisfied, Laughing Crow spoke to Malone in a hushed voice. "I don't know if we can trust the Wichitas any more. Why this Long Talon brazenly slaughters *our* buffalo and threatens our people is a mystery to me. We are on friendly terms with many Wichitas and often trade our goods with them." Laughing Crow stopped abruptly to listen to a loud screech in the distance and then he glanced at Malone.

"It's just an owl," assured Malone.

Malone offered more information to the leader. "I've heard that Long Talon has separated himself from his band to follow a path of hunting and raiding, turning his back on the old ways—the trading and farming traditions of his family. Many of the young warriors have chosen to follow him."

"Then they will follow him to the grave. Our justice will be swift...and final," snarled Laughing Crow. "Any other Wichitas outside of his group who choose to follow his foolish path will also be silenced."

The restless war horses snorted impatiently. Their riders tried to calm their nervous gaits, but with little success.

"It's been a while since we heard from Silent Weasel. Maybe they plan to kill the Wichitas without us," suggested Laughing Crow, half joking, though he believed they could do it.

Silent Weasel and Little Owl were men of extreme patience and acute sensitivity to detail. They could paint their bodies to blend in with their surroundings or mask their scent with animal oils. They could move on the ground without rustling a bush or snapping a twig, or climb a rock without disturbing loose rocks or dirt. They could kill a dog or a man instantly, silently with a bow or knife. They could calm a restless horse. They mastered mimicry of animal and bird sounds to communicate. He respected and appreciated his men of stealth and camouflage because they had skills he could never master and he recognized their invaluable contributions to his war party.

"It's a calm night. I can see clearly, like the owl sees, because the moon is bright." Malone looked around at the stars and moon as he spoke.

"It's a killing moon, Malone. It gives us a great advantage," said Laughing Crow. Entering warfare with a clear advantage was one of Laughing Crow's sacred beliefs. *One man lost is one too many.*

Suddenly, the loud bark of a dog cracked the calm night air. It was the sound they were waiting for—the call to war.

From the west, the Nokoni riders thundered towards an open seam in the Wichita camp, led by Laughing Crow, Malone, and the other Blood Riders; all clad in buffalo head-dresses. The Wichita warriors emerged from their tipis, confused and in disarray, scrambling for their weapons and looking in every direction for the attackers they heard but could not see.

The Wichita men had tattoos all over their bodies, composed of long, flowing lines of many colors. Large black tattoos also surrounded their eyes. The *Noomah* often described them as the men with the "raccoon eyes."

Like the turbulent force of a waterfall, Laughing Crow and his warriors descended upon them, determined to eradicate most of them with the first wave of attacks. Launching a volley of arrows, the black-faced Nokonis injured six of the overwhelmed Wichita men before switching to lances and tomahawks for the finishing blows. The screams of the Wichitas coupled with the cheers of the Nokonis pierced the droning rumble of hooves. With help from Silent Weasel and Little Owl, who were attacking on foot with their knives, the remaining Wichitas were slaughtered before the dust of the horses settled. The ambush was executed to perfection.

The war-whoops of the victorious Nokonis filled the night sky. Laughing Crow's men severed the scalps they had earned, and maimed the bodies of their enemies with their lances. Their leader claimed two of the fourteen scalps for himself. The Wichitas' bows and French-made tomahawks were gathered up by Malone and the other Blood Riders, as were the horses.

Malone brought the weapons to Laughing Crow and offered them to him, but he declined. Then he turned to the other men. "Who needs weapons? These steel toma-hawks and Wichita bows, made from the French tree, are excellent weapons," offered Malone, inspecting one of the bows.

Laughing Crow knew that the Wichita bow was made from the wood of the French-named Bois de Arc tree, which was very hard, yet flexible. It was the finest bow known to the *Noomah*.

Several of the Blood Riders and other fighters came up to Malone and accepted the weapons. They nodded to Malone and to their leader to show their appreciation.

"Laughing Crow, I can't recall when you took any rewards for yourself."

"I have weapons and horses, Malone. The scalps I take are enough of a prize," he added with a smile. "It's leading the men…and the blood rush from combat that are the true re-wards. If the new weapons help to sharpen the men's fighting skills, then it benefits us all."

"Your generosity breeds loyalty. Like buzzards following a successful wolf pack, men will follow a generous leader," said Malone to his friend.

The spirits of the men rose like nighthawks in the deep night sky.

Later that night, the Nokoni men were seated around a large, crackling fire. They had roasted one of the Wichita horses earlier and had just finished their hearty meal of horsemeat. It was common for them to kill and eat a spare horse if other food wasn't available.

"Silent Weasel, our esteemed Blood Rider, tell us your story," said Laughing Crow, feeling relaxed and in a pleas-ant mood after his filling meal. He enjoyed listening to Silent Weasel tell his stories of trickery and stealth. Silent Weasel was a squat, muscular man—the shortest of Laughing Crow's warriors. Like the weasel, his spirit animal, he could easily overpower men much larger than himself.

Silent Weasel stood up and spoke. His face was streaked with blood over faded war paint.

"It was dark as Little Owl and I approached the camp. The moon poured enough light on our path so that we could see a good distance ahead of us. We moved slowly, cautiously, on the tops of our feet as we stalked, with our bows cocked, among the sleeping Wichita horses. From earlier scouting, we knew there were three dogs in the camp."

He gestured towards his fellow Blood Rider. "Little Owl spotted the first dog, lying in the grass. He raised his bow to eye level with the fluid motion of a stalking cat and released the arrow. WHOOSH! The arrow tore into the dog's chest, killing it instantly, silently."

Silent Weasel's eyes widened as he told his story. He walked on quiet feet around the fire, engaging all the men.

"I saw the second dog walking among the horses. It was looking in Little Owl's direction, following the sound it must have heard, but it was silent, undecided. I raised my bow slowly, with the speed of a stalking turtle." Silent Weasel smiled and waited for the light breeze to carry away the men's laughter. "I launched my magic arrow at the dog. It fell to the ground without making a sound, without disturbing the soothing breath of the Great Spirit as he blew his breeze through the forest. Only one dog left."

Silent Weasel moved to the other side of the fire and continued his story.

"I signaled to Little Owl that I would be moving closer to the camp. Next to the tipis, I spotted two men and the third dog sitting around a fire. My plan was to try to lure the dog away from the camp, without alarming it, and kill it quickly. Taking a fist-sized chunk of rabbit meat from my bag, I tossed it towards the camp as quietly as I could, hoping the dog would pick up the scent. The dog's ears shot up instantly when the meat landed. It stood up and immediately barked an alarm."

The Nokoni fighters were leaning in now, completely taken in by Silent Weasel's story. The flames of the cascading fire reflected in their eyes.

"I yelled loudly and released an arrow at one of the men who was standing and looking for me. The force of the arrow knocked him off his feet. Little Owl responded with a shot to the other man's back." Silent Weasel pulled out his long steel knife. "The angry dog lunged at me with the speed of an angry rattlesnake, but I slashed its throat, leaving it to wallow in a pool of its own blood." Silent Weasel imitated the motion with his knife.

"When the stampede of mighty Nokoni warriors arrived," Silent Weasel flung a wry grin at a few of the men, "I saw one of the Raccoon-Eyes run away from the camp into the trees and disappear into the darkness. I immediately chased after him. I could see glimpses of him only when the moonbeams sneaked through the fortress of trees. The only sound I heard was the blending of steps and breathing as we weaved between the trees. He ran quickly with the grace of a deer, but I was not far behind and was gaining on him. Suddenly, his shoulder grazed a small tree, which knocked him off balance just enough for me to catch up to him. I pounced on him like a hungry wildcat and slammed him to the ground. I wrestled with him for some time and then pinned his throat to the ground with my left hand while I wrapped my legs around his like a king snake around a rattler. With my right hand, I tore my knife from my leg sheath and dug it deeply into his side. He screamed and found enough strength to knock me over. He climbed on top of me and tried to hold back my knife, but I was too strong. I sank the knife even deeper into his stomach flesh. He gasped as blood gushed from his mouth onto my face and then his body went limp. I carved the scalp off this brave warrior and returned to find you celebrating at the Wichita camp."

Laughing Crow laughed and cheered with the other men as Silent Weasel returned to his place next to the fire.

"That massive knife you use, Silent Weasel, probably ripped the dog's head completely off," Malone said as he stood up and walked over to the scout. "May I see it?"

Silent Weasel handed him the knife and Malone inspected it.

"This is beautiful craftsmanship. I've never seen a knife so long. It's as big as the short swords of the Spanish captains." Malone handed the knife back to the scout.

Silent Weasel's story was one of many that night.

The next morning, most of the men in the camp woke up late. The previous night's victory had left them tired but in sky-high spirits.

The lightness of the moment soon ended for Laughing Crow as he realized he needed to think about the looming Pawnee situation in the north. The Pawnees had not harmed any of his people, but he had been told that they were encroaching on *Noomah* buffalo lands. The Pawnees were primarily a farming people, but they always took trips each year to harvest large amounts of buffalo from the lands north of the Rio Rojo.

Unlike the young, inexperienced warriors of Long Talon's Wichita band, the Pawnees would be tough adversaries. Their people were fearless warriors who were very skilled using their horses and weapons.

"Silent Weasel, I need you and Little Owl to ride north to watch the Pawnees. We need to know how many men and horses they have and what their activities are, so we can uncover their weaknesses. Take your time. The more we know about their routines, the better chance we have to defeat them with minimal losses. They are skilled fighters, not to be taken lightly," commanded Laughing Crow.

"Little Owl and I will leave at sunset, so we can ride with the cool breeze and the safety of the stars," said Silent Weasel.

"Good," replied their leader.

Hungry Mouths

Many Wolves returned to his village just as the sun was setting.

"Grandfather, look what I killed!" He dangled the headless rattlesnake in front of Yellow Feather's face. His grandfather was sitting in the family's lodge, cleaning his pipe.

"Is it a gopher snake or a rattlesnake?" asked his mother, looking up from her seated position where she was grinding pinion nuts in a stone bowl.

Yellow Feather teased his daughter by making a rattling noise with his mouth and tongue.

"It's a rattlesnake. I killed it over by the rock pile east of the village." Many Wolves lied about the spot where he killed the snake to keep the location of the den secret.

"I don't want you playing with rattlesnakes, Many Wolves. They are very dangerous! I want you to promise me you'll leave them alone from now on," demanded his mother.

"Just be careful," interrupted Yellow Feather. "How did you kill it?"

"I *was* careful. I used a snare-stick like you taught me. Once I had the snare around its neck, I smashed its head against a boulder several times, and it was dead." Many Wolves downplayed his fear since he didn't want to worry his mother any more than she already was.

"I'm proud of you, Many Wolves. It took a lot of courage to confront a snake like that," said Yellow Feather, placing his hand on his grandson's shoulder. "I think you're ready to help your father bring fresh meat to the fire pit."

Painted Wings sighed. "Give me the snake. I'll skin it and cook it up for us."

Yellow Feather winked and smiled at his grandson.

"I want to show it to Father first. I'll be right back."

Many Wolves ran off towards Walking Free's lodge to find his father.

Many Wolves woke up at sunrise the next morning to get an early start on what he expected would be a busy day. After a quick meal of ground pinion nuts and dried buffalo meat, he immediately set out to check on the young birds. He found the rocks, which covered the den's opening, undisturbed and was relieved to see the fledglings sitting quietly inside.

"Well, let's see if I can catch some food for you," he said to himself.

The previous night he made a new snare-stick, which was smaller than the one he used for the rattlesnake. He had caught many lizards with snare-sticks like this. So, he began his hunt for blue-bellied lizards, which were the most common, and stripe-tailed lizards too. The blue-bellied lizards were frequently found around yucca plants, so he started his search there.

It didn't take long for him to hook his first victim by the neck and bring its wiggling body back to the den. He killed the lizard quickly by banging its head against a rock and then thanked the Great Spirit for the life he had taken. He impaled it on a long stick with a sharpened point. Reaching into the nest, he offered the morsel to the birds, but they were too frightened to take the offering. They just stared at him with wide-open eyes and gaping mouths. After trying for some time to coerce them to eat, he scraped the dead lizard off the stick and left it in the burrow. *Maybe if I leave them alone, they will eat.*

Many Wolves spent a good part of the morning looking for small animal tracks and burrows. He placed snare-traps along paths where he saw many rabbit tracks and scat, using mesquite bushes to anchor the traps in place. He also found several gopher and squirrel holes where he set snare-traps near the entrance. He tied the other end of the snare to a mesquite log, which would prevent the snared gopher or squirrel from retreating to its burrow.

While he prepared his traps, he checked in on the birds from time to time to see if they had eaten the food he left for them. Finally, after half the day was behind him, the lizard had disappeared. "They ate it! They ate it!" He jumped up and down with excitement. *I need to find them more!*

When dusk arrived, he had caught six more lizards— four blue-bellied lizards and two stripe-tailed lizards—and brought them all back to the den. He also saw a big-headed lizard during his trip, but he couldn't bring himself to feed the "hunter of other lizards" to the birds. He placed the day's catch at the entrance to the burrow and then walked a short distance to a spot where he could see the dead reptiles without being seen by the birds. Once he was completely out of their sight, he watched them grab the food eagerly and devour it whole. He felt pleased that his birds accepted the food he was providing.

As the days passed, the three young birds became more and more accustomed to his presence and so he began to speak to them often. He fed them food with a stick, mostly lizards, but once in a while he offered rat, gopher, or squirrel meat that he caught with snare-traps. He cut up these larger animals into smaller pieces for the birds to swallow. Often, he wet the food before feeding it to the birds, to ensure they were getting enough water. Eventually, after many failed attempts, they snatched food from his hand with their strong beaks. He made sure his hands never got too close to their sharp talons. *We are becoming friends!*

The smallest, weakest bird had recovered well from its injuries. Many Wolves decided to name this one Chiquito, which means "Little One" in Spanish. He had learned many Spanish words from Lupita, a Mexican woman who lived in his village. She had named all of the dogs in his village, and so he decided to give his birds Spanish names as well.

The two bigger birds were more aggressive, constantly lunging at the food when they saw it, so Many Wolves made sure to feed Chiquito while they were distracted with their own meals. His grandfather had once told him that female hawks, falcons, and eagles, were larger than the males, so he decided to name the largest of the baby hawks Reina— "Queen." He named the other female Cazador, which means "Hunter" in Spanish.

The birds were growing, adding feathers and shedding their down. They became more active inside the den as their legs developed more strength and coordination. At the same time, Many Wolves gained more skill with his bow and provided a steady supply of rabbit and squirrel meat for them, relying less on lizards. He had greater success killing rabbits when he found them sitting in their hiding places. Once they bolted, however, it was nearly impossible to hit them with an arrow. Rock squirrels were easier to find and kill, since they let him come close before diving down their holes. He continued to check his snare-traps at sunrise to see if he caught a hopping rat or a gopher or a rabbit foraging for food during the night.

Now that the birds were bigger, their appetites increased and their screams of hunger became louder and more frequent. Their wing feathers started to grow out and they spent most of the day exercising their flight muscles. At one point, Many Wolves brought back a live gopher to see if they would kill it. After snapping one of its back legs to immobilize it, he tossed it into the den and Cazador immediately pounced on the crippled animal, squeezing it to death with her powerful claws. Many Wolves was amazed at the strength of her talons. From then on, whenever possible, he fed them live prey so they could practice killing it, though he still had to feed Chiquito separately with small pieces of meat, since he was reluctant to attack a live animal.

Over time, Many Wolves also fed them the bones and fur with their meal. He had seen wild birds swallow small animals whole, so he figured this roughage was healthy for them to eat. After eating a meal like this, they would spit out a small, egg-shaped stone the following morning, which was made entirely out of bones and fur. He recalled finding these fur-stones near perches used by wild hawks and owls. It was a useful trick for discovering what these predators were eating, especially owls who hunted in the darkness.

One evening, Many Wolves returned from feeding his birds and paused outside his home as he heard his mother and grandfather talking in the family's lodge. He could see the outlines of their bodies through the thatched walls, backlit by the flames of their fire pit. His mother was busy grinding nuts while his grandfather was smoking his pipe, as he often did when the sun disappeared at the end of the day.

"Many Wolves seems to be keeping himself busy these days. We never see him anymore. He leaves at sunrise and doesn't return until dark," said Painted Wings with concern in her voice. Many Wolves knew his mother was growing suspicious, but he had to keep his secret hidden. He wasn't ready to tell anyone about the birds.

Yellow Feather assured her, "He's a young man learning the ways of nature. I was a lot like him when I was his age. I would worry much more if he was spending his days with the women and old men of the village!" His grandfather laughed and continued. "You've noticed that belt of rabbit ears haven't you? He wears it proudly like a warrior wears a belt of scalps! I'm certain that he's cooking those rabbits and eating them during the day. You know how he loves to eat! I'm pleased he's using the fire-making sticks that I made for him."

"That certainly explains why he doesn't eat as much as he used to," added Painted Wings, returning to her arduous task.

"Learning to survive alone is a valuable skill. Someday, he may be a scout and tracker for the village, like I was when I was younger. I spent many days on my own in the wilderness, hunting and cooking alone. The best way to learn survival skills is to practice them often. There is only so much I can teach him."

Yellow Feather paused to take a puff from his pipe.

"Your son Hollow Leg is becoming Many Wolves," said Yellow Feather, exhaling a cloud of smoke.

The War Party

On a late fall morning, Laughing Crow combed the dark brown mane of his favorite stallion behind his lodge. The Nokoni leader repeatedly curried and stroked his horse with great care, meticulously removing every tangle, every burr from its shiny mane. He spoke gently to it as he worked. It responded with playful nickering, nudging its owner affectionately with its nose. Laughing Crow enjoyed spending a part of each day with his war horse. It was during this time that he did some of his deepest thinking and did not permit interruptions unless it was of the utmost importance.

Laughing Crow had found the horse with his former owner, a Spanish captain, after a raid. The man was slumped over the saddle, bleeding to death. The horse was unharmed, but completely blanketed in the captain's blood. A French trader, after hearing the story, suggested that Laughing Crow name the horse Cheval-Sang, which means "blood horse" in his language. He was so enamored by the name, which to him exemplified greatness and strength, that he used it from that day forward.

Like all of the war horses of the Blood Riders, Cheval-Sang was a painted stallion—his colors were primarily brown on white. The pinto horses like him were bred specifically for their athleticism, hardiness, and looks—a desirable mix of white with reds, browns, and black. Cheval-Sang was one of the fastest horses in the village, and like the other painted horses, was agile, sure-footed, and could survive on a minimal amount of food, water, and rest. In Laughing Crow's mind, these traits, along with their ability to execute grace and control when confronted with physical hazards like stampeding buffalo and exploding gunfire, made them the favored breed for hunting and warfare.

Laughing Crow pulled out a bone pick from his belt pouch and began picking out rocks, manure, and other debris from the bottom of his horse's hooves. He didn't want to chance a serious injury from some kind of obstruction. Once finished, he returned to stroking his animal affectionately.

Suddenly, Cheval-Sang perked his ears, alerting his keeper of the arrival of Silent Weasel and Little Owl on horseback. The two scouts dismounted and greeted their leader with a respectful nod.

"I hope the trip went well, my friends." Laughing Crow finished grooming his horse and was now stroking its nose and neck.

"Any trip is a good trip when we return in the flesh and not the spirit!" said Silent Weasel, in a pleasant tone and slightly out of breath. "*Namunewapi*, you give more attention to your horse than any of your wives!"

"Cheval-Sang does not speak and does not need to be ordered more than once," said Laughing Crow with a balanced mixture of seriousness and humor. "What have you learned of the Pawnees?"

"As you suspected, they have been moving with the herd, frequently killing many buffalo to fortify their winter stores. They have about twenty-five men and an equal number of women and children to help prepare the slaughtered buffalo for travel. All the men have horses and carry bows and tomahawks. They have many extra horses for hauling the buffalo back to their village when the hunt is over. I expect they will be there for a few more sleeps, since they still have horses to load."

"They are taking *our* buffalo. We must not let them return home with them," responded Laughing Crow. "Can we ambush their camp?"

"I don't think so. Their tipis are always set up on the open prairie and they have many dogs guarding the camp."

"Silent Weasel, I will send you out tomorrow and then I will decide when to attack. We will need at least fifty men. Have Malone join us here so we can begin the call for arrows to assemble a war party."

The next morning as the sun peeked over the hills to the east, Laughing Crow and his war party of fifty-four men rode out, hoping to find the Pawnees before darkness.

As they rode, Laughing Crow was working out plans in his mind, trying to imagine how the raid would unfold. With the moon in a dark phase, attacking at night would be unwise, especially in unfamiliar territory. Waiting for a moonlit night might mean risking an attack in Pawnee territory, since they would be well on their way home by then. The only real option left was a swift, decisive attack in daylight, but that would put many of his men at risk. If he could trade good horses or high-quality buffalo hides for more time or a brighter moon, he would, but all he had to parlay were the lives of his men.

After sending his scout in advance, Laughing Crow and his riders waited for him to return to their agreed meeting place, a large oak on the hilly grasslands near the last location of the Pawnees.

Silent Weasel arrived at dusk and reported his findings to his leader. "*Namunewapi*, the Pawnees have finished with the hunt and are heading north to their village. Their travel is slowed by loaded horses and they will stop to camp when darkness falls. If we leave at sunrise we will be upon them at midmorning."

Laughing Crow paused to digest the information while his men, who waited in silence, gathered around him.

"We will camp here and get some rest, along with our horses," he yelled in a booming voice. "Be prepared to spill Pawnee blood when the sun rises." The men whooped with excitement, shaking their bows and lances above their heads. Laughing Crow knew that his men hated the Pawnees, almost as much as they hated the *Navoonah.*

"Malone, I wish to speak with Mocking Bird," directed Laughing Crow.

Malone left to find him.

Mocking Bird was included in the war party because he spoke many of the dialects of the other plains people: *Navoonah,* Wichita, Pawnee, as well as fluent Spanish and some French. Malone often said that he "sang the language of many birds." Mocking Bird could remember everything he ever heard and retell it in great detail. Needless to say, he was an invaluable member of Laughing Crow's war party.

The Nokoni village was a melting pot of different cultures. Many captives were brought back from villages that were raided by the Nokonis, offering Mocking Bird every opportunity to develop his linguistic skill. Learning new languages was his passion and he was pleased that his two sons wanted to learn from him.

Although Mocking Bird almost always accompanied the warriors on their raids, he was kept out of combat. His fighting ability was feeble at best, and Laughing Crow wisely regarded his services as hard to replace. Because of his lanky appearance and unorthodox movements, he was often the brunt of many jokes among the warriors, but his good-natured wit and superior intellect earned him the respect and friendship of the other men.

"Mocking Bird, I expect we will have some Pawnee survivors tomorrow. Some we will keep as slaves to trade to the

French pigs, and others we will send home to their Pawnee village. I want them to deliver a message to their leaders that I will not tolerate their presence on our lands. The Pawnee leaders should hear this message through the terror-stricken faces of their own people. You will tell them this before we release them."

"I will, Laughing Crow," said Mocking Bird, respectfully.

"You can go now. Prepare yourself for tomorrow."

The Flame

The next morning, midway between sunrise and noon, Silent Weasel and Little Owl reported to Laughing Crow that they were in striking range of the Pawnees. The horses were rested and the men were ready.

Laughing Crow felt the time was right to present his plan to his men and force the attack. He rode a prancing Cheval-Sang up and down the row of Nokoni riders, looking into the eyes of each of his painted warriors, and projecting his words in a calm, confident voice:

"Warriors, the Pawnees move north as I speak, getting closer and closer to their lands, which are strange to us. We will give up the advantage of darkness, which has been taken from us by the dark moon, to pursue the fight on *Noomah* lands. The Pawnees are experienced fighters; we must treat them with the greatest respect. Trust your skills as a rider to make their aim difficult, and keep your shields up. Do not spare the life of any who raise a weapon against you."

Cheval-Sang shifted directions, still prancing, as the leader continued to speak.

"I will lead the Blood Riders with the first strike. Stands Alone and Three Drums will ride with us on the front line. The rest of you will follow. Keep moving at all times and we will prevail!"

Laughing Crow then raised his shield towards his men.

"Look to the Thunder-Bird, the true spirit of war, for strength and courage, and he will deliver it!" Etched in his shield was the large symbol of a black bird with its wings outstretched. Around his neck was an eagle-bone whistle, decorated with red and yellow feathers, which he used to hail his men in battle. The shrill sound of the whistle cut through the rumble of horses and the yells of men. "You will hear the call of the eagle whistle if we need to retreat, or to call upon the power of the great Thunder-Bird to aid us in our time of need."

Laughing Crow lowered his shield and directed his dancing horse to circle around and face the enemy. Cheval-Sang was neighing and snorting anxiously.

"Let them crawl and bleed in the afterlife!" yelled Laughing Crow, urging his horse to lead the charge of the Blood Riders.

The eleven warriors, most of whom were draped in buffalo headdresses, reached full stride in less than thirty heartbeats, with Laughing Crow pulling ahead of the rest. The line of men were separated by several shoulder-widths as they rode across the flattened prairie, with the rest of the warriors spread out in a wider formation several horse-lengths behind.

In less than sixty strides, Laughing Crow saw the closest Pawnees and heard their barking dogs. He and his elite fighters locked onto their first targets, bows drawn. The first wave of Nokonis launched a barrage of whining arrows at their enemies, then quickly covered up with their shields, which were fastened to their forearms, leaving their hands free to grip their weapons. Five Pawnees were hit and three of them were finished off with the swipe of a lance or tomahawk. The Blood Riders, unscathed at this point, directed their attack at new targets, still moving at full speed, as the second wave of Nokonis swept in on their original targets.

The Pawnees looked distinctly different with only tufted scalp-locks for hair, which streaked along the top of their heads. None of them carried shields, but most wielded bows and French-made tomahawks or lances. Some of the women and boys were huddled around the pack horses, shooting arrows sporadically at the swift raiders. The black-faced Nokonis ignored them and focused their attention completely on the greater threat—the mounted Pawnee warriors.

From the corner of his eye, Laughing Crow saw Malone riding beside him. Malone was one of the most skilled *Noomah* horseback riders he had ever seen. While maintaining full speed, Malone dropped to one side of his horse while riding past a Pawnee warrior, using his horse as a shield from his adversary. After he passed his attacker, he pulled himself up just enough to fire an arrow at his enemy's back. Laughing Crow had watched his friend use this technique repeatedly in raids.

With riders from both bands swirling around in every direction, the scene was utterly chaotic. The cadence of barking dogs was drowned out by the sounds of war. The high-pitched screams of the men, in mixed tones of rejoicing and pain, blended with the low, thunderous rumble of hooves to create a rich orchestration of sound. The Nokoni riders yelled "Aaa-hey" when they pierced their enemy with an arrow or struck them with a lance or tomahawk as a way to claim recognition for the blow.

Dust and grass were thrown in all directions by the powerful war beasts, which snorted violently to keep their flaring nostrils clear of debris. Every so often, Laughing Crow heard the wailing scream of a horse that was pierced by an arrow or lance, followed by the loud crash of horse and rider being slammed to the ground.

In the midst of the havoc, Laughing Crow was hit on the left shoulder with an arrow and then knocked off his horse with a violent blow from a Pawnee tomahawk. The force of the weapon had overpowered his shielded arm, which was weakened by the arrow wound. He jumped to his feet, grasping his shield and pulling his large, steel-bladed battle-axe from the rawhide harness strapped to his back. Consumed by rage, he yelled as he broke the shaft of the arrow, leaving the arrow point embedded deeply in the left side of his upper chest.

His first thought was to signal Cheval-Sang to return to his side, but he feared his shoulder would hinder his ability to mount. Fighting on foot was not a disadvantage for a skilled fighter like Laughing Crow. In fact, he welcomed the intimacy to better see the look in his enemy's eyes as he bludgeoned the life out of him, to feel the warm blood of his victim as it spattered like paint across his body, and to hear the gasp of a last breath. He yearned for up-close killing, which was beyond what a man could see or hear from a distance.

The wound in his shoulder accelerated his heartbeat. The threat to his survival improved his focus and heightened his senses. He saw his enemies with greater clarity, as if they were moving at half their normal speed, and the smell of his own sweat and blood seemed almost overpowering. He shoved the acute pain out of his mind, refusing to be mastered by it, and then blew his eagle whistle loudly to harness the power of his deity, the Thunder-Bird.

Malone, within range of his call, reacted to Laughing Crow's vulnerability and concentrated his attacks on any rider approaching his friend. Working in unison, Malone fired upon the charging attacker, hoping to injure or stun him moments before Laughing Crow slashed the distracted Pawnee with his axe, knocking him off his horse for the final blow. His weapon was much larger than a tomahawk, a two-handed weapon for most men, but he needed only his powerful right arm to swing it. Laughing Crow fought with the ferocity of a cornered wolverine as he took on one Pawnee rider after another. The Pawnees were drawn to him like a moth to the flame, sensing an advantage, and hoping to seize the life and the prized scalp of the Nokoni leader. But with his mounted guardian watching over him, Laughing Crow felt invincible.

Several snarling dogs also rushed at the leader, fangs bared, but they, too, were cut down by Malone's arrows. One of them reached Laughing Crow, but he bashed it down with his shield, then severed its back leg with his axe, leaving the paralyzed dog howling in pain on the grassy field.

Malone exhausted his supply of arrows, so he hurled his lance at the next Pawnee attacker and knocked him off his horse. A swift blow to the head from Laughing Crow's axe quickly ended this man's life. Laughing Crow grabbed a quiver full of arrows from the fallen Pawnee and tossed them to Malone, who instantly loaded a new arrow.

The attacks against Laughing Crow subsided and he saw that the battle was turning in their favor. The hard-fighting Pawnees, now noticeably outnumbered, were falling one at a time to small assault groups of up to four Nokonis. Any Pawnee who made a run for it, out of fear or shortage of arrows, was quickly hunted down by three swift *Noomah* riders, including Mocking Bird. It was their job to patrol the perimeter of the fight and take down any runners. No Pawnee escaped.

Once most of the Pawnee riders were dead or injured, the Nokoni war party turned their attention to those that remained, the women and children. Using their native language, Mocking Bird yelled at the remaining Pawnees to lay down their weapons or die. The ones that refused were slaughtered mercilessly. The others were led to an area away from the weapons and horses.

Knowing that victory was at hand, the Nokoni fighters released a series of war-whoops and began to congratulate each other by banging lances or shields. There had been loss of *Noomah* life as well, but Laughing Crow believed that dying in battle was the greatest honor a warrior could hope for, because his spirit would then rest gloriously in the afterlife. There was much to celebrate.

The sounds of war yielded to the wailing cries of the Pawnee women and the piercing barks of their dogs.

Laughing Crow, smothered in blood from his wound and the blood of his enemies, summoned Malone and his Blood Riders, who had begun collecting scalps and retrieving their arrows from the Pawnee bodies—arrows that were marked with each warrior's unique pattern or symbol. Placing his war shield on the ground, which had five Pawnee arrows embedded in it, Laughing Crow gave his sore left shoulder some much-deserved rest.

"Malone, how many did we lose?"

"We lost eleven warriors, including Three Drums and Seven Horns," answered Malone. Seven Horns was a Blood Rider, and Three Drums was recruited to replace Prowling Coyote. "And five of our horses were lost."

"A trade we had to make. How did Stands Alone fight?" asked the leader.

"He fought bravely, two kills I believe."

"Good," uttered the Nokoni leader, fighting the searing pain in his shoulder, which was growing more difficult to suppress.

"Also, Thorn Bird showed much skill with the bow and lance. He collected four scalps for himself," added Malone.

"That doesn't surprise me. He is still very young, but has proven himself again in battle. When we arrive home, we will initiate Thorn Bird and Stands Alone into the Blood Riders. Bury those who died here so their bodies will lie close to where their spirits rose," said Laughing Crow. "And make sure the bodies are hidden well so the scavengers of the plains will not find them."

"Laughing Crow, what should we do with the dead Pawnees?"

"Cut their eyes out, but nothing more. They will not have their eyes to see in the afterlife, but they will still have their ears to hear and their tongues to scream and taste the blood in their mouths. Then leave them to bleed for the horseflies." Laughing Crow held his breathing, trying to suppress the pain.

"And Malone, have Mocking Bird bring his medicines," he added, reluctantly.

Mocking Bird not only served as the party's translator but as the medicine man as well. Though he wasn't one of the Nokonis' primary healers, he tended to minor wounds in a pinch. Most warriors who suffered serious injuries would rather die with honor.

Shortly after, Malone arrived with Mocking Bird. After dismounting, they approached Laughing Crow.

"Laughing Crow, here is the great warrior, Mocking Bird, who killed his first man in battle today!" said Malone, delightedly.

"Well done, Mocking Bird. Was the man running away or half dead on the ground when you killed him?" added Laughing Crow with mock humor, to disguise the grip of pain.

Malone and some of the other men laughed.

"Well, he was running away...at first," began Mocking Bird, and the men laughed some more. "Then he turned and faced me with his tomahawk. That's when I shot an arrow in his chest."

"Keep that scalp in a safe place then, Mocking Bird," added the leader. "Have you spoken with the Pawnee captives like I instructed you?" said Laughing Crow, changing the subject.

"Not yet."

"Pick the two oldest women and take them to a place well away from the others. Give them a horse and some food and send them home," ordered Laughing Crow. He didn't want the other captives to know they were spared. "Mocking Bird, do you have a medicine skin for my shoulder?" He fought to keep his voice steady, but he was feeling dizzy and cold. He did not want his men to see any weakness.

"Yes. Let me pull the arrow out and wrap the wound. That should slow the bleeding some," said Mocking Bird, who removed a willow stick from his quiver and broke it in half. After shaving down the broken edges, he slid both ends down along the broken shaft of the arrow buried in Laughing Crow's shoulder. He plunged the divided willow stick deep into his wound and dug the shaved ends of willow into the barbs of the arrowhead. The pain was excruciating, but Laughing Crow gnashed his teeth and pushed it back into the recesses of his mind. Once Mocking Bird felt satisfied that the barbs would hold, he locked his grip on the willow sticks and arrow shaft and quickly extracted the arrow point.

He cleaned the wound with water and applied the medicine skin, a piece of softened rawhide, to the shoulder wound to contain the bleeding. One of the warriors had found some firewater on one of the dead Pawnees and brought it to Malone, who offered it to Laughing Crow. He grabbed the container and quickly drank most of the liquor.

Using his right hand, Laughing Crow awkwardly mounted his war horse. Malone cleaned his friend's bloody battle-axe and placed it in a strap on Cheval-Sang's saddle. Then, he yanked the arrows from Laughing Crow's shield and handed it to the leader, who strapped it on his right forearm.

"Malone, tell the men to load the women and children onto the extra Pawnee horses. They should not be harmed, especially the women. They're our captives for now, and the French traders will want them in good condition, without cuts and bruises. We will get good value for them in trade. When they are finished loading, we'll begin our journey home."

Laughing Crow sat on his painted stallion and observed the aftermath of war. The incessant droning of dogs in the distance amplified the throbbing pain in his shoulder. At this moment, he only wanted to rest in a quiet place.

"Silence the dogs!" he hollered. He couldn't stand their grinding noise any longer.

Little Steps to a Big Purpose

As the three birds grew larger and stronger, Many Wolves was faced with the reality that they could not live in the cozy den forever. They would need more space to exercise their legs and wings and prepare them for the day when they would take to the air. He decided that each morning, before feeding time, he would take each of them outside of the den to see what they would do with a taste of freedom.

The following morning, he placed Reina in his bag and carried her down the hill to a grassy meadow below. Slowly taking her out of the bag, he placed her gently on the ground and then walked over to a rock nearby to sit and watch the young bird. As she did in the den, she sat there looking at him and screaming with a cry of hunger: "Feed me! Feed me!"

He cut a small piece of meat from a dead rat that he had snared the night before and tossed it towards the noisy bird, after calling her by name. Seeing the food, she instantly hoped over to grab the morsel, swallowing it eagerly. He repeated this exercise many times, each time increasing the distance between the bird and her food. Her reaction was always instantaneous until eventually she was no longer hungry after eating about half the rat meat. The screaming had stopped by this time, so he knew that she had had enough. Many Wolves gathered her up into his bag and returned her to the den.

He duplicated the same feeding process with Cazador with positive results as well, saving a small chunk of the remaining rat for the littlest bird. Chiquito's response, however, was much more hesitant. He seemed a lot more distracted by the giant new world around him. It took a while, but finally he took some of the rat pieces, though he was unwilling to go very far to get them.

As the days passed, he could see that the birds were learning to come to the food, just as Half Leg had come to get the nuts from Yellow Feather. When they were hungry enough, they responded well to his calls. When they weren't hungry, it was difficult getting any kind of response from them at all. Usually, they were hungry at least twice a day, so that gave him plenty of opportunity to train them. With time and practice, he hoped he could teach them to come to him whenever he called them, hungry or not.

His grandfather had once taught many of the village dogs to obey a handful of his commands, like "come," "wait," "go," and "easy." He would call a dog to "come" to get his food, have it "wait" before eating the food, then "go" to let it eat. He would use the "easy" command to teach dogs not to snatch food from his fingers or to calm an agitated dog when approaching it while it ate. He would always call the dog by name before using a command, and whenever a dog was far away, he'd use a bone whistle to get its attention, since the sound of a whistle could be heard from greater distances than a voice.

From then on, Many Wolves decided that the young hawks would need to earn their food, either by killing the animal or coming to get it from him, while reinforcing the "kill" and "come" commands. No more free handouts. Also, whenever he wanted them to obey a command, he would always call their names and then follow with the command word, hoping they would become familiar with these words. *Would a bird be able to learn the commands that a dog could learn?* He had no idea, but figured he'd try to teach them the most important commands first and then progress from there.

With fall upon them, the days became shorter and shorter. Many Wolves was becoming more proficient with his bow, so hunting no longer required as much of his time. Killing a single jackrabbit would provide enough food for him and the three birds for a day. Any leftover meat could be stored in a rawhide bag and then hung from a tree with strong sinew in a well-hidden location. He had learned from Red Arrow and Yellow Feather that hanging food like this would protect it from many predators, like foxes, coyotes, and raccoons, who would love nothing more than an easy meal.

The shortened days also meant that Many Wolves spent more time at night with his family. In the evenings, he learned to make weapons from his father, or learned about medicines from Desert Flower, or learned about life's many lessons from his grandfather. In the back of his mind, he knew he would eventually have to tell his family about Reina, Cazador, and Chiquito because the village would soon be moving for the winter hunting grounds.

"Grandfather, do you think it would be possible to train a bird like you would a dog or a horse?"

"Many Wolves," his grandfather was getting used to using his new name, it seemed. "I guess anything is possible. If the bird were raised with people, then perhaps it would lose its fear of us and open its mind to friendship. Dogs and horses are pack animals, so they relate well to people. They do a great service for our village: horses carry us and haul our goods, while dogs are the village sentinels to warn us of any danger. In serving the village, it helps them to bond with us. Possibly a crow or raven could bond with us in this way, since they are pack birds and very smart."

"What about a wolf hawk?" said Many Wolves.

"I don't know. They are social animals and very intelligent. I don't know of any stories about them being tamed by our people. With Half Leg, I was able to gain his trust and teach him to eat from my hand. It took patience on my part and an understanding of what he wanted. I felt as though Half Leg could understand some of the words I was using with him. So, maybe a person could build this level of trust with a wild animal, especially a younger one, and possibly tame it. Of course the bird could also choose to fly away at any time."

Yellow Feather lit his tobacco pipe and began to smoke, allowing Many Wolves to inhale his smoke and words.

"So then you don't think it would be against nature to try to tame a wild animal like that?" Many Wolves was trying not to sound too persistent with his questioning.

"The dog and the horse have their place in our world. I guess if the wolf hawk could serve a useful purpose for us, then it would be worth the effort to tame it. Without knowing what this purpose is, it's best to let them stay in the wild, to help maintain the balance of living things."

Hearing this, Many Wolves decided that he would keep his birds a secret as long as he could, until he found out what this purpose was. For now, they provided friendship and laughter, but nothing of value beyond that. He was spending much of his time hunting for them.

Many Wolves sat quietly watching his grandfather smoke his pipe, imagining what it would be like if he could teach his birds to hunt for him. In this way, they could be of service to the village. Then he heard his mother call to him above the rhythm of the crickets and he knew it was time to sleep.

The Blood Rider Initiation

Two days after the Pawnee raid, Laughing Crow's warriors were warmly received by the people of his village. Sorrow filled the eyes of the women and children whose loved ones had not come back. Nothing was spoken of the ones who had fallen. Still, most of the villagers were jubilant to see so many of their fighting men return, which meant the raid had been a success.

After he arrived at his lodge, Laughing Crow unpacked his weapons and removed the light buffalo hide saddle from Cheval-Sang. One of the other Riders took the headman's prized war horse and led it, along with his own horse, to a nearby creek to drink. The two stallions would join the rest of the herd later to rest and graze.

Laughing Crow's injured shoulder, which was still very painful, allowed him only limited use of his left arm. Mocking Bird had done a skillful job of cleaning and dressing the wound, but the injured leader was hoping to get a stronger remedy from his old friend, Snake Tooth.

"Malone, have Snake Tooth come and tend my shoulder. Tell him to bring his best medicines," commanded Laughing Crow, his body tired from a day's travel on the arid plains.

Snake Tooth was one of the oldest men in the village, a small man with long gray, disheveled hair and a hunched posture. His selfish disposition and eccentric behavior made him more enemies than friends, but Laughing Crow respected him for his healing talents. One time, when his blood burned with fever from a rattlesnake bite, one of the other healers tried to remedy his ailment, but his condition did not improve until Snake Tooth treated him. The old shaman had been away from the village on one of his spiritual journeys until Silent Weasel found him and brought him back to see Laughing Crow.

Snake Tooth's treatments consisted of a mixture of strange medicinal ingredients and bizarre spiritual rituals, which utilized his talents as both a medicine man and shaman. Most of the villagers preferred the other, more traditional, healers who treated them kindly, with a mother's love. To hold their status, these healers often remarked that Snake Tooth's unusual remedies were nothing but concoctions created by a madman. But to Laughing Crow, *they* were the makers of false medicine.

Snake Tooth had once told the leader that he didn't have the patience to care for old women and children. He preferred spending most of his time experimenting with different medicines and delving deep into the spiritual world.

He arrived at Laughing Crow's tipi in no apparent hurry. "So, what have you done this time?"

"Just a small wound to the shoulder," said Laughing Crow, downplaying the injury.

"Let me have a look at it," grumbled the old medicine man in a voice that sounded more like a growling dog. Many of his teeth were disfigured or missing, causing him to slur as he spoke. He examined the wound after removing Mocking Bird's blood-soaked medicine skin. "I'll apply some of my healing herbs. That should cleanse the wound and kill the evil spirits."

Snake Tooth pulled out a small container of a thick, reddish liquid and began applying it slowly to Laughing Crow's shoulder. The odorless liquid looked like a mixture of herbs and some type of animal blood. Laughing Crow did not care what was in it as long as it healed his wound. As the medicine man administered the remedy, he sang quietly to the spirits, occasionally raising his hands to the sky as he pleaded with them to empower his medicine. The strange liquid stung when it touched Laughing Crow's lesion, but he didn't flinch. He believed that the harder the medicine bit, the quicker it would heal him.

Snake Tooth concluded his medical treatment with a long, silent pause and then a loud cry out to the spirit world. "The power of the medicine should heal your wound quickly, Laughing Crow. Don't wash it off for the next few days."

"Your medicine better work, crazy old man, or I'll hang your scalp on my lodge," threatened the leader, half-jokingly, pointing to the scalps ringing his tipi. "Also, we'll be initiating two of our most promising warriors as Blood Riders later tonight. Make the necessary preparations for the ceremony."

Later that day, after the sun had departed and the women and children were asleep, Snake Tooth and the Blood Riders gathered around a roaring fire to begin the initiation of Stands Alone and Thorn Bird into the elite Nokoni group. Two of the young men from the village were invited to provide drum rhythm, fulfilling a prestigious role in the ceremony. They bowed and thanked Laughing Crow profusely for the honor. He always insisted that an even number of drummers play at his ceremonies. He believed that using odd numbers was bad luck.

The seven Blood Riders and the two drummers were seated in a half circle around the fire, with Laughing Crow seated alone opposite to them. The Riders' faces were painted in many colors, a sharp contrast to the stark black they reserved for war, and they each wore a buffalo horn headdress. Snake Tooth was draped in a full buffalo hide coat. He placed a tortoise shell of animal blood and a buffalo tail in front of each Rider and placed eight eagle feathers next to Laughing Crow. The initiates had not yet arrived. They were waiting for a signal from the old shaman.

Snake Tooth left the fire and returned moments later with a large ceremonial staff and a small bag of herbs. The handle of the wooden staff had been carved into a rattlesnake head, and over a dozen large snake rattles hung from the shaft, attached by strands of sinew. He tossed cuttings of aromatic cedar and blended herbs to make the fire crackle and spark. Laughing Crow thought that he did this to rouse the spirits and draw their attention. With his hand, the shaman directed Stands Alone and Thorn Bird to sit on either side of their leader.

"Let us begin," muttered Snake Tooth. He stood motionless with his arms folded across his chest, his eyes closed, and his head directed towards the sky. No sounds were heard but the crackling fire, a concordance of chirping insects, and a distant, howling coyote.

"Spirits rise!" shouted Snake Tooth, opening his eyes as if shaken by the blast of a long gun. Awakening like a moth from a cocoon, he nodded to the drummers to begin a loud, steady beat. He raised his arms to the night, one hand clutching the staff of rattles, and began to dance in front of the fire. After offering a brief prayer in each of the four directions, he began to speak lucidly, driven by the rhythmic drumming, circling the fire and looking into the eyes of the men as he passed.

I fly...with the wings of an insect...darting up and down.
I fly through the mesquite and sage...but where I am going...I do not know.
My wings grow tired. So tired...I cannot lift them anymore.
I fall to the earth...to the dust.
Suddenly, darkness...

The old shaman stopped and raised his arms to the sky, then shook his rattling staff, which had been silent. Then he continued with his incantation.

> *I rise...from the darkness with renewed strength.*
> *I bask lazily on a large rock.*
> *My eyes see blurred movement and I run from it.*
> *I run, bounding from rock to rock...but where I am*
>   *going...I do not know.*
> *Darkness finds me again...*

Once again Snake Tooth stopped and shook his staff towards the sky. Laughing Crow could see the spirits working through him. The shaman's body looked like a man half his age and he spoke with a loud, clear voice, a voice with thunder in it. His eyes reflected the bright flames of the blazing fire. The men appeared mesmerized by the ritual as Snake Tooth began circling them again.

> *I rise again into the light on feathered wings.*
> *I dance gracefully, stirred by the shifting winds.*
> *I soar, spiraling high into the clouds...but where I am*
>   *going...I do not know.*
> *I grow weary from the climb and feel the earth pulling me*
>   *down.*
> *I rest on a large rock overlooking a vast canyon.*
> *The darkness reaches out to me, once again.*

Again he rattled his staff at the sky then motioned for the wide-eyed drummers to drum louder and faster before he circled the flames again. He raised his voice to higher levels.

> *I rise again on powerful legs and paws.*
> *I climb down the rocky boulders of the canyon's ledge.*

Down...down...down I go...but where I am going...I do
  not know.
Breathing hard, panting, I stop to rest when I reach the
  canyon floor.
On my right, I hear small rocks tumbling down.
As I turn to see what made the noise...the twang of a bow-
  string, a rush of air, and then a piercing pain in my
  chest...and...darkness.

Snake Tooth signaled the drummers to stop. In the silence, he directed Stands Alone and Thorn Bird to stand next to the fire, and then the shaman began dancing around them as he chanted.

Rising now, I am the hunter.
With two shots of my bow, I have captured many spirits:
  the devil cat, the hawk, the lizard, and the locust.
With every spirit I grow stronger.
As a hunter of men, I will grow stronger still.

Snake Tooth danced one last time around the two initiates, shaking his snake staff. Then he stopped in front of them, raised his arms, and closed his eyes. He stood before them in silence, breathing hard, for a long time before opening his eyes. Then he spoke. "Your spirit must be strong...to be hunters of men."

At this point in the ceremony, Snake Tooth lit two pipes filled with tobacco and handed one to each initiate. He spoke to Stands Alone first. "Take this pipe and offer it to each Rider. When they blow smoke to the spirits above, we will know they are speaking the truth. Then they will offer you the blessing of blood as a sign of their acceptance."

Starting with the Rider on the left, Stands Alone presented the pipe to each of them. Each took a single puff and blew smoke to the sky. Then taking the buffalo tail that Snake Tooth had left by their side, they dipped it in the animal blood and spattered it on the chest of the initiate several times, uttering these words of approval: "Let the blood of your enemies protect you." This process was repeated with each of the Riders and then Thorn Bird took his turn.

Once this ritual was complete, Laughing Crow stood up, directed the two young men to stand before him, and then addressed them solemnly, as the light from the fire cast a rich glow on their faces.

"Warriors, you have been chosen to join the Blood Riders, an honor which you have earned with your courage and mastery of skills in battle. You will take orders without question, even if it threatens your life. Do not give your life away easily or be afraid to die. To lose your life in war is the highest honor you can receive and you will be rewarded as a great warrior in the afterlife. There is no greater glory than this. From this day forward, you will ride into war with us, the first line of attack. Your enemies will see the buffalo headdress which you will wear into war and see your fearless eyes which offer no mercy to them, and they will know you are Blood Riders."

Laughing Crow then took his knife and handed it to Stands Alone. "Let us take an oath in blood." The Nokoni leader directed them to slice open their palms with the knife and then he did the same. Clasping hands, Laughing Crow sealed the oath with each of them. "The blood we share today becomes one blood, for one people."

Laughing Crow smiled, releasing a flood of tension from his body.

"My brothers, as Blood Riders you will have your choice of the painted horses from the herd. Take these feathers and decorate the mane of your war horse so that your horse will go swiftly and bravely into battle, guided by the spirit of the eagle." Laughing Crow handed them each four eagle feathers.

"Take these wolf-tooth earrings and wear them proudly so that our village will know you are Riders." Laughing Crow handed them each an earring. "As you already know, the spoils of war are offered first to the Riders. You can take any unclaimed woman of the village as your wife. Their family will not oppose you. Have many children, especially sons. We want the blood of our bravest warriors to be the blood of our people."

"Welcome, Stands Alone… Welcome, Thorn Bird…to the Blood Riders!"

Snake Tooth and the Blood Riders congratulated the new members with loud cheers and warm embraces. With beaming smiles, the initiates whooped with excitement. Stands Alone and Thorn Bird were then invited to sit around the fire with the other Riders. The men danced, and smoked, and told great stories of brave deeds from past hunts and battles until the sun rose to welcome a new day.

Laughing Crow was pleased to see his men relaxing and enjoying themselves. They would need to ride again to the south in two days time. Although Laughing Crow's shoulder was hurting badly, it eased his pain to know that the Blood Riders were at full strength again, though he hated having to replace good warriors. He was especially proud that Thorn Bird, his oldest son, was one of them.

A Show of Strength

The falling sun cast the outstretched shadows of the Nokoni riders over the dusty plains just east of a Lipan village. Laughing Crow heard dogs barking and boys yelling as he and his men approached slowly and in plain sight. It was his intention to show strength and to attract the attention of the outnumbered *Navoonah*, like a male prairie chicken who displays a puffed-up chest.

The procession was led by Mocking Bird, who carried a white flag atop his lance. Laughing Crow knew that there was an unspoken acceptance of the Spanish "peace flag" by plains people of all skin colors. Following the flag carrier a few horse-lengths back was a line of ten Blood Riders, including Laughing Crow and Malone, whose decorated war horses pranced and neighed as they trotted shoulder-to-shoulder towards the village. Ordered to remain within arrow range, a wide swath of Nokoni warriors flanked them. All the Nokoni men carried bows or lances, and some wore shields strapped to their forearms.

Laughing Crow's men were not dressed for war, although they were prepared for it. Their faces were painted with two colors, red and yellow, but not black. Laughing Crow and the other Blood Riders did not wear their bulky buffalo headdresses, but instead, a single eagle feather, or two, hung from the back of their scalps.

Laughing Crow draped a buffalo skin around his chest to cover up his shoulder wound, though the weather was still too warm for winter clothing. Most of the pain was gone, but the shoulder was still stiff and weakened by the deep cut of the Pawnee arrow point. His Thunder-Bird shield adorned his left arm.

The Nokoni headman raised his shield, signaling his men to halt, while Mocking Bird, the lean warrior with the peace flag, continued to ride towards the village. Laughing Crow saw the *Navoonah* men approaching in a single line, shoulder-to-shoulder on horseback, forming a barrier between their village and the Nokonis. He counted seventeen riders. The women and children of the village gathered a short, safe distance behind them.

The *Navoonah* riders were led by two older, gray-haired men, whom Laughing Crow assumed were the village leaders. One of the men had a distinctly large nose and wore a red bandanna as a headband while the other wore his hair in thick braids and had wrapped a strip of deerskin around his head. Both men were dressed only in breechcloths and deerskin leggings, which covered most of their legs. They each carried an undecorated spear, which was much shorter than the *Noomah* lance. The other mounted *Navoonah* carried bows, but no shields.

The one with the braided hair yelled out strange words and instantly the boys of the village rounded up the noisiest dogs and tied pieces of rawhide around their noses to silence them. Laughing Crow saw that one of the boys had white skin, a rare sight among the native people of the Southern Plains.

Mocking Bird, speaking in *Navoonah*, called out his request to the Lipan elders, who were still several horse-lengths away from him. "Laughing Crow, leader of the Nokonis, wishes to speak with your leaders."

The elder with the red bandanna responded hesitantly in a rough, even tone. Once the man spoke, Laughing Crow immediately recognized him, the confident bravado of his foreign voice was unmistakable. He was the *Navoonah* leader that his people named "Chasing Coyote." Long ago, before Laughing Crow was leader, Chasing Coyote and his men stole many horses from the wary Nokonis. Laughing Crow remembered him as a cunning trickster who would follow the Nokoni war parties across the Rio Pecos and wait, often for many days, for the right moment to steal their spare horses. The Nokonis named him this because he followed like a begging coyote who follows men to grab scraps of unguarded meat.

Mocking Bird translated the elder's words: "Let him come, but his men must stay where they are. If any Nokoni draws his weapon, then your leader will die."

Laughing Crow looked at the two leaders and nodded his acceptance. On his command, Cheval-Sang strode confidently towards the *Navoonah* leaders. Malone also accompanied him. Mocking Bird remained still, awaiting their arrival. The two *Navoonah* leaders moved slowly towards Mocking Bird as well, putting some distance between them and the mounted men of their village.

Looking directly at the big-nosed Lipan, Laughing Crow began to speak, gesturing to each of his men as he introduced them. Mocking Bird translated all the words between them.

"I am Laughing Crow, leader of the Nokonis, and this is Malone. The one who speaks your words is Mocking Bird."

"I am Silent Thunder and this is Walking Free. We are the leaders of this village," the braided elder declared.

Laughing Crow had not remembered that Chasing Coyote's *Navoonah* name was "Walking Free" until he heard it in Mocking Bird's voice.

The Nokoni headman addressed the elders with a calm, eloquent voice, "I have come to offer you peace on my terms, or death should you chose it. I do not wish to shed the blood of your people. Unlike the Wichitas and Pawnees, the people of your village have not shown aggression towards us or taken more than their share of the buffalo. However, with four of our riders to your one, we are in a position of strength, so there will be a price to pay for our peace."

As Mocking Bird translated, Laughing Crow studied the mounted *Navoonah* warriors. Most were healthy and strong with no fear in their eyes. He tried to guess which of them were the bravest fighters.

"What are the terms of your peace?" asked Walking Free, glaring at Laughing Crow with squinting, wrinkly, old man eyes.

"Our peace will cost you twelve horses," answered Laughing Crow. His people didn't need the horses, but it would weaken the *Navoonah* village, and tilt the odds in his favor should his men choose to attack by another moon. He examined the reactions of the Lipan elders, hoping to uncover their thoughts, but they remained expressionless, shrouding emotion like clever gamblers.

"Twelve horses is a steep price to pay," retorted Walking Free. "How do we know you won't take our horses and then kill us when the moon is bright?"

"I am a man of my word, Walking Free. I do not speak with the double tongue of the Spaniard or the French. I only kill those who shed first blood or who are greedy killers of our buffalo," said Laughing Crow. Cheval-Sang shifted nervously until calmed by his rider.

"Storm Feather did you no harm, nor was he greedy, but you cut him down," said Walking Free in an even more forceful voice.

"He was hunting close to where our women and children sleep. He knew the boundaries and stepped over them at his own risk—a fatal decision on his part. How was I to know he was after only the buffalo?" Laughing Crow said, pleased with his twisted words.

"A greater leader would have offered him a warning and not an arrow in the back," Walking Free shot back with contempt.

There was a momentary silence. The snorts of the horses filled the void. Laughing Crow assessed the poignant words of the Lipan elder and then looked at Malone and cracked a subtle, satisfied grin.

"Laughing Crow, you rule with your weapons and not your wisdom. What will you do when you are too old to ride with your men into war?" said Walking Free.

Laughing Crow stroked the mane of his war horse as he contemplated his response. He was reminded of the elders of his village and their old-fashioned notions. *The plains are filled with buzzards.*

"I will not grow old. I will live bravely and die young. That is the life, and death, that I choose." Laughing Crow was beginning to tire of the conversation. Looking past the *Navoonah* line of men, he nodded towards the village.

"Who is the *taibo*?" Laughing Crow fixed his gaze on the white-skinned boy, who was standing with the other children.

"He is an adopted son of our village," answered Silent Thunder, glancing at Walking Free.

"What is his name?" asked Laughing Crow. He wanted to know about the white-skinned boy. He wondered why the Lipans hadn't sold their captive. The white traders would pay handsomely for one of their own.

The elders hesitated and looked at each other, and then Walking Free spoke. "His name is Many Wolves." The contempt had left his voice.

"That's a strong name for such a weak-looking boy," the Nokoni leader said with a laugh. "A better name would be Many Horses, since that's what I could get for him in a trade with the French!" Malone and Mocking Bird laughed along with him. Mocking Bird knew not to translate these words.

Silent Thunder shifted on his horse, agitated by the laughter while Walking Free continued to stare at Laughing Crow, unflinching.

"Walking Free, I grow tired of our talk. We will leave the peace flag in plain sight of your village. If you accept our offer of peace, then bring twelve horses at sunrise tomorrow and leave them next to the peace flag. If you refuse, then I will see it as a sign that you want war with us. Our attack will be guided by this moon or the next or even the one after that, but you will not know. This is my promise to you."

Laughing Crow and Malone turned and trotted back towards the other Riders. Mocking Bird galloped out to an open area on the grassy prairie and stuck the lance with the peace flag into the ground, then rejoined his commander.

The Nokoni leader stopped his horse, and abruptly turned towards the two elders. Still within earshot, he yelled, echoed by his translator: "And leave the white-skinned boy with the peace horses…we will take him too!"

Painful Acceptance

"Father, what's wrong? Are the Northerners attacking?" Many Wolves woke up startled and disoriented.

"Don't be afraid, Many Wolves. Walking Free needs to speak with you," said Red Arrow calmly. Painted Wings and Desert Flower were also awake inside the family's lodge and seemed equally alarmed by the late night visit.

Many Wolves heard Walking Free and his grandfather talking to each other with hushed voices, but he couldn't make out their words. The medicine man entered their home and began speaking solemnly. "Many Wolves, you need to leave the village tonight. It's not safe for you here anymore."

"Why? Why is it not safe for me?" asked Many Wolves, feeling scared and a little light-headed. *What have I done wrong?*

Walking Free sat down next to him and looked at him with his soft, aging eyes. They were eyes of experience and wisdom. "Laughing Crow, the leader of the Northerners, values you highly for your white skin. When dawn breaks, he wants to take you away from our village. We do not have enough warriors to protect you. You must pack some clothes and weapons and leave right away."

Many Wolves felt a surge of heat rush to his head. *Is this a bad dream?* He sat there staring at Walking Free in disbelief. Tears welled up in his eyes. He wouldn't be able to hold them back for long. His mother began to sob.

"What will they do with me if I go with them?"

"I don't know," replied Walking Free. "Laughing Crow might make you a slave or sell you to the French or Spanish for horses and white man's goods. Either way, we feel you would have a better life in the wilderness."

"But…what will they do to the village if I'm not here when the sun rises?"

"Laughing Crow will be angry, but I will tell him that you are not for barter and we will give them the horses he wants. We will show him that we are ready to fight. I want you to be far, far away from the village when they come."

"I hate my white skin! I wish I was never born with it! I wish I could take a knife and peel it all off!" Many Wolves screamed with frightened tears streaming down his face. His distraught mother put her arms around him and comforted him, then caressed his hair with her gentle touch. It was the same comforting touch that soothed him when he woke from his bad dreams.

Walking Free placed his warm hand on the crying boy's shoulder. "Do not be afraid for us. I don't think Laughing Crow will risk the lives of his men for one white-skinned boy. He bears no grudge against us."

"Can't I just hide away for a while until the Northerners leave?" Many Wolves pleaded.

"No. You must journey far away from us so they will not find you. Head northwest along the Rio Pecos until you reach the high country. There are many places to hide where you will be safe from them. You know enough about hunting and tracking to survive on your own. This will be a great test of your skills." Walking Free looked him squarely in the eyes and brushed away a tear that was rolling down the boy's face. "You are ready to become a man. You must make preparations. There isn't much time before sunrise. The Northerners will be watching our village and our horses, but you can take the northwest path without being seen."

Red Arrow interjected his words, "Like Walking Free said, if you head northwest from either of the creeks near our village, they will take you to the Rio Pecos. You will know when you reach the big river because it is much larger than the creeks. It is so wide that you will not be able to shoot an arrow to the other side. It is fast-moving and very deep, so do not try to cross it. It is especially dangerous in the late winter and spring with the rains and snowmelt feeding it."

His father continued, speaking with more urgency now, relaying many details about his son's journey. "Along the eastern banks, you will find many rock shelters to hide in. Stay out of sight. Build only small fires at night, never during the day, because the smoke plumes will surely be seen by Northerner eyes. And stay off the well-traveled horse trails. After many days of travel, you will reach Horsehead Crossing."

"Why is it called that, Father?" Many Wolves asked, sniffling.

"The area around this part of the riverbank is littered with skulls of horses and buffalo and men that died there. Their intense thirst drove them to drink the salty river water too quickly. Horsehead Crossing is the easiest way for men to cross the Rio Pecos, and it is used frequently by the Northerners, so you must be careful as you pass it. As you head further north, you will start to see more and more trees along the river. This is the beginning of the high country."

The boy could not remember when his father had spoken so many words before.

"My son, we must prepare supplies for your journey. You will be leaving soon," said Red Arrow, and then he left the lodge abruptly with Walking Free.

Reluctantly accepting his fate, Many Wolves gathered up his clothes and began to load up the pole-drag they had left for him outside of his family's lodge.

With tears streaming down her cheeks, Desert Flower handed him a small leather pouch. "These are some of my best herbs. Use them like I taught you. Be safe, little brother," she said, hugging him as she wept. She called him "little brother" for as long as he could remember, though she was not his sister.

His mother had packed some dried meat, an assortment of nuts, and some supplies for cooking and sewing. "We will miss you, my dearest son. I know this is not the path you have chosen, but the Great Spirit will be with you. We will be with you, always." His mother embraced him and kissed his forehead, then rubbed her soft, wet cheek against his face. Releasing him, she immediately burst into tears again. Desert Flower grabbed her sister's arm and helped her into the family's hut.

When his father and Walking Free returned, Many Wolves was standing outside the lodge. "Many Wolves, take this bow and these arrows. You are not strong enough to use it yet, but when you can draw it with a steady hand, you will be a man. Do not try to kill deer or elk or other large animals until you can use this. Use your smaller bow for now," said Red Arrow as he handed him a large mulberry bow and eight arrows, which he had made himself. "And I want you to have this coyote-skin quiver. It can easily hold your bows and arrows and other supplies, like your fire-making sticks," his father added as he put the new bow and arrows inside it.

"I want you to take this. The Mexicans in our village call it a *libro*." Walking Free handed him a heavy, tattered object that looked like it was very old and made somewhere other than the village. "We found this when we found you as a child. There are white man's symbols in it, which we don't understand, but also some pictures of birds and animals. There were other *libros*, but they did not have pictures, so we left them. This one may tell you something about your past—about your white-skinned family. I was going to give it to you when you started your journey into manhood, but your journey begins now."

Many Wolves had never seen a *libro* before, but he packed it tightly in his clothes, which were tied to the pole-drag. He thanked Walking Free, the leader of his village and his close friend. The medicine man embraced him, reminded him of his words, and then walked away into the darkness.

It was impossible for the young boy to hold back the tears now as he said his final goodbyes to the people he had lived with all his life. It felt like a large stone was pulling his heart to the ground. He wanted to believe that he would see his family and Walking Free again, but nothing was certain anymore.

Red Arrow tied the pole-drag to the dog, Amarillo—the dog that was chosen for his son—and embraced him one last time. There were no tears, only sadness, in his father's eyes. He too walked away into the night.

His grandfather accompanied him to the edge of the village, to the northwest path, guided only by the light of a half-moon. The night was silent except for the hundreds of desert insects that chirped in unison. As they walked, Yellow Feather reiterated many of the lessons of survival that he had once shared with his grandson. There was so much more he wanted to ask his grandfather, but there was no time now.

"Of all the boys of our village, you are the most prepared to journey into the wild alone," said his grandfather in a subdued voice. "I am pleased that Amarillo will be with you. Take good care of him. He's a strong pack animal who does not tire easily. His sharp ears and keen sense of smell will find danger that you cannot. He is a brave dog and sometimes a little too crazy for his own good. I once saw him stare down a bear. Larger animals will not attack you when they do not sense fear in you or your dog. Keep him well-fed, because you will want him to be strong and healthy at all times."

His grandfather walked with him towards the gurgling sounds of the creek. "This is as far as my old legs will take me, Long Drink. I wish I could go with you, but my body is just an old bag of bones. I would just be a burden to you. Your father would go with you if he could, but he is sorely needed to provide for our family and to protect our village."

"Would my father really want to come? He seems to be so busy with hunting and making weapons. He never really talked to me like you and Desert Flower and my mother."

"Your father cares for you very deeply, Long Drink. He's not one to use many words. Expressing feelings with words is just one way to show you care. He provides food and clothing for you and he spends time showing you how to make tools and weapons. That is how he expresses his love."

Many Wolves and his grandfather arrived at the creek. Stopping, Yellow Feather turned to his grandson and continued to speak. His words weighed heavy with emotion. "I remember when your father first heard of your new name. It made him feel so proud. He was pleased that you received a strong animal spirit that would protect you. He doesn't often smile, but he did then. I will never forget that moment and neither should you."

He felt his father's love and acceptance like he had never felt it before. "Thank you for telling me this," said Many Wolves with appreciation. "I will always remember what you have said about my father."

Many Wolves wiped another tear from his face. "Grandfather, I have something for you." Many Wolves removed the rabbit ear belt from around his waist and handed it to the man who had molded him and brought him so much joy.

"I will treasure it always, Long Drink." His grandfather smiled and looked at his grandson with sparkling eyes and a single tear crawling down his cheek. "May the great eagle of the north watch over you always, Many Wolves, and may you walk with wolves on your journey."

Many Wolves hugged his grandfather tightly, his closest friend, bringing a fresh surge of tears to his eyes. He felt his grandfather's warm, welcoming arms and smelled the familiar tobacco smoke embedded in his rawhide shirt, in his long, tangled gray hair, and on his breath, for perhaps the last time.

Yellow Feather motioned for his grandson to go on without him, into the dark. Many Wolves watched his grandfather cover up their tracks with great care and he thought to himself as he turned and walked away: *I hope my memories will not be covered so easily.*

A New Family

It was a very tiring night for Many Wolves because he had barely slept. After leaving his grandfather, he hiked further into the rocky canyons west towards the Rio Pecos. He had remembered a large crevice from his earlier exploration of the canyon. It would make a well-concealed shelter for him, at least for the first day. He was careful to cover his tracks as his grandfather had taught him.

The toughest part of the journey was crossing the two creeks, which were cold, but shallow enough to walk across without sinking. He had crossed each three times during the night and early morning hours: the first time to safely get Amarillo and the pole-drag across, and the second and third times to bring the three birds, packed carefully in his bag, from their den to his hideaway in the canyon. On his way back to the birds, he retrieved his hidden cache of fresh rabbit meat and many of the snares he used for trapping small animals.

When he returned to the hideaway he saw that Amarillo was resting and still secured to a large rock by his rawhide lead. He had no idea how the dog would react when he saw the birds, so he felt it best to keep him tethered. Before letting the birds out of the bag, he cut off a moist piece of rabbit meat and tossed it to Amarillo, who eagerly began to bite off pieces.

While the dog was occupied with his reward, Many Wolves slowly took each bird out, some distance away. Once on the ground, they immediately stared at the strange animal eating in front of them. Amarillo raised his head briefly to look at the birds and then resumed his meal, keeping a distrusting eye on them as he chewed.

"Don't worry, Amarillo. They won't take your food. You need to get used to them, they're part of our family now."

Many Wolves cut off a sizable portion of rabbit for each bird. Reina and Cazador immediately began to feast, forgetting all about the dog, who didn't appear to be threatening them. Chiquito was more suspicious, and took his piece of food to a spot away from the other two birds and the dog. Without the den to confine them, Many Wolves hoped that the birds would not run off on their own or get too close to Amarillo. There was no way to constrain them. Like the young children of his village, they would have to learn to stay close to their family.

He was relieved to see the birds eating and Amarillo staying calm. He was very tired, wet, and cold after the night's events. He was hungry too, but could wait until later to cook the remains of the rabbit for himself. He laid out the buffalo-skin robe that his grandfather gave him, and went to sleep.

When Many Wolves woke later that morning, the sun was shining and the warm weather soothed his cold skin, his clothes still damp from the previous night. Amarillo was lying quietly next to him, still attached to the lead. Reina and Cazador had hopped up to a higher spot on the rocks, while Chiquito was still sitting in the spot where he had eaten his meal. Many Wolves was elated that they hadn't tried to leave the hideaway.

The birds had grown up since that day he rescued them from the crows. Most of their fledgling down had shed away, and was replaced with dark brown plumage. Their feet were still gangly and oversized, but they could now walk with more confidence and balance. They constantly flapped their wings, building up flight muscle. It wouldn't be long before they took to the air. He wondered more each day if they would just fly away and never return. *Is the lure of the wild stronger than any bond they share with me?*

"Quite the little wolf pack we are, my friends," he told them, trying to feel cheerful. His thoughts drifted back to the home he left behind. *Amarillo surely would have barked if he had heard any screams coming from that direction.* He had to believe that all was fine and that his people were safe. Walking Free knew how to protect the village.

"It's my turn to eat. I thought the leader of the pack was supposed to eat first?" Chuckling to himself, he ventured out to find some wood to burn in his cooking fire. Returning soon after with an armful of mesquite, he quickly got a small fire going using his fire-making sticks and began cooking the leftover rabbit by dangling it on a stick.

As he was looking for some cooking tools in his pack, his hand felt the *libro* that Walking Free had given him. He pulled it out and began to look at the pictures and symbols. Most of the little symbols were strange-looking and unlike anything he had ever seen before. There were also bigger symbols too. Pictures of things that were familiar to him, like hawks, and men, and other kinds of animals. In many of the pictures, the men and the hawks were together, as if they were friends. It reminded him of how men and dogs were friends. *Maybe my birds could be my friends?*

He found many other interesting pictures in the *libro*: hawks attacking rabbits and birds, hawks wearing funny-looking headdresses, hawks with leads on their feet, and hawks sitting on a man's covered hand. Though there were many pictures of hawks, none of them looked like wolf hawks. *Did the men use magic to tame them?*

Many Wolves was so distracted by the pictures that he had forgotten about his food. His rabbit was now badly overcooked, but it was still good enough to eat. Hunger brought out the best flavors in food.

After finishing the rabbit, he realized he would have to hunt again soon. He would need to be extra careful in broad daylight to avoid being seen. He would hunt in low-light conditions, at sunrise and dusk, and stay away from open areas; traveling only at night by the light of the moon or by day if tall bushes or trees gave him cover.

He felt confident in his ability to survive in the wild alone. However, surviving in the wild with four more mouths to feed and no village to come home to would make his life much more difficult. Amarillo would earn his keep, but what about the birds?

Maybe the pictures could help him figure out their purpose.

Child of the Wind

M any Wolves woke before sunrise to prepare for his day's journey. His plan was to travel upstream along a creek that would eventually lead him to the Rio Pecos. Using the trees for cover, he journeyed as far as he could until he found another hidden shelter to camp in.

His present dilemma was to find a way to transport the birds. Carrying them in his hunting bag for too long was unsafe; they needed fresh air during the warmer part of the day. In the *libro*, he had seen a picture of a wooden structure that birds were perched on; but trying to build a frame like that would take time and would be awkward to carry. Maybe if he could find a young willow or cottonwood tree along the creek, he could use a branch as a perch by tying it to his pack on the pole-drag. At the moment, it was the best idea he could come up with.

He attached Amarillo to the pole-drag and placed each of the sleepy birds in his bag and started off along the creek. The sun had not yet fully risen, but there was enough light to travel by. The only sounds were the sporadic chirping of a few waking birds and the constant trickle of creek water as it gently rolled over a cluster of rocks. The hawks had settled down after the brief shock of being awoken and handled. Now, they were numbed by the darkness of their enclosure. Sounds and smells meant little; it was light that pumped life into them.

As he walked along the bank with Amarillo, he marveled at the dog's willingness to accept his arduous task. While Amarillo hauled the burden of his material belongings, Many Wolves shouldered the burden of responsibility for his new family. Each day, he would need to find food and shelter for them in unfamiliar places, leaving him with little time for anything else. The carefree days of his childhood were packed away in his memories.

The sun had cleared the horizon and still he hadn't found a small tree or branch that was sturdy enough for a perch. He began to feel hungry and he knew that the rest of his family felt the same. He needed to hunt before the sun rose too high. One of the large oaks along the creek would provide the shelter he needed, so he loosened Amarillo and hauled the pack to the base of the oak tree. Still tethered, his tired dog eagerly lapped up water from the creek.

With Amarillo loosely secured by a lead to the frame of the pole-drag, he let the birds out of the pack one by one. Instantly, they screamed at him with their raspy cries of hunger.

"All right, you crazy beggars, I'll try to find some food," he told them. "Amarillo, stay here and watch the camp. Make sure coyotes don't get into our food bag!"

He took his small hunting bow and an arrow out of his quiver, and slung the rest over his shoulder. He ventured out into the sage and mesquite to find rabbits or other small game. His grandfather had taught him that locating fresh tracks and scat would eventually lead to rabbits. The trick was to first locate the tracks and then stalk quietly around the surrounding area to try to locate a sitter—a rabbit sitting or eating quietly in the brush. It was too difficult to hit a bolting rabbit with an arrow.

After walking a short distance into the mesquite, he flushed out a small white-tailed rabbit, which dashed into a burrow. *There are rabbits here.*

He walked on the balls of his feet, avoiding noise-making objects like dead twigs or dried leaves, and scanned the brush for white-tailed rabbits or jackrabbits, both masters of hiding. His bow was ready, but not drawn, as he searched the ground ahead for targets. Every fifteen steps or so, he froze and looked carefully around him. He noticed more and more pellet-shaped rabbit droppings scattered about his path.

Then he spotted his first target, a white-tail. In one smooth, fluid motion, he drew his arrow and released. The arrow struck the hind leg of the rabbit, knocking it down. A perfect strike wasn't necessary because often the force of the arrow was enough to weaken or stun the rabbit so it couldn't escape. Many Wolves ran to it quickly and quelled its screams of pain by stabbing his bone knife into its neck, giving thanks to the Great Spirit, *life for life*.

He continued to hunt. After flushing out another white-tail, which escaped easily, he killed the next one instantly with a shot through its chest. He stashed the second rabbit with the first in his hunting bag and headed back to camp.

A red-tailed hawk circled overhead, watching him. "I'll only take what I need from your hunting grounds, great bird of prey," he said respectfully. The hawk followed him for quite a while, occasionally screeching its familiar battle scream before flying off.

On his way back to camp, he found a large cottonwood branch on the ground. It was smooth, thick, and straight, like one of the poles on the pole-drag. It seemed sturdy enough to support the weight of the birds, who weighed much less than other animals their size because of their feathers and hollow bones. *My luck has been good so far.*

Once back at camp, Amarillo greeted him with an enthusiastic tail wag. Cazador and Chiquito were perched on low rocks nearby, squawking at him for food. "Where is Reina? Where is your sister?" He looked all around the camp for her. *Has a predator killed her?* He didn't see any tracks in the dust. Then a thought occurred to him: *Did she fly away?* He checked the oak tree and the trees nearby, but nothing. *She is gone!*

He didn't have time to look for her right now with hungry mouths to feed. He cut a rear leg off one of the rabbits and tossed it to Amarillo, who received it eagerly. With a sizable piece of rabbit liver in his hand, he blew on his whistle and called "Cazador!" Immediately, she came lumbering over, using her wings for balance. He fed her and told her to go "back" to her perch as he had done many times before. He repeated this exercise several times and each time she performed it perfectly, while Chiquito watched. He ended Cazador's training by calling her from a much greater distance than before and rewarding her with a rabbit foreleg.

The training session did not go as smoothly with Chiquito. Working with him always tested the boy's patience. Many times Chiquito would just sit there on his perch after his name was called and look around, distracted, as if he was frightened. Worse still, Many Wolves had to carry him back to his perch most of the time. He offered the smallest and weakest of the fledglings a small treat or no treat at all if he failed to obey his instructions. Eventually, Chiquito got through his training, but it took much longer than with Cazador.

With the two of them fed, Many Wolves returned to his concerns for Reina. If she was still alive, she might be close by. He walked to a clearing near the camp and whistled and called for her, remaining careful not to be too loud.

From a distance came the faintest of sounds. *Reina!* He rushed towards the sound, calling to her periodically, trying to pinpoint her location. He realized that the call was coming from a clump of oak trees upstream.

When he reached the trees, he heard her scream again and then saw her perched in the middle of one of the larger trees.

She must have flown there! Her wings were spread and her mouth was open, but she looked unharmed. He knelt down, took a piece of the rabbit meat out, and called to her. She flapped her wings, screeched at him, and then with a great leap of faith, launched herself towards him. Gliding downwards on unsteady wings—a child of the nurturing wind—she landed awkwardly on a branch just above him and then jumped to the ground to grab the piece of food from his hand. It was amazing to see her fly. His heart pounded with excitement. *This beautiful, wild creature has flown to me!*

"Reina, I'm glad to see you, sister!" he said. "I thought I had lost you!"

As he walked back to camp, she followed him, flying low to the ground, sometimes landing clumsily on a rock or tree limb next to him. He gave her a small treat each time she followed. He led her back to the camp and gave her a rabbit foreleg as her final prize. She flew to a low branch on the oak tree and ate the rest of her meal.

Reina was growing up. She was free to go as she pleased. Like her, he thought, the other birds would learn to use their wings. *Would they be harder to train? How would they learn to hunt?*

The Scent of Death

"Should we have searched for the white-skinned boy?" asked Malone. "He is worth as much as the horses they gave us."

It was a cool, fall day. Mounted on their painted horses, Malone and Laughing Crow enjoyed a panoramic view of endless prairie from the top of a large hill near their village.

"I did not want to anger Walking Free and his people, Malone. Though their numbers are small, they are fierce warriors like the Pawnees. In a head-to-head fight, we would have lost many men. It wasn't worth the risk. Besides," Laughing Crow added, "it is time for us to hunt the buffalo and harvest their hides. If the hunt goes well, we will collect many hides that will be worth as much as the white-skinned boy."

The Nokoni leader knew that when the leaves fell from the trees, the buffalo hides were in prime condition, covered with a freshly grown coat of dark brown fur with no lingering residue of the previous winter's hair. The hides were perfect for making winter coats and robes and could be traded for desirable French goods, like steel knives and war axes, cooking pots, sewing implements, and vermillion.

"When should we begin our preparations for the hunt?" asked Malone.

"Tomorrow. Let the men know that if they wish to join us, they need to be ready at sunrise. The women and children should also be packed and ready."

"I'll have Silent Weasel and Little Owl ride out tonight to scout the herds and report to us in the morning," Malone said.

"Good. Tell Snake Tooth and the elders that I will not attend the hunting ceremony tonight. I prefer to be alone, so I can prepare my weapons." Laughing Crow was bored with the singing and dancing at most of the village ceremonies and he did not want to be bothered by the incessant tongue-flapping of the elder buzzards.

Two mornings later just before sunrise, the two scouts met with Laughing Crow and Malone. The night before, the women and children had prepared the camp, which was located near a running creek surrounded by various trees: cottonwoods, aspens, and poplars. They would follow the men to the hunt once they found the buffalo.

"How is your shoulder, Laughing Crow?" asked Silent Weasel.

"It's stiff, but I can pull my bow well enough for the hunt." Despite the lingering pain and stiffness, Laughing Crow felt obligated to lead the men. He knew that his absence would be seen as weakness. He was hoping the blood rush from the hunt would help him to forget the pain.

"I'm not used to seeing you hunt without your lance," Silent Weasel said, grinning.

"When my shoulder is stronger, I will use it again," said Laughing Crow. He preferred to hunt buffalo with a lance, since it provided a quicker kill and a greater challenge, earning him the respect of his men.

"A large herd is just over the bend to the northwest," reported Little Owl. Using rocks as landmarks on the ground, he described in fine detail where the buffalo were located. "They are grazing on flat land with no hills or gullies in the area. We should have plenty of space to ride safely."

"The lay of the land is good, Little Owl, and the Great Spirit has blessed us with a clear day." Laughing Crow signaled for the other hunters to approach and form a line in front of him. The men carried bows or lances; some carried both. They were dressed in breechcloths only and none of them carried shields as they did in war. Their faces were painted in varying patterns of white, blue, and yellow, except for the Blood Riders, who were painted with blood-red vermillion.

Laughing Crow addressed the twenty-four men of his hunting party with a raised voice. "We will approach them quietly, in a single line, with the wind in our faces to cover our scent. When they start to run, ride fast and hard and attack from the right side. Aim your arrows and lances at their hearts to kill them quickly. We don't want the meat to spoil. Be aware of other riders around you. After our horses have lost their first wind, we will prepare what we have killed for the ride back to camp." As he spoke, Laughing Crow rode back and forth along the line of men. Cheval-Sang was prancing with giddy anticipation. Laughing Crow knew the body language of his favorite horse so well that it was as if their thoughts were from one mind.

Laughing Crow fell into the middle of the line, between Malone and Thorn Bird, and gestured for the men to move forward cautiously. The pungent aroma of fresh buffalo excrement permeated the air. Within moments, the most distant members of the massive herd appeared from the other side of a low slope and slowly the rest of the herd unfurled before them. Many of the buffalo stopped grazing, alerted to the approaching riders. In a steady wave of motion, the closest animals began to flee.

Raising his bow, Laughing Crow signaled for his men to charge with a loud yell. The horses launched into a full gallop driven by the cries of their riders. The rumbling hooves of buffalo and horses meshed into a beat-driven feast of sound.

Dung and dirt flung into the faces of the riders as they approached their closest targets. The twang of a bowstring, sometimes more than one, was followed by a moaning animal scream and then the earth-shaking crash of a great beast as it slammed into the ground; the sequence ended with a hunter's triumphant yell and soon the cycle of sounds began again.

Laughing Crow, who had killed one buffalo bull, was watching the other riders and keeping a rough head count of the kills, when Malone yelled to him.

"Laughing Crow, Thorn Bird is down!"

He watched as Malone cleared himself of the herd and circled back. Laughing Crow followed, tortured by the thought that his son was hurt, or even dead. Riding against the flow of the herd, Malone launched himself back into the stampede, which was sparser than it had been moments ago. Now at full speed, he slumped over the side of his horse and grabbed Thorn Bird's arm and in one smooth, powerful motion, hoisted the larger warrior across the back of his horse. Separating himself from the rampaging herd, Malone rode to a safe place, dismounted, and rested Thorn Bird's limp body on the ground.

Laughing Crow arrived soon after, trying to prepare himself for the worst. "Is he alive, Malone?"

"His heartbeat and breathing are strong. I think he was just knocked out from the fall," said Malone, who was on his knees examining Thorn Bird.

Relieved, Laughing Crow dismounted and approached his son. Though he had seen many dead and injured men, seeing his son like this stirred an emotion he had never felt before.

Moments later, Walks Loudly approached them and slid off his horse.

"Is he all right?" asked the young warrior, older brother of Stands Alone, one of the Blood Riders.

"He's lost his wind," answered Malone, who was pouring water on the young man's forehead. Then he stood and turned to Walks Loudly. "What happened? I saw you riding next to Thorn Bird when he fell."

"He was trying to kill a large bull, but the animal wasn't slowing down, even after Thorn Bird pierced him with three or four arrows," he said. "I rode up next to the buffalo and fired an arrow at him from the other side."

"From the *left* side?" Laughing Crow interrupted.

"Yes, from the left side. I always attack from the left because I draw my bow with my left hand," remarked Walks Loudly nervously, as the Nokoni leader strode towards him.

"What happened then?" asked Laughing Crow.

"The bull…the bull bucked to the right and then it fell… and knocked Thorn Bird off his horse," said Walks Loudly, his words quivering.

Laughing Crow paused and then spoke. "Attacking from the left is not *our* way. Do you choose to ignore my words, or is your mind as slow as the desert turtle?" Laughing Crow was feeling a fury build up inside him as he stared down the young warrior. "Your skills as a warrior are a shame to your family! You live in your brother's shadow. He commands the respect of my men, but not you!"

As beads of sweat rolled down his face, Laughing Crow continued to berate the man, who was struggling to look in his eyes. "I see you standing before me in all your weakness and my son, one of the bravest of our warriors, lying motionless on the ground because of your stupidity!" Laughing Crow grabbed him by the shoulders and slammed him to the ground.

Rage gripped his senses with the unrelenting grasp of an eagle's talon. It was unstoppable, uncontrollable. Laughing Crow knelt down on one knee beside the trembling man. "This weakness, this carelessness, I cannot accept and will not tolerate!"

With speed and precision gained on many blood-soaked battlefields, Laughing Crow drew his knife and slashed the throat of the man he deemed worthless. He watched as Walks Loudly choked on his own blood, unable to scream. He wiped his victim's blood off his face, as if it were a stinging poison, and then he spit on the dead man and walked away.

"Malone, find Stands Alone and tell him to take care of his brother. Tell him what has happened here."

Malone nodded, still tending to Thorn Bird.

The Nokoni leader walked over to the carcass of the bull he had killed, wiped his bloody knife on its belly, and then cut into the animal's side. Ripping the liver out, he hoisted it above his head and squeezed the blood into his dry, dust-bitten mouth to quench his thirst.

Walking back to where his son was lying, Laughing Crow spoke to Malone again.

"I will take my son back to the village when he awakes. Snake Tooth will know how to take care of him. Lead the men in my absence. The hunt is over for me."

Malone nodded again. "I will take care of it."

Laughing Crow noticed buzzards starting to circle, smelling death. Only a few of them now, but soon there would be many. *The scent of death reaches far. Smoke cannot hide it. Wind cannot blow it away. Rain cannot cleanse it. Once it's released, it cannot be recalled. It always finds the buzzards whose survival depends upon it. And they always come.*

A Piece of Hope

The elation of Reina's first flight soon lost its luster for Many Wolves. He continued to worry about how to transport his birds. He decided that he didn't want to carry them in the bag again, so he attached a cottonwood branch to the pole-drag, but the birds wouldn't stay on it, despite all of his training efforts. He held the branch low to the ground, with a small piece of food on it, but they simply grabbed the food and jumped off. With no other choices left, he decided that he would leave the oak tree camp only after all of them could fly. If they followed him after that, it was their choice.

Cazador was now airborne like her sister. Many Wolves watched her fly around the camp the previous day with the same awkwardness that Reina demonstrated on her first few flights. He was relieved to see that the two sisters were becoming more independent, although he feared they would someday leave him for the call of the wind and the sky. *Now, there is just Chiquito.*

Many Wolves woke up at sunrise with an idea burning in his head. He dug into his bag for the white man's *libro*. He flipped through the thin, leafy pieces until he reached the picture he'd studied the day before. It was a picture of a man with a bird perched on his covered fist—a "fist-perch" was what he called it. The hand was covered by some sort of animal hide that was shaped like a hand. It seemed strange to him that a bird would perch on a man's fist. He had always fed the birds from his fingertips or tossed the food on the ground for them. He didn't want those sharp talons near his bare hands and arms, for he had seen how deeply they punctured the skin of small animals. *Maybe wrapping his hand with deerskin—a fist-perch—would make it less painful.*

He emptied the bows and arrows from his quiver and wrapped it around his hand, covering the wrist and knuckles, but leaving the thumb and fingers exposed. Using his other hand, he reached into his food bag and ripped off a small piece of rabbit meat from the previous day's hunt and hid it in the palm of his fist-perch. The birds launched into a screaming frenzy when they saw him reach for their favorite bag. "Easy does it, you little beggars!"

Keeping the food hidden from their sight, he walked a distance away from them. Then he raised the fist-perch above his head with the food held between his finger and thumb, like he had seen in another picture, and called to Reina with a whistle. Without hesitation, both she and Cazador flew towards him, but only Reina landed on his fist. She eagerly gulped down the food. Cazador flew to a rock and waited for her turn. The flightless Chiquito meandered towards him on gangly legs, wings outstretched and screaming in protest, but remained a safe distance away knowing his place in the feeding order.

Many Wolves lowered his fist-perch slowly and Reina looked at him and watched his other hand carefully as if to ask, "Where's the rest of my food?" Once she was nearly at eye-level with him, she flew off to land in a tree nearby. "Don't worry, sister. I'm not going to eat you!" He laughed.

With his fist lowered this time, he placed a piece of rabbit meat on his fingertips and called her and again she flew down to the fist-perch and grabbed the food, then flew off. *I can hardly feel those claws!* He wanted to continue the training with the fist-perch, but he was running low on food and needed to hunt again. *The quiver works well as a fist-perch, but I need it to carry my bow and arrows.*

"Reina and Cazador, it's time to hunt. You can stay here and scream with your brother or come with me. You'll get fed sooner if you come," encouraged Many Wolves, knowing that words were as strange to them as the symbols in the *libro* were to him.

He grabbed his bow and arrows, filled his quiver, and walked towards his favorite hunting spot. He hoped the birds, driven by their hunger, would follow; but either way, he had to hunt.

After looking for some time, he finally shot a sitting jack-rabbit. He squelched the wails of the dying animal with his knife. Suddenly, from behind him came a familiar scream. Cazador was perched just beyond his reach, looking at him and at the freshly killed rabbit.

Many Wolves smiled. "So, the great hunter has come for a handout! I guess I should reward you for following." He cut off one of the front legs of the rabbit and tossed it to her. Usually she hopped away from him with the food clutched in her claws, but this time she stayed next to him and ate. He was delighted that she was sharing the kill with him. "You'll be safe with me, sister. A coyote or eagle won't try to hurt you or steal your food as long as I am here." He packed the rest of the rabbit in his bag, sat down, and watched her eat. *I wish my grandfather could see this.*

Moments later, he heard Reina's screams coming from a mesquite bush nearby. She was still hungry. *I should try the fist-perch again.* He emptied his quiver and like before, wrapped it tightly around his left hand. He cut off the other front leg of the rabbit, held it in his covered hand, and then stood up and whistled for her. Instantly, she flew at eye-level towards him, focused on the fist-perch and the food.

She landed on his fist, ripped off a chunk of rabbit flesh, and immediately flew to a bush next to him. She repeated this exercise many times, gradually settling on the fist-perch for longer and longer periods of time. "Your hunger makes you brave!" He sat motionless and watched the bird eat from his hand. With every bite, the fear she felt for him was melting away. Soon, all that was left was a bone on the desert floor, unaffected by the rain and wind and heat, permanent, like friendship and family.

Every day his heart ached for his family. Often he cried himself to sleep at night, thinking about them and praying to the Great Spirit that they were still alive and in good health. The place in his heart where they once lived was now occupied by the growing fear that he would die alone in the wilderness or that the Buffalo People, who still haunted his dreams, would find him and kill him.

Today, he felt a little stronger, a little less lonely, a little less fearful because the bond with his birds was growing, filling his heart with hope.

Their Kill

"Chiquito, if you don't start flying soon, we'll have to leave you here all alone!" teased Many Wolves. He was sitting at his camp under the oak tree, cleaning up two jackrabbit skins he had soaked in the creek the previous day. With the backside of his knife, he scraped away the hair that hadn't been washed away by the water. He planned to use the skins to make a crude cover for his hand and lower arm, to protect them from the birds' sharp talons. While his quiver was useful as a fist-perch, it was difficult to shoot his bow while his hand was wrapped with it, and he needed his quiver to carry other hunting supplies.

Once most of the hair was removed from the hides, Many Wolves intended to use the brains of the rabbits to tan the hides into rawhide leather that could be softened and stretched. He had watched his mother and Desert Flower do this many times with animal hides, but this was the first time he had tried it himself. He was not concerned too much about the final appearance of the leather covering, only that it would be durable and protective.

"This is hard work, Amarillo! The women of the village must have strong hands!" Amarillo, resting next to him as he worked, perked his ears up as Many Wolves spoke. "I think I need a break, my hands are getting sore," he complained, trying to stretch the stiffness out of his aching hands. "I think I've scraped most of the hair off. It doesn't need to be perfect."

He stretched the hides out on a large, flat rock in the sun and spread a coat of the warm rabbit brain-water on each of the hides. The mixture had been sitting in the sun in one of his water containers. The horrific smell of rotting brains made it difficult to work. He needed to walk away from time to time to escape the suffocating stench and fill his body with clean air. He wondered if he would ever be able to use that container again for drinking.

"Cazador and Reina, let's get away from here and go hunting somewhere...anywhere!" Many Wolves grabbed his quiver and bow and walked down to the creek to wash his hands and face thoroughly, and to drink. Looking back, he yelled, "Chiquito, keep exercising those wings. Soon the sky and the wind will be your brothers!" Amarillo waited behind with Chiquito, enjoying the shade of the oak tree.

With the quiver wrapped around his left hand, he practiced calling the birds to his fist-perch for small morsels of rabbit flesh as he walked out towards the hunting area. The birds were becoming more and more accustomed to it. He fed them a large portion of their meal the previous day with his hand covered this way.

As each day passed, the birds were transforming from helpless babies to full-fledged members of his family. Their dependency on him for food still nourished his link with them, but soon they would be able to hunt for themselves. He hoped a new, stronger bond would be forged between them, not based on need, but companionship. He had to make them believe that they were better off with him than on their own in the wild. He hoped this would happen after many successful hunts together.

As Many Wolves approached the spot where he found rabbits before, he removed the quiver from his hand, put all the arrows inside, except for one, and slung it over his shoulder. He loaded his bow and began stalking, scanning the sandy loam for any signs of small animals. Reina and Cazador watched him intently from their low mesquite perches. "Someday, you'll be finding the rabbits, not me," he muttered to himself.

He spotted a large jackrabbit and then drew his bow and quickly released an arrow, hitting it on the backside. The rabbit tried to run, but its movement was impeded by its injured rear leg, and it was only able to run at half speed. Many Wolves chased after the laboring rabbit, when all of a sudden, a flash of brown, winged fury passed him on his left. *Cazador has joined the hunt!* A short distance ahead, the young hawk tucked her wings in and dove straight to the ground from a height just above the mesquite, unleashing the penetrating scream of a rabbit struggling for its life.

Sprinting towards the sound, Many Wolves caught up to the two, one of them fighting for its life and the other just trying to hold on. Cazador's talons were locked onto the lower back of the rabbit, but the great strength of its powerful legs dragged the bird along the ground. The rabbit tried in vain to free itself from the young predator's grip. After two failed attempts to grab the rabbit, Many Wolves finally subdued it and ended its pain with a quick stroke of his knife.

"Cazador, you did it! You are a hunter!" Many Wolves's heart was racing like a hummingbird's wings. He sliced open the chest of the rabbit and scooped out two of the bloodiest organs, the heart and the liver, and offered them to the fledgling hunter, who devoured them in a hurry.

"Today we hunted like wolves, Cazador, together, as a pack."

Reina arrived soon after, looking for her share of the prize. "Reina, your sister has become a hunter. I always thought you would be the first to catch prey, but Cazador has proven me wrong. Now, you can learn from your sister." Many Wolves tore off a front leg for Reina. "If you help with the kill like Cazador, then you'll get the heart and liver, the juiciest parts."

As he spoke, a deafening blast of thunder filled the air and rain began to pour all over them. Late-afternoon thunderstorms were common in the fall. Many Wolves loved the rain, which swallowed the dust and cleansed his body. His grandfather had once told him that the wailing groans of the Earth Mother could be heard in the roaring thunder as she wept and mourned the loss of the falling, dying leaves. Many of the people of his village were terrified of the thunder and lightning, but to him, it reinforced the belief that there were greater spirits alive in the world. It was a loud, crashing reminder that it was their world and not the world of men.

"Let's head back to camp, sisters. Perhaps we'll find your brother high up in a tree so our journey to the Rio Pecos can continue." With that, he gathered up the remains of their kill and stashed it in his hunting bag, then walked back home in the pouring rain, feeling renewed in body and spirit.

Extracting the Poison

"Laughing Crow, the *paraibo* and his council are ready for us," said Malone with graveness in his voice.

Buzzards. "I was wondering when they would want to peck at my carcass," Laughing Crow said coldly. He was sitting in his tipi shaping dogwood shoots into arrow shafts, using a piece of buffalo bone with a hole punched through it. He knew that he would inevitably have to face Gray Elk, the peace leader, the *paraibo* of the village, and the rest of the elders.

The Nokoni war leader walked over to Gray Elk's lodge where the elders were gathered in a half circle outside, still carrying his shaping tool and the arrow shoots. Stands Alone, the brother of the man Laughing Crow had killed three days earlier, and Malone were seated facing the elders, who sat on the other side of the council fire, while other men of the village surrounded them. The women and children were also present on this mild fall day to witness the events.

Gray Elk stood up and began to speak. "Laughing Crow, it is the desire of this council to resolve matters between Stands Alone, his family, and you with regards to the violent, unexpected death of his brother. Please be seated next to Malone." Gray Elk motioned for Laughing Crow to sit on Malone's right. Stands Alone was seated on Malone's left.

Laughing Crow sat down facing the council and continued working on one of his arrow shafts, listening selectively. *What could they do to me?*

Gray Elk was a tall man with long, straight gray hair. He always wore two eagle feathers in his scalp-lock, like many of the Nokoni men. He was dressed in deerskin leggings, deerskin boots, and a buffalo robe. His most distinctive facial feature was his large, bulbous chin, which Laughing Crow thought was sufficiently shaped to grind corn.

"Malone, this council wishes to hear what you saw that led to the death of Stand Alone's brother," said Gray Elk, returning to his seat. Standing directly behind him were two warriors, one of them his son, who were armed with lances.

Malone stood up and spoke to the council.

"I was riding with Laughing Crow, in the middle of the stampeding buffalo, when I looked to my left and saw Thorn Bird fall from his horse. Immediately, I turned around and rode back to pick him up, fearing he would soon be trampled. I grabbed him off the ground and rode to safety in a clearing where Laughing Crow joined us. Thorn Bird was alive and his breathing was strong. Shortly after, Stands Alone's brother arrived. He said he was trying to help Thorn Bird kill his buffalo when the large bull knocked Thorn Bird off his horse." Malone hesitated before continuing, "Then Laughing Crow became very angry and accused him of carelessness. I saw Laughing Crow push him to the ground and say some words I did not hear. Then Laughing Crow reached for his knife and slashed his throat. That's all I saw."

Malone sat down.

Gray Elk nodded to Malone and then stood up. "Laughing Crow, tell us with your words what happened," requested Gray Elk.

Laughing Crow stuck the carving knife in the dirt and dropped the arrow to the ground, stood up, and faced Stands Alone. Through the silence around him, he could hear the tail-swishing of Gray Elk's horse as it lashed at flies.

"Stands Alone, you are a brave hunter and warrior, that is why we made you a Blood Rider. You bring honor to our village as a provider and protector." Laughing Crow paused to choose his words carefully. He looked at Stands Alone and then turned his attention to the people gathered around him. "Your older brother, however, was not like you. He was not skilled with the lance or bow or as a horse rider. I tolerated his weaknesses and let him ride in my hunting parties because I did not want to dishonor you."

Laughing Crow turned to the council and spoke to them more fervently. "Stands Alone's brother was light in the head. He was forgetful and chose to ignore my directions, and not just this time, but many other times as well. In war, if you fail to follow simple instructions you endanger the men who ride with you. You become as dangerous and unpredictable as the enemy." Laughing Crow felt the anger burning inside. "His carelessness almost killed my son. This is why I took my knife to his throat."

There was murmuring in the crowd.

"Silence!" barked Gray Elk.

"Is there anything else you wish to know?" asked Laughing Crow, defiantly facing the elders, his long late-afternoon shadow spilling darkness on the elders. "If not, I wish to return to my lodge."

"We are not finished, Laughing Crow," Gray Elk said, standing up. "Is it your belief that any man who disobeys your orders must die?" asked the peace leader. "If Thorn Bird or Malone disobeyed you, would you take your knife to their throats?"

"Gray Elk, you try to speak with the coyote tongue…with words of trickery," retorted Laughing Crow. "Thorn Bird and Malone do not endanger men with mindless actions. The difference between them and Stands Alone's brother is that they have learned from their mistakes, while he continued to fail."

The Nokoni leader looked at each of the elders with disgust and then returned his attention to his accuser. "Gray Elk, when was the last time you commanded a war party? Can you remember an order you gave that would endanger men if it wasn't followed?" snarled Laughing Crow, glaring at the big-chinned man. "You buzzards! You sit around your fire and feed off the flesh that my men bring to the village and then criticize the way I lead them! Gray Elk, was it your blood that was spilled—" Laughing Crow reached down, picked up his carving knife, sliced his palm, and showed it to Gray Elk "—or was it *this* blood that was spilled so you could ride one of the finest horses on the plains and wear that ornate buffalo robe?" *What do these buzzards know of war!*

Gray Elk stood up and faced Laughing Crow, flanked by his two armed guards, but he chose not to answer.

"I find it laughable that one who bears no scars or scalps from battle can judge *me* on matters of war!" thundered Laughing Crow, taunting a response.

"Is that all you have to say to this council?" said Gray Elk, his voice trembling.

"I am finished," said Laughing Crow, returning to his seat.

Gray Elk leaned over and whispered words to the elder on his left. The elder nodded in approval. "Stands Alone, what do you ask from Laughing Crow as payment for your brother's life?"

Stands Alone stood up and answered. "I want his war horse as payment and if he is unwilling to part with it, then I want him to leave the village and never return."

Again, there was more buzzing from the throng of onlookers.

Gray Elk looked back at the other council members who all nodded. "Stands Alone, that is a fair offer…"

"That offer is absurd!" yelled a woman from the back of the crowd. As she walked forward, pushing her way through the crowd, Laughing Crow saw that it was Prowling Coyote's widow. "If it were any other man of the village, the barter would be death! It is the tradition of our village to punish murderers with death! This snake of a man does not deserve easy treatment!" The widow was yelling uncontrollably as she pointed at Laughing Crow.

"We cannot take Laughing Crow's life because Stands Alone did not ask for it. Please return to your place with the others and remain silent," commanded Gray Elk. Two of the men dragged her back towards where she was standing, but she continued to curse and holler, so they carried her thrashing body far away from the gathering so she could not be heard anymore.

"Laughing Crow, will you give what Stands Alone requires?" said the peace leader.

"I would rather die than give up my best war horse," answered Laughing Crow. "I can offer him five good horses and nothing more. That is my offer. Cheval-Sang stays with me." Laughing Crow began digging in the dirt with the point of the arrow he was shaping, which was now bloodied by the cut in his stinging palm.

"That is an insult!" said Stands Alone. "You have forty horses? ...Fifty horses? Or more! Five horses mean nothing to you! You are not bartering with some white trader for knives or arrow points! Your war horse is what I demand for my brother's life! He didn't deserve to be slaughtered like a dog!"

"Laughing Crow, if you are unwilling to pay what Stands Alone asks for, then you must leave the village," Gray Elk said in a tone laced with satisfaction.

Laughing Crow stood up and threw the arrow to the ground. "I would rather leave this village of scavengers than pay him a single horse!"

"Then it is agreed," said Gray Elk, his voice now firm and confident. "You and your family will leave before night falls and never return. You can take one horse with you, but the rest must be left behind as your payment to the village."

Somewhere in the middle of the murmuring crowd, Laughing Crow heard Sun Sparrow let out a muffled cry.

Gray Elk walked towards Laughing Crow and spoke to him directly. "For too long you have been a rattlesnake in our village, spreading your poison to all living things. Now, your poison has killed and we are glad to be rid of it. If you return without our permission, you will be killed," he pronounced.

"Old buzzard, in five winters' time I will lead a village greater than yours. Where I go, men will follow. They hunger for strong leadership and thirst for glory in war. Like a tick, your leadership will suck the life out of the men who stay, making them weak and unable to protect themselves, like a toothless predator!"

Laughing Crow walked closer to Gray Elk so he could feel the old buzzard's breath, but he felt Malone grab his arm to restrain him. Gray Elk's guards closed in with their lances drawn and ready.

"When I return you will be the first to die, old man! I will hang your gray-haired, buzzard scalp inside my lodge, so that each night before I sleep, I can look at it and smile, knowing that your spirit is tortured in the next world." With that, Laughing Crow picked up his knife and arrows, spit on the council fire, and stomped off back to his lodge. *How easy it will be to take your power, old buzzard. Just like I took Crooked Twig's.*

Soon after, the Nokoni headman arrived at his lodge. Dusk was fast approaching and Laughing Crow wanted to put this day and this village far behind him.

Malone approached him. "Laughing Crow, I will find the warriors that are still loyal and we will follow you with our families. You will not be alone."

Laughing Crow put his hand on Malone's shoulder and gripped it firmly.

"Many will follow us, Malone. There is only rot and decay where buzzards circle."

The Big River

Three days had passed since Many Wolves left his camp under the large oak tree and even longer since Chiquito had finally flown for the first time. Their days were spent traveling or hunting. If hunting went well, then they spent more time following the creek, which he knew led to the big river. Often, the birds made it difficult to travel when one of them refused to follow, but he was compelled to keep moving, to reach the Rio Pecos and the safety of the high country beyond it.

Many Wolves had tied the large cottonwood branch to the pole-drag to give the birds the option to perch, but they rarely stayed on it for long. Now that their wings had liberated them, they seemed to prefer higher perches. *The pole-drag perch is too low.*

Cazador and Reina continued to hunt with him and though they both chased after the rabbits and rock squirrels he flushed out, neither of them was able to repeat Cazador's previous hunting success. Catching a rabbit in a full sprint or a squirrel dodging from rock to rock proved to be too difficult for them without a slowing blow from one of his arrows. But, he did see some progress each day. They were gaining speed and agility as flyers, making it harder for animals to escape their concerted attacks. They were maturing and learning. It was fascinating to watch them turn into predators.

"Chiquito, let's go! Don't be a lazy bird! The creek is much wider here. We must be getting close to the big river." Many Wolves was growing more and more impatient with his smallest bird for not keeping up. When the bird was hungry, he would follow closely, but otherwise, he seemed distracted. "Maybe if you miss a meal or two, you'll learn to stay with us."

As he walked along the dusty path, weaving around the numerous mesquite bushes with Amarillo pulling his pole-drag close behind, the sound of rushing water grew louder. The big river was close now. Overwhelmed by excitement and curiosity, Many Wolves ran towards the sound.

When he reached a low overlook, the gigantic river presented itself to him. The creek that had led him for many days, like a tracker leading a hunter to a prize animal, now yielded to its majestic, hard-flowing brother. With Amarillo at his side, Many Wolves sat and watched the mighty Rio Pecos, in awe of it. A light breeze carried the refreshing mist to his dry, dust-caked face. Reina and Chiquito were perched on mesquite bushes nearby, while Cazador flew out to scout the river more closely. "I made it," Many Wolves said to himself, pleased and relieved.

"Look, Amarillo! See how the river carries that tree trunk with ease? Imagine what it would do with a man or a horse!" Many Wolves looked across the water. "It's so wide! I don't think I could shoot an arrow to the other side!"

Reina flew out over the water to get a closer look, joining Cazador. He watched as the two birds flapped and soared, repeatedly circling the big river, spiraling higher into the sky. No longer awkward, they now flew with grace and power. As he watched them go higher than ever before, he thought perhaps this was their way of greeting the river.

The flight of his two female birds was both beautiful and terrifying. They flew with a spirit of freedom and independence. They were truly free to choose their path. He started to feel insecure as they sailed further into the horizon. *I should call them back.*

Many Wolves stood up and nervously put on his rabbit hide fist-perch. Placing a small chunk of rabbit meat in his hand, he raised it to the sky and yelled, "Reina! Cazador!"

The birds did not respond. They continued to sail high above the river, drifting away like a leaf being carried by the southeastern breeze. *Did they hear me?*

"Reina! Cazador!" He called to them and blew his bone whistle as loud as he could.

The birds continued to glide along the wide swath cut by the Rio Pecos until the two dark specks were completely absorbed by the horizon. A rush of heat filled Many Wolves's chest, breeding panic. He felt completely helpless, like the day he left his home. But he had to cling to the hope that the birds would return. *Could they really leave me and Chiquito?*

After drawing a deep breath, he said, "Chiquito, Amarillo, let's find shelter along the riverbank before they come back." He felt comforted that they were still with him. He wondered why Chiquito hadn't flown away too. *Is he afraid to fly with them, or does he feel safer with me?*

He walked along the eastern bank of the big river and bent down to inspect the water. The water was dirty and clouded, compared to the clear water of the creek. He cupped some of it in his hands and sipped it slowly. It tasted gritty and salty. Amarillo also drank from the muddy river.

"This is the water we will have to drink from now on. We better get used to it," he said to Amarillo and then resumed walking north along the riverbank. Further up, he saw many different rock formations on either side of the river, shaped over time by smooth blades of rushing water.

As he walked, he noticed bones and skulls of animals that the water had spit out on its shores. *Did the river kill these animals?* He recognized the remains of buffalo and horses, mostly. *Did they drink too much of the salty water, or did they die trying to swim across the river?* The river was fast-moving and appeared too deep to walk through. It would be impossible to reach the other side, he thought.

Further on, Many Wolves found a large depression in the rock. It provided a windbreak and overhanging protection from the hot sun and late-afternoon thundershowers—already, the looming clouds in the west were beginning to harness their moisture.

"Amarillo, wait here. I need to hunt for us." He gathered up his bow and arrows and signaled for Chiquito to follow him.

It took him some time to finally kill a rock squirrel. The terrain around the river was more barren than he was used to and was decorated with a tapestry of mesquite, sage, prickly pear, and sotol cactus plants. He fed Chiquito with a sizable portion of the squirrel. After that, Chiquito lazily followed along as his provider stalked and killed a jackrabbit with a quick shot of his bow. *It is lonely hunting without Reina and Cazador.*

He returned to his camp and began digging out a fire pit with a sharpened piece of cedar. Suddenly, Amarillo started to growl—a low rumble of a growl that Many Wolves knew as a signal that a larger animal was nearby. Often coyotes followed him back to camp after a hunt, smelling the aroma of a fresh kill. "Easy, Amarillo, it's probably just another coyote looking for a handout."

After he made the fire pit, he rubbed his fire-making sticks in dried sage, which he often used to tinder his fires. Amarillo continued to growl, louder and more frequently until at last he erupted into excited barking.

"Easy, boy, easy..." Unlike in the past, his comforting words had no effect on his companion.

"What brings a boy to these barren lands?" said a soft, raspy voice from behind him.

Hadakai

In one swift move, Many Wolves lunged for his knife and turned to confront the person speaking to him. Amarillo strained against the rawhide lead that was stretched around his neck, and barked even louder at the stranger.

"Don't be afraid. I wish you no harm." An old man dressed in only a tattered breechcloth showed Many Wolves that his hands were empty and then brought the open palm of his right hand to his heart in a gesture of friendship.

"You are Lipan?" asked Many Wolves, inspecting the elder's slouching figure, and still gripping the knife with his sweaty hand. Amarillo's frantic barking forced him to raise his voice.

"No, but our words are similar. I am Mescalero and my band lives far across the river to the northwest," he said. Many Wolves could see that his frail body was not the body of a warrior, but rather a man whose physical strength and youthfulness had been sapped by the suns of many summers. His long, gray matted hair covered his leathery, sun-beaten skin and shaded his elongated ears and the sides of his face. He appeared to be even older than Walking Free and Yellow Feather.

"Amarillo! Easy…" Many Wolves commanded his dog with a firm voice and a hand signal. Immediately, his dog stopped barking, but resumed his low growls, unwilling to be completely silenced.

"Are you alone?" asked the boy, still not completely convinced of the old man's harmlessness.

"I am alone and have been for quite a long time now," he replied, with the hint of a smile in his tone. "May I join you? It's been a long time since I've heard another voice."

Many Wolves gestured for him to come closer and then placed his knife down at his side. The old man approached slowly and then sat down, but kept more than a body's length of space between him and them.

"What name do I call you? A white-skinned boy with long brown hair who wears a Lipan headband, speaks Lipan words, and makes peace with the wild birds," he said, glancing at Chiquito as he finished his sentence.

"My name is Many Wolves. I grew up in a Lipan village. This is my wolf hawk. His name is Chiquito," he answered, pointing to his smallest bird who was sitting on a large rock. He wished he could show his visitor his other birds. "This is Amarillo," he added, gesturing towards his dog. "What do I call you?"

"You can call me Hadakai," replied the old man, whose head ticked nervously from side-to-side.

"What does it mean? I've never heard this word before."

"It means 'One Who Walks' in the ancient language," replied Hadakai, his voice wheezing from the strain of breathing, though he didn't seem tired. "Many of the old words have been replaced by the newer words that you know. I learned them from my father and grandfather and the elders of my village."

"My grandfather used words like this when he spoke with the other elders, but he never taught them to me."

"What brings a young one like you to this desolate place?"

Many Wolves gathered his thoughts, still studying the man's sagging cheekbones and eyelids, which resembled the face of an old dog. *It's good to hear a voice again.*

"After a group of Northerners threatened our village, the leaders of my village believed that it would be safer for me to leave and head up north along the Rio Pecos until I reached the high country, where the Northerners could not easily find me."

Hadakai watched him carefully as he spoke. Although he was old, he seemed alert and full of life.

"I need to make a fire. Would you like to share this rabbit with me?" asked Many Wolves, feeling more comfortable with the stranger. Amarillo also seemed more relaxed. His growls were reduced to an occasional "woof," which sounded like a rush of air from his stomach. Now it was Chiquito's turn, and he began to screech loudly.

"Fresh rabbit would be a welcome change from the snakes, lizards, and fish I usually eat. Thank you." Hadakai nodded and smiled to show his appreciation. "I have some hearts from the sotol cactus that I can share with you," he added, removing a few of the bulb-shaped hearts from the pouch that hung around his waist. "Try this."

Many Wolves was blowing on a small ember, which was nestled in a bundle of dried grass. Once the small flames began, he took the sotol heart from Hadakai and nibbled off a small piece. "This is so tender and it has a different flavor than the sotol I am used to," he said, before taking another, larger bite.

"I cooked them slowly on a bed of hot rocks, which I covered with prickly pear pads to prevent them from charring and drying out. They soften up nicely and are much easier to eat if you cook them slowly for a long time. I added sage and mesquite for flavor." Hadakai took a bite from another one of the sotol hearts. He ate with his mouth open to aid his labored breathing.

"I don't remember the women of my village cooking them this way," said Many Wolves, savoring every bite as the juice ran down his chin.

"Why is your bird screeching?" asked Hadakai.

Many Wolves glanced up at Chiquito. "I don't know. He usually screams when he's hungry, but I've never heard this kind of scream before. Perhaps he's not used to you or maybe he misses his two sisters."

"He has sisters?"

"Yes. I raised him and his two sisters after a strong wind-storm blew them out of their nest. Crows were attacking them and their parents had abandoned them. I had to save them from the crows. His two sisters, Reina and Cazador, flew away from us earlier today when we first reached the Rio Pecos," said Many Wolves, speaking with his mouth half full. "I'm worried that they are far, far away and won't return. I've tried many times to call them back, but my words and whistles go unanswered."

"This is a test of your friendship. The spirits of animals are difficult to tame."

Many Wolves prepared the jackrabbit for cooking, strip-ping the skin from the flesh—the cold smell of rabbit slammed his face, like dust kicked up by a swirling wind. After the skin was removed, he skewered the rabbit on a large, sharpened stick and hung it over the small fire.

Chiquito still seemed agitated and unsettled. The bird's screams echoed the loneliness Many Wolves felt for Reina and Cazador. He hoped that somehow Chiquito's calls would reach his sisters and he prayed silently to the Wind Spirit to deliver Chiquito's pleas to them.

"Why do you live here and not with your village?" asked Many Wolves, still distracted by Chiquito's droning cries.

Hadakai grinned. "I left my village when I was very sick. Like an old buffalo, I wanted to leave my people and go off to die by myself. I believed that it was my time to die. That was over three winters ago." Hadakai laughed. "I believe the salty waters of the Rio Pecos somehow healed my ailments and now I am afraid to stray too far from the river."

"Was it hard to survive here on your own?"

"The river and the desert provide all I need. There are plenty of rock shelters along the river to hide in. I can forage for sotol, agave, and prickly pear and dig up plenty of roots to eat. There are many snakes around the rocks here, especially rattlesnakes. There's nothing tastier than a plump rattlesnake that has been cooked slowly over a fire." Hadakai closed his eyes and nodded his head approvingly.

"You aren't worried about the rattlesnake's bite?" Many Wolves's mind flashed back to the encounter he had with one at the den. Those deadly, beady eyes were now burnt into his memory forever.

"It's easy to kill them if you know how. I use this stick to uncoil them and then I spear them just behind the head, pinning them to the ground with the forked end." Hadakai showed him the long stick, which he also used for walking. "Then I slice off the head with my knife and cook the meat after I remove the skin. And if one bites me, then I will die as bravely as a warrior in battle."

"But how can you find them in the winter when they hide?" asked Many Wolves.

"You have to know where they sleep," said Hadakai. "Deep underground, many snakes will sleep together in a winter den. If you know where their dens are, you can crawl down carefully, with a small flame to light the way, and kill many of them. They are very sluggish in the winter."

As Hadakai spoke, Many Wolves tended to the roasting rabbit, rotating it occasionally to ensure that it was cooked evenly. The succulent aroma of cooked rabbit settled in the camp along with the long shadows, precursors to the on-coming sunset. Many Wolves prayed that Reina and Cazador would return before the sun vanished for the day, but the despair in his heart was slowly extinguishing the glimmer of hope that he had earlier.

Revelations

"This is tasty," said Hadakai as he chewed on a mouthful of freshly cooked rabbit. "It's been a long time since I've had meat like this."

"Rabbit is mostly what I've eaten since I left my village." Many Wolves had just devoured a hind leg and was ripping into the other one. "They're easy to find and it's good food for Amarillo and the hawks."

There was a period of silence as the two hungry wanderers shared their meal together. Many Wolves enjoyed talking to Hadakai, and at certain moments, he saw his grandfather in Hadakai's place, though sitting around the fire listening to his grandfather's stories seemed like a distant memory to him now.

"Do you see many other people out here?" he asked Hadakai.

"You're the first person I've seen around this part of the river. Further up north, near Horsehead Crossing, many people cross the river during the fall when the river is low." The old man took another bite from the large piece of rabbit he was eating.

"My father told me of that place. He said there are bones of horses and cattle scattered around the riverbank there."

"Your father speaks the truth, Many Wolves. My people call it 'Skull Crossing' because of all the skulls there. Not just bones of animals, but of men too—men heading west through the desert whose strength has been sapped by the heat, without the mercy offered by shade, and sapped by thirst, without rain or river to quench it, only to fall victim to predators who lie waiting to slash their parched throats." Hadakai spoke deliberately, pausing frequently to catch his breath.

"Predators?" asked Many Wolves.

"Laughing Crow and his Nokonis. They use the crossing as a camp in the fall to launch their attacks on people and villages further to the west."

"Laughing Crow? You have seen him?" Many Wolves was curious to know as much as possible about the man he was running from.

"Yes, I've seen Laughing Crow and his Blood Riders many times, but only from a distance as I watched them from a concealed spot. He is feared by many people: the Mescaleros, the Pueblos, the Spanish, the Mexicans, and your people, the Lipans. I have heard many stories about this devil-man."

Hadakai took another bite. He was in no hurry to collect his thoughts. "Laughing Crow's men believe that his *puha* is so powerful that he cannot be killed."

"What is *puha*?"

"It is the Northerner word for spiritual power or medicine," said Hadakai.

"Do you believe he cannot be killed?"

"If you shoot an arrow through a man's heart, he will die. That is what I believe."

"Who are the Blood Riders?"

"They are the small group of brave fighters that ride with him. A warrior of my village once told me that the Blood Riders are the most skilled fighters he has ever seen. They are expert riders and deadly with the bow. He was one of the few survivors of a small Mescalero village that was wiped out by Laughing Crow and his men." Hadakai caught his breath and continued, "He says he'll never forget the men with black faces, riding painted horses and wearing buffalo headdresses. He remembers the leader, Laughing Crow, as the large, ferocious man with the Thunder-Bird shield."

Instantly, Many Wolves's mind raced back to his most painful memory. *The buffalo people.*

"The buffalo people! Laughing Crow and the Blood Riders are the buffalo people!" Many Wolves blurted out his revelation. He had become accustomed to speaking his thoughts aloud in his solitude.

"Who are the buffalo people?" said Hadakai.

"They are the men I see in my dreams. They killed my white-skinned parents. I saw Laughing Crow and his men talking to the leaders of my village on the day I left. He had a large shield with a bird symbol on it, just as you described. I never thought that *he* was one of the buffalo people in my dreams, because I didn't see their faces clearly." Many Wolves was both excited and terrified by his discovery, but it all made sense. "It was Laughing Crow who killed my mother and father."

He stood up and began walking around, pondering the truth that had been revealed to him and dispelling the nervous energy he felt in his body. The old man sat in silence and watched the boy. Finally, Many Wolves turned to him and spoke. "Hadakai, why didn't Laughing Crow attack my village when he had the chance?"

"Like any other great war leader, he will only attack if he knows the odds are weighed heavily in his favor and that there is much to gain with victory. Perhaps he felt that your village was too strong to attack directly."

"Our village gave him half of our horses as a peace offering."

"You see, then, Laughing Crow got what he wanted without losing any of his men. With fewer horses, he believes that your people are no longer a threat to him," explained Hadakai.

"You don't think he would attack our village?" said Many Wolves, seeking reassurance so desperately.

"Once you've taken the fangs from the rattlesnake, you can let it crawl among the children."

Many Wolves hoped that there was truth in Hadakai's words and that his family and his people were safe. It concerned him to hear that Laughing Crow and his Blood Riders were great warriors. Though they had killed his parents, it worried him more what they could do to his village. He wished there was a way he could know if they were safe.

"Many Wolves, may I have a closer look at your hawk?" said the old man, motioning toward Chiquito.

"Let me get a little food for him." Many Wolves reached for his bag. He pulled out a small, uncooked rabbit leg, stripped most of the meat off with his knife, and then put on his fist-perch.

He held the nearly fleshless bone in his covered hand and called to Chiquito, who had calmed down considerably since night had descended. He was sitting with one leg tucked in his roused feathers, preparing for his nightly slumber. Immediately, upon hearing the call, he woke up and flew over to the fist-perch and began picking at the remaining scraps of flesh still clinging to the leg bone.

"I've never seen a live hawk this close before," said Hadakai as he slowly moved closer to Chiquito, who paused to observe the old man and then continued eating once Hadakai stopped moving. "Their eyes are much bigger when you see them up-close." Hadakai studied Chiquito with keen interest. "Your dog protects your camp and pulls your pole-drag, but what does this bird do for you?"

Many Wolves smiled. "Besides friendship, I'm not sure yet. One of my other birds helped me to kill a rabbit by pouncing on it when it tried to run away, but that happened only once. I hope these birds…" Many Wolves paused to correct himself, "...this bird will help me to hunt rabbits and squirrels. Until then, he is as good a companion as Amarillo here." He stroked his dog, who was lying on his right side.

"Your hawk is a handsome creature. The other two birds will return home to their brothers, you will see," said Hadakai as if reading Many Wolves's mind. Then, he backed away from the bird and the boy and returned to his original sitting place.

"Many Wolves, your friendship with wild animals reminds me of a story my grandfather once told me," began Hadakai, his face glowing from the flames.

"A long time ago, before my people had horses to hunt with, there were men who tamed the wild beasts. They captured young bears, wolves, even mountain lions, and raised them as a mother raises a child. They were patient men who felt a close bond with nature. They preferred life in the wilderness to village life and most did not have wives or children. In time, after much hardship and sacrifice, they trained the animals to hunt with them. They hunted deer, elk, and buffalo with much greater success than the men in the village. Though they were considered outsiders because of their solitary habits, they were well respected by the people because they provided a steady supply of meat, especially when times were lean. The people called them *nantan tsetahgo danlinihi*, which means 'masters of the wild.'"

Hadakai took a few deep breaths before continuing. Many Wolves's attention was strung tightly around each of the old man's words. Chiquito remained focused on cleaning every scrap of flesh from the leg bone. The boy would periodically rotate the bone to expose new rewards for his bird.

Hadakai continued, often pausing to let his breath catch up with his words.

"It is also believed that these 'nantan' shared a special medicine which allowed them to speak with the animal's spirit. This medicine only worked with animal companions who had not lost their wild spirit, unlike most dogs and horses that were tamed by the village. I've heard this medicine is a mixture of buttons cut from the roots of the peyote cactus and petals from the white lion's paw flower."

"Are these things easy to find?"

"Peyote is commonly found around the Rio Pecos and the white lion's paw is found deep in the mountains, in treacherous, rocky terrain, where it blooms in the spring."

Hadakai gazed up at the thousands of shimmering stars spread out across the clear night sky and then took a few swigs of water from his water pouch. "From the first moment I saw you with your hawk, Many Wolves, I was reminded of this story and I wanted to share it with you."

"Do you think I should try to make this medicine?"

"It's up to you. I have no proof that it is real medicine. I'm only passing on this knowledge to you as once it was passed to me by my elders." Hadakai looked at him and smiled with bright eyes entrenched in saggy eyelids. His ears and nose seemed larger than Many Wolves would expect for such a gaunt face. He noticed this, too, with his grandfather and Walking Free. Perhaps it was because they were so old.

Hadakai continued to speak to him. "There is something else that was told to me about this rare flower. It is protected by ferocious guardians—a bear my people know as 'Old Man-Beast' and is also called 'grizzly.' Many people believe these bears are our ancient ancestors because they walk upright like men, eat the same food as men, and use their minds to figure things out like we do. Most are fiercely protective of their territories. Only the bravest of hunters should try to take down these powerful animals and many have died trying. One swipe of their giant claw can kill a man. The best way to escape them is to climb a tree. So, be warned, Many

Wolves, if you go to the high country, you must be aware of Old Man-Beast."

"I once saw a black bear near our village at night, but it ran away when it saw me. It didn't seem much bigger than a buffalo."

"It probably wasn't Old Man-Beast. Most of them are larger than buffalo and are dark brown. Like men, these bears have many different personalities. Some are timid and shy and will run away from you, while others are aggressive and will attack when they see you. They mostly live in the high country."

"Have you seen them before, Hadakai?"

"Indeed I have. When I was younger, the men of my village used to hunt them when they came near us to feed on berry bushes. There were always at least eight hunters, and one was chosen as the runner. Once we found one of these great beasts, the runner would lure it to where the rest of us were waiting with our bows. We aimed at its legs and shoulders to slow it down because they run with the swiftness of a deer. The only way to kill it quickly was a hard shot to the head. Whoever made the kill shot was awarded the bear's claws to make into a necklace or armband, the highest symbol of courage in our village, even above the scalps of men."

Hadakai's story reminded him of the many buffalo hunt stories his grandfather used to tell him. "Did anyone ever die or get hurt?"

"Yes. I remember two men who died on our hunts. It was an honorable way to die. There were also many times when the trees were our safe haven. I never saw Old Man-Beast climb a tree."

It was getting late. The moon and stars were now firmly planted in the night sky. Many Wolves could sense that Hadakai was growing weary, fighting to keep his eyes open in between stories.

"Sleep here tonight, Hadakai. Tomorrow I can hunt more rabbits for us."

"You are very kind. The way you treat your animals is proof of that," said Hadakai as he cleared rocks away from a level spot in the camp. "I will stay tonight, but I must leave at dawn to return south to my rock shelter along the river. I want to arrive there before the heat of the day is upon me."

"All right. Good night then, Hadakai," said Many Wolves and then he added, "Thank you for the stories."

Moments later, Hadakai was asleep. Many Wolves laid his buffalo robe out on the dirt of his camp and curled up on top of it. Amarillo was already asleep too, lying on his side snoring, and Chiquito's head was tucked deeply in his feathers.

I hope Reina and Cazador are all right. Many Wolves prayed silently to the Great Spirit that he would see them again.

From the Heart
of the Sunrise

A s the orange sun was just beginning to breach his camp, Many Wolves was shaken from his sleep by the loud, raucous cries of birds. *Familiar cries!* He looked around and found all three of his birds squawking at him like crows scolding an owl in the daylight.

"Reina! Cazador! You're back!" he yelled as his heart pounded like a thumping wing against the inside of his chest. "The Great Spirit has returned you to me!" Chiquito was screeching louder than usual; perhaps it was his excitement over their return. The birds were perched on different rocks around the camp and their eyes were completely locked in on him. Even Amarillo seemed more animated, his tail swinging wildly from side to side as he barked vigorously.

"So, are you happy to see me or are you just hungry?" asked Many Wolves. He wanted to believe it was friendship that brought them back, but their begging cries were the sounds he was well acquainted with. "Let me get some of the rabbit left over from last night." As he said this, he realized that Hadakai was nowhere to be seen. The only sign of his presence was a small pile of sotol hearts that he had left behind.

He returned his mind to the task in front of him and fitted his fist-perch to his hand and began cutting pieces of rabbit with his knife, keeping the food hidden from them as he worked. He sensed their focused attention as they tightened their circle around him and curiously watched with cockeyed looks of hunger.

"It's coming, my friends. You made me wait for almost a day and now it's your turn to show some patience." He started with a serious tone but ended with a smile and a hearty laugh. He felt like a huge weight was lifted from his mind. "I hope you two enjoyed your little adventure. You drove me crazy. I thought the Wind Spirit had taken you away forever."

Clutching a large piece of rabbit meat in his fist, he called for the queen of his birds, "Reina, come." Both she and Cazador flew to the fist-perch for their morning meal. Reina grabbed her sister by the neck, asserting her dominance. Cazador knew the pecking order and withdrew to a rock nearby, still screaming, while Reina gorged herself on large chunks of rabbit meat. Many Wolves watched with heightened joy as she ripped apart large pieces of flesh and bolted it down in one swift motion. He rationed the food, not allowing them to fill their stomachs, because he wanted them to have appetites for the hunt later on.

Once Reina was finished, he cast her off his fist-perch and instructed her to go back to the rocks. Then he called Cazador to his hand with a new piece of meat. As he watched Cazador tearing off pieces of flesh, he reminisced about his visit with Hadakai. He had learned many new things about cooking, and hunting, and about the man who killed his parents. After hearing about Laughing Crow, one question rose in his mind above all others: *Is my family safe?* He couldn't drive this thought from his mind. The fall sun could burn away the morning chill, but it couldn't melt the chill in his heart.

Hadakai's visit made him realize how much he missed contact with other people. It had been more than a moon's lifetime since he had last seen his family. Every night before he slept, he tried to remember moments he had with them so he wouldn't forget. He remembered his grandfather's stories and helping his mother with her work. He remembered making arrows and bows with his father and his many talks with Walking Free. Day after day he replayed these memories, but no matter how hard he tried, the details slowly eroded away as the pangs of loneliness grew.

Gratefully, his birds had returned to help relieve the sadness he experienced when he knew that Hadakai would leave. Each day he would have to confront his loneliness, which was as unrelenting as the scorching desert sun, the chilling midnight winds, and the constant threat of hunger. Like a refreshing late-afternoon thundershower, Hadakai's visit had provided a temporary relief from these realities, but soon they would return and he would have to confront them with all the strength in his mind and body.

"My wild friends, the generous spirit of the sunrise has brought us back together.

We must continue our journey north. We must carve a path along this great river and make our way to the high country. It is the path that the Great Spirit has chosen for us."

Part II

Drawing a Man's Bow

Many Wolves drew his bow slowly, took careful aim at a gnarled manzanita about thirty steps in front of him, and let loose a blunt-tipped arrow towards a target in the middle of its trunk. The arrow crashed into the tree, breaking off pieces of reddish bark, exposing the softer, lighter-colored bark underneath. His arrows had already shredded most of the rotting tree bark in one small patch barely larger than his outstretched hand.

"Chiquito, my aim is improving! I'm hitting the target and my arrows are knocking away pieces of bark with ease," he said. He often talked to his smallest bird because, unlike Reina and Cazador, he was almost always within earshot. Chiquito was perched in a juniper tree just above his right shoulder. "Soon, I'll be able to shoot this as well as my other bow!" He was using the ash bow now, which his father had made for him four winters ago when he left his village—a bow that was much larger than the rough, dogwood bow he was accustomed to.

It was a warm fall afternoon and Many Wolves was shirtless and dressed in a deerskin breechcloth. He wore the buffalo-tooth necklace his father had given him around his neck, and a deerskin headdress covered his head to keep his long, sun-bleached hair out of his face and eyes.

As he again drew back his father's bow, the well-defined muscles in his arms and shoulders carved out distinct striations in his lean body—the same, once-frail body that had lost so completely to Kicking Bull in a village wrestling match. It seemed like a lifetime had passed since then, as he stood holding the bow steady, with scarcely a quiver in his hands before driving another arrow into the manzanita's trunk. He had honed his archery skill by killing small animals, like rabbits and squirrels. He recalled what his father had once told him when he gave him the bow: "Once you can draw this bow, you will be ready to hunt larger animals."

"Chiquito, let's head back home," Many Wolves instructed his bird while he gathered up his arrows. As he walked the well-beaten animal path towards his camp, Chiquito flew out ahead of him.

The rock shelter he chose for his camp was a short walk away from the turbulent waters of the Rio Pecos and was surrounded by all kinds of large trees: junipers, pines, oaks, and manzanitas. He had chosen this particular camp because it was well-hidden and provided a comfortably large, rock-covered area to protect him from the beating sun and violent thunderstorms. For Many Wolves, his three birds, and Amarillo, it was home.

Arriving at the camp, he found Amarillo lying on his buffalo robe and Reina and Cazador perched in trees next to the shelter. "Amarillo, you old lazy dog, we need to get some food. The berries and nuts I gathered are not food for you and the birds." Many Wolves hid his father's bow in the back of his shelter and packed the other in his coyote-skin quiver. He did not need a powerful bow to hunt jackrabbits and tree squirrels, the staples of his family's meals, and he was not yet strong and accurate enough to use it reliably on moving prey. Depending on his mood, he would hunt either jackrabbit on the open desert floor or tree squirrels in the pine forests. The foothills around him provided easy access to each habitat and an abundance of these prey animals.

The birds watched with great interest as Many Wolves packed his quiver and prepared his equipment and provisions. They knew it was time to hunt. The puffy, relaxed birds, perched one-footed on nearby branches, quickly transformed into lean, alert hunters.

The mottled brown, tan, and white chest feathers of immaturity had been stripped away during the birds' first full molt as yearlings, replaced by a solid, grayish-brown, almost-black plumage. The chestnut coloration, which was once just smattered on their shoulders and thighs, now completely covered those areas. The only patches of white that remained were on the base and tip of their tails. As young hawks, they were easily mistaken for young red-tailed hawks, but as adults, they no longer resembled their larger cousins. They were truly distinctive among the hunting birds of the desert.

He strapped on his crude rabbit-skin leggings, to protect his legs from briars and thorns, and one of his many rabbit-skin fist-perches on his left hand, and then set out for the pine groves in search of tree squirrels. His birds followed along, flying from tree to tree. Amarillo also joined them, not wanting to be left alone. He was much more useful at flushing out jackrabbits than tree squirrels, but Many Wolves always liked having him along for protection. The dog's sensitive nose and ears could find danger long before Many Wolves's human eyes could see it.

Many Wolves led his pack to a favorite grove of trees. This hunting spot had very little underbrush covering the ground, making it harder for the squirrels to escape if pushed from the safety of the trees. Like a seasoned war leader directing his men to battle, Many Wolves whistled for Chiquito and Cazador to fly up. Once he and Reina were in position to patrol the ground, the hunt would begin. Chiquito and Cazador had learned after many hunts that they were the finders and chasers, while Reina waited near the ground to grab the squirrel when it fell from above.

Many Wolves loaded his bow with one of his crude, blunt-tipped arrows—arrows that were easy to make and often lost. His role was not to kill, but to flush out squirrels from their nests or to knock them off tree trunks or branches so the birds could chase them.

As he walked along the edge of the grove, he watched the two higher birds intently as they flew from tree to tree in search of prey. Their eyes were much sharper than his, so he relied on their skill above his own. Suddenly, both birds were staring down at a conspicuous clump of sticks between two trees, with their heads twitching and bobbing on their outstretched necks. Many Wolves recognized it as a gray squirrel nest and suspected that there was a squirrel hidden inside it.

This was his cue to act.

Aiming his bow upwards at the nest, he released the arrow, which whirred past the nest. *Too high.* The two birds flicked their wings, momentarily anticipating the start of the chase, and then rested again, still concentrating on the nest.

Loading another arrow, Many Wolves shot again and struck the nest near the center; the sound of cracking sticks echoed through the silent forest. A small gray squirrel emerged from the nest, jumped onto a branch, and dashed for the nearest tree trunk on its left.

From above, Chiquito dove towards the squirrel, forcing it to scamper further down the trunk and across to another branch. Many Wolves saw that the squirrel, now frozen on the branch, was watching Chiquito as he flapped quickly to regain a position above it. Chiquito's tighter wingspan and rapid wingbeats allowed him to accelerate and maneuver more quickly than either of the other two birds.

As the squirrel was watching Chiquito, Cazador came crashing down on it from behind, grabbing hold of its head with her sharp talons. Together, the hunter and hunted tumbled down towards the ground. All the while, Cazador used her wings and tail to slow her descent and keep her balance as best she could. Once they hit the ground, Reina slammed into the rear end of the squirrel, which was on its back trying to bite Cazador's feet.

Many Wolves ran to Cazador's aid. He knew that squirrels had dangerously sharp teeth which could easily sever a bird's toe. Chiquito had lost a toe this way and was now very cautious about jumping into a wrestling match with any squirrel. Also, their hides were tough and their bodies extremely muscular, making them difficult to kill.

"Hold on, Cazador…just hold on!" said Many Wolves firmly.

He began squeezing the small mammal's chest with his hand. The squirrel, open-mouthed, struggled to bite and breathe. He held the squirming animal in this death grip for many moments until he sensed that its breath was gone and it was dead. *Life for life.* The birds allowed him near their prey because they knew he could kill this dangerous animal faster than they could. They were a well-organized hunting pack with each member knowing his or her role.

He cut off one of the rear legs of the dead squirrel and called Reina to his fist-perch. She obeyed, and then with his right hand, he tossed the leg a short distance to move her away from the kill. Then, he cut open the white chest of the squirrel and rewarded Cazador with the heart, liver, and other organs, since she had caught it. Chiquito was given the animal's other back leg as his reward for the chase.

"Well done, Cazador, the great chaser!" He watched her dig into the squirrel's chest with her bloody beak, gorging on the warm flesh after eating the organs. After a short time, he cut off one of the front legs and offered it to her. She accepted the trade and he moved her away from the remains of the squirrel, stealthily stashing it in his hunting bag while she and the other birds were distracted by their meals.

Many Wolves had discovered on previous hunts that if he didn't hide the remains of the kill, the birds would eventually fight over it. He was careful not to overfeed them. He wanted them motivated for the rest of the hunt and needed them to kill at least two more squirrels, so there would be enough food for all of them, including Amarillo.

Up a Tree

"Let's get another," said Many Wolves after the birds had finished their rations. The late-afternoon shadows of the trees were stretching further and further across the forest floor. The breeze was stirring and whistling between the trees. Dusk was not far away.

He continued to walk along the edge of the trees and called for Chiquito and Cazador to fly up and find more squirrels, while Amarillo and Reina followed along as ground sentries. He noticed that Amarillo was repeatedly sniffing the air as if he discovered a new, interesting scent.

"What is it, Amarillo?" The dog slowed his pace and searched the air for new smells. To Many Wolves, the only scent was the clean, medicinal aroma of pine. Amarillo started to walk more briskly with his tail swaying and his nose pinned to the ground. *He's found something.* Many Wolves followed close behind, his eyes searching in the direction that his dog was leading him.

Then Amarillo stopped and began digging at a bed of pine needles that had been arranged in a mound. Many Wolves bent down and started brushing away the debris to see what was buried underneath.

It was a dead elk. Many Wolves touched the dead animal and realized that the body was not stiff. *It hasn't been dead for long.* He brushed more of the pine needles away and found that much of the elk's chest and neck had been eaten away.

The bite marks were larger than those of a coyote or even a mountain lion. Then he saw long, thick claw marks across the elk's back. He knew instantly that the elk's killer was a bear.

Amarillo turned and faced the trail ahead and began to growl. Many Wolves spotted the huge bear emerging from the trees. It stood up on its hind legs and swayed back and forth with its nose in the air. He had seen big predators like mountain lions and bears before, and Amarillo's barking had always chased them away. This time, the predator did not run away.

Suddenly, the bear charged towards them. Its jaw was dropped, its ears were flattened, and there was a ridge of fur raised on its back. Many Wolves panicked at the sight. "What should I do? What should I do?" Then Hadakai's words flashed in his mind: "These bears don't climb trees."

Many Wolves could hear its growls and grunts, as the bear cut the distance between them with astonishing speed. He spotted a big, sturdy tree behind him, which had a low-hanging branch. *Is it strong enough?* He didn't have time for second-guesses. He dropped his quiver and ran for the tree, jumping up to grab the lowest branch, and then he pulled himself up.

The bear was closing in. Many Wolves looked back and saw the massive leg and shoulder muscles expand and contract as it charged, and its large, pointed fangs chomping up and down as drool rolled over its chin. He pulled himself up to the next branch and looked down.

Amarillo was between Many Wolves and the bear and he was standing his ground. "Amarillo, run!" he shouted as loudly as he could. "Run!"

Amarillo glanced over at him, as if considering a retreat, and then planted himself deeper into a hunched position. He was barking and growling, preparing himself for the charging beast. Like the bear's, his hackles were raised and he was tensed and ready to fight.

The bear was undaunted by Amarillo's threats and redirected his charge toward the dog. Amarillo gnashed his teeth and growled loudly as he lunged at the oncoming animal. The bear slashed him with his massive claw and battered him to the ground like a child's doll. Amarillo whimpered and staggered to his feet, but the bear clamped down on him with his claw and sunk his fangs into the dog's neck. Amarillo cried out and then went silent. The bear loosened his huge jaws, releasing the limp dog, and then turned his head to look up at Many Wolves. Amarillo's blood dripped from his mouth.

Many Wolves was iced by the sight. He couldn't move or think. All he could do was stare back at the cold, terrible black eyes of a killer. The bear growled again, a slow rumble of a growl, baring his fangs as he turned his body to face Many Wolves. He lowered his head and looked back at the dead dog, and then stared at Many Wolves with his squinty eyes. The gray coloration in his face contrasted with the dark brown fur on his huge body. Behind his neck protruded a large, muscular hump of furry flesh. He kept staring and snarling, his lip uncurling each time he refreshed his growl.

Then the great beast suddenly bolted for the tree and leaped up against the trunk. Many Wolves snapped out of his stupor and held on tightly to the shaking tree, terrified, praying that the bear couldn't climb the tree or knock it down. The tree held its position, supporting the bear's full weight. The raging animal tried in vain to climb, its powerful claws tearing off chunks of pine bark, but it could only pull its massive body up a short distance, less than a body length. Many Wolves hung on.

Eventually the bear gave up and retreated to the ground. It began pacing in front of the tree, still snarling in anger and looking up at Many Wolves. He felt a small current of relief flow across his mind as he realized that it could not climb the tree. Taking his eyes off the animal momentarily, he looked through the trees to see his three birds picking at the elk carcass, completely detached from the danger he was in. Apparently, they didn't possess the same protective instincts as Amarillo, who had given his life for him.

Many Wolves tried hard to fight off the tears as the bear paced anxiously around the base of the tree. He was scared and he had lost a dear friend. He struggled to think clearly. *How am I going to get out of this?* He braced himself in the tree and tried to rest his troubled mind.

The bear spotted the birds at the elk carcass and ran towards them, chasing them into the trees. *At least the birds are safe.* It lumbered back to the tree, staring at him, guarding him. Many Wolves sensed that the gray-faced bear wouldn't be leaving anytime soon.

Gray Face

Dusk descended on the pine forest, and the cool, refreshing breeze Many Wolves had enjoyed earlier was now chilling his bare flesh as he tried hard to position himself comfortably in the tree. Gray Face, his name for the large bear, was feasting on the elk carcass a short distance away. Many Wolves figured that the bear had cached the elk in the forest and that he had trespassed on its sacred feeding ground.

His birds had filled their bulging crops with elk meat and were roosting comfortably in tree branches above him. Cazador was preening herself, seemingly without a care in the world. "Cazador, you little beggar, don't shed a feather worrying about me!"

Gray Face had been eating for quite a while and had consumed most of the carcass. Many Wolves had never seen an animal eat so much food at one time. *He must be preparing for his winter's sleep.* The bear was less agitated, resting on his haunches as he ate, yet still intent on keeping the young human in his sights.

Many Wolves had finally calmed his nerves, feeling safe and a little bolder in his pine sanctuary. "Gray Face! I didn't take your food, so leave me alone!" Many Wolves hoped that somehow the bear would understand his words and accept his suggestion. Undisturbed by the taunt, Gray Face kept eating and staring in his direction. Many Wolves knew that Gray Face was a male bear from his large, bulky size. Also, he believed that the bear was fairly old from all the gray hair on his body. *Maybe he'll leave when he's finished.*

Eventually, Gray Face stopped eating and began to groom himself, meticulously licking his front paws clean of blood and flesh. It was hard for Many Wolves to imagine that this was the same violent, ferocious animal that killed his dog and chased him up a tree. He kept as still as possible, afraid to do anything that would trigger the bear's rage.

Once Gray Face was satisfied with his grooming, he covered up the remains of the carcass by swiping dirt, leaves, and pine needles over it. Then, he ambled over towards the tree where Many Wolves was bracing himself. Looking up at his captive, he roared loudly. His fangs seemed as long as Many Wolves's fingers. He dropped down on all fours and spread his body out on the ground at the base of the tree. *He's not going to leave!*

Many Wolves felt despair well up inside him. There was no way of knowing when the bear would leave. He wouldn't be hungry for a while after that feast. Even if he closed his eyes to sleep, his sense of hearing and smell would remain sharp—bears were like dogs in that way. *If I had my bow, I might be able to scare him off.* Unfortunately, his bow and arrows were lying on the ground near Amarillo's body and he didn't want to risk leaving the safety of his lofty perch or making any movement at all. *I'll have to wait it out.*

It wasn't long before the bear's eyes began to close as he rested peacefully on the ground. Many Wolves remained silent in the tree, with his legs wrapped around a long, thick branch, his back resting against the tree's heavy trunk, and his arms clenching his chest in an effort to stay warm in the cool night. Unlike Gray Face, Many Wolves could not sleep. His head was humming like a beehive as he tried to figure a way out of his predicament. *If I try to run, he'll hear me and chase me up another tree.* The water container was about half full and he had a few pieces of dried rabbit meat in his waist pouch, so he was all right for a while.

Hopelessness was tearing at his insides. He wanted to cry, hoping that somehow his father or grandfather would hear him, but he knew they were far, far away. *I have to be strong.* He began to plead with the Great Spirit: "Show me a way out of this! There has to be a way!" Prayers were all that he had left. Amarillo was dead and he felt so alone.

Half the night had passed and Many Wolves could hear Gray Face snoring in his sleep, his huge body heaving with every breath, illuminated by the rays of the half-moon. With every moment that passed, the night was growing colder. He felt the need to relieve his bursting bladder, but was afraid to do anything that might wake up the slumbering beast. He huddled tightly in the tree, trying to stay warm and to hold his body-water in. The pressure on his bladder was causing a painful cramping in his legs. He wasn't sure how much longer he could hold out.

"I should just spray all over you, Gray Face," he whispered to himself. "You killed my dog and now you want to kill me! Why should I let you sleep peacefully while you starve me to death in this tree?"

Defiantly, he stood up, pulled up his loincloth, and released his body-water on the bear. "Now, you will have my scent all over you!" he scorned at the old bear as he aimed his stream at Gray Face's head.

The bear woke up, raising his sensitive nose to the air, inhaling the pungent odor of body-water that was not his own and was dripping down the sides of his head and back. Suddenly, he rose to his feet and bellowed loudly in anguish. He shook his body and head violently and continued to wail loudly. His shaking body reminded Many Wolves of Amarillo who used to shake himself dry after swimming in creek water.

Gray Face looked up at Many Wolves and snarled, his hateful gaze crashing into his captive's mind like a bolt of lightning into a dried-out tree. Then, without warning, the huge bear ran away. Almost as fast as he had charged at Many Wolves earlier, he was gone.

Many Wolves saw this as his chance to escape. He rushed down the tree and jumped to the solid ground below. His legs were stiff and tingling from sitting motionless all night. Grabbing his quiver of arrows and his bow, he ran for his life, away from Gray Face and towards his home. The hot blood flowing through his body protected him from the biting chill of the air that rushed past him as he ran. He didn't stop to look back, he just kept running. *I must get home!*

While stranded in the tree, he had worked out a plan if he could somehow make it home. He remembered there was a big pine tree near his camp with a sizable branch overhanging a flattened rocky ledge above his camp. If he could get to it, he would be safe from Gray Face.

Finally, he arrived at his camp, breathing gulps of stinging cold air into his thirsty lungs. He bent down for a few moments to catch his breath. *I need to hurry.* He grabbed his hunting bag and put two handfuls of dried rabbit meat and the full water pouch inside. Then he gathered up his father's bow and arrows and crammed them into his quiver. He slung the hunting bag over his left shoulder and the quiver over his right. He ran over to the pine tree and pulled himself up on the lowest hanging branch, still laboring to breathe. With ease, he climbed up three more branches until he reached the limb that stretched out towards the ledge. He reached up and clung onto it with both his hands and pulled himself across it one hand at a time, with his legs dangling and swinging from side-to-side. Once he was above the ledge, he dropped down and landed on the large, flat rock.

He removed the hunting bag and the quiver from his shoulder and placed them against a wall on the ledge. Feeling the chill of the night wind against his skin, he shivered and realized that he needed his buffalo-hide blanket. He looked around and listened carefully to the seemingly peaceful world around him. He heard nothing and saw nothing. *I need to go back down!*

He started to climb down, feeling his fatigue, but still driven by the hot blood rushing through his body like the Rio Pecos. Reaching the lowest branch, he jumped down to the ground and ran to his shelter to get his blanket, which was spread on the ground.

Suddenly, the blood-curdling screech of an owl pierced the silence of the dark forest. His heart jumped. He looked up into the darkness, but could see nothing. Then he saw the flashing form of a small owl fly silently past him. *What startled it? Is Gray Face here?*

Quickly, he draped it around his shoulders and ran back to the tree. Climbing the tree with the heavy blanket was more difficult than he had anticipated. His foot slipped, but he caught himself by grabbing hold of another branch. *I can't fall now. Great Spirit, help me.* Eventually he pulled himself up to the ledge, completely exhausted.

He sat down and leaned back against the rocky wall, covering his legs with the warm blanket, sweat dripping from his forehead and chest, and his heart racing like a chased jackrabbit. *What do I do now?* He was too tired to find the answers. For the moment he felt safe. He had food, water, a warm blanket, and a weapon that could kill large animals.

Fear in His Eyes

Many Wolves woke up at sunrise in a cold sweat, with the residue of his worst nightmare—Laughing Crow and the Blood Riders—still polluting his mind. Though the dream was much less frequent now than it had been when he left his village, it was still just as terrifying. He shook his head to try and rid himself of the horrible images. Then, he looked around and realized he was on the rocky ledge above his camp, his blanket wrapped around his shoulders and legs. The vivid memories of the bear attack and Amarillo's violent death quickly pushed to the forefront of his mind. *What am I going to do about Gray Face?*

After pondering this question for some time, he arrived at two possibilities: He could run away from this place and never return, or he could kill Gray Face. *If I run away and find another home, will the same thing happen there? Will I always have to keep running?* He knew deep in his heart that running wasn't the answer. *This is a test that the Great Spirit has put before me. I must kill Gray Face. It is the only way.*

Chiquito landed in the tree next to the ledge and looked at him, turning his head inquisitively from one side to the other. Many Wolves smiled. "Look at you, Chiquito! You act as if nothing happened last night, your body still bulging from your last meal! I wish I could fly away from bears!" He felt relieved to see that Chiquito was all right. "I'm sure your two sisters aren't far away. They're probably sleeping off their meals!" Many Wolves laughed.

He pulled out some dried rabbit meat and the water pouch from his hunting bag. The squirrel carcass was missing from his bag. *I must have lost it when I was running or climbing.* His mouth was parched, and though the water was lukewarm from sitting in the early morning sun, it was still refreshing. He bit off a small piece of the rabbit meat and began chewing on it. It took a while to grind the hardened meat into small enough chunks to swallow. He ate several pieces, but still felt hungry.

Suddenly, Chiquito started screaming, not the droning, periodic cry of hunger, but a higher-pitched, excited scream. Cazador and Reina joined the chorus of sounds. He heard them, but couldn't see where they were. "What is it, Chiquito?"

His bird was looking down towards the center of the camp—a spot blocked from Many Wolves's view by the rocky ledge. He stood up and looked over the ledge, but saw nothing. It was hard to hear anything over the cries of the birds. *Something is down there.*

"Is Gray Face back?" he mumbled to himself, horrified. He still could not hear or see anything, but the birds certainly did. If it was Gray Face, he knew he had to stay on the ledge. He reached back for his quiver and pulled out his larger bow and one of his father's arrows, nocking the arrow. The large obsidian arrow point reflected the morning sun's rays into his eyes. He moved closer to the edge of the drop-off. *If it is Gray Face, he smells me and knows I'm near.*

The bear lumbered out towards the middle of his camp. Many Wolves ducked back away from the edge to avoid being seen, though he felt almost certain the bear could hear his pounding heart. Gray Face roared, a deafening howl, and then Many Wolves heard huge claws rush towards him, scraping against the hard dirt and kicking up a cloud of dust.

The beast began ripping out the bark of the tree that Many Wolves had used to reach his sanctuary.

Many Wolves snuck over to a portion of the rocky slab closest to the tree, and prepared to fire his bow. Peering over, he saw one of Gray Face's giant claws shredding the tree trunk and then his massive gray head. The bear paused to look up at him, snarling ferociously and baring his fangs before resuming his futile, frenzied efforts to climb the tree.

Many Wolves struggled to steady his bow with his trembling hands. The sweat on his palms was making the task more difficult. From his vantage point, he had an unobstructed shot at the bear's head and one of his claws, but both were moving frantically. The potent musk of the bear engulfed his senses. As he withdrew the bow and began to take aim, the arrow slipped from his hands and fell to the ground. He closed his eyes and took a deep breath. *Calm down. Great Spirit, help me.*

He pulled another arrow from his quiver and loaded it carefully into position. He saw that Gray Face was no longer scratching the tree trunk, but was pacing back and forth at the base of the tree, roaring in frustration. Many Wolves drew back the bow and took aim. Still shaking, he held his breath and steadied his aim, tracking the animal as he moved about the camp. The muscles in his sinewy arms were straining to keep the bow steady with enough tension to hopefully break through the bear's thick hide. *I need to bury this arrow deep into his body; it doesn't matter where.*

Once Gray Face moved into position for a clear, close shot, Many Wolves released the arrow cleanly and on a straight path, exhaling just after the arrow took flight. The arrow's point tore through the bear's rear leg and embedded itself deep in the animal's body.

Gray Face shrieked and swung his head to see what caused the pain in his leg. Many Wolves watched as the bear tried several times to pull the arrow from his leg with his teeth. Then, in an instant, his focus shifted back to the young man. He roared up at Many Wolves and, just as before, tried to charge up the tree. Many Wolves fell back away from the edge, surprised by the bear's quick recovery. *I will not be chased away from my home again!*

He found another large arrow and set it in the bowstring. He moved to another part of the ledge where he gained a better angle. He peered over to see Gray Face, now silent and solely focused on trying to rid himself of the painful annoyance. He drew his bow and took aim at the bear's right shoulder. He pulled it back even further, knowing that he now had a greater distance to his target. The arrow struck the bear in the shoulder, but didn't burrow very deeply into his flesh. Gray Face turned around, screaming in pain, and then instantly shattered the shaft of the second arrow with his left claw. Looking up at Many Wolves again, he bellowed, spraying the drool and foam from his mouth all over the ground in front of him, and then limped off into the forest.

For the first time, Many Wolves saw fear in the Man-Beast's eyes.

A Trail of Blood

Many Wolves rested on the rocky ledge, contemplating his next move. Although it had been several winters, he could still recall Hadakai's words about the self-healing power of the grizzly:

These beasts have magical healing powers. Many times after we inflicted serious wounds with our arrows, the Man-Beast ran away. Often, we found him some time later almost completely recovered. They know how to make strong medicine to heal themselves.

"I need to track down Gray Face and kill him before he can heal himself," Many Wolves said to himself. He knew that the bear could not wander far on an injured leg. If he didn't find any huge footprints, then surely he would find a trail of blood.

He loaded up his quiver with his father's bow and what was left of the arrows his father made him. He replenished his waist pouch with dried rabbit meat and filled his small water container, the one he used for hunting.

Many Wolves climbed back down to the ground. His birds were silent, so he felt confident that Gray Face wasn't nearby. He walked over to a small pool of the bear's blood and dug a hole in the reddish dirt, leaving the loose dirt inside. Then he poured some water into the hole, mixing it up with the dirt and blood to make a thick, muddy mixture. He applied it to his face, then his arms, and then the rest of his body. *I must cover my scent.* He felt empowered by the blood of his great enemy.

Once he had finished, he walked off in the direction of the blood trail. Chiquito followed him, but the other two birds remained at camp, not feeling hungry enough to join the hunt. Many Wolves listened carefully as he walked, filtering the sounds of the trees as the breeze flowed through them, staying alert to any sudden, rustling noise. *I'm glad Chiquito is with me; he'll see Gray Face before I do.* He scanned the ground carefully, noticing broken branches, crushed twigs, partial footprints, and drops of blood left on the trail by the injured bear.

Many Wolves followed the bear's trail most of the morning. The heat from the midday sun caused his face to sweat and dried the mud on his body, which was beginning to itch. He found a small creek and drank some cool, fresh water. He wanted to wash the mud off his body, to remove the itch, but knew he couldn't. *If I keep my scent covered and approach from downwind, I might be able to surprise him.*

Refreshed, he crossed the creek and immediately found bear prints heading south. The rear footprints looked like a man's: a similarly shaped foot with five toes, except that these were nearly twice the size of an average man and the toes had large claw marks at the end of them. The front footprints were not nearly as elongated as the flat-footed rear ones. The dirt around the prints was loose. *Gray Face is not far.*

Suddenly, up ahead, he heard a man yelling and a horse grunting, then the roar of the huge bear. He sprinted towards the sound and spotted a clearing in the trees ahead. He was close enough now to hear the thumping hooves of a single horse. Gray Face was snarling and growling. Chiquito shrieked in alarm.

Many Wolves reached the edge of the trees and looked into a large grassy meadow. He saw a man on a white horse circling Gray Face and firing arrows. The bear had at least four arrows protruding from his body, one of them Many Wolves recognized as his own. Though the grizzly's movements were slowed by injuries, his assaults were unrelenting. The muscles rippled under his shimmering coat each time he burst into another attack.

The man who faced him had long, straight black hair and two large feathers dangling from his scalp-lock. His face was painted with yellow and red and he was wearing deerskin leggings and a deerskin shirt. He rode his horse with great skill, stopping, starting, and changing directions quickly and fluidly. He was able to fire his bow easily and accurately while riding, more skillfully than any Lipan Many Wolves had ever seen. *He's a Northerner.*

Many Wolves felt a gust of heat rush through his head. *Is he from Laughing Crow's village? Will he try to kill me, or take me away if he finds me? I must stay hidden.*

Gray Face charged the Northerner repeatedly, but the rider quickly redirected his horse to evade the bear. Retreating from one of these charges, the Northerner unloaded another arrow into the middle of the bear's body and Gray Face screamed. Many Wolves noticed that the Northerner held his bow with his right hand as he fired, unlike any man he had ever seen.

Roaring, Gray Face charged the rider again. The man yelled, commanding his horse to retreat, but the horse's front foot dipped deeply into the ground, and it stumbled and crashed down on top of the man. The hunter wailed in agony. The frightened horse rolled upright and galloped off.

The man turned over on his stomach and covered his head with his arms, preparing for the bear's attack. Gray face charged.

Many Wolves felt sympathy for the man who was lying helpless, even though he was a Northerner, his enemy. *I have to do what I came here to do. Gray Face must die.* He pulled his bow from his quiver, loaded an arrow, and ran towards the bear. Gray Face began slashing and biting savagely at the man's back and head, bellowing between bites. Many Wolves yelled at the bear to try to divert his attention, but with no success. Within firing range, he stopped, took careful aim, and released an arrow into the bear's flank.

The beast turned to face him.

The grizzly snarled at his taunter and charged. Many Wolves realized that he was too far from the trees to make a run for it. He pulled an arrow from his quiver and faced the rampaging animal. He loaded the arrow and pulled the bow back as far as he could.

Gray Face raced towards him with his ears retracted and his fangs bared. The bear's eyes bored into Many Wolves like large black thorns. He held the bow steady and aimed at the bear's head. *I have one shot and I have to kill him.* He took a deep breath and waited for the bear to come closer.

When the bear was about three horse-lengths away, he released the arrow. It struck the bear's head, on the left side just below the eye, and dug deeply into his skull. Gray Face howled in pain, stumbled, and crashed to the ground at Many Wolves's feet. Groaning, the great beast took his last breath and gave up his spirit.

Gray Face was dead.

The Fortress

From an overlooking vista, Laughing Crow spotted a single plume of smoke rising from a distant dwelling. The lodging backed into a large mesa, but otherwise it sat in a flat, barren wasteland, with just the occasional patch of mesquite and cactus. The Rio Bravo loomed beyond it.

Laughing Crow had ridden south most of the day, from Horsehead Crossing. Seven of his most loyal warriors, who had followed him into exile, were with him. They had found what they were looking for—signs of human habitation. The Nokoni leader knew that water always led to men and the Rio Bravo was no exception. Where there were men, there were horses and women and children.

"What do you think, Malone?" A cool fall breeze had dried the dust-encrusted sweat on his face.

"It looks like just one or two dwellings, and not a village. Probably Mexican farmers working the land. I don't think they will have many horses."

"It's not just the horses we want, but the women and children. We cannot grow our village with horses, but we can with women who can breed and children who can work and learn to fight with us."

Just then, Silent Weasel arrived on horseback after surveying their target. "*Namunewapi*, they are Mexicans—about three families and four horses. I did not see any men with weapons aside from the knives in their belts," he said, chasing his breath.

"How many young women and children?" asked Laughing Crow.

"I saw two young women and several children."

"Good." This was what Laughing Crow was looking for—women and children with few men to protect them. Even a young boy could kill a buffalo calf without a bull to guard it. They must have mistakenly thought that no one, not even the skilled Nokonis, would find them in this desolate wilderness.

"Thorn Bird and Silent Weasel will ride out ahead. Kill the men who have knives and bind the rest. Cut them off before they reach their shelter."

At his word, the two black-faced riders launched themselves down the hill with their bows in hand and shields ready. Laughing Crow and the remaining men followed the billowing streams of dust at a three-quarter's pace. He had every confidence that two of his best warriors would be able to handle any man who threatened them, especially ones without long guns.

Alerted to the oncoming attack, the three men who were working the land began shouting and running back to their lodge. Thorn Bird caught up to the first one, quickly switching from his bow to a tomahawk, and then slowing his horse down just long enough to jump off without stumbling. The Mexican turned on him, knife drawn, but Thorn Bird's tomahawk crashed down in a single, powerful stroke.

Meanwhile, Silent Weasel launched an arrow into the next man's back, knocking him down. He then began tracking the last one, who was running but still carrying a large shovel. The man turned to face his attacker and raised his tool threateningly, shouting a challenge in Spanish. The Nokoni scout screamed a war cry, as he rode up to him, then leaped off his horse. His large, gleaming knife was protruding like a spider fang from his right hand. Silent Weasel drove his knife deeply into the man's neck before he had a chance to swing the shovel. The Mexican fell to the ground hollering in pain as his blood gushed all over his chest.

With a squeeze of his legs, Laughing Crow directed his horse at the one with the arrow in his back, who was on his feet again, running and yelling for help. The Nokoni leader swung hard at him with his battle-axe as he galloped past him. The Mexican flew off his feet from the force of the blow. Surrounded by a burst of spraying blood, the man yelled out, and fell to the ground in silence.

By this time, the others who were outside the dwelling ran inside. They sealed the door and closed all the openings. As Laughing Crow rode up to it, he heard the frantic cries of women and children and the voice of an older man shouting orders. The brownish adobe lodge was plain-looking but well-built. The outer walls were smooth and the contours were straight. There was a hole at the top for smoke to leave and enough room for more than one family.

After his men arrived, the headman turned to them and barked, "Check the back for openings," pointing to two of his men. Then, to Silent Weasel he said, "Climb up and check the top." Everyone quickly went to work. They banged on the walls and the roof with their axes and tomahawks, looking for any kind of weakness. There was none.

"The only large opening is the fire hole on top, but I can't crawl down," said Silent Weasel. "There are holes in the walls, but too small to put an arm through. It's sealed like an armadillo."

Laughing Crow rode around the dwelling, inspecting it for himself. He saw several fist-sized holes in the wall, but no other openings. The ground was hard; it would be difficult to dig through.

He heard a child whimpering inside, and then nothing until a man started to speak in Spanish. "You will never get into our fortress!"

Laughing Crow understood Spanish well enough from living with Spanish-speaking people. But he did not speak it as well as Mocking Bird and Thorn Bird, who had learned it from his mother.

The leader returned to the front door and spoke to Mocking Bird, "Tell him that he has built a strong home, but he is still not safe. We will get in or his family will die in there."

The man answered Mocking Bird, "We would rather die in here than be stung by *Avispa Negra*! We have food and water to last us for days. I have built many forts in Mexico. These walls will protect us."

"He calls you by the name of the Black Wasp," said Mocking Bird.

The nickname was not unfamiliar to the Nokoni leader. Laughing Crow did not doubt that this man had built a fortress here. He just needed time to figure out how to break in or flush them out.

"Malone, how many horses did we capture?"

"Four."

"Then have the men kill the weakest one and build a fire pit here."

Malone selected three of the men to prepare the meal. Laughing Crow dismounted and led Cheval-Sang to a pot of water near the lodge. Silent Weasel and Mocking Bird also got down and led their horses to drink.

"What is your name, *viejo*?" asked Laughing Crow with Mocking Bird translating.

"Ferdinand."

"How many in your family?"

"I will not tell you. You know there are at least four. The three men you murdered besides me." The man's voice was deep and gruff, but unsteady—the voice of an older man.

"Say what you want. I will find out soon enough," mumbled Laughing Crow. He sat down next to the front wall of the lodge, which was shaded from the late-afternoon sun. Thorn Bird and Thunder Voice led the horse to the newly prepared fire pit and the leader's son thrust his knife into the horse's neck. The horse screamed and crashed to the ground.

"Ferdinand, won't you join us for a meal? Your horse will soon be ready to feast on," taunted Thorn Bird, wiping his bloody hands on the dead horse's hide.

"I would not eat my own horse, unless I was starving. I am not a savage like you!"

"Well, I am a starving savage!" Both Laughing Crow and Mocking Bird laughed at Thorn Bird's response. "Let me get something for you and your *familia* to eat, Ferdinand."

Thorn Bird walked away while Thunder Voice and Mocking Bird began butchering the dead horse. He returned shortly after carrying a bloodstained bag. He walked to a corner of the lodge, reached into the bag, and shoved two human hands through a hole at the top of the wall. "Here, you can eat this, Ferdinand. Your amigo's fingers still have plenty of meat on them! The buzzards haven't picked at them yet!" Laughing Crow heard women screaming from inside the wall.

"*Bestia fiera!*" yelled Ferdinand.

Laughing Crow and his men laughed even louder this time. It gave him an idea. He considered using smoke or fire to scare them out, but he didn't want to risk injuring what he came for. *I will use fear to flush them out of their fortress.* He called for Silent Weasel and Thunder Voice and revealed his plan.

The Sound of Death

"Silent Weasel, I see you caught one." Laughing Crow was pleased, eager to test his plan.

"Yes, *namunewapi*. But I won't be able to eat anything with this thing in my hand."

"Just hold it until darkness comes, and keep it quiet. It won't be long."

"Did Thunder Voice find one?"

"No, he's still looking," said Silent Weasel, keeping his distance from the rest of the group.

Laughing Crow and his men sat around the fire eating pieces of roasted horsemeat. "It's good to have fresh meat again," he said to Malone, as he cut another bleeding slice with his knife.

"There's nothing like it when you're far from home. It sure beats pemmican," said Malone in agreement.

The warmth of the day was slipping away with the sunlight. Laughing Crow felt refreshed by the cool breeze on his face and the warm meal in his stomach. He was biding his time, waiting for the sun to hide.

He heard chanting. The voices of women and children repeated Ferdinand's words. "Mocking Bird, what are they doing in there?"

The thin Nokoni translator stood up and walked closer to the front door. "It sounds like they are praying to their god."

"*Viejo*, tell me, where will you go when you die?" barked Mocking Bird as he leaned against the door, following his leader's instruction.

The praying stopped and Ferdinand answered, "I hope that God will send me to heaven."

"What is this heaven?" Laughing Crow remembered hearing other Mexicans in his village talk about it.

"It is *paraiso*, where everyone is kind to one another. Everything you need, God will provide for you. There is no place in heaven for killers like you, *Avispa Negra!*"

"Everyone is kind?" grunted Laughing Crow as he brushed his oiled black hair out of his eyes. "It does not sound like a good place to me. Is there another place to go?"

"It's either heaven or hell. Hell is for sinners—those who break God's laws. Hell is where you burn for eternity."

"That's not a good place either. I don't think I like your god, *viejo*." Laughing Crow looked at Malone and Thorn Bird, eyes gleaming with humor.

"What are the laws of your god?" asked Thorn Bird, speaking fluent Spanish. Mocking Bird continued to translate for the leader.

"A man should not kill or steal or tell lies."

Laughing Crow shook his head and his men grumbled in disagreement when they heard Mocking Bird repeat these words. "How can you gain respect if you don't kill men or steal horses? You are speaking crazy talk, *viejo*."

"Wouldn't you rather live in a world where everyone is friends?"

"That is not possible. If you trust everyone, you show weakness, and eventually, you will die by the lance or the bow," said Laughing Crow. "What you speak of is not a real world, just like your heaven is not real. It's only in your mind, *viejo*."

Silence followed and Laughing Crow returned to his meal. What this man was saying made no sense. You earned power in this life from your brave deeds like killing and stealing, so you would be rewarded in the next life. This was the way of his people—the way of the world.

"Laughing Crow, Thunder Voice is ready," said Malone.

"Good. It will be dark soon."

When the blackness of night came, all was quiet except for the crackling fire.

"Mocking Bird, make a torch so the men can see," ordered Laughing Crow, looking at Silent Weasel and Thunder Voice. "We must be ready for them to come out," he said to the rest of his men.

Then, Laughing Crow grabbed Thunder Voice's lance and readied himself by the door. Thorn Bird stood next to him with his tomahawk in one hand and a coil of braided horse-hair in the other.

When Silent Weasel walked over to the dwelling, the rattling sound of an agitated snake cut through the night like the screeching cry of an owl. Thunder Voice followed him, holding the rattlesnake he had caught, one hand grasped firmly around the snake's neck and the other holding its squirming, muscular body. The sound of death was in the air.

Mumbled words, laced with fear, seeped through the walls of the lodge. Finally, Ferdinand yelled, sensing the situation, "You are a savage, *Avispa Negra!*"

Laughing Crow grinned and pointed. "Put one on this side and the other one over there."

Mocking Bird, holding a torch, led Silent Weasel and watched the scout push the head of the snake through a hole in the wall and let go.

With a scowl, Laughing Crow bellowed, "This world is not your heaven, *viejo!*"

The women and children screamed when they heard the snake hissing and rattling. Ferdinand tried to calm them down in the darkness. "Stay next to me!"

Thunder Voice squeezed the head of his snake through a hole on the other side and pushed its body through so that the captives were trapped between the two reptiles.

"Kill them, Ferdinand!" echoed the voice of an older woman. Another, younger woman shrieked in panic.

"Help us, *abuelo*, help us!" cried a child.

"I can't see them. It's too dark! Just don't move," yelled Ferdinand. "They will not harm us if we stay perfectly still."

The *Noomah* war party gathered around the door, expecting their terrified captives to burst out at any moment, but they did not. Somehow, Ferdinand had calmed them, except for the one frantic woman who still continued to shriek.

"*Viejo*, do not let your women and children die the horrible death of poison. Come out and we will kill the snakes for you," said Laughing Crow.

"Calm down, Maria. You have to calm down!" pleaded Ferdinand, but still she screamed as if she had lost her mind. He raised his voice even more: "*Avispa Negra*, we would rather die from the poison than from your torturing knives!"

This surprised the Nokoni leader. He thought they would have run out by now. He didn't want to starve them out because then the women and children would not be healthy and he'd have to return to his village without any captives. Chasing them out with rattlesnakes was still his best plan, but the rattling had stopped and his hostages had settled down, except for Maria.

"Maria, I promise you that you will not be harmed. Let us kill the snakes for you," said Laughing Crow in a calm, restrained voice. Mocking Bird used a similar, soothing voice when he spoke.

"Don't listen to him! He has already killed your brother and your husband! You cannot trust this man!" shouted Ferdinand.

"They are dead because they raised a weapon against us. Come out now and we will offer you mercy," said Laughing Crow. He could hear whimpering and labored breathing inside.

"I feel it crawling on me, Ferdinand!" Maria yelled.

Laughing Crow knew she was suffocating in pitch-black darkness.

"I can't stay here!" she added.

Suddenly, there was rattling and the hissing sound of a striking snake, followed by the panicked movements of everyone fumbling in the dark. Their scattered footsteps kicked clouds of dirt from the floor, which shot through the holes in the wall. They cast an eerie glow against the torchlight. Then, there was a thumping sound against the door.

"I think it bit me, Ferdinand!" screamed the older woman.

"Don't do it, Maria!" shouted Ferdinand, his voice just on the other side of the door. She was crying and yelling uncontrollably, igniting further panic in the others. Laughing Crow heard a large piece of wood banging against the door. *She's trying to open it.*

"No. I can't take this anymore!" Maria shouted.

"Help me, Ferdinand, it bit me!" yelled the older woman, again.

At that moment, the door cracked open, just a little bit, but enough for Silent Weasel and Thorn Bird to push it in. Thrown off balance, Ferdinand and Maria tumbled to the dusty floor inside. Silent Weasel grabbed her by the hair and dragged her outside, while Thorn Bird and another warrior hauled Ferdinand outside, one on each arm, and threw him to the ground. The men quickly bound their hands and feet. The rest of the family remained inside, huddled in the darkness.

Mocking Bird lit the entrance with torchlight, revealing a coiled snake and the faint images of women and children on the other side of it. Silent Weasel reached in with his knife and flung the snake further inside the lodge, clearing a path to the captives. Then he, along with Thorn Bird and Thunder Voice, rushed inside and pulled the others out quickly. They tied them up as well. The women and children screamed and struggled, but to no avail.

"Strap the two younger women and the three children to the extra horses and cover their eyes. Cover her mouth," ordered Laughing Crow, nodding at Maria. "Leave Ferdinand and the older woman here."

Besides Maria, who was tall, gaunt, and in her twenties, there was another younger, much calmer woman who was even taller and stronger-looking, with an attractive face. Of the three children, two of them were boys, and all of them were between six and ten years old. The children were crying, but not as frantically as Maria and the older woman, who Laughing Crow guessed was Ferdinand's wife. He could see the snake bite on her leg. Ferdinand was a tall man with long gray hair, weathered skin, and dark brown eyes. He appeared to be in his late forties. All of them were dressed well in brightly colored clothing.

"Silent Weasel, check the lodge for blankets, clothing, pots, cups—anything that our women can use. Leave the snakes in there, but be careful."

"Yes, *namunewapi*. I will throw a blanket on them for now."

"Are you going to kill us now, *Avispa*?" asked Ferdinand. "You savage bastard!"

"I'm not going to kill you, *viejo*. I will let you choose how you want to die," said Laughing Crow, in a cold tone.

"At least let me draw the poison from my wife's leg."

"No, it will be quicker if she dies from the poison. You will need to decide, *viejo*, if you want to die from thirst or from poison. That is your choice. Your fortress will be your dying place," Laughing Crow said with a smile just before Mocking Bird translated it.

"I am not afraid to die, *Avispa Negra*. Your time will come, too, and my hell will be waiting for you!" Ferdinand yelled. He stopped for a moment, collected his thoughts, and began speaking again, calmly. "I remember when I was a little boy. We had red-skinned savages like you as workers in our plantations. Most were lazy. They had to be whipped for a good day's work. Despite our attempts to teach them, they did not want to learn our language, or to read or write to preserve their heritage. They didn't care. Your people are lazy like those savages. When the Spaniards march north from Mexico, they will kill all of you. With no written history of your people, you will decay like bones into dust, forgotten forever! Your time is coming, *Avispa Negra*! It is coming soon!"

Ferdinand stared into Laughing Crow's eyes, but received no reaction. To the Nokoni leader, these were just words, empty words of a desperate, dying man. "You're a lucky man, *viejo*. You won't be able to see the poison suck the life out of your wife. The darkness will be your friend." Then he said to his men, "Put them inside. The stench of this place sickens me."

Thorn Bird and Silent Weasel, led by Mocking Bird's torch, dragged the couple inside the lodge and tied them to a table. Ferdinand's wife began screaming again. The rattlers, now uncovered, resumed their death chant as the three men closed the door behind them.

"Your time is coming, *Avispa Negra*!" yelled Ferdinand, repeatedly.

"Let me have the torch," said Malone.

Mocking Bird handed him the torch and mounted, as did Thorn Bird and Silent Weasel. Laughing Crow knew exactly what his friend was going to do and he did not stop him.

Malone opened the front door. He pulled the knife from his leg sheath and disappeared into the dwelling. The screams of the old woman stopped first and then Ferdinand's voice went silent. He walked back outside, rubbing the bloody knife on his leggings. "They are not our enemies," he said, looking up at Laughing Crow.

"Let's go, my friend. We have a long ride ahead of us," said Laughing Crow, offering a smile to his merciful friend.

In the Great
Spirit's Hands

Many Wolves sat for a moment, trembling next to the lifeless body of the magnificent bear he had just killed. The bear's head was enormous. His front claws were enormous. Everything about him was enormous. The largest animal he had ever seen before this was an elk his father had killed near his village and Gray Face was as big as three of those. Then, after taking in several deep breaths, his body stopped shaking. *The Northerner!*

He stood up and saw that the man was still motionless on the ground. Cautiously, he walked over to him. As he approached, he bent down and saw that the Northerner was still breathing, but unconscious. His deerskin shirt was ripped apart and blood covered his back where Gray Face had slashed him with his knife-like claws and punctured him with his fangs. He had gashes on both of his arms and deep bite marks on his right arm. The Northerner looked much younger up-close, perhaps as old as twenty or twenty-five winters.

Knowing that other predators like wolves, mountain lions, or other bears, would soon pick up the scent of the dead bear's carcass, Many Wolves realized he needed to get the Northerner to a safe place. He grabbed the man's arms and began dragging him along the ground towards the pine forest. The man's limp body was heavy, but eventually he brought him to the tree line, to a flat spot that would make a good camp. *This is far enough away.*

Many Wolves cut away the shreds of bloody leather that remained on the back of the Northerner's shirt. Two claw wounds were bleeding profusely, as well as the deep puncture wounds from the bear's fangs. The man's breathing was labored, so he rolled him over on his side so he could breathe a little easier, and then pulled away the rest of his shirt, which was dry. He wasn't exactly sure what to do, but he knew he had to try to slow the gushing blood, so he wrapped two of the drier strips of deerskin around the man's arms. Using the clean piece of shirt, he applied pressure to the two deep cuts and held it until the shirt was completely soaked with blood.

Now that the bleeding had slowed, he pulled out a bone needle and some thin sinew from his bag, which he used for stitching rabbit hide. He threaded the needle and stitched the loose skin together on the two large gashes, just as he had seen Desert Flower do before on him when he had cut his leg. The stitches were crude, but they would reduce the blood loss even more and help him to heal. He carefully washed all the man's wounds with the water from his pouch. The man's skin was cool and damp to the touch. *I have nothing to cover him with, to keep him warm.*

He saw that the Northerner's horse had returned, but was keeping a safe distance from him. "Maybe he has some supplies I can use," Many Wolves said to himself. He walked over to the creek that had led him to this meadow. He cleaned the Northerner's blood off his hands and washed the dried mud from his body. It felt good to strip away the itchy layer of dirt.

He stood up and walked slowly towards the white horse, remembering what his father had taught him about approaching horses. Since he was a stranger to the horse, he expected it to spook easily, so he walked up to it at an angle, speaking quiet words. "Easy. Don't run on me. Easy." The horse was grazing, and he could see that it was a stallion. "Easy, my friend, easy." He ripped a large handful of grass out of the ground and held it out, as he approached the horse from the right side.

The horse was nervous and ran away from him. Many Wolves tried to approach again with his offering, but every time the horse ran away. "You must smell the blood and the bear, that's why you are afraid." After several more attempts, the horse finally allowed him to stay near.

"Hello, my friend. Here, eat this." The horse gently took the grass and began chewing. Many Wolves rubbed his hand against the side of the horse's face and along its smooth neck and bristly mane. He continued to talk softly, "That's it, easy."

It had been a long time since he had been close to a horse. He saw a light buffalo-hide saddle pad with short stirrups and a long strand of braided horsehair attached to its mouth as a lead. This horse was well cared for and in excellent condition, apparently unharmed from the fall it had taken. There was no other equipment on the horse, just the saddle pad. So, he led the horse to where his rider lay, removed the pad, and covered the man's body with it.

His deep hatred for the Northerner was melting away as he stared at the helpless man, fighting for every breath. He had no idea if this man even knew Laughing Crow, his proven enemy, but he felt compelled to help him. This man had not harmed him and so he couldn't leave him to die.

"This is all I can do for you now," he told the Northerner. "Your life is in the Great Spirit's hands. I can pray for you and take care of you, but I can't heal you." Then a new feeling crept into his mind. *If you recover, maybe we can be friends.*

As he was covering the man's body, Many Wolves noticed a knife sheath attached to his right legging. He pulled out the knife and noticed the hard, shiny metallic blade. Some of the men in his village had knives like this. He was told they were made by white men. The edges were much sharper and they didn't dull nearly as easily as the bone knives he used. *This knife will make it much easier to skin Gray Face.*

Many Wolves walked over to Gray Face's carcass and looked it over. He started pulling the arrows out of its thick hide. Some came easily, while others he had to cut out with the knife. He removed nine arrows; four of them were his. Two of the arrow points from his arrows were completely shattered from impacting bone, while all the Northerner's points were still intact.

Then, he positioned himself on the ground beside the bear and, with all his strength, pushed its body so that it was lying on its back. He knew it would be easier to skin this way. He cut each of its claws off. The hide was extremely tough, but the metal knife sliced through it easily. It would have been much more difficult with his bone knife. Then he cut an incision from the bear's throat to its tail and made four more cuts along each leg. Large flies were buzzing all around him, capturing their share of the feast, and the merciless late-afternoon sun rained sweat into his eyes.

After a final cut around the bear's neck, he peeled the skin away from the flesh, leaving only the skin on its head. *How quickly will the scent of pooled blood bring out other predators?* Finally, he cut into the flesh of the animal's rear leg and stripped off a piece of fresh sinew.

He dragged the weighty hide back to the forest, to a spot some distance away from the makeshift camp, and stretched it across the ground, anchoring it with four pointed sticks he found on the forest floor. He also hung the sinew from a tree, so it would dry. He rinsed the bear's blood off his hands, arms, chest, and legs.

Returning to the carcass, he removed the bear's liver, which was still lukewarm, and took a big bite from it. The liver was tender, moist, and delicious. The bear's blood ran down the sides of his mouth as he ate. He felt a little bit of strength return to his body with each mouthful.

He cut out the rest of the bowels and buried them in a large hole he dug with the knife. From his experience hunting rabbits, he knew that the bowels would eventually taint the flavor of the meat and had to be removed immediately.

When he was finished with the entrails, he cut a generous piece of breast meat and carried them back to camp, along with the bear claws and arrows. *This is all I need to take for now. I can butcher the rest of it in the morning, before the sun gets too high.*

Back at the camp, he cut a chunk from Gray Face's heart and called Chiquito down to the fist-perch on his left hand. The hawk tore into the glistening heart voraciously. "This is the heart of the great bear that killed Amarillo. Enjoy it, Chiquito," he said. "I will need to lead your sisters here and bring more supplies before the darkness comes. With the man's horse, it shouldn't take me too long." As he sat watching his bird eat, the Northerner mumbled a few unrecognizable words in his sleep. *He must be having a bad dream.*

Once Chiquito was finished, he flew up to a branch, satisfied with his meal, and began to preen. Many Wolves washed his hands in the creek, drank some water, and cleaned the arrows he extracted from the carcass, returning the two arrows that were still usable to his quiver. He left the Northerner's arrows in his camp. They were some of the finest arrows he had ever seen; smooth, straight shafts and sharp, metallic points.

With his quiver slung around his shoulder, and the remains of the bear's heart in his waist pouch, he again approached the white horse from the side. He couldn't remember the last time he had ridden a horse. After some hesitation, he breathed deep and mounted. The horse snorted curiously, shaking his head from side-to-side, but did not protest the strange rider.

With his legs and knees, Many Wolves signaled the horse to walk, guiding it with the horsehair lead. It felt good to be on a horse again. "Chiquito, stay here. I'll be back soon," he told the bird, not really knowing if he understood his words. Besides, the bird was preoccupied with grooming himself. Many Wolves prompted the horse to trot and began his short trip home.

Ten Arrows

At dusk, Many Wolves rode back to the makeshift camp, hauling the supplies he thought he would need. Reina and Cazador followed close behind. He had forgotten how exhilarating it was to ride a horse and how useful they were as pack animals. The trip would have taken much longer otherwise.

The Northerner lay on his side, breathing hard in his sleep. Many Wolves unrolled his buffalo robe and pulled out a large deerskin bag full of tools and cooking items and his large water pouch, which he refilled with water from the stream. He pulled the saddle pad, now spotted with blood, off the man and covered him with the buffalo robe instead. *I'll use the saddle pad to sleep on.* He collected logs, sticks, and some dry grass, which he used to tinder a fire. His birds were perched on branches around the camp, each with one leg tucked away, preparing for sleep.

As Many Wolves watched the fire dance in front of him, he thought about what he needed to take from the bear carcass tomorrow, knowing that the scavengers would come the next day: coyotes, buzzards, and maybe a larger predator of some kind. He would also need to scrape the flesh and fat off the bear hide to prepare it for tanning. It would make a nice sleeping pad for his home.

Night crawled into his camp, bringing with it the constant chirping of crickets and the occasional screech of an owl. The white, heart-faced owls were his favorite. Their sound was a drawn-out, raspy screech, like the scream of a pained animal. He often saw them flying along the tops of the trees at dusk. Other people in his village believed they were restless spirits searching for a resting place and were bad luck, but he didn't agree. He couldn't imagine any kind of bird bringing bad luck.

The Northerner mumbled strange words again, but it was just another dream. *When is he going to wake up? What am I going to say to him?* Many Wolves realized that his words would probably be strange to this man. *I know some hand signs; maybe he will know them.*

He was beginning to feel hungry again, so he pulled out a piece of meat he'd cut from the bear's breast, impaled it with a sharpened stick, and hung it over the flames. He had eaten bear meat once or twice before, but it was a long time ago and he didn't remember what the flavor was like. As his meal sizzled over the fire, the aroma overwhelmed his senses. Knowing that the flesh was Gray Face's made it even more appetizing. Once it was cooked to his liking, he let it cool for a few moments, then took a small bite. It had a different flavor than the rabbit he was used to, but it was good. It was thick and juicy and there were no bones to worry about. He ate all of it, savoring every bite.

Then he glanced over at the Northerner, and saw that the stranger was awake and staring back at him. Startled, Many Wolves felt a shiver run through his body. He stood up and backed away. The man tried to move his arms, but winced and moaned, then gave up. *His pain must be great.*

Many Wolves put his food down and made a sign with his hand. His grandfather had taught him that it meant "friend." Then, he showed the man that his hands were empty. He repeated himself two more times, but the Northerner didn't respond; he just locked his eyes on Many Wolves.

Then Many Wolves picked up his water pouch and asked, "Water?" The man nodded slightly, accepting the offer. Many Wolves walked over slowly and placed the pouch next to the injured man, within his reach, then backed away. The man winced again reaching for the water, brought it to his mouth, and took a small sip. He took a few more small mouthfuls, spilling much of the water on the ground, and then placed the pouch back where he had found it.

The man motioned his hand, making the same sign as Many Wolves, and then he uttered a strange word softly. Many Wolves guessed that it was the word "friend" in his language. Then, the man spoke the word "friend" in Lipan. Many Wolves nodded his approval, expressing his relief with a smile.

"You speak Lipan?" asked Many Wolves.

"A little." The man signaled the word "little" with his finger and thumb as though he were about to pinch them together. As he moved, he grimaced from pain.

Many Wolves reached for his drinking-shell and filled it with water. He took some finely ground pieces of mescal and a few purple coneflower petals from his medicine pouch and sprinkled them in the water. Then he placed the drinking-shell near the fire. Desert Flower had taught him that this medicine would take away the pain.

It had been a long time since he had spoken words to another person. It felt strange. Ever since he had last spoken to Hadakai, he reminded himself to use his words so he wouldn't forget them. Talking to Amarillo and his birds had helped keep the words alive.

"Are you Nokoni?" Many Wolves asked the question that was burning in his mind.

The man looked at him, tried to stretch his leg, and then winced again. "Penateka," he answered.

Penateka. Many Wolves sighed in relief. He remembered Walking Free telling him about the Penateka Northerner band. He said that they lived further east than the Nokonis and had greater numbers than either the Lipans or the Nokonis. They were all Northerners to his people. Unlike Laughing Crow's band, the Penatekas had never raided or even threatened the Lipans around the Rio Pecos. *This man is not from Laughing Crow's band.*

"Talk *Navoonah*, but not *Navoonah* skin," the Northerner said.

Many Wolves nodded. "Yes. White skin, *Navoonah* spirit." He paused briefly to check on the mescal tea and then returned his attention to the ailing man. Pointing to his chest, he said, "My name is Many Wolves."

The Northerner looked confused. "Name?"

"Many Wolves," he repeated. But still, the man looked perplexed.

Then Many Wolves howled loudly like a wolf and said, "Wolf."

The man repeated in Lipan, "Coyote?"

"No, wolf." Many Wolves spread his arms out to express "bigger."

"Wolf!" The man cracked a subtle, understanding smile.

Many Wolves nodded his approval and then started pointing to the ground in many places, counting "One… Two… Three… Four…" and then kept pointing to new spots without counting. When he was done pointing, he made a ring with his arms and surrounded the area where he had pointed and said, "Many."

The Northerner nodded. "Many… Many Wolf!"

Many Wolves smiled approvingly. "Yes! Many Wolves! That is my name!" He saw that the tea was steaming, so he carefully pulled the hot drinking-shell away from the fire and let it cool for a few moments. Then he offered it, saying, "Medicine. It will make the pain go away and let you sleep." He didn't expect the man to understand all of that, but he did echo back the word "medicine" as though he understood what it meant.

The Northerner slowly sipped the tea and then set it aside. He pointed to the arrows that Many Wolves had pulled from Gray Face's carcass.

Many Wolves asked, "Arrows?"

The Northerner immediately nodded and then pointed to himself and said, "Arrows." Then he held up one finger and Many Wolves said, "One," and then he said, "Two" and "Three" as the Northerner held up more fingers. Many Wolves kept counting as he held up more fingers: "Four... Five." Many Wolves continued with more numbers: "Seven... Eight... Nine... Ten."

Once Many Wolves said, "Ten," the Northerner repeated, "Ten. Ten Arrows," and then pointed to himself.

Many Wolves nodded to show that he understood. *His name is Ten Arrows.*

Ten Arrows picked up the mescal tea and drank the rest of it quickly and then set the empty drinking-shell down. He tried to make himself as comfortable as possible while lying on his side, keeping the pressure off his back. Each time he shifted, the wrinkles of pain returned to his face.

Many Wolves sat silently watching him and staring into the hypnotic motion of the dancing fire. The constant crackle of flames was embellished by the occasional screech of a nighthawk searching the meadow for insects.

Like stones, the mescal tea weighed down the drooping eyelids of the injured Northerner, erasing the pain lines from his face. Many Wolves continued to watch as Ten Arrows slowly drifted off to sleep.

Progeny

Laughing Crow and his men arrived home at midmorning and were welcomed by the cheers of the women and children. The men held their lances high as they rode into the village, some displaying the scalps they had taken on the tips of their lances. The scalp that Laughing Crow claimed was hanging from his Thunder-Bird shield. The men were smiling and whooping, their white teeth in stark contrast to their dark, dust-covered skin.

Laughing Crow's fifteen-year-old son, Walks On Feathers, took Cheval-Sang's lead as the leader dismounted. He always insisted that his son greet him after raids or hunts. He wanted him to witness how much the village respected and celebrated their warriors.

"I heard the raid went well, *Ahpu*," said Walks On Feathers, his adoring eyes focused on his father. "You have another scalp!"

"Yes, it went well. No injuries to our men and we lost only one horse to a broken leg," said Laughing Crow, calmly, with a hint of a smile. "Take Cheval-Sang to the creek and find him some fresh buffalo grass."

The other warriors also dismounted and led their mounts, as well as the seven new horses they had captured, to water and food. The two Mexican women and three children they had taken from Ferdinand's dwelling were bound by horsehair. Their ankles were also strapped to the ponies they rode, making it impossible to escape.

"Malone, take the women to Rosa so she can take care of them. Tell her that I am interested in the tall one," said Laughing Crow. He knew that Rosa's whip would quickly prepare them for slavery in the village. He wanted her to go easy on the tallest Mexican woman because he wanted to couple with her when he felt the time was right.

"And you want her to take the children also?" asked Malone.

"Yes, let the women take care of them," answered Laughing Crow. The girl captives usually fit in well with other girls around them. The boys were treated with much cruelty. If they could endure beatings and prove their worth to the village, then they had a chance of being adopted and receiving the benefits of full membership in the Nokoni band. By contrast, the weaker ones were castrated and forced to work with the horse herds as slaves. Laughing Crow's village called them "pony-slaves."

"You like the tall one, *namunewapi*?" asked Silent Weasel.

"Yes, she looks strong and healthy, unlike the other one."

"She is not nearly as pleasing to the eyes as the other one," continued Silent Weasel.

"I do not want sons who are pleasing to the eyes, Silent Weasel," said the Nokoni leader, grinning. "You better let Rosa know you are interested in the pretty little one before she whips the prettiness out of her."

Hearing this, Silent Weasel hurried off to find Rosa.

Laughing Crow walked to his tipi and was greeted by Sun Sparrow and two of his other wives, who were Mexican. Walks On Feathers was also there. "Do we have any fresh meat to cook?" asked Laughing Crow.

"Only pemmican and some dried buffalo meat," Sun Sparrow answered.

"I have two rabbits I killed this morning," said Walks On Feathers, proudly.

Laughing Crow smiled. "You've become quite the hunter, my son. Sun Sparrow, roast his rabbits and have the women kill the brown Mexican horse so the village will have some fresh meat to celebrate our return."

Sun Sparrow handed the rabbits to one of the wives to cook and then rushed off with the other one to make arrangements for the horse to be slaughtered and roasted over a large fire pit.

"My son, I've been eating a lot of your kills lately." Laughing Crow squeezed his son's shoulder affectionately. "Soon, you will need to take your journey into the wild and learn to hunt bigger animals, like deer and elk. Then we can take you on your first buffalo hunt."

"I think I'm ready for that, *Ahpu*," said Walks On Feathers; his voice was growing deeper each day. Soon, it would be a man's voice.

"It's too close to winter to go now, but it will be a good time to leave when the green returns to the hills."

"Broken Nose and I have been talking about journeying west to the mountains to hunt deer and elk."

"You don't need to go that far to hunt them," interrupted Thorn Bird, the oldest brother, who had been listening in on the conversation.

"But I want to hunt wolves too, Thorn Bird. Broken Nose says that the wolves on the plains are too hard to approach and that the wolves in the mountains are bigger and have softer coats from the cold winters. He has a wolf-skin quiver, and I want one made from a wolf that I will kill."

Laughing Crow nodded. "That would be a good journey for you. Capturing the spirit of the wolf makes a man strong—it is very good medicine. Silent Weasel has taught you how to track and how to stalk silently. This will help you in a wolf hunt, and later on, when you hunt men."

"*Ahpu*, I will tell Broken Nose that we can leave in the spring," blurted Walks On Feathers and ran off.

"You didn't let me take a friend when I journeyed my first time," said Thorn Bird, in a challenging tone.

"You and he are different. You learn things well on your own without help. In this way, you are like me. It will help him to have a friend along on this journey. They will be going much further into the wilderness than you ever did at his age."

"You are making it too easy for him. Broken Nose is already a skilled hunter!" Thorn Bird yelled. "You have always beaten the path ahead of Walks On Feathers, because he is your only full-blooded *Noomah* son and I am a half blood!"

Laughing Crow walked closer to Thorn Bird and glared into his eyes. "Thorn Bird, I have accepted you as a warrior and a Blood Rider, and this is how you show your thanks? Get out of my sight! Leave now before you regret it!" roared Laughing Crow, the veins bulging from his forehead.

Close by, Malone was congratulating a few of the warriors. He quickly walked over to his friend. "Is everything all right?" he asked, gently.

"Thorn Bird knows how to get under my skin. Like a little tick, he feeds off my blood," said Laughing Crow. "He is a great hunter and one of our most powerful warriors, but I worry that his impatience and his temper will not make him a good leader. Stands Alone was his only real friend and now that we have been driven into exile, he is our enemy. Thorn Bird hasn't made any new friends since we left."

Laughing Crow paused to wash the dirt off his face and hands. He heard a horse scream in the distance, causing his mouth to water. "Walks On Feathers is different. He will someday be a great hunter and a strong warrior. Everybody likes him and listens to him when he speaks. He will be a leader of men."

"Thorn Bird has always tried hard to please you, harder than your other son. Do you remember when he was younger how he would hunt rabbits and squirrels and hang them on sticks around your lodge?" said Malone.

"How could I forget, Malone; that's how he got his name. He is like the butcher bird who hangs its prey on thorns to attract mates."

"Yes, but he did not do it to find his mate, but to please his father."

"Lupe, I wish to bathe. Bring those bathing herbs that I like," ordered Laughing Crow. Lupe was one of his Mexican wives and the mother of his only daughter. She was once his slave, but he married her after she bore a child for him. Laughing Crow considered her a dutiful wife and a caring, yet strict, mother of his children.

Lupe nodded and rushed over to one of Laughing Crow's other tipis to get the bathing herbs.

"I want you to go to Rosa and return with my new slave, the tall Mexican," said Laughing Crow after she had come back with the herbs. "I wish to spend some time with her. I want you to teach her what she needs to learn and I want her to learn *Noomah* words just as you have. I will be waiting for the two of you at my usual bathing spot where the dam slows the creek."

Laughing Crow always bathed after a raid or hunt and it was one of his favorite times to enjoy the company of women. He hoped to breed with his new slave as soon as possible, forcing himself on her if necessary. She would assimilate more easily to the Nokoni lifestyle with a child to occupy her thoughts. Lupe and his other wives would take good care of her.

From the moment he first saw the tall Mexican woman with the broad shoulders, he knew he wanted her to be the mother of his next child. He wanted his next son to be tall and big.

A Blood Rider Returns

A brisk breeze flowed like rushing water through the Nokoni camp, dousing the waves of heat caused by the scorching late-afternoon sun. The heat was most intense at this time of day and the breeze refreshed Laughing Crow's people until the large mesa west of the village blanketed them with its cooling shade.

The breeze also spread the aroma of roasting horseflesh from the large fire pit near the center of the village to all the hungry villagers. It was a welcome change from their usual meal of pemmican and dried buffalo meat.

Laughing Crow felt relaxed after finishing his bath. All the dirt and blood had been scrubbed from his body and the lingering aroma of Lupe's bathing herbs erased all traces of his sweaty odor. His coupling with the tall Mexican captive had been a gratifying release of tension. She did not accept his advances gracefully, scratching deeply into the skin on his back with her sharp fingernails, but eventually he silenced her screams and overpowered her will. He had planted his spirit seed deep inside her and that was enough for now. He was pleased by her fiery spirit and proud of the numerous scratches on his back, because they were evidence of his conquest.

Laughing Crow, Malone, and Silent Weasel sat around Laughing Crow's fire pit enjoying pieces of his son's freshly roasted rabbits, a small snack before the horsemeat was ready. The rest of the rabbit meat was shared among Laughing Crow's wives and children, who ate outside his other lodges.

Suddenly, two boys ran through the village towards Laughing Crow. They were yelling, "Little Owl is here! Little Owl is here!"

Hearing the commotion, Laughing Crow stood up to greet them.

"Little Owl is coming! His family is with him and their horses and supplies!" blurted out one of the excited boys.

Laughing Crow smiled. "Bring them here." He motioned and the boys ran off. Silent Weasel left with them.

"Silent Weasel can't wait to see his good friend," said Malone, laughing.

"It certainly is good luck, Malone, if he returns to us. Little Owl is a skilled warrior and a valuable scout."

After the crowd had dispersed, Laughing Crow spotted the three horses walking towards him. Little Owl was leading one of them and holding his daughter's hand. His son was leading a second horse, and Silent Weasel was leading the third, which pulled a pole-drag filled with their family's possessions. The village greeted them with smiles and cheers.

Laughing Crow embraced Little Owl. "It's good to see you, my old friend," said Laughing Crow, beaming from ear to ear.

"It's good to see you, *namunewapi*," answered Little Owl in his usual calm voice. Little Owl was a quiet, soft-spoken man. Unlike most of the other men who freely told stories of their courageous exploits, Little Owl preferred to let others like Silent Weasel speak for him. It was difficult to coax words out of him. Despite his quiet disposition, he was extremely well-liked and respected by the villagers, especially the warriors. "My family and I would like to live in your village. I would like to be Laughing Crow's scout again," said Little Owl, humbly.

Laughing Crow laughed heartily. "Little Owl, my old friend, you are always welcome here. I only wonder what took you so long!"

"My wife died of a fever last summer. I honored her family's wish to stay in Gray Elk's village and not follow you, until now."

"You can stay with us. My family will help take care of your children and you can choose another wife—we have many women here," said the Nokoni leader, staring into Little Owl's eyes and gripping his shoulders with his large hands. "You will ride again with us as my scout and fellow Blood Rider. It is good that the Invisible Ones will be together again."

"I will serve you well, *namunewapi*," said Little Owl, bowing his head.

Malone also embraced him, smiling. "Welcome back, my friend. I am sorry for your loss."

"Join us at my fire so that we can enjoy a smoke and a meal." Laughing Crow motioned for him to follow. "The women will set up your lodge and watch your little ones."

Laughing Crow led Little Owl and Malone to a small fire pit inside his tipi where the flames lingered at a low level in the sweltering heat. Silent Weasel and Thunder Voice, the newest Blood Rider, seated themselves around the fire with the others. Laughing Crow sat across from the tipi's entrance, the traditional place of honor for the host.

"Sun Sparrow, bring us some ribs," barked Laughing Crow, "and fill these water pouches with fresh water." He turned to Little Owl. "You and your children look healthy. Food must be abundant at Gray Elk's village." Laughing Crow filled his favorite pipe with white man's tobacco, packing it tightly in the smoking chamber with his finger. The pipe was marked with the symbol of the Thunder-Bird and adorned with several small feathers.

"The buffalo have been plentiful. Gray Elk has been moving the village often to follow the herds and keep the horses near fresh grass and water."

"Have there been many war parties?" Laughing Crow lit his pipe with an ember from the fire.

"Not many since you left. Gray Elk believes in keeping peace and will only fight to protect what they have," said Little Owl. "I have not taken a scalp since your departure, Laughing Crow."

"The old buzzard is weak!" growled Laughing Crow. "He fears for his own skin."

"We have seen signs of Pawnees and *Navoonah* on our lands, but Gray Elk's warriors do not pursue them. I would follow them for days, but Stands Alone, who is the war leader, does not want to risk the loss of life."

"The horse herd is thriving?" asked Malone.

Laughing Crow took a puff from his pipe and passed it to Malone on his right.

"Yes, Malone. We have raised many ponies. We have lost some horses to the Pawnees, but many more were taken by the great horse thief, Silent Weasel." Little Owl laughed and pushed Silent Weasel playfully.

"Did Gray Elk suspect me?" Silent Weasel raised his eyebrows and beamed a smile, which filled the huge lodge.

Little Owl chuckled. "No, he thought it was the Pawnees, but I knew it was my old friend. The Pawnees aren't clever enough to pick the finest war horses."

"Silent Weasel hasn't stolen from Gray Elk's herd in over two winters!" Laughing Crow said, after the men had finished laughing. "We have plenty of good war horses now and a healthy breeding stock. I don't want to be burdened with finding fresh grazing lands for our herd." A serious tone had returned to his voice.

After each man had smoked from the pipe, Laughing Crow handed it to Sun Sparrow. "Bring us our meal."

The men stopped speaking as Sun Sparrow and the other women passed around large pieces of bark filled with choice cuts of roasted horsemeat. Most of the men selected slices of tender, reddish rump meat and a couple of rib pieces each. They sunk their teeth into the meat, like ravenous wolves tearing into a fresh carcass, the bloody juices dripping down their mouths.

"Laughing Crow, your village is prospering. Have your men been raiding?" asked Little Owl, holding a piece of rib in his hand.

"On occasion we have attacked villages that do not have many men to protect their people and horses, but we choose them carefully," said Laughing Crow. "Our war parties are small, so we need to focus on smaller raids against villages with weaker fighting men, like the Mexicans and Pueblos."

"What about our enemies, the Lipans and Pawnees?"

"We will only fight them if they provoke us, but we haven't had to since I left Gray Elk's village. We need more warriors. I wish we had the magic to make our sons grow faster." Laughing Crow grinned and then took a bite.

"Gray Elk has made peace with the Penatekas since you left, but his men never join their war parties." Little Owl threw the remainder of his rib bone to the begging dogs waiting around the men. Three of the dogs raced for the bone, growling, until the biggest dog wrestled it away from the other two and ran off.

"So, the *Noomah* buzzards flock together," remarked Laughing Crow. "They probably need each other's protection."

"That's what I believe," continued Little Owl. "Gray Elk's men are experienced buffalo hunters, not warriors. Most of the bravest Nokoni warriors are here with you."

"Wolves will follow a good pack leader," said Malone, putting his hand on Laughing Crow's shoulder, "because they know he will quench their thirst for flesh and blood, and keep the pack healthy." He looked over at Laughing Crow and smiled, then sank his teeth into a tender piece of roasted horsemeat.

Life Taken and Given

The chill of the air greeted Many Wolves when he awoke early the next morning. The sun was barely peeking through the trees. It chased away enough of the darkness to allow him to see the glistening dewdrops resting on the blades of grass in the meadow before him.

He loved the peaceful mornings at sunrise when the Earth Mother woke her daylight creatures, inviting them to begin their day. The hungry cries of his birds had become part of the morning landscape. Animals and birds busied themselves in search of that first morsel to eat. Lizards and snakes sought out rocks to warm their cool, sluggish bodies. They all had plans, things they wanted to get done before the blazing hot afternoon sun rose to its peak. It was the same way with him too. He hunted or worked on laborious tasks in the morning, so he could seek restful shade in the afternoon.

Ten Arrows was sleeping nearby. Several times during the night, Many Wolves heard him roll over onto his back and moan before rolling back over to his side. It was hard for him to imagine how much pain the wounded man was suffering.

Many Wolves didn't like to leave the Northerner alone for long, but he needed to butcher the remains of Gray Face's carcass. He grabbed his friend's knife and a long pole for carrying the meat back to camp. He knew that the warm air of the midmorning sun would carry the scent of dead flesh to animals all around him, so there was no time to waste. Nothing ripened meat like the hard beating sun.

As he walked towards the carcass, he saw the buzzards already gathering in the nearby trees, waiting for the morning sun to burn away the moisture from their outstretched wings.

Working quickly, he cut large strips of lean flesh from the carcass and draped them over the pole. The meat had stiffened overnight, but still bled as he cut into it. The fetid stench rising from the large gut pile overwhelmed his senses. The flies buzzed all around him in frenzied unison. He focused on cutting the leanest pieces of meat, knowing that the fatty parts wouldn't preserve as well.

Once the pole was covered with meat, he carried it back to camp and hung the meat on branches that were exposed to plenty of sunlight. After several strenuous trips, he felt satisfied that most of the lean meat had been stripped off the carcass. There was still plenty of flesh left for the scavengers. Finally, he cut through the thick skull of the bear, removed the brains, and placed them in a large turtle shell. They would be useful later for tanning the bear's hide.

When he was completely finished with the carcass, he cut small pieces of bear meat and offered them to his birds, who grabbed them greedily and flew to separate perches to eat in solitude. Then, he walked over to the creek and thoroughly washed all the dried blood, guts, and bear hair from his hands and body. After the birds had finished eating, they sat with him around the camp.

The sun eventually burned away the morning dew and warmed his chilled bones. The buzzards gorged themselves on Gray Face's carcass until two coyotes chased them away and enjoyed their fill. Though they were just barely in sight, he could tell they were coyotes from their barks and yips. Crows and ravens also visited, sneaking away mouthfuls while the coyotes weren't looking. Once the coyotes had finished, the growing mob of buzzards, crows, and ravens swarmed the corpse.

The scene reminded Many Wolves of times in his village when someone died and the rest of them said their final goodbyes to the dead person's body. In the same way, the animals of the forest were saying farewell to the great Man-Beast, who was the uncontested leader of their world. Gray Face had taken life from the forest and now he gave it back. *Would life be better for them now?*

Ten Arrows woke up, moaning and wincing, his eyelids still weighed down from his long slumber. He pointed to the drinking-shell cup and uttered "medicine" in a low, tired voice.

Many Wolves had already prepared more mescal tea, but he wanted to warm it up, so he set it next to the modest fire, which he was using to dry some of the bear meat. Once it was hot enough, he handed the cup to Ten Arrows.

After a few sips, Ten Arrows asked, "Horse?"

Many Wolves pointed behind him towards the meadow where the Northerner's white horse was grazing. Ten Arrows twisted his head around to see the animal. He seemed pleased and muttered a few words Many Wolves didn't understand.

Then, he looked at Many Wolves and signaled with his hands, "Two. Two Horses."

"Two?" Many Wolves repeated. *Is there a second horse?*

Ten Arrows pointed to the northwest and said, "Horse. Two Horses." Then he pointed at Many Wolves and then to the northwest again.

"Want me to get the horse?" asked Many Wolves.

Ten Arrows nodded as if he understood. Then, he took more sips of mescal tea and rested his head on the ground. Many Wolves noticed that every time he tried to stretch his leg, he grimaced in pain. He must have broken a bone in his leg or foot, Many Wolves thought. *Broken bones always take a long time to heal.*

Many Wolves mounted the white horse and directed it to walk. Suddenly, in the distance, the throng of birds that were feasting on the carcass flew away—the crows cawing in protest. Squinting his eyes, he spotted what looked like a large mountain lion beginning to devour the bear's flesh. *Even the great cat wants to pay its respects to Gray Face.*

He commanded the horse to gallop and headed off towards the trees to the northwest. He felt rejuvenated by the fresh air blowing past him, blasting away the stagnant odor of Gray Face's rotting corpse. He didn't know how far he needed to ride, but it didn't matter; riding was exhilarating. He kept his eyes peeled in front of him for any sign of the other horse.

As he rode deeper into the pine forest, his mind wandered. Would his companion heal completely? How long would it take? Would he stay through the winter or leave as soon as he could ride? Many Wolves relished the human contact, as he had with Hadakai, though it was very difficult to communicate with Ten Arrows. How long would it take before they could speak freely without a language barrier? *Will I have to learn the Northerner's language?* The more he thought about it, the more the idea appealed to him. *I will have Ten Arrows teach me his language.*

Finally, up ahead, he saw the silhouette of a horse. As he approached, he could see that the horse was tethered by a long lead. It was a dark brown horse with a white patch down his nose. The horse did not seem afraid of him, perhaps because he was with the familiar white horse. They greeted each other with nodding heads and snorts.

Many Wolves looked around the area and found that the horse had stripped a large amount of bark off the surrounding trees, since there was very little grass to eat. He also found a neatly packed pole-drag on the ground. He dismounted and greeted the horse by gently stroking its face and mane.

He untied the tether and attached it to his mount, and then secured the pole-drag loosely to the second horse.

When he arrived back at the camp, Many Wolves removed the pole-drag and placed it next to Ten Arrows, who was awake. He untied the brown horse and left both animals to graze freely in the meadow, checking to make sure the big cat was nowhere in sight. Surely, the horses would alarm him if a predator were near, just like Amarillo used to do. It appeared that the scavenger birds were once again in control of the carcass.

With much difficulty, Ten Arrows untied the pack and pulled away the large buffalo hide that wrapped his supplies. He had many tools and cooking items, most of them made of the white man's steel. He tossed Many Wolves's buffalo hide towards him, motioning him to take it, now that he had his own. He grabbed his water pouch, which was empty, and asked, "Water?" Many Wolves took the pouch and filled it with creek water, then returned it.

While Ten Arrows was drinking from the pouch, Many Wolves asked, "Northerner words? You teach me?" pointing at Ten Arrows and then at his own mouth.

Ten Arrows nodded and smiled.

That night as the two men rested around the fire, Many Wolves learned the Northerner words for "horse," "water," "bear," "fire," and "cup" as Ten Arrows pointed each of them out to him, repeating each word several times. He also learned "hello," "goodbye," and "thank you" from his new friend, who seemed to also know many common Lipan words.

Rain and Tears

The water poured from the sky, a giant waterfall from an afternoon thundershower, forcing the people in Laughing Crow's village into their shelters. Usually they soaked the village for a short time and then departed as quickly as they came, but this storm lingered on into the warm night.

The constant, pelting rain was accented with loud, booming thunder and lightning, which cracked periodically from the clouds. It illuminated the horizon one flash at a time. The villagers respected the Spirit of Thunder and feared the Spirit of Lightning. Their magic was stronger than any man's magic. It was best to stay hidden until they moved on.

Laughing Crow was resting in his tipi, waiting the storm out, when one of his pony-slaves arrived out of breath. "Men are coming! Men with weapons!" Usually the village dogs sounded the alarm, but Laughing Crow knew that the heavy rains could easily mask the scent and sounds of men.

Laughing Crow bolted to his feet, grabbed his battle-axe and shield, and ran outside. "Where are these men? How many?" Thorn Bird was awake now and was with them, his tomahawk in his hand.

As he said that, he heard the screams of women and children and spotted the lightning-flashed silhouettes of men entering his camp. Only the closest villagers were waking up because the screaming was muffled by the raging storm. The shirking dogs now began to alert everyone else with their cascading barks.

"You and the other pony-slaves must move the horses to the mesa. Go now!" barked Laughing Crow. The boy ran off in the dark.

Laughing Crow and Thorn Bird bellowed screams of war as they charged at the intruders. Silent Weasel, not far behind them, yelled, "Pawnees!" and sent an arrow whistling through the air, striking one of the attackers in the neck, knocking him down. Laughing Crow blocked a tomahawk with his shield and countered with a slicing blow to the Pawnee's lower torso. Then he kicked his attacker and watched him splash into a large mud puddle. Finally, he drove his battle-axe deep in the man's chest, killing him.

The Nokoni leader looked for his next opponent and heard Thorn Bird's steel tomahawk crash solidly into flesh. His son yelled "Aaa-hey!" to claim the kill and then charged at another Pawnee. The hissing arrows were more frequent now, as Malone and Thunder Voice launched their attacks on horseback. Silent Weasel and Little Owl fought on foot with knives, using their quickness to avoid the Pawnee attacks.

Laughing Crow heard one of the Pawnees yelling words he did not understand. *This man is the leader.* They spotted each other at precisely the same time. Their eyes locked in combat. The man's large, sturdy body was painted in bright red and yellow, along with the right side of his face. Several large eagle feathers hung from his scalp-lock, and his shield bore the symbol of a Fire-Bird. Like Laughing Crow, he was dressed only in a breechcloth.

In the distance Laughing Crow heard the loud, wailing scream of his second-in-command. He didn't know what was happening to Malone, but he had never heard him scream like that before.

The Pawnee leader pointed at one of Laughing Crow's men lying dead in the mud and then pointed at him, yelling words he did not understand.

"This one is mine!" yelled Laughing Crow to claim his opponent and then he charged. His battle-axe came crashing down on his adversary's shield, a blow that would have knocked an ordinary man off balance. The Pawnee leader held his ground and then whirled around, taking a backhanded swipe at Laughing Crow with his steel tomahawk. Laughing Crow blocked most of the blow with the handle of his weapon, but a part of the sharpened blade still cut into his upper arm. The rainwater thinned the blood as it oozed from his wound.

Laughing Crow backed away and once again heard Malone yelling a short distance away. From Malone's direction, he heard beating hooves and singing arrows against the backdrop of falling rain. Most of the fighting was over there. Laughing Crow was alone with the Pawnee leader as they stared once again at each other.

The Nokoni headman blocked out the sounds from the other fight and refocused on the enemy in front of him. The stinging wound threw him into a rage. He attacked the Pawnee with a series of frenzied blows, forcing his opponent to retreat and defend himself against the onslaught, blocking the attacks with his shield. A sudden surge of energy suppressed Laughing Crow's fatigue as he continued to strike without pause. The force of his blade cut through the Fire-Bird shield, weakening it with every blow, until finally it was a severed mess of wood and animal hide.

The Pawnee leader threw the shield away. Laughing Crow did the same with his shield. The Nokoni warrior swung three more times at his enemy, but the man ducked and dodged to avoid the blade. Suddenly, a wave of exhaustion hit Laughing Crow like a strong gust of wind. He was breathing heavily, fighting to keep the rainwater clear of his nostrils and mouth. The two men stared at each other as they circled, plotting their next move. The Pawnee's eyes were intense, fiery.

The Pawnee leader yelled and charged at Laughing Crow, tackling him to the ground. The Pawnee was on top, with each man's free hand holding the other's weapon in place. Neither man could overpower the other. Suddenly, in one fluid motion, Laughing Crow kicked his right leg up against the Pawnee's left arm. Laughing Crow released his axe to grab the knife from his leg sheath, and plunged it deeply into the backside of his opponent's left shoulder. The man screamed out in pain.

Laughing Crow retracted the knife and slammed the Pawnee leader to the ground, reversing their positions. Then he stabbed his knife through the man's right forearm, forcing the weapon to fall from his hand. He moved his adversary's tomahawk and his knife out of reach and began choking him with his right hand. The man flailed, but his arm and shoulder were severely weakened from injury.

Sensing the life slipping away from the Pawnee's body, Laughing Crow leaned in closer to feel the man's final, choking breaths. Laughing Crow's long, wet hair draped down on either side of the man's face, blocking out the surrounding world. He saw the fear in his enemy's flaming eyes, although he continued to quiver beneath Laughing Crow's powerful hold. Life was dimming, as his eyes and face swelled and he fought desperately for each breath. "My enemies will die in this world and suffer in the next," whispered Laughing Crow. His words were poisoned with hatred, as he stole the Pawnee's last breath, melding the great warrior's spirit with his own.

Laughing Crow then rose to his feet, reentering the dark world around him, which was oblivious to him during those final, killing moments. Dogs were barking, women were crying, and in the distance, the only war cry he heard was Malone's. He sounded like he was still vigorously pursuing

Pawnee runners in the distance. The rains continued to pound the earth around him. The thunder and lightning had stopped.

Thorn Bird approached him. "It is over."

"Who have we lost, besides these men?" asked Laughing Crow, pointing to two of his dead warriors and preparing himself for more bad news.

"Silent Weasel was injured, but no other men were lost," answered Thorn Bird.

"How bad is his injury?"

"He was knocked out and cut badly in the arm. Snake Tooth is looking at him now."

"Did we lose women or children?"

His son hesitated and then spoke so softly that Laughing Crow had to lean in to hear him over the hissing rain. "Malone's wife and daughter were both killed."

Laughing Crow felt the wind leave his body and heat flash in his head. Malone's family was very close to his own, and he knew how much Malone loved them. His friend had only one wife and his daughter was the pride of his life.

Thorn Bird continued, "Malone has killed many men in his grief, *Ahpu*. It's like a bloodthirsty demon has taken his spirit."

"He is dealing with his grief. Killing will ease his sorrow for a while, but the pain of his loss will eventually return. Where is he now?" asked Laughing Crow. Malone's war screams had faded away into the darkness.

"He's looking for runners and trying to find their camp, *Ahpu*."

"He rides in the darkness and rain? The clouds have swallowed the moonlight and there's barely enough light to see!" said Laughing Crow in disbelief. "Have Little Owl find him and bring him back. I do not want to lose another warrior."

As Thorn Bird began walking away, Laughing Crow called to him. "Thorn Bird, you fought bravely tonight."

His son turned his head momentarily, nodded to his father, and smiled gratefully, before continuing on.

Some time later, deep into the wet, sleepless night, Laughing Crow and Thorn Bird were alerted by the village dogs that riders were approaching. Laughing Crow heard Little Owl's familiar whistle and relaxed when he realized it was him. He saw that Malone was riding with him.

The riders dismounted and led their horses to where Laughing Crow and Thorn Bird were standing in front of Laughing Crow's lodge.

The rain had slowed to a steady drizzle.

Laughing Crow embraced Malone and then began to speak to him with his hands resting on his friend's shoulders. "Are you all right?" he said, looking deeply into his friend's eyes. Laughing Crow looked at the solemn face before him; the drops of rain were running like tiny creeks over his high, jutting cheekbones. He could see thicker, slower-moving drops falling from his pain-riddled eyes.

"I have killed many tonight, my friend… Too many," said Malone in a melancholy voice. He looked up to the sky, then looked at Laughing Crow again. "I wish to be alone."

There was silence as Malone walked away towards his lodge.

"Malone, I have six of your scalps. What do you want me to do with them?" Thorn Bird called to him.

"Save them for me, I will bury them with my family," said Malone, without stopping or looking back.

"Did you find the Pawnee camp?" asked Laughing Crow, looking at his scout.

"Yes, it's not far from here to the southwest," said Little Owl, who paused before speaking again. "Laughing Crow, he killed them all at the camp…the young boys…the women… the children. Malone killed them all."

Casualties

When morning came, the rain had subsided, but the ground was still damp and muddy around Laughing Crow's village. The clouds still crowded the sky, not allowing the sunlight to pass. The air was fresh and brisk.

Laughing Crow breathed in the clean, dust-free air and thanked his god, the Thunder-Bird of War, that his village had survived the Pawnee attack. His men had once again demonstrated their skill and bravery on the battlefield, though the odds were bent against them. He felt fortunate to have warriors like Thorn Bird, his son, and Malone, his closest friend, at his side.

Today would be a difficult day. There would be funerals for his lost warriors and his best friend's family. The men who died, died bravely, and would be rewarded with a full, rich existence in the afterlife. He did not mourn for them. Malone's wife and daughter would find a safe haven in the next world, and keep a lodge warm and ready for when Malone joined them. He did not worry about them, but he worried greatly for the one they left behind, his friend and second-in-command.

The Nokoni leader believed that certain men killed for pleasure. They looked forward to hearing the screams of their tortured victims. They killed women and children without remorse and without any doubt that it was the right thing to do. Laughing Crow knew he was that kind of man, as was Thorn Bird. But Malone was not. He couldn't recall a time when Malone killed or even raped a woman, or raised an angry hand to a child, or tortured one of his victims. It wasn't in his nature. Malone took life only when his own life was threatened. The way he acted last night was just as Thorn Bird said: "As if a demon had taken his body."

Lost in thought, Laughing Crow didn't notice his men arriving. Little Owl, Thunder Voice, and Mocking Bird were leading two strings of horses. A boy was bound and riding on one of them. Thorn Bird joined his father from his lodge nearby when he saw the party approach.

The men dismounted and Little Owl spoke, "Laughing Crow, these are the horses and supplies from the Pawnee camp. We also found this boy wandering around near there."

Little Owl untied the child's legs and pulled him off the horse. His hands were still tied behind his back. The scout pushed him closer to Laughing Crow. The boy's lips were quivering as he stared defiantly at the Nokoni leader. There was a familiarity about him, especially his eyes.

"Little Owl, take the horses to the pony-slaves. We will divide them up later among the men who took scalps. Mocking Bird, ask him if his father was the Pawnee leader," said Laughing Crow, staring at the dust-covered child, who looked like he had lived through twelve winters.

Mocking Bird used Pawnee words to speak to the boy. He turned to listen to Mocking Bird and then returned his gaze to Laughing Crow, not responding to the question.

Laughing Crow walked over to his tipi and returned with what was left of the Fire-Bird shield. "Is this your father's shield?" he barked, as he threw it at the young Pawnee's feet. Mocking Bird translated the question.

The boy looked at the shield and tears welled up in the corners of his eyes. Then, with eyes that burned, he looked at Laughing Crow and spit on his feet.

Laughing Crow motioned for Thunder Voice to hand him a throwing stick that was lying on the ground near his lodge.

He struck the boy across the face with it, knocking him down. The boy looked up at him fearfully, but did not cry, then he stumbled to his feet. Blood was dripping from his mouth.

"You will learn to respect us, little man, or you will die," commanded Laughing Crow, motioning for Mocking Bird to translate.

Laughing Crow gave the stick back to Thunder Voice and looked at the defiant child. "I like his spirit. He is strong. Maybe someday he will ride with us, if we don't kill him first. Thorn Bird, have Walks On Feathers look after him and teach him the Nokoni ways."

Thorn Bird grabbed the boy and started to walk away when Laughing Crow called after him, "One more thing. We will call him 'Fire Eyes' because he has the eyes of his father."

It was late afternoon and the sun was still hidden by the overcast skies. Laughing Crow had just finished cleaning his scalps and hanging them around his tipi when Malone approached him. Laughing Crow hadn't seen his friend since the previous night. Malone's usual cheerfulness had evaporated like the rain.

"Laughing Crow, I have decided that I must leave the village."

"For how long?" asked Laughing Crow, not surprised by his decision.

"However long it takes for the Great Spirit to help me decide the path I must walk," answered Malone.

"Malone, it will not be the same village without you. What would we have done without you last night?"

"I don't know what came over me. I was angry...and sad. I deeply regret many of my actions," said Malone, with sorrowful eyes.

Laughing Crow tried to comfort him by stroking his shoulder. "How can you feel guilty about protecting your village and avenging your family? Most men would have reacted the way you did."

"It's not the killing of men that saddens me, but the killing of the defenseless ones. I kept seeing my family die in my mind, over and over again, as I killed the Pawnee women and children. It was as if my spirit was outside my body watching me kill them."

It was difficult for Laughing Crow to understand Malone's remorse. Killing was survival. There was no emotion associated with it. Kill or be killed, it was that simple. If he saw some value in sparing a woman's or child's life, he would, just as he did with Fire Eyes. Otherwise, there was no reason to let them live, especially if there was a chance their sons would rise up against him.

"You must journey, my friend, to find your path and your peace," said Laughing Crow. "There will be a celebration and a great feast when you return to us."

Malone bowed his head. "I will leave tomorrow at sunrise, after I bury my family tonight."

Thorn Bird walked over to his father. "Is Malone leaving the village?"

"Yes, my son."

"He did nothing wrong. He fought bravely. We should dance and sing of his great deeds around the victory fire tonight." Thorn Bird raised his arms to the sky and shuffled his legs in a mock dance.

Laughing Crow looked at him in disbelief, realizing that his son had not yet attained the wisdom to understand the situation. Then he stopped himself from speaking his mind, reflecting on how he would have behaved at Thorn Bird's age. *Only age will teach him this wisdom.* Then, he paused and continued speaking to his son, "There will be no celebrations tonight, only mourning for our lost ones."

"*Ahpu,* who will replace Malone as our second leader?"

"I do not know, Thorn Bird. It may be almost impossible to replace such a gifted warrior and a great man."

A Midwinter's Sun

Many Wolves sat with Ten Arrows under the rocky shelter that he called home. A small fire kept the two of them warm during a cool, overcast afternoon in late fall. Only a few withered leaves remained on the deciduous trees of the foothills and Many Wolves sensed that the first storm of winter was coming soon to blow the straggling foliage away.

Ten Arrows had healed from most of his wounds, though he was still unable to put his full weight on his fractured left leg. He was resting by the fire, stroking the end of one of his arrows. "We use three feathers so the arrows fly further and straighter," said the Northerner, making a whooshing sound and holding the arrow in his hand as if it were in the air. He laughed. "The men of my village make shafts mostly from dogwood branches."

"What kind of feathers?" Many Wolves had learned enough of the Northerner's language to follow most of Ten Arrows's words. He talked slowly as if his words were thickened by mud.

"Turkey feathers are best if you can find them."

"I use hawk feathers," said Many Wolves, a little surprised. "My birds lose many feathers in spring. They make good arrows that fly straight and far."

Ten Arrows shook his head. "But hawk feathers are ruined easily with blood."

Many Wolves laughed. "Well, I never get blood on my arrows!"

Ten Arrows nodded in agreement. "That's because you only kill small animals. You don't need arrows when you have sharp claws to hunt for you!"

Many Wolves had grown fond of Ten Arrows, of his infectious smile and calm temperament. It had taken some time for Many Wolves to feel comfortable with the Northerner, but now their friendship warmed his lonely existence like the sun on a midwinter's day.

"Ten Arrows, how did you get your name? Did a medicine man give it to you?"

"I'll tell you the story. In my village, we often played games of skill with the bow and arrow. We had contests of accuracy and distance, but my favorite was the speed-shooting contest. I could shoot arrows quicker than anyone in my village."

He pulled himself to his feet, then continued. "The shooter would start his turn by launching an arrow high into the sky with all his strength." Ten Arrows acted out the story as he told it to Many Wolves, arching his back and aiming at the sun. He spoke slowly, often repeating or substituting words when he sensed that Many Wolves did not understand. "While this arrow flew, he would fire as many arrows as he could before the first arrow landed on the ground. The highest mark that I knew of was eight arrows. You have to be strong and fast to do this."

Ten Arrows hobbled slightly to regain his balance. "Then one summer day, with a nice breeze on my back, I told my father and my friends that I would shoot ten arrows into the sky before one fell to the ground. I had spent much time practicing a strong, quick release and I was feeling very confident, though I hadn't actually shot into the sky since the last contest many moons before. My father was the only one who believed I could do it, so he placed many bets on me."

Ten Arrows picked up his bow and used imaginary arrows to show Many Wolves. "They painted one of my arrows red, so they would know it was the first. Then, I loaded up five arrows in one hand and five between my teeth, took a deep breath, and launched them into the sky. Whoosh! Whoosh! Whoosh! Whoosh! Whoosh! Each release was perfect and every arrow was shot with the force of a bull's charge. I snatched the other five from my mouth and shot them with five blinks of a hummingbird's eye. Just after I had shot the last one, one of the spotters yelled out that the red one had landed. My father and I shared in all of his winnings!"

"That's amazing!" said Many Wolves. "I remember your quick arrows with Gray Face."

"I will teach you to shoot quick arrows, Many Wolves. I will need more turkey feathers. If you can't find them, then buzzard feathers will work."

"I've seen turkeys by the creek. I'll bring one back for you," promised Many Wolves.

The thought of Gray Face reminded Many Wolves that he had something to give Ten Arrows. He walked over to his bags and pulled out two necklaces.

"Ten Arrows, I have a gift for you." Many Wolves handed one of the necklaces to his friend and sat back down. "I have been making these for some time while you slept and your body healed. They are made from Gray Face's claws and teeth. There's one for me and one for you. We both killed Gray Face." Many Wolves was pleased that the right words seemed to rise from his tongue.

"This is remarkable, Many Wolves. The claws are huge!" Ten Arrow's eyes lit up as he stared at the enormous black claws dangling from the necklace and separated by the shiny white teeth and fangs of the great bear. "I still can't believe that he didn't kill me." Ten Arrows looked at Many Wolves. "I will only accept this gift if I can give you one in return." The Northerner reached over to his quiver and pulled out a bow. "This bow was crafted by the most skilled bow maker in my village. It is made from the Osage orange tree. They make the strongest bows. The wood is sturdy and flexible. It will never break."

Ten Arrows handed Many Wolves the bow and one of his arrows. "Try it."

Many Wolves stood up, loaded the bow, and fired an arrow at a tree about twenty steps away. The arrow dug in deeply, shattering the pine's bark. "It's not as hard to load as my father's bow. The arrow flies with power."

"Trust my words, it will make you a better hunter," said Ten Arrows, looking up at Many Wolves. "Your arrows will fly faster and rip through the toughest animal hide."

Many Wolves sat back down and inspected every part of the bow. It was light and well-balanced. The sleek, dark wood was smooth to the touch and shaped meticulously. The bow was as much a ceremonial piece as a hunter's weapon.

"This is a bow that shoots arrows from the right, but you shoot arrows from the left?" said Many Wolves.

"I brought that bow with me so I could learn to use it. My village thinks it strange that I use a bow that shoots arrows from the left, but it is always how I have done it. This is the first time I have taken it out of my quiver since I started my journey. I don't think I will ever use it."

"It is a very generous gift, Ten Arrows. Thank you."

Ten Arrows inspected the necklace and hesitated as if lost in thought, until finally he spoke. "Many Wolves, this necklace can only be worn by one who has killed a great bear. I would dishonor myself and the spirit of Gray Face if I wore it."

"But you helped kill Gray Face and you have killed bears before."

"Not a powerful bear like Gray Face. I must kill one on my own—that is my journey. I wish to stay with you through the winter and kill a grizzly bear when the blossoms fill the trees and he rises from his winter sleep. My journey will not end until then." Ten Arrow's voice was solemn.

Many Wolves was pleased to hear that Ten Arrows would stay with him until spring. He was worried that when Ten Arrows's leg healed, he would return to his village, leaving him alone again in the wilderness. Winter was the hardest time to be alone.

"When spring comes, I will help you find a bear," said Many Wolves, "a bear that will test your skills and your courage. Gray Face is the only Man-Beast, or what you call 'grizzly' bear, that I have seen around here. I think most of them are in the mountains to the north. We will go there."

Many Wolves set the bow down on the ground and picked up his necklace. "And I will not wear this until you pull your arrow from the bear's body and your journey is at an end."

The Northerner offered Many Wolves his hand in friendship with a wrestler's forearm grip. "We will go together to the high country when the flowers tell us it is time," vowed Ten Arrows.

Many Wolves recalled what Hadakai had told him about the white lion's paw flower. "Ten Arrows, I have a journey to make as well," began Many Wolves, his eyes focused intently on his friend. "I wish to find a flower that looks like a white lion's paw. I was told it could be found near steep rocky cliffs in the high country. I was told it is for a special medicine."

"The old man by the river told you this?" asked Ten Arrows.

"Yes, it was Hadakai. Most of his words about finding roots…about grizzly bears…have been true."

"What does this medicine do?"

"I don't know exactly, but he says that it will allow me to bond with my animals in a new and different way," answered Many Wolves.

"Then we must find my bear and your medicine," said Ten Arrows. "My journey does not end until yours does."

Shining White

The air nipped at Many Wolves's skin like a hungry horsefly. Huge, dark clouds floated past the tree line, driven by the relentless winds, which whistled through the forest. A storm was approaching from the north, a big storm.

"The snow will be here soon," said Many Wolves, looking up at the sky. "We should head back to the rock shelter." He had just finished feeding his birds their share of the squirrel take for the day.

Ten Arrows, his leg almost fully healed, was mounted on his white horse. He carried the remaining three squirrels in his saddlebag. The Northerner followed the young hunter on his daily hunts and Many Wolves enjoyed showing him how to kill rabbits and squirrels with "sharp claws" instead of sharpened arrow points.

Arriving back at camp, the two men took shelter from the gusty wind by moving underneath the rocky ledge, the same one that once protected Many Wolves from Gray Face. He revived the morning's fading fire by placing dry grass and twigs on the hot embers, while Ten Arrows began stripping the skin off the squirrels they had killed.

"Many Wolves, you hunt with your birds like brothers hunt with each other, using the unspoken language of instinct. When the hunt begins, each brother knows what their role is; a role they have earned with their physical abilities and through the experience of many hunts. It is a great joy to watch you hunt with them."

Many Wolves felt an immediate rush of warmth. Over time, he began to regard the Northerner like an older brother and one whose respect he desired and cherished.

"I feel I know my birds like they are my family. I don't know how I could have survived on my own without them. We learned to survive together."

"How were you able to tame their wild spirits?" asked Ten Arrows. "I have never seen this kind of medicine before."

The first sprinkles of powdery snow began to drift in with the wind. Many Wolves blew on the fire to feed the flames. Once the fire spread itself across the fire pit, he answered his friend.

"I don't know exactly. It just happened. Like any family, we grew up together and our survival depended on each other. I find them food, they chase it and catch it, and I kill it. They warn me of danger and I protect them. If one of us fails, then the rest of us go hungry, but we try to correct our mistakes the next time."

Many Wolves paused to catch his breath and then continued. He was pleased that the Northerner words flowed easily from his tongue without having to think about the words in his people's language first.

"I'm amazed at how clever they are. They learn from their mistakes like men do. They learn how to gain height when they need to gather speed for an attack. They learn to read the wind so it will aid their flight. They learn to grab prey by the head to control it safely. Most importantly, and what fascinates me the most, is that they learn from each other and they are driven to succeed together, as a pack. They will attack much larger animals if they know that the pack is there to support them…and I am there to protect them."

Many Wolves gazed at the swirling snow for a moment and then looked at Ten Arrows before adding a final thought.

"I often wonder if their behavior is any different than wolves…or men."

As the day passed, the snow blanketed the ground in a thin coat of white. The forceful wind shattered the snowflakes into small white particles filling the air like a cloud of dust from a stampeding buffalo herd, and it howled and whined like a hungry coyote pup awaiting its mother's return.

Many Wolves and Ten Arrows huddled together in the shelter, wrapped in their buffalo hide blankets and sitting on the huge bear-skin rug that they used as a sleeping pad—another gift from Gray Face. They felt safe from the freezing weather and warmed by the fire.

"Why haven't you returned to your village?" asked Ten Arrows.

The question caught Many Wolves by surprise, forcing him to retreat in thought. He had never seriously considered returning to his village.

"I'm afraid to go back. I fear that the Nokonis will find me and I'm afraid of what I might find if I go back," answered Many Wolves.

"This is the sixth winter since you left your village. Aren't you lonely?"

Many Wolves clenched his knees to his chest and looked out at the rushing, white world around him. "Yes, it does get lonely in the wilderness. I feel like there's a large splinter in my heart because I miss my family so much. But another part of me enjoys the solitude. There are animals and places that I see out here that I would miss if I still lived in my village. I can choose where I want to live and where I want to go. I don't have to face the other boys in the village, who have been unkind to me. I feel I belong in the wilderness."

As the men talked, Chiquito flew from a nearby branch and landed on a log next to Many Wolves, one of the smallest hawk's favorite perches. Many Wolves believed that he enjoyed the warmth of the fire, unlike the other birds who always stayed outside the rock shelter, unless they were called in for a meal. *You will want to stay warm tonight, my friend.*

Ten Arrows smiled. "I understand the peace you feel out here, but I sorely miss the village life: the touch of a loving partner, the laughter of children, the friendships of men." Ten Arrows stretched his hands out towards the bristling fire and then rubbed them together. "Was it difficult growing up as a white-skinned boy in a Lipan village?"

It felt strange to Many Wolves to answer questions about himself, but it also felt good to put his feelings into words.

"It was hard at times. I felt as though I had to always prove that I belonged and that I was good enough to be a Lipan. I didn't want to disgrace my family. I was weaker than the other boys and they constantly taunted me. I didn't have any friends my age, just my family, so I ended up spending most of my time alone. The wilderness became my friend and a haven for me."

Ten Arrows continued with his questions. "You said you were worried about what you might find if you returned to your village. What did you mean?"

"I fear that Laughing Crow and the Nokonis have raided my village and killed my family. When I was a child, I dreamed that he and his men killed my white-skinned parents. I had that dream again and again. I still have it once in a while, but not as much. Part of me feels that if I stay far away from my village, and if I can stop this dream from haunting me, it will keep them safe."

Ten Arrows reached over and put his hand on Many Wolves's shoulder. "Many Wolves, I've been told that Laughing Crow is no longer the leader of the Nokonis; instead it is Gray

Elk who leads them. Gray Elk and the elder council banished him for killing a man. Laughing Crow lives in a smaller band now with only his family and some men who are loyal to him." Ten Arrows rubbed his friend's shoulder briefly and then removed his hand. "My village has found peace with Gray Elk and his people now that Laughing Crow is gone. You should worry less about him because he does not have the force to attack large villages anymore."

Many Wolves was relieved to hear that Laughing Crow was no longer in power. It gave him hope that his village was safe.

"Do you think I should go back?"

"You should go back, if only to visit, then you can return to the wilderness if you choose. Your family would be over-joyed to know that you are healthy and well and it would bring peace to your heart to know that they are safe," said Ten Arrows.

Many Wolves thought carefully about his friend's words. He would dearly love to see his family again. A short visit wouldn't endanger them or him, he thought. *Perhaps I should return next summer.*

"How are the Penatekas different than the Nokonis?"

"We share common *Noomah* bloodlines with the Nokonis and share a common language with them. The Nokonis are wanderers. They will travel far to raid other villages or to find buffalo herds, and many of their men wear the picture of the snake on their arm or chest." Ten Arrows pointed to his body and waved his fingers as if to draw a snake. "They also mark their horses with the snake."

"Why do they use a snake?" asked Many Wolves.

"A long time ago, before my grandfather's time, there were no *Noomah* on the Staked Plains, only Shoshone peo-ple who lived in the northern mountains. The other people of the plains called them 'the Snake People.' I do not know why. They had many horses, but mountain living was very difficult. The antelope that lived in the mountains were very fast and difficult to hunt, so many people starved. Faced with starvation, a band of Shoshones split off from the main group and migrated south to the Staked Plains. They found many buffalo to hunt and plenty of food to gather. It was a much easier living, so these people stayed and formed my band, the Penatekas. Soon after, other bands like the Nokonis came down from the north as well to live there. The Nokonis honor a tradition of their Shoshone fathers by marking their skin and horses with the sign of the snake. They are the only *Noomah* band that I know who do this."

Many Wolves thought about all that Ten Arrows had told him as he prepared some peppermint leaf tea to share with his friend. Both men conversed late into the night, huddling close to each other next to the blazing fire. They watched as their previous world of browns and greens transformed completely to a shining white.

The Frost Bites

For five days, the icy winds blew thick layers of snow onto the foothills surrounding Many Wolves's home. During this time, the two men worked diligently using a hollowed-out tree trunk to push the snow away from the entrance to their rock shelter. The snow was everywhere, smothering the ground and the trees. The sun, which had become a stranger, peeked in on them sporadically between the scattered clouds, like a timid child who wasn't ready to reveal himself.

"Ten Arrows, I need to hunt for the birds. They have not had nuts and dried meat to eat as we have during the storm," said Many Wolves as he stood with Chiquito on his fist-perch. Small clouds of steam burst from his mouth and nose as he exhaled. He felt Chiquito's breast with his fingertips. "His chest bone is sharp and he really needs to eat. They all need to eat." He set Chiquito back down on a log and began dressing himself with his winter clothes.

Many Wolves was especially worried about Reina since she had not eaten for several days now. He had never seen her refuse food before. He knew that the birds needed more food in freezing weather to hold their weight.

"I will go with you, Wild Man. I owe those birds some meals for all the times they fed me," said Ten Arrows, grabbing his quiver. Many Wolves liked his nickname "Wild Man." He thought of it as a sign of affection, reminding him of when his grandfather used to call him "Long Drink."

Many Wolves was dressed in rabbit skin—moccasins and leggings covered his legs and thighs and he wore fur covers to keep his hands warm. A headband covered his ears. He draped his buffalo-skin robe around his shoulders and arms as well. Compared to Ten Arrow's finely crafted buckskin outfit and buffalo robe, Many Wolves felt like an unkempt man of the wilderness.

"Here, put these on. I made them for you, knowing that winter would be here soon. They will help you walk in the snow." Many Wolves offered Ten Arrows a pair of what he called "snow feet"—a flat arrangement of sticks tied together like a cage. "Tie them to your moccasins," he instructed as he began attaching his pair to the bottom of his moccasins.

"I won't need them. Our people do not walk when there is a horse to ride!" Ten Arrows grinned and finished strapping his buckskin leggings on. Then he slipped his knee-high, wooly buffalo-skin moccasins over his leggings for extra warmth. "I have ridden horses and ponies even before I could walk. My horse's legs are my legs. No other people of the plains grow up on horses like *Noomah* do."

"All right, then try to keep up!" said Many Wolves as a playful challenge.

Ten Arrows laughed. "You don't need to worry about Ten Arrows, Wild Man. I have ridden in snow much deeper than this before!"

Many Wolves whistled to his birds as he set off in search of squirrels. Ten Arrows followed closely on his white horse, whom he named Cloud for his color and the way he "floated lightly on his feet." Chiquito and Cazador joined them, but Reina lingered, her puffed-up body clinging to a low pine branch. *I must get her some food.*

Chiquito spotted the first squirrel, sitting motionless halfway up the trunk of a pine. He pumped his wings upwards, above the squirrel, and then tumbled down after it. The squirrel evaded the attack by darting to the other side of the large tree trunk. Cazador stooped towards it, but was unable to get a clear attack.

Many Wolves sensed that the birds were having more difficulty than usual with this large red squirrel, perhaps because Reina was not there to help them. Their repeated attacks failed to flush the stubborn squirrel out into the open. He pulled out his bow, the one that Ten Arrows had given him, and loaded an arrow with a small flint point, not one of the blunt arrows he usually used on squirrel hunts. Most times, he wanted the birds to make the kill and not his arrow, but he was growing impatient with them and they needed the fresh meat.

"Wait, Many Wolves. Let me kill it," interrupted Ten Arrows, who quickly loaded an arrow with his left hand and launched it whistling towards the squirrel. The arrow cut into the squirrel's flesh and carried it into the snow a short distance behind the tree. The birds dove after it.

Many Wolves ran over to find both birds tugging at the dead squirrel's carcass.

"Easy, you two. Let me get this arrow out." Many Wolves extracted it with one quick, jolting motion. He cut off one of the rear legs and tossed it aside for Cazador, and the other for Chiquito. The two birds tore into the meat enthusiastically, as squirrel blood encased their beaks. Many Wolves then cut open the remaining carcass and divided the organs—the liver, heart, and lungs—between the two birds.

When they finished feeding, Many Wolves looked up and saw that Ten Arrows had ridden away. He saw Cloud's tracks in the snow leading deeper into the forest, but he couldn't see Ten Arrows.

"Ten Arrows!" he yelled, but there was no reply, only a faint echo returning his words back to him. "Chiquito, Cazador, let's go!" Many Wolves packed Reina's share of the squirrel carcass in his bag and then rushed off in the direction of the tracks. Ten Arrows had always stayed with him during their previous hunts.

Many Wolves trudged through the clumpy snow following the horse tracks, which weaved between the pine trees. The crisp air nipped at his cheeks and earlobes. Though his hands were covered, they felt damp and cold from the squirrel hunt. The wind and snow had ceased completely. Fortunately, it seemed like the blizzard was over.

"Ten Arrows!" he yelled again.

"Over here," replied Ten Arrows.

Many Wolves spotted him near a break in the trees. His white horse blended in seamlessly with the snow-covered world around him. Ten Arrows was hunched over on the ground looking at something.

As Many Wolves approached, he saw a mound of brownish fur in the snow at Ten Arrow's feet, with an arrow protruding from its midsection. It was a dead buck.

"Look what I got for us, Wild Man!" shouted Ten Arrows, laughing heartily. "While you were feeding your birds, I scouted around the area looking for another squirrel, but found fresh deer tracks leading deeper into the forest. Then I spotted him in this opening between these trees." Ten Arrows ran his hand along the buck's powerful leg muscles. "He just stood there looking around and eating. He was hungry. I came up to him slowly and got a clear shot from over there." Ten Arrows pointed at a pair of large pine trees near the edge of the clearing. "I was lucky that there was no wind to carry my scent to him. My arrow cut through his lung, killing him instantly." Ten Arrows showed him the small wound in the deer's chest where the arrow protruded. "A quick kill helps to preserve the meat."

The Northerner made a small incision, a bit larger than his outstretched hand, in the deer's chest. He reached inside the chest cavity, felt around for a few moments, then pulled out the buck's liver. He took several ravenous bites and then laughed loudly. "The snow will help us, Wild Man. We will be able to track more of these, and the cold weather will hide our human smells."

Ten Arrows handed the remaining portion to Many Wolves, who enjoyed a few delicious bites from the tender liver; its moist warmth melted in his cold-bitten mouth. He handed it back to Ten Arrows.

"A nice change from dried bear meat!" Ten Arrows said excitedly, then gorged himself on the rest of the liver.

"Help me load this buck on Cloud, so we can take it back to camp," said Ten Arrows. With his knife, the Northerner cut the arrow free from the dead animal, wiped the blood off in the snow, and returned it to his quiver.

Together the two men hoisted the large deer carcass onto the back of the Northerner's horse. Ten Arrows tied the buck's body securely to the horse, grabbed his quiver, and mounted.

"Now, I can make you some *Noomah* clothes," said Ten Arrows, smiling.

When the two men arrived at the camp, Many Wolves called for Reina, but didn't see her. He looked around the camp, up and down every tree, but still did not see the hawk. He whistled and called her name again, and again, but there was no reply.

Then he walked back over to where she was last perched and saw her crumpled body lying in the snow. His heart tightened, as if a strong hand was squeezing it. He knelt down beside her lifeless body. The chill bit at his bones as his tears trickled like melting icicles onto her frigid body.

"How could this happen?" Many Wolves cried out loud as he looked up to the sky, addressing the Great Spirit, the giver and taker of life. "No..." he moaned, softly, and continued to weep over her body. He shivered. His Reina, the leader of his bird family, was dead. The only warmth he felt in this freezing moment was the comforting arm of Ten Arrows around his shoulder.

La Fontaine

It was a cool, overcast winter's day in Laughing Crow's village. The leader was enjoying a late-afternoon nap when two of his men woke him up.

"Laughing Crow, we have just spoken with a Wichita scout carrying a peace flag just outside of camp," said Mocking Bird. Little Owl was with him.

"I was wondering why the dogs were barking. What does he want?"

It was rare for visitors to wander near Laughing Crow's secluded winter village. Since the Pawnee attack, he had moved everyone several times, attempting to keep his people hidden and safe from hostile bands of Utes and Pawnees. This particular camp was located in a small, timber-filled valley with a meandering stream crawling through the middle.

"He speaks for another, a white man, a French trader named La Fontaine. This white man wishes to speak to you about trade and peace," said Mocking Bird. "He has asked for your permission to camp outside the village."

"How many are with him?"

Little Owl spoke up. "There are three white men and five Wichitas with his party, including him and this scout, and they all carry the French long guns. Also, they have several horses pulling pole-drags filled with supplies."

"I have heard of this Fontaine from our visits to the French trading posts. He does not pose a threat to us. Tell the scout that Fontaine is welcome to bring his party and his goods to us at sunset and stay the night outside our village, but in the open area west of our camp," instructed Laughing Crow.

"We will tell them." The two warriors rode off.

Thorn Bird approached his father. "Should our hunters kill another deer for tonight?"

"If they can; otherwise we will slaughter a horse for our guests. Have the pony-slaves round up seven or eight of our older mares and stallions and bring them to my lodge. Have them load twenty buffalo skins on some of the horses. They can get the skins from our winter storage."

Thorn Bird nodded and walked away.

Laughing Crow sat alone in his tipi, engaged in thought. He enjoyed the white man's goods, but did not understand their desire to make peace with the people of the plains. Most leaders made treaties with other villages to protect themselves from a greater enemy. He had never felt the need to ask for help. He did not want to feel like a dog begging for scraps. But what did the white man want with treaties? Most of their people were far across the seas.

It was times like this that he missed his conversations with Malone. His closest friend understood things he did not about the white man and his strange ways and would explain them to him. Malone believed that the white men, the Spanish and the French, were great enemies in their lands across the sea and the French wanted the dark-skinned peoples to fight against the Spanish, who wanted to expand their territories eastward from Nuevo Mexico.

Laughing Crow would listen to the words of the white man Fontaine and decide what was best for his people. After knowing Malone for so many years, he hoped that he could think Malone's thoughts without hearing his words.

The grayness of daylight snuck closer to darkness without much warning from the hidden sun. Laughing Crow and his village were prepared to receive their guests. The men were dressed in their finest ceremonial outfits. Most wore buckskin leggings, which extended from their buckskin moccasins and attached to a belt on their hips. Their shirts were made from deerskin, with a neckline shaped like an arrow point, and hung loosely over their belts. Both shirts and leggings were adorned with long fringes of buckskin strings, which were accented with many colored beads and pieces of shiny metal. The women wore buckskin dresses with long fringes that were decorated with colored beads.

In addition to his outfit, Laughing Crow draped a buffalo robe around his shoulders, which was painted with red designs of flying birds on the front. The symbol of the Thunder-Bird of War was emblazoned in red on the back of the robe. His was the only painted robe in his village—the robe of a leader.

Laughing Crow sat alone in his lodge facing the entrance, with a small fire burning mesquite and buffalo dung in the middle. He listened to Mocking Bird talk to his guests outside his lodge in words he did not understand. Thorn Bird entered first and sat at Laughing Crow's right side, and then Silent Weasel followed on his left and sat. Little Owl took his position on Thorn Bird's right. The four Nokonis sat with legs crossed on a fine buffalo-skin rug.

Mocking Bird showed the four guests to their seats on the buffalo-skin rug opposite to Laughing Crow. Mocking Bird seated himself next to Silent Weasel. Next to him sat a young Wichita warrior who translated Mocking Bird's words to the white men. An older, distinguished Wichita man with gray hair sat next to the young warrior and then two white men sat to his right—both of them had hair covering their chins and the skin beneath their noses. The older of the two white men had a familiar face.

"Laughing Crow, I will introduce our men to them and then they will follow," said Mocking Bird. As he introduced Laughing Crow's men, he pointed to each as he spoke, finishing with his Nokoni leader. Then the younger Wichita man spoke and pointed to his men as Mocking Bird interpreted.

"The one who speaks is Running Creek," translated Mocking Bird. "The younger white man is called Jean-Pierre Dubois. The older Wichita is Smoke Cloud. He is the leader of the Wichitas northeast of the Rio Rojo. The older white man is Claude La Fontaine." As each man was introduced, they nodded at Laughing Crow.

"Laughing Crow, La Fontaine wishes to speak to you," said Mocking Bird.

"Let him speak," said Laughing Crow in a tone that did not offer friendship.

La Fontaine began to speak, followed by Running Creek, and then Mocking Bird who translated for Laughing Crow. The Nokoni headman watched the white man with a scrutinous eye.

"My friends, I send greetings from my leader across the Great Sea and thank you for your kind hospitality. I am honored to share words with a great warrior and leader. Laughing Crow, your deeds are known well by all people of the Southern Plains. You are both feared and respected—the numerous scalps that decorate your lodge are proof of this." La Fontaine paused momentarily before continuing.

La Fontaine was a stout man with broad shoulders, and was roughly the same age as Laughing Crow. There was no leanness in his body, which led Laughing Crow to believe that his meals were gathered and prepared for him. His hands were large and soft, with bulbous fingers—not the hands of a person who labored or crafted. He wore a bright white shirt made from a thin cloth material that only the white man could make. The shirt was decorated with puffy material around the neck and hands. His leggings were dark brown and tight-fitting, ending just past the knee. La Fontaine's hair was light gray with two large curls covering each ear and ended in a small ponytail. It didn't seem like his own hair. The other white man's hair was dark brown and wavy and seemed more natural-looking. It draped over his ears and shoulders and was longer than La Fontaine's.

"Laughing Crow, we share some common friends on the Southern Plains: the Wichitas," La Fontaine pointed to Smoke Cloud, "the Penatekas, the Nokonis, the Osages, and the Pawnees. We also share common enemies: the Spanish, the English, and different bands of Apache people like the Lipans and Mescaleros. I believe that the people of the Southern Plains must join together peacefully to repel the threat from our enemies. Each day men from Spain and England arrive on large boats from across the Great Sea with the sole purpose of taking your land away and making you slaves. We need you as brothers in war to push them back. My country does not offer you men who can fight, but instead, the best weapons to fight with and many useful goods for your people. At this time, we ask for fair trade for our goods—whatever horses and animal skins you can spare. Our continued alliance will reward you with more favorable trades in days to come. We ask you to join my people and our common friends on the Southern Plains as brothers in war and trade."

La Fontaine bowed his head, indicating to Laughing Crow that he was done speaking.

Silence fell over the lodge, amplifying the crackling wood in Laughing Crow's fire pit. The Nokoni leader paused for several moments, organizing his thoughts. He was not surprised by La Fontaine's offer, but did not fully understand what the white man would gain from this alliance. *If his country is enemies with the other white men, then why don't they fight on their own land?* He needed to decide what was best for his village.

Laughing Crow began to speak. As he spoke, his words were echoed first by Mocking Bird in the Wichita tongue and then by Running Creek using the white man's words. He paused frequently to allow the trail of translations to catch up.

"The white man, Fontaine, has come peacefully to offer us a fair deal of friendship and trade. I have never had reason to fight with his people, so I consider him my friend. I offer my peace to Smoke Cloud and his people and the Osages as well as to my brothers, the Penatekas. It is very difficult for me to offer peace to your other friends, Fontaine. My people feel deep hatred towards the Pawnees and no words of peace could heal the wounds they have inflicted on my people. I will not be like the overfed dog who is fattened with promises of peace only to leave his bulging belly exposed to a Pawnee tomahawk as he sleeps."

Laughing Crow paused to look at each of his four guests as Running Creek addressed them with his words, measuring their reactions as intently as he would the sharpness of a blade.

He continued with his speech, his lips curled in a snarl.

"Though we share the same bloodlines as Gray Elk's Nokonis, I will never call them friends. If Gray Elk were here at this council, I would decorate the rug you sit on with the blood from his throat! We have survived this long because we know who our enemies are and will never trust them."

Laughing Crow breathed deeply to hold back some of his intensity.

"Fontaine, we share common enemies, the Lipans and the Spanish. I would willingly fight side by side with my Wichita, Osage, and Penateka brothers to wipe out these enemies and purge them from our lands forever. But, I refuse to offer the lives of my men to any war party with Gray Elk's warriors or with men who wear the Pawnee scalp-lock. I am not at war with Gray Elk or with the Pawnees as long as we respect each other's lands, but still, I will not ride with them."

La Fontaine nodded over and over as he heard the words from his translator.

"Fontaine, I hope that we can be friends and that good trade can flow like a river between us. I will trade fairly for your goods. I have several horses and many freshly taken buffalo skins that I can offer you in trade if your items are of interest to me. As my friend, I invite you and your men to join us now for a generous meal as our guests. If my words are acceptable to you, then we will enjoy a smoke together after our bellies are full. We can exchange goods in the improved light of morning."

Laughing Crow extended his arm to La Fontaine, inviting him to respond.

"Laughing Crow, I understand your reluctance to extend friendship to the Pawnees and Gray Elk. They are your enemies just as the Spanish and English are ours. Smoke Cloud and I graciously accept your offer to smoke the peace pipe and we thank you for your hospitality. When the spring arrives, I will arrange a council with the Penatekas and the Osages to advance our peace efforts. My leader across the Great Sea will be pleased to hear of our progress towards peace."

Laughing Crow was satisfied that his compromise was accepted. Since he was no longer the leader of large war parties of forty or fifty men, the security of an alliance with the Penatekas and Wichitas would be welcome. In time, perhaps he could turn them against the Pawnees and further protect Nokoni lands from one of its greatest threats. He was further satisfied that the agreement didn't force him to sit on a council with Gray Elk and his buzzards. As far as he was concerned, they were dead. *Malone would be pleased with this peace.*

"Mocking Bird, let the women know we are ready to eat," he commanded.

French Goods

Dreary, overcast weather greeted Laughing Crow and his village the following day. The women and children bustled with activity, working quickly to finish their morning chores. Laughing Crow sensed the excitement in their bubbling voices. He knew they were racked with curiosity, trying to anticipate what new items the French traders would bring. Most of the white man's goods were superior to what his villagers could make with their hands.

The bantering rose to a controlled hysteria as the traders approached the village on horseback, pulling three pole-drags. La Fontaine, Dubois, and Smoke Cloud rode in while three other Wichita men, including Running Creek, walked alongside.

Mocking Bird instructed them to lay out their goods next to Laughing Crow's lodge. After spreading blankets over the moist dirt, they unpacked each pole-drag and arranged the items neatly on the covering.

The villagers surrounded the traders and their goods, watching their every move with widened eyes. Every so often one of the women would gasp with excitement, reacting to a piece of jewelry or a steel cooking tool. The boys reacted with wild screams and cheers when weapons were revealed and placed on display.

Once La Fontaine and his men had emptied their loads and were satisfied with the presentation, the distinguished white man spoke through the two translators to Laughing Crow.

"Laughing Crow, here are the goods I offer to my friend."

Laughing Crow motioned to Walks On Feathers. "Go get the trade horses."

Walks On Feathers ran off, forcing his way past the throng, and returned with a pony-slave leading a chain of horses loaded with buffalo hides.

One of the Wichita men looked over each horse carefully, inspecting its nose and eyes, its feet, and feeling its leg and back muscles. While he checked out the horses, another Wichita scrutinized each buffalo skin in great detail. When they were finished, one of them spoke to the Wichita interpreter who relayed the message to La Fontaine.

Mocking Bird, overhearing their comments, spoke softly in Laughing Crow's ear.

"They said that no one cares for horses like *Noomah* and the hides have been worked with gifted hands."

Laughing Crow smiled discretely.

"Laughing Crow, we are very pleased with the horses and the hides. Take what you want for yourself and your people," said La Fontaine with a broad smile, extending both his arms.

Laughing Crow and his wives and children approached the blankets. Sun Sparrow gathered some iron pots and pans and handed them to the other wives. Laughing Crow selected a long, steel-bladed knife and handed it to Walks On Feathers. "You can use this when you journey to your hunting grounds in spring. The blade will stay sharp much longer than the blades we make with bone or flint."

"Thank you, *Ahpu*."

Laughing Crow picked up a mirror, inspected it closely, and gave it to Thorn Bird. His oldest son looked in the mirror, groomed his hair, and made a serious face—a mock imitation of his father. Laughing Crow and the other villagers erupted in laughter and cheers for Thorn Bird.

Walking along the showcase of items, Laughing Crow picked up one of the several long guns that were on display. "Mocking Bird, ask Smoke Cloud if he would like these long guns for his people."

Mocking Bird did as he was instructed. Smoke Cloud looked at Laughing Crow and nodded his acceptance.

"Tell him that I would accept any bows that he can spare, especially ones made from the Osage orange tree. If he has none for trade, then have him accept the long guns as my gift."

Mocking Bird again delivered the message through the Wichita.

"Smoke Cloud wishes to know why you do not want to keep them for your village," said Mocking Bird.

"Tell him that the white man's long gun is too slow to reload and is hard to aim on horseback. A skilled Nokoni warrior can fire twenty arrows in the time it takes to load one of those. Also, tell him my village cannot make the exploding powder and metal balls. The weapon is useless without them."

Hearing Laughing Crow's response, Smoke Cloud barked strange Wichita words to one of his men, who promptly mounted one of their horses and rode off.

Laughing Crow picked up a small clay bowl, half filled with vermillion, and handed it to one of his Mexican wives. It was strong dye for decorating skins and weapons. It was also used for painting the horses and bodies of his warriors as well as the faces of the women.

Finally, the Nokoni headman approached the display of metal arrow and lance points and hesitated before picking any up. He recalled how Malone had chosen the best arrow points for the both of them, relieving him of this tedious work. Malone always had a more discerning eye for hand-crafted items than he did.

"Thorn Bird, choose enough of these for the both of us," he said.

Thorn Bird cast a self-satisfied grin back at his father. It was a great honor to be asked to do what Malone had done before. He inspected the arrow points carefully and chose the ones he felt were of the best quality.

"Is there anything else you would like, Thorn Bird?" Laughing Crow asked after his son was finished selecting arrow and lance points.

"I am satisfied," replied Thorn Bird, holding his head high.

As Laughing Crow began to walk away from the blankets, he heard the rumble of hooves. The Wichita warrior who had been sent away by Smoke Cloud returned carrying four bows. He dismounted and handed them to Smoke Cloud, who in turn, gave them to Laughing Crow, nodding graciously.

Laughing Crow returned a nod of thanks and spoke to Thorn Bird.

"Do you need one of these?"

"No, I have two already," said Thorn Bird. "I do not want to be burdened with carrying another. Two is all I need."

The Nokoni leader carefully selected a smaller one from the bunch and handed it to Walks On Feathers. "Take this on your journey. It's made from the Osage orange tree and crafted by skilled Wichita hands."

Walks On Feather's eyes lit up as he took the bow from his father, thanking him.

Laughing Crow placed the other three bows on the blanket for the villagers to take.

The Nokoni leader's family finished selecting the items they wanted. The order of choosing was always based on family status in the village. It saddened him to think it should have been Malone's turn. In many ways, Malone was like a brother to him—his family. It had been many days since Malone had left the village and Laughing Crow was wondering if he would ever see him again.

"Silent Weasel, you and your family can take what you want."

Awaken

It was the second day of their journey to the high country and the third straight day that the early spring sun beat down on the backs of Many Wolves and Ten Arrows. The bitter winter weather had dumped a generous cover of white over the browns and greens of their world. Now, the sun was painting the colors back and warming all living creatures, bringing the dormant back to life. Birds gathered twigs and pine needles to fortify their nests. Squirrels scampered on pine branches foraging for nuts to replace their depleted winter supplies. Many Wolves knew that all these signs meant the Man-Beasts, the grizzly bears, were awakening from their winter slumber.

"Many Wolves, do you think we could find another bear like Gray Face?"

"We didn't find Gray Face, he found us!"

Ten Arrows laughed. "Yes, he did and with great ferocity! I expect we won't need to read the prints in the snow or the scratches on the bark to find such a beast. If we float our scent, like a falling leaf on the spring breeze, it will bring him to us."

Ten Arrows rode just ahead of Many Wolves, who rode his friend's spare brown horse. Ten Arrows called him "Elk Dog" because he looked "half dog and half elk." The horses followed an animal trail that wove in and out of snow patches along a sloped ravine and then descended into a valley carved out by the Rio Pecos. The two hawks followed Many

Wolves, flying from tree to tree, occasionally rising to greater heights to circle above the men. The pine trees dominated the landscape, leaving the oaks, manzanitas, and dogwoods to populate the lower foothills behind them.

"I don't want to kill a cowardly bear that runs from us or one that is the mother of cubs," continued Ten Arrows. "I want to kill a bear that is a leader of bears. The kind of bear who is old and lives alone because the other grizzlies fear him. He kills the offspring of others so he can breed with the mother and he challenges other males that enter his territory…and he challenges men too. Gray Face was this kind of bear."

Many Wolves understood his friend's desire to kill a "leader of bears," but part of him was deathly afraid of seeing a bear like Gray Face again. At the time, an escape didn't seem possible. He had only one choice—to kill the powerful animal. With the help of the Great Spirit, he has been able to overcome an overwhelming challenge that seemed far beyond his abilities. Certainly, his chances were better now that Ten Arrows was at his side, but he had never confessed to his friend just how close Gray Face had come to killing them both and how traumatic the encounter had been. Now, every step of their horses brought him closer to confronting this terror again.

"Ten Arrows, aren't you afraid to face a bear like Gray Face again?" asked Many Wolves, scouring the ground and tree trunks for signs of a bear's presence.

"Yes, a part of me is scared, Wild Man, but after what Gray Face did to me, I have to cure myself of this fear. I have to trust that my skills as a hunter will not fail me again. I would rather die than live with this fear. You must understand that killing a lesser bear does not ease the pain of that failure."

The frequency of bear signs increased as they rode deeper into the high country, just as Ten Arrows had predicted. They found footprints of many smaller bears in the snow, but Ten Arrows did not want to track them.

"In the spring, there are many more bears here than in the lowlands. They awaken from their winter sleep, starving, and spend most of their days and nights searching for food," said Ten Arrows. "Here, in the land that is close to the sun, they dig roots and forage for many kinds of plants and grasses and catch fish in the streams and lakes."

"But I thought grizzlies were great predators?"

"They will also hunt large animals, like elk and deer, which have been weakened by winter starvation and are easily killed or scavenged. But why risk injury from a fight when easier food can be found."

"So a bear would not understand why we are hunting him?"

Ten Arrows chuckled. "Probably not, Wild Man. Probably not. There are many things I'm sure a bear does not understand about men."

"Why did you come to the lowlands in the fall to hunt them?" asked Many Wolves.

"In the fall, many of them come down from the mountains to feast on berries, which are abundant in the foothills. This is how they fatten their bodies for the big winter sleep."

The two men approached a sprawling, grassy meadow and Many Wolves spotted movements in the distance, and instantly, he knew what it was. He guided his horse to a halt and looked out over the meadow.

"Look! Wolves!" Many Wolves whispered excitedly, pointing towards the northwest part of the grasslands. He tried not to raise his voice because he didn't want to startle them.

Ten Arrows stopped to look, holding his hand over his eyes to shield them from the late-morning sun. "I've never seen the larger mountain wolves before, only the smaller ones that roam the plains," said Ten Arrows.

"Neither have I," said Many Wolves. "I have only seen coyotes around my village, but wolves are much bigger."

"Look over there. You will see there are at least two pups with them," added Ten Arrows, pointing with his left hand.

All the wolves were standing, looking around with ears pricked high in the air. The one closest to them was reddish and clearly the largest of the pack. It stared in the direction of the two hunters, not moving or turning away.

"I believe the red one is the leader. See how he raises his tail higher when another wolf approaches," said Ten Arrows. "He's keeping an eye on us, protecting his family. Since they have pups, they probably have a den near here. They won't wander too far from their offspring."

"They're beautiful," said Many Wolves. "The red one is the most impressive." He had always been captivated by the creatures that his grandfather and Walking Free had described to him in stories. He remembered what Walking Free had said the morning after he'd been given his new name: *There is much to admire in our brothers, the wolves.*

Besides the red wolf, two of the others were dark brown, almost black. Another was light brown and the last one was gray. One of the darker wolves was playing with the two pups. The western breeze carried the yipping sounds of the pups and the occasional bark of an adult to the onlookers.

Many Wolves and Ten Arrows sat motionless for a long time watching the wolves. While most of the pack seemed unalarmed by their presence, the red one remained fixated on them. His wariness reminded Many Wolves of a dog from his village named "Mulo," who had big ears like a mule. Mulo was always awake, with his large ears upright, tuned for distant sounds. He was always the first dog to sound the alarm when strangers approached their village. When Many Wolves was young, he often played a game where he tried to sneak up on Mulo as quietly as he could, but the vigilant dog always heard him and barked before he could get close.

"We should keep moving, Wild Man."

"I could watch them until the sun sets," said Many Wolves, commanding his horse to follow Ten Arrows, who had started up again.

The two men rode deep into the afternoon without speaking until they reached a small creek that was no wider than a horse. They stopped to drink and let their horses rest.

"Do your people hunt wolves?" asked Many Wolves.

"Many have tried, but wolves are wary and alert. It is very difficult to approach them within range of an arrow's flight. The white traders will trade many good items for wolf skins."

"My grandfather says that they are intelligent, like people," said Many Wolves, "and that there is no reason to hunt them. He said that killing a wolf is bad luck."

Ten Arrows drank the cool, spring water from his cupped hands.

From his friend's silence, Many Wolves suspected that the Northerner did not agree with his grandfather. He wondered if Ten Arrows had hunted wolves before, but was afraid to ask because he did not want to stir up a disagreement with his friend. The Northerner seemed to know a lot about the animals he hunted, like bears and deer.

"Ten Arrows, how come you know so much about bears and yet you've never killed one?"

"My father did not want me to hunt bears until after I had killed many buffalo. My father used to hunt bears when he was younger. He has shown me the claws and skins of some of the large bears he killed. He would tell me his hunting stories late into the night in front of a blazing fire."

Ten Arrows looked at the surrounding meadow and then looked up at the jagged mountain peaks over his shoulder before turning his attention back to Many Wolves. His eyes were glazed in moisture. "I miss my father's stories."

The Lure of Blood

In the late afternoon of the next day, Many Wolves and Ten Arrows had followed the same trail deeper into the mountains. They uncovered signs of deer and elk, but no sign of a large bear. They caught a glimpse of a small black bear, but it quickly dashed away once it saw them.

As the trail leveled off, the two men saw fewer and fewer trees. Green grass invaded areas where the snow had melted. The mountain peaks were marked by many jagged rock formations. They had seemed distant a day earlier, but were now within reach. To Many Wolves, the sun felt closer. His birds still followed closely behind and used rocks, which jutted out of the snow, as their perches. After some time, the two men came to another creek.

"This one leads to that lake down there," pointed Ten Arrows. "Let's follow it downstream. There may be fresh tracks around the shoreline."

After allowing the horses to drink, they rode down to the lake and began searching for tracks along the water's edge, one of them heading north from the inlet and the other south.

"Ten Arrows, look at this!" shouted Many Wolves, dismounting and then crouching down on one knee.

Carved into the muddy earth were large bear tracks leading away from the lake. They were as large as Gray Face's and the front footprints were elongated with five toes like a human. Many Wolves felt certain that this is what his friend was looking for.

Ten Arrows arrived in a gallop, dismounted, and examined the footprints.

"They are fresh, from earlier in the day. The edges of the prints have not hardened," said Many Wolves.

"Wild Man, you have brought me luck again! A female could not make large prints like this. It is too late in the day to track him now. We will set up camp downwind of here. I feel confident that he will return to this water for his daily bath."

Ten Arrows led Many Wolves to a stand of trees on the other side of the lake. The lake was not large enough to hide its opposite shore, and the spot that Ten Arrows chose provided a clear view from one end of the lake to the other. Many Wolves welcomed the safety of the trees.

"This is a good spot to build a camp and let the horses rest. I must begin my preparations for the hunt tomorrow."

Ten Arrows built a small fire as darkness covered their camp. Many Wolves ate a few strips of dried meat, but Ten Arrows did not eat anything. *He is fasting for the hunt.* He watched as the Northerner checked and double-checked the tips on all of his arrows. Then Ten Arrows painted yellow stripes on each of the arrow shafts.

"Why are you painting them yellow?"

"So the Great Spirit will protect them from winds that bend their paths."

As they drifted deeper into the night, Ten Arrows continued his hunt preparations. Many Wolves found it difficult to close his eyes knowing that another bear like Gray Face was nearby, but eventually his fatigue overwhelmed him and forced him to sleep.

"Many Wolves, wake up!" whispered Ten Arrows.

Startled, Many Wolves looked up from where he was lying on his buffalo robe and almost didn't recognize the painted face looking down at him.

"What is it?" answered Many Wolves, his morning dream still etched in his mind. He had dreamed of hunting rabbits with his three birds. The images were vivid and the movements of his birds chasing the fleeing rabbit were all at half speed. He experienced dreams like this before, but not since Reina had died. In this dream, she chased the rabbit only for a short time and then she disappeared. Now that she was dead, he wondered if the dream would be like this from now on.

"Quiet. There's a buck over by the trees there. You see it?" said Ten Arrows, pointing across the lake.

Ten Arrows was wearing buckskin pants and leggings, but no shirt. His face and chest were painted with thick, streaky lines of red and yellow. Many Wolves had seen his face painted like this before, when he first saw him, but not since then.

Many Wolves sat up and looked across the lake, still groggy. "I see it." The morning sun, which was fighting its way through the darkness, lit up enough of the surroundings to expose color and detail on the silhouetted landscape.

"The scent of freshly killed deer will draw this bear, and plenty of buzzards, to us! I would enjoy some fresh meat myself." Ten Arrows moved into the trees with silent steps.

Many Wolves just sat with his buffalo robe wrapped around his shoulders and watched the deer eat peacefully. The air was brisk and his body wasn't yet ready to leave the comforting warmth of the robe. Chiquito and Cazador were also awake. They sat quietly in their arboreal perches, waiting for the warming sun, and not wanting to waste their energy on movement.

Many Wolves got up slowly and walked over to a spot in the trees away from the deer's keen eyesight to relieve his bladder. Just as he was finishing, he heard the twang of a bow and the distant whistle of an arrow, which cut the crisp morning air like a stone shattering the surface of a still lake. He looked up and spotted the flashing movement of the buck as it bolted into the trees. He quickly tied the drawstring on his buckskin and ran towards the lake.

Ten Arrows whistled for Cloud and yelled to Many Wolves, "The buck is injured and I need to follow it!"

Many Wolves hurriedly slipped on his buckskin shirt and leggings, slung his quiver over his shoulder, and mounted Elk Dog. He rode after Ten Arrows, who was inspecting the spot where the buck had been eating.

"I hit it high, on the right shoulder. I should have tried to sneak closer. See the dark blood?" Ten Arrows kneeled down and pointed at blood marks on the ground. "My arrow didn't cut it close enough to the heart, but I don't think it can go far. We can follow the blood path," he continued as the frost chased his words. "Let's go."

Ten Arrows guided Cloud to move west, in the direction of the injured buck. Many Wolves followed close behind on Elk Dog, while Chiquito and Cazador flew after them. Ten Arrows stopped to let his friend take the lead. Many Wolves was pleased that Ten Arrows trusted his tracking skills over his own.

The blood trail wasn't hard to follow. When blood marks were absent, there were tracks to guide him. Eventually, the evidence left by the injured deer led them upwards into tree-less, cascading rock formations, which were covered in melting snow, most of it icy from the sun's exposure. Rough pieces of broken stone littered the ground where the snow had melted completely. The deer's path followed along the base of an unclimbable slope on the left, but it was much less inclined on the right, opening into a clearing littered with rubble.

Higher and higher they climbed towards the mountain's

peak. Clouds buried the sun and a hazy mist descended on them, obscuring their visibility to a distance a man could throw a stone.

The young tracker followed the buck's hoofprints into a small rocky crevasse. He spotted the buck's body lying in the snow, tucked in a small niche.

"Here it is," he yelled to Ten Arrows, as he dismounted to take a closer look.

Ten Arrows walked over to the deer and stroked its body. "It hasn't been dead for long."

Many Wolves looked at the deer's shiny, lifeless eye and spoke softly. "It's in a better place now where hunters can't follow." He closed his eyes briefly and thanked the Great Spirit for giving them this gift.

The Northerner hunter sang a song in celebration, then unsheathed his knife from his leg strap and cut a small incision in the buck's side, large enough to insert his hand. Reaching in, he pulled out the deer's liver and bit into it ravenously. He handed it to Many Wolves, motioning for him to take a bite.

Many Wolves enjoyed the taste of the warm, succulent liver. Chiquito and Cazador glided over towards him and perched on the rocks nearby, keenly interested in what he was eating.

"Share it with them. I have shared in many of their kills," said Ten Arrows, with his mouth still full and blood streaming down his chin.

Many Wolves cut off a generous piece for Cazador and cast it a short distance away. The female hawk leaped with her wings outstretched and her talons extended and grabbed the liver morsel. She immediately started ripping off chunks. He pulled his fist-perch off his quiver, where it was strapped, and offered a small piece of liver to Chiquito with his covered hand. Chiquito flew to it and began gorging on the bloody liver, which he could easily tear into small, bite-sized pieces.

He gave the remaining liver back to Ten Arrows, who groaned with pleasure after each bite.

Suddenly, the horses began stirring and grunting, their ears flickering nervously. Ten Arrows stood up and looked down the slope, then yelled, "Get on your horse! Go!"

Many Wolves looked in the direction of Ten Arrows's eyes and saw a large bear charging towards them, kicking up gravel with every step. Pushing through the mist, its jowls were extended and its dark pig-eyes burned, resurrecting the frightening memory of Gray Face.

The birds screeched and flew to higher perches. The two hunters grabbed their quivers and ran to their horses. Once mounted, they headed off in opposite directions. Many Wolves yelled for Elk Dog to run as he watched the bear close in on him from the left. The horse screamed as his feet dug into the gravelly earth. Many Wolves heard the bear grunting as it grew closer. He didn't want to look. He focused his attention straight ahead. *Faster. I need to go faster!*

The grunts, the heavy breathing, and the thumping footsteps were gaining on him. He could see the massive beast from the corner of his eye. The bear lunged at him and he felt its sharp claws cutting into his left thigh, tearing a gaping hole in his buckskin pants. The pain shot through him like an arrow to the brain. Elk Dog almost stumbled from the force of the giant bear's weight against him, but managed to somehow recover to a full stride. Many Wolves glanced down at his aching leg and saw several large gashes.

Suddenly, he heard the twang and whoosh of Ten Arrows's bow and the anguished cry of the bear. The monstrous footsteps stopped and the bear roared in anger. Many Wolves redirected his horse so he could see the fearsome predator, a mass of fur and muscle. The bear diverted its attention now to its attacker and rose on its hind legs briefly before charging at Ten Arrows, who was shooting repeatedly. *Whoosh! Whoosh! Whoosh!*

The bear snarled loudly each time an arrow struck its body. One of the arrows must have penetrated its shoulder or leg, because the bear's movement slowed abruptly from a horse-catching pace to a limping trot. It stopped and stood again on its hind legs and roared at Ten Arrows, who continued to unleash a fierce volley of whirring arrows, striking it over and over again.

Ten Arrows rode towards it with an arrow drawn, steadying his aim. He halted Cloud and continued to aim his arrow high, at the bear's head. The weakened bear dropped to all fours and again roared at its attacker. The Northerner's loaded arrow tracked the target and then the hunter drew his bow back even further, paused for several heartbeats, and released. The bear bellowed loudly when the arrow ripped through its head. Its wailing howl turned into a moan as the animal collapsed, its powerful legs no longer able to support its deadened body. The massive grizzly was motionless and silent.

Ten Arrows looked to the sky and yelled a primal scream, which echoed like thunder, proclaiming his victory to the highlands. Then, he climbed off his horse to get a closer look at the giant animal he had brought down.

Many Wolves rode over to his friend, the pain swelling up in his body. The blood was gushing from his leg, soaking into the buckskin, and he began to feel light-headed and woozy; his heart was thumping in his chest.

"Is it dead?" Many Wolves asked, trying to catch his breath.

"Yes, the Cloud Eagle has found its spirit," said Ten Arrows, looking up at Many Wolves, who was slumped over his horse.

"Wild Man, your leg doesn't look too good. Let me see it." Ten Arrows helped his friend off his horse. "Sit down over here in the shade and don't move." Many Wolves leaned on Ten Arrows's shoulder while he hobbled to a spot near a large pile of boulders. After tearing off the loosened remnants of the tattered buckskin, Ten Arrows cleaned the excess blood and dirt from each cut with water then pulled a large piece of softened rawhide from his saddlebag and gently covered the wound with it. Then, he wrapped two long leather strings around the rawhide to hold it tightly against the damaged leg. "It's a good thing you wore these leggings or the wound would have been much deeper."

"Who is the Cloud Eagle?" asked Many Wolves, wincing each time his leg was touched or moved.

"The Cloud Eagle is a great bird who carries an animal's spirit to the next world. Grasping its spirit with his giant talons, he sails through the clouds on gigantic wings until he drops it in its final resting place," said Ten Arrows as he cleaned off the remaining blood that hadn't soaked into his companion's leggings.

"I feel funny. My head feels hot and it's hard to see clearly."

"Just don't move, Wild Man. Here, drink some water. It will help you feel better." Ten Arrows offered him water from his drinking pouch and Many Wolves drank a few gulps, after shaking off the fist-perch that was still on his left hand, then poured some of the water over his head. He returned the pouch and rested his back and head against the large boulder behind him.

"You got your bear, Ten Arrows."

"Yes, I did. It was not the kill that I had envisioned," said Ten Arrows. "Facing that bear with my bow drawn is a moment I will never forget. Staring into its dark eyes, it felt like death was reaching out for my spirit and I had one last chance to answer it. The wind and the birds and all living things stopped to experience that frozen moment between man and animal. Then, all the hurt, the stinging pain in my heart, which was left to me by my father's death, was carried away by that last, fatal arrow. I know now that my father's spirit will live well in the afterlife with no fear of the great bear that killed him in this world."

"I am honored to have witnessed it."

Many Wolves was tired. It had been a long day and his wound was sapping his energy. Though the throbbing remained in his leg and the pounding footsteps and grunts of the bear lingered in his memory, his body was overcome by the injury and he drifted off to sleep.

The Earth Gives

Many Wolves woke up the next morning with the icy frost biting at the gash in his leg and a pulsing pain in his head. Ten Arrows sat by his side and tended a small fire, which was close enough to warm them both.

"How is the Great Spirit treating you this morning, Wild Man?" the Northerner asked.

"The Great Spirit is pounding my head with stones and pouring hot embers on my leg," Many Wolves joked.

"Your aching head is telling your body that it needs water. Here, drink up. I found a creek near here and filled our pouches." Ten Arrows handed him his pouch and Many Wolves drank a few swallows.

"Have you seen my birds?" asked Many Wolves.

"Yes, Cazador nearly took my hand off." Ten Arrows showed him the deerskin bandage on his hand.

"What happened?"

"I held out a piece of meat for her, just like you always do, but instead of grabbing the meat, she dug her claws into my hand!"

Many Wolves started to laugh, but it made his head ache even more. "You should have used the fist-perch."

"It's not as easy as I thought. I guess I'm not a master of the wild things like you, my friend," Ten Arrows said with a grin.

"You are the master of many things, Ten Arrows, but leave the birds to me." Many Wolves repositioned his sore leg on the buffalo robe, but it only brought more discomfort.

"Some tea will be ready for you as soon as the fire heats it up. You can try some *Noomah* medicine for a change!" Ten Arrows laughed. "I have packed the horses with the bear and deer hides and as much of the meat as they can carry. I'll come back for more later after we get back to the lake."

Along with tea, which he heated up in two drinking-shells, Ten Arrows was roasting a hearty portion of venison over the fire.

"The deer will be ready soon," said Ten Arrows. "I had a feast last night while you slept. There's nothing better than fresh meat after eating dried bear jerky for many days. Do you feel like eating?"

"Yes, I'll eat," muttered Many Wolves. He knew that it was important to eat, even when he wasn't feeling well or wasn't hungry, to keep his strength up. "Funny, how it's you who is taking care of me now."

Ten Arrows smiled.

"I have something for you...a gift from the mountains." Ten Arrows pulled something from his pouch and held it hidden in his clenched fist.

"What is it?"

Ten Arrows slowly uncoiled his hand and handed his friend a flower. "I believe this is the flower you have been looking for. The white flower that looks like a lion's paw."

Many Wolves examined it. "Where did you find it?"

"I found the first one tucked between two boulders next to the deer carcass." Ten Arrows stood up and pointed to the surrounding area. "I found more in the rocks over there and over there too. They're hard to see, unless you know what to look for. They grow on the east side of large rocks to soak in the early morning sunlight."

Ten Arrows handed Many Wolves a pouch full of white lion's paw flowers.

"Hadakai was right," Many Wolves mumbled softly.

"What was that?" asked Ten Arrows.

"Hadakai was right," he repeated in a louder voice. "He said they would be hidden among the rocks in the high country and that they would be guarded by grizzlies."

"Well, then, they must be the ones he spoke of. The old seer's words have been like stars leading you through the darkness to this lovely, glowing flower. Look at it! It shines whiter than the snow on the mountaintops!" said Ten Arrows, holding one of the flowers up to the sky. "What does this flower medicine do?"

"I don't know. Hadakai said that long ago men who tamed wild creatures used it in mysterious ways to bond with their animals. He said they would mix it with peyote to make a medicine that allowed them to communicate with the animal's wild spirit. That's all I remember."

"Peyote is very strong medicine, Wild Man. It must be taken with great care. There are some old men in my village who use it recklessly and it has made them as crazy as fever-stricken horses."

"Have you ever taken it, Ten Arrows?"

"No. Some men need it for spiritual guidance, but I prefer fasting and solitude to reach my inner spirit."

Many Wolves had collected many buttons from peyote roots while he traveled in the desert, hoping he would find a use for them someday. He had never tried eating any of them or mixing them in his tea because his grandfather had always told him that peyote was only for men with "strong, well-trained minds" and was dangerous to the young. He also said that medicine men used it to achieve wisdom in spiritual rituals.

"Is your leg well enough to ride?" asked Ten Arrows, interrupting the young man's thoughts.

"I don't know. I feel weak. Some of that *Noomah* tea and a cooked meal might help."

"We'll try to ride after we eat and you have finished your medicine tea."

Riding back to the lake was a grueling ordeal for Many Wolves, but he suffered through the pain knowing that at the end of the trip he could rest more comfortably with his buffalo robe wrapped around him. He knew that when the crisp mountain air crept in for the night, warmth would be a welcome friend and his best medicine. He was relieved to finally see the beautiful blue lake again.

As the horses walked around the lake, the mild pain relief from the medicine tea began to wear off. He tried to block the discomfort by occupying his mind in thought. He wondered what the peyote was like and what would happen if he mixed it with the white flower. So far, most of Hadakai's words had come true. *He must be right about the white flower medicine too.*

His mind drifted to many paths, like offshoots from a big river, but one thought grabbed his attention and wouldn't let go. *Ten Arrows has killed his bear. Will he return to his Penateka village?* More severe than the agony he felt in his leg was the thought of his friend's departure. *Will the loneliness be greater than before? Should I return to my family?*

"When we get back to camp, I'll need to stretch these skins for tanning and dry the meat with smoke," said Ten Arrows, riding alongside. "It will take several sleeps to finish the skins. I'll make you some new buckskin pants to replace the ones that were ruined."

"Will you return to your village after that?" said Many Wolves, fearful of the answer and trying to suppress the shiver in his voice.

"When you have healed, I will return home. My journey is over now that my father's spirit is at peace."

Many Wolves felt sad. *I will be alone again.*

The two riders arrived at the camp around midafternoon. Ten Arrows helped Many Wolves off his horse.

"Rest, Wild Man, while I unpack the horses and make us a small fire. Then, I'll make you more medicine tea."

"What do you put in that tea?"

"A mixture of grasses and some tobacco," said Ten Arrows. "Does the *Noomah* tea kill the pain as good as your remedy?"

"It's good medicine—they're both good medicine—but I like the taste of yours better," said Many Wolves.

Ten Arrows cracked a smile at his friend's response.

Many Wolves laid down on his buffalo robe and rested. *What would I do if Ten Arrows wasn't here to take care of me?*

Spirit Walker

The crescent moon melted the twilight away, leaving its snowy reflection imprinted on the mountain lake near the two men. A cool breeze lifted the flaming embers of their hearty fire, like butterflies floating into the pine canopy around them.

"I want to try Hadakai's medicine, but I'm afraid of what it will do," said Many Wolves.

"It's your choice. I'll be here if you need my help," Ten Arrows assured him. "I think you should try it, Wild Man, but just don't use too much of it."

"Should I eat it or make tea with it?"

"Most of the men I know chew on the peyote buttons, but they say it has a very bitter, unpleasant taste. They say it's easier to swallow if taken with tea. I'll heat up some water for you," offered Ten Arrows. "It will need to be boiled for a while to soften the buttons."

"How many buttons should I take?"

"I would start with two or three, since it's your first time. You don't want to make it too strong."

Many Wolves removed two of the fingertip-sized buttons from his medicine pouch and mixed it with one of the white lion's paw flowers in his empty drinking-shell. When the water began to boil, Ten Arrows poured the mixture from the drinking-shell to the pot of water and added some herbs from his medicine pouch.

"The medicine men say that peyote can make you feel a sickness in your stomach. It is good to soak the buttons until they soften. If you don't eat anything else until then, less food will rise from your stomach if you get sick."

Many Wolves knew that this was the best time to at least try it once. Ten Arrows would soon be leaving him and he didn't want to try it alone.

The deepest part of the night had crawled into their camp. Ten Arrows stirred the concoction in the boiling pot and examined it. "I think it's ready. Do you still want to do this?"

"Yes. The throbbing in my leg is like an early morning woodpecker that will not let me sleep."

Ten Arrows poured the tea into his friend's drinking-shell and offered it to him. "Let it cool and then drink it down quickly," he instructed.

Many Wolves swirled the tea and inhaled the pungent scent. It was potent and harsh, but softened by the aroma of mint. "You added mint leaves."

"They will help improve the flavor."

After letting it cool, Many Wolves took his first taste. The flavor was extremely bitter and unpleasant. He had an urge to spit it out, but instead, he gulped it down quickly to get rid of the taste. He drank the rest of the tea with the same large, quick gulps.

Within moments, queasiness entered his body and he had to fight hard not to vomit.

"Just let it go, Wild Man, don't hold it in. Some of the unpleasantness will soon go away."

Many Wolves vomited several times and gradually the nausea wore off. His face and neck muscles tightened and his head felt as if it was burning. He closed his eyes and saw a myriad of bright colors blossoming in his mind, floating and fading in and out of focus. There were colors he had never seen in flowers or sunsets, but there were also colors that were familiar to him: fiery yellows and deep sky blues. The patterns that flashed in his head were as varied as the rocky formations along the Rio Pecos, which Hadakai had said were carved out over many years by the spirits of the river.

He opened his eyes and looked around. Everything seemed magnified and close-up. He picked up his drinking-shell and studied it. He saw shades of purple and blue that he had never noticed before. The surface of the shell was smooth and round, like the perfection of an egg. He saw patterns of animals in the shell's contours: deer, lizards, and snakes.

His body felt invigorated and without pain. Ten Arrows reminded him to call out to his birds to see what would happen, but their heads were tucked away in a deep sleep and his calls would not wake them.

His mind's journey lasted most of the night. He studied many different objects: arrow points, rocks, leaves. Each of them exhibited nuances and details that he had never seen before. He felt as though he were seeing these objects for the first time, as if through a child's eyes.

The rays of dawn welcomed him back from his journey. With the sun came the pain of his injury, an awakened hunger, and the shock of cold air. The flames of their fire had gone out, but the embers were still hot. Many Wolves tossed a couple handfuls of dried leaves to rouse the flames and then added a dried pine log for them to chew on. Ten Arrows, who was still sleeping, had left the remains of their skewered venison next to the fire pit, so Many Wolves placed it over the fire.

His senses slowly returned as he sat by the warming fire, cooking his morning meal. The mind-journey he had experienced was strange and uncomfortable. One part of him was frightened by losing control of his thoughts and actions while another thoroughly enjoyed the free-flowing river of boundless thoughts. Was it possible to see his birds differently, to notice details about them as never before? Could he learn to truly communicate with them as Hadakai had said? *I will have to take this mind-journey again when my birds are awake.*

Once the meat was warm, he ate it, ravenously.

Late morning, the following day, Ten Arrows was scraping and cleaning the skin of his bear while Many Wolves rested around the camp's fire. The Northerner hunter sang a song to himself as he sat immersed in his work.

"So, Wild Man, are you ready to take another ride on the peyote horse?" Ten Arrows asked and then laughed heartily.

"A part of me is ready and another part is scared to death. I'm ready to try, but I'm worried about what will happen."

Ten Arrows grinned. "Well, if you start jumping around like a mouse-chasing coyote, then I'll have to throw your medicine pouch into the lake! Let me get the hot water started."

"I haven't eaten since last night. The birds ate the whole squirrel you brought back this morning." Though it was difficult to pass up a meal, Many Wolves wanted to be ready to try the mind-journey medicine again. He handed his friend two peyote buttons and one of the white flowers from his pouch. "I don't want to try more than two."

"The visions will last longer if you take more, but it seemed like two was enough for you to feel the effects," said Ten Arrows.

Many Wolves noticed that Chiquito was perched on a tree just above him, so he put his fist-perch on and called to him. The hawk plunged down to him instantly.

"I don't want to waste any time looking at rocks and shells," he joked. "Add one of those mint leaves, if you can spare it."

"It's already in there, Wild Man. Only the best for my adventurous friend."

Once the water had boiled, Ten Arrows moved it away from the fire to let it cool. Then he poured the concoction into his young friend's drinking-shell.

Many Wolves took the drinking-shell and looked into the bright sun, which was peeking between the treetops. Then he raised his drink, asked the Great Spirit for guidance and good health, drank, and cast the drinking-shell aside.

As before, nausea filled his body. Dizziness forced him to relinquish what little food was left in his stomach. He cleaned his mouth and nose and drank some water.

Soon after, he began to feel better and sensed the world closing in around him. He saw Ten Arrows, the flames of their fire pit, and Chiquito on his fist-perch, but everything else was a blur. He studied the cracks and wrinkles of Chiquito's yellow feet. The curved black claws appeared like jagged pieces of obsidian jutting out from his toes. He was afraid to touch them, fearing they would slice his hands open like the blade of Ten Arrows's knife. He examined Chiquito's stumped middle toe, whose claw was lost because of a vicious squirrel bite. He tried to imagine how much it must have hurt Chiquito to lose a toe. It was probably more painful than his leg injury. He looked at his bird's dark brown chest feathers and noticed how they stuck out from his body like a forest of leaning trees. Next, he studied the powerful, hooked yellow beak with its pointy tip, which looked like a sturdy, needle-sharp thorn.

Chiquito's head was swiveling, constantly looking at the world around him. He looked up towards the sky, drawn by the movements of birds or large insects, and then back down again. His eyes were always working, always searching for food or danger.

Many Wolves closed his eyes.

This time he only saw the festival of colors briefly. Then the world came into focus, in much greater detail than ever before. He looked up at a blue jay in a tree and it seemed as if the bird was right in front of him, close enough to touch. Then his sight shifted to another movement, a chipmunk running along the ground. He could see the striped pattern on its back with great clarity. Then he looked up at the sky and watched a buzzard fly over his head. He could see the claws on the scavenger's feet and the red, fleshy skin on its face.

Then, he saw himself. He was sitting with his legs crossed and his eyes closed.

It was strange to see himself not as a reflection in the water. His face was smooth, mostly, except for the high cheekbones, which poked through his light skin. His jaw lines were straight like the blade of a knife, not rounded like Ten Arrows. His face was much narrower than his friend's as well. His nose was long and straight. The curves of his upper lip looked like a heron in flight, with one wing slightly higher than the other. A few small hairs rose from above his cactus-green eyes—the ones he hadn't plucked yet. His dark brown hair, which was thick and wavy and wrapped in a red headband, was much different than Ten Arrows.

Many Wolves looked to the sky and suddenly felt like he was rising, getting closer to the trees and the sun. He was moving. He was flying. He had dreams like this before, that he was an eagle or a hawk. This time, however, he saw wings beating on either side of him, pulling his spirit higher. He looked down and saw his body sitting with Ten Arrows by the fire. His spirit circled the camp, floating higher and higher. Then it soared over the lake, above the tree line, with the sun burning down on his back and the wind rushing past his face. He saw trees and rock formations from great distances as he glided, and once in a while he looked back to see his camp with him and his friend sitting there together.

He flew for a long time around the lake, but didn't go too far away from the camp. This dream seemed more vivid than the others. It almost seemed real. Then, all of a sudden, he opened his eyes, and he was sitting in front of the fire with

Ten Arrows in front of him. It felt like he had been thrust from a great distance in the blink of an eye.

Chiquito is gone.

"Are you all right, Wild Man?"

"Yes, but that was a strange vision. It felt like my spirit was lifted by the wings of a bird. I looked down over you and me as we sat here by the fire. I flew around the lake and I could see things from a great distance. I have had dreams of flying like a hawk or an eagle before, but this was…different."

"It was different, Wild Man, because you were sharing the journey with Chiquito." Ten Arrows paused. "He flew around the lake while you were sitting here, just as you described it."

"I don't understand. What does it mean?"

"I don't know, but somehow your spirit joined with his," said his companion. "I remember a story that my father once told me. He knew an old shaman who could walk into the minds of others. My father said that this shaman had saved the life of a dying young man, when other medicine men had failed, by reaching into his mind and bringing him back. All others thought this young man was lost. His lungs and heart still lived, but his mind was numb. This healer joined with the man's spirit and led him out of the darkness and back to life. From that day forward, the people of the village called the old shaman, 'Spirit Walker.' Wild Man, your experience reminded me of this story."

Birthmarks

Many Wolves bathed in the chilly lake water near his camp, removing the dust and soot from his body. His mind wandered back to the journey he took with Chiquito two days earlier.

He thought about the strangeness of it and considered Ten Arrows's words. *Did the flower medicine allow me to soar with Chiquito's spirit?* The more he thought about it, the more it made sense. He'd felt as if he was looking through Chiquito's eyes and not his own. He always knew that his birds could see things from a greater distance than he and his mind-journey showed him that vividly. When he saw himself up-close, it felt as if it was Chiquito looking at him from his fist-perch. Chiquito flew around the lake at the same time he was on his mind-journey. *Were we sharing the same flight?* Hadakai had said that there was something special, something magical, about the lion's paw flower and his words had always proven true.

The brisk water began to bite at his body. He rested awhile on the shore to let the hot late-afternoon sun warm him. Once he felt he had thawed out enough, he walked back to the camp and found his friend packing his supplies.

Ten Arrows looked up at him. "Wild Man, now that your leg has healed and you can hunt again, I must return to my village." Then, the Northerner loaded his rawhide bag and the rolled-up bear hide into a bundle and attached it to his pole-drag.

Ten Arrows's words shattered his introspective moment, like a large stone cracking the surface of a tranquil lake, and reminded him that he was going to be alone again. A part of him had not wanted his leg to heal so quickly, so his friend would not leave. The pain in his leg could never hurt as much as the pain in his heart once his friend was gone.

"Come with me, Many Wolves. Come to my village and live with my family."

Many Wolves contemplated the offer. He felt close to Ten Arrows, but he wasn't sure he was ready to embrace his friend's people and to forget what they had done to his white parents. Although Ten Arrows's people were Penateka, not Nokoni, they were still Northerners and the Lipans hated them. As tempting as the offer was, he knew that his decision was already made.

"I cannot. They are your people, not mine, and my family sees them as their enemy. I will live alone in the wilderness until the snow has completely melted. If the threat from Laughing Crow and his men has lessened, then perhaps it will be safe for me to return to my village."

"I understand, my friend," said Ten Arrows, softly. "Once blood has stained rawhide, it is impossible to remove. Know that you will always be welcome in my village. Many Wolves is my friend and a friend of the Penatekas."

Many Wolves sat down and started cleaning the wet dirt from his toes and the bottom of his feet, so he could put on his moccasins. "I think I will head south when you leave and try to find that wolf pack with the red leader, so I can study them. I want to know more about how they hunt, how they take care of their family, and how they interact with each other. I've heard many stories about them and I want to see for myself which of these stories is true. After that, I will stay at the Gray Face camp until it is time to return to my village."

Silence fell between them. It wasn't an awkward silence, not like those first few days when they shared a camp and struggled to understand each other's words. It was a comfortable feeling, the same as when he sat with his grandfather or Walking Free in silence. Ten Arrows was family.

Barely a word was spoken for the rest of the day. Many Wolves watched his friend shoot a target on a tree trunk as he rode his horse back and forth past it. Ten Arrows could ride and shoot at the same time with greater accuracy than Many Wolves could achieve standing still. Ten Arrows fired four of his practice arrows from various distances from the target and then retrieved them and repeated the practice over and over again. Usually, he repeated the same exercise with his other horse, Elk Dog. He said it was important to run the horses like this each day to keep them fit, which he always did when they weren't hunting. Many Wolves never tired of watching him.

After Ten Arrows finished his shooting practice, he began packing his horse for his journey. Meanwhile, Many Wolves led his birds to the nearby woods, looking for squirrels. This time, however, he found a covey of quail hiding in the thickets. He flushed them out of the brush so his birds could attack. He flushed them again when they landed, then repeated this several times until his birds had caught and killed three of the plump, ground-dwelling birds. He fed one of the quail to his hawks and the other two he brought back to camp.

"The birds caught two quail for us to cook," said Many Wolves. Using a small steel-bladed knife that Ten Arrows had given him, he cut a slit along the breast of each quail and peeled off the skin and feathers. He placed some rocks over the low-flaming fire to heat them up. When they were hot enough, he set the two quail on top of them.

"I have prepared a gift for you," said Ten Arrows. Many Wolves couldn't imagine a greater gift than friendship, or certainly that beautiful wood bow that Ten Arrows had given him last winter. Ten Arrows reached into one of his travel bags and pulled out two bear-claw necklaces. "These are the necklaces you made. I have added the claws of the bear I killed to each one. Each of us will have a necklace with claws from the bears we killed together. The strength of two bears, not just one, will protect us."

The Northerner handed one of the necklaces to Many Wolves and continued to speak. "I will wear this necklace always to remember the two warrior bear leaders that we killed together. I will not forget that these claws tore through our skin, but did not kill us, because we had a friend to protect us and keep us from death. The scars we share will be like birthmarks—signs that two strangers from enemy villages can be reborn as brothers pulled from the loins of Mother Earth."

Many Wolves felt the wind leave his chest and water come to his eyes. He had never had a friend, or a brother, like Ten Arrows. It was overwhelming for him to hear such kind words and to feel accepted by someone outside his family—someone whom he respected as a hunter and a warrior.

"This necklace will remind me that I am protected by two powerful animal spirits and that my friend is with me wherever I go," said Many Wolves. Then, he slid the necklace over his head, tying the loose ends into a strong knot. He caressed the sharp claws with his fingertips. It was hard to believe that these claws had not torn deeper into his flesh than they did. "I can finally wear this necklace now that you have killed your bear."

The hunters sat and enjoyed their last meal together. They spoke of many things: hunting, animals, their villages. They exchanged stories that had been passed down to them by their fathers and grandfathers. Many Wolves did not want the night to end.

The sunrise and the aroma of warm berries woke Many Wolves and instantly dropped a heavy stone on his heart. Ten Arrows was sitting by the fire drinking some steaming-hot berry tea.

"There's some hot tea left in the pot, Wild Man, so help yourself."

With his buffalo robe wrapped around his body, Many Wolves walked over to the fire and poured himself some tea.

"Cloud and I are ready to begin our journey home," said Ten Arrows. "I will leave Elk Dog with you. *Noomah* brothers share weapons and horses and wives. I would like to give Elk Dog to you as one brother would give to another."

"Don't you need him to pull your pole-drag?"

"Cloud will pull it for me. You will need a horse to take you home and it's not hard to see that you and Elk Dog have become good friends."

"Thank you," said Many Wolves. "I will care for him like you care for Cloud." Many Wolves was deeply touched by the gift. A horse would make his life easier and be another companion to help ease the loneliness.

Ten Arrows emptied his cooking pot and packed it into a saddlebag along with his cup, then mounted Cloud. "Thank you, my friend, for guarding my life…for sparing the life of one who is your family's enemy. You have the great spirits of the two bears to give you strength and the spirits of your birds to walk with you, Spirit Walker. As your life brother, I hope the day will come when I can return the life that you have saved. May the Great Spirit guide you in your travels."

Having said these words, Ten Arrows rode off along the lakeshore. Many Wolves stood and watched as his friend departed. He touched the claws of his necklace because he needed to feel connected somehow to the Northerner. He felt the cold loneliness creeping in like a cloud blocking the sun.

Once Ten Arrows was on the other side of the lake, he stopped, looked back at his white Lipan brother, and yelled across the glassy lake: "Many Wolves, when the wilderness calls to me again…I will find you!"

Twilight Calls

After a full day of travel on horseback, Many Wolves found the meadow where he and Ten Arrows last saw the wolves. A strand of thickets and small trees outlined a path through the southern end of the grassy plain. Like thirsty animals, the foliage lined up on either side of the small, running creek, which meandered through the grasslands. Many Wolves followed the rippling water to a stand of pine trees at the edge of the clearing. He dismounted, washed his hands and face in the creek, and then drank from his cupped hands. *This is a good spot to rest for the night.*

Many Wolves unpacked his supplies to relieve Elk Dog of the burden and then began searching the forest floor for dried grass, pine needles, and brittle, dry pieces of pine to build a fire with. Once gathered, he assembled what he found in a nest-like bundle and used his fire-making sticks to carefully bring the flames to life. He made sure to keep the smoke hidden. Ten Arrows always built larger fires, seemingly unafraid of sending a signal out to anyone else who might be watching them. *I must be careful again.*

"I bet that you two are tired." He looked up to see Chiquito and Cazador perched on the low branches of a pine tree. They had flown much of the way, pumping their wings from one perch to the next, only soaring occasionally to save energy or to investigate areas away from the path.

Many Wolves saw the spot where he had first seen the big red wolf looking back at him, unflinching and vigilant, but it was too dark to look for the wolves now. He hoped to study him and the rest of the pack. Settled in his camp, he fed his two birds the remaining squirrel meat—freshly caught when the animal tried to bolt away from Elk Dog's huge hooves. As he huddled next to the warming fire, he ate dried venison while his eyes fixated on the dancing flames.

The next morning, Many Wolves roused shortly after sunrise. He refrained from his normal morning meal, thinking that he might want to try the mind-journey medicine again. There was inherent danger in weakening his body with fasting, especially without Ten Arrows to take care of him, but the hunger to know what the medicine would do to his body and mind made him want to take the risk.

He walked around the area and looked for signs of wolves. He checked the needle-covered ground around the trees and found some tracks. They were a few days old from what he could tell and they looked like coyote or dog tracks, yet bigger and narrower, and they had the four claw marks of a predator. *Wolf tracks.*

He continued to make his way along the edge of the meadow and found more footprints, some bigger than others. The largest set he guessed was from the paws of the red wolf, which he had decided to name "Rojo." He found several markings near the creek as well, but none of them were less than a few days old. *The pack must be moving around, not staying in one place for too long.*

As he explored, he inadvertently flushed out a rabbit, which Cazador pounced on and held in a death grip until Many Wolves could kill it. He cut open its chest cavity and offered the birds their reward. He sat watching Chiquito eat and an idea occurred to him: *The mind-journey medicine can help me find the wolves through Chiquito's eyes. If I could do that, then I would know it wasn't just a dream.* He let the feathered hunters eat until their crops were bulging. He stashed the rest of the rabbit carcass in his hunting bag and returned to camp.

Many Wolves filled a small cooking pot, which Ten Arrows had left for him, with water and placed it in the fire. He called Chiquito over to sit on his fist-perch. His hawk shook its body, rousing its feathers, and began to preen itself. Many Wolves had learned that this was a sign of contentment. "Don't get too relaxed, Chiquito. I need to know if our journeys are real or just a dream. If you can fly me to the wolves, then I will know that our spirits are walking together."

After adding three of the peyote buttons and crumbled pieces of the white lion's paw flower, he let the tea boil for some time before pouring it into his drinking-shell to let it cool. He added an extra button because he remembered what Ten Arrows had said: "The more peyote you use, the longer the effect will last." Chiquito was still perched on his hand, relaxed.

Many Wolves swallowed the tea quickly and felt the heat rush to his head and the soreness in his stomach. He heaved, unable to hold it in, but only a mouthful came up from his stomach. The horrible nausea faded away slowly. He closed his eyes and focused his thoughts on what he wanted to do. *Chiquito, find the wolves...find the wolves.*

Suddenly, the darkness opened up to a blue sky as he climbed towards the treetops, driven upwards by the beating of wings around him. Once above the trees, his ascent leveled off as he steadied himself with the horizon. *Keep soaring, Chiquito. Follow the creek towards the mountain where the sun rises. Find the wolves.* The world all around him—around them—was sharp and full of detail. Small, faraway objects came closer as if reaching out to them, and then fell back into a distorted background. It was always a moving object that came into view: a squirrel, a covey of quail, a weasel. They could see the winding creek below, and the mountain where the sun rises was in the center of their vision. Chiquito was soaring in large circles, though his movement was advancing eastward. Many Wolves gazed at the world below him in astonishment. It was breathtaking to see the world through his bird's eyes. *It must be a dream if Chiquito understands my thoughts.*

From above came the familiar cry of a red-tailed hawk. Looking up to the right, they saw a large hawk diving straight towards them. They plummeted in a dizzying spin, the world around them rushing past in a blur before they leveled off. In those free-falling moments, Many Wolves felt as if the inside of his body was falling out. It was exhilarating and frightening, and he was happy when it was over. *Chiquito is used to this, not me!* They looked up again to see the screaming red-tailed hawk circling above them. Chiquito's wings rapidly pumped the air to escape the danger, racing towards the mountain of sunrises.

With the aerial danger behind them, they resumed circling, scanning the ground below for movement, using the eastward flowing waters as their guide. They spotted more small animals and some deer, but nothing else. Most of the landscape was covered by a dense tapestry of pine trees pinching the creek from both sides. *Chiquito, let's go back to the meadow and head towards the mountain of sunsets.* Instantly, they reversed direction after a sweeping turn and began heading west, back to where they came from, guided by the path of water flowing against them.

Chiquito flew past the meadow and the spot where Elk Dog was grazing in front of their camp and fell again into a circling pattern. The path of water led them through the grasslands and into a thick pine forest, making it more difficult to see objects on the ground. As they scanned towards the westward mountains, Many Wolves saw a break in the tree line. *Chiquito, follow the water to the break of trees.* Chiquito broke out of his spiraling flight path and headed further west. They found another clearing, even larger than the one they had started from, and discovered a large lake of greenish-blue water where the creek ended. The lake had an irregular shape. A narrow passageway flowed down the middle with many branches extending from it, like fingers from a hand. Guarding the lake, like a giant sentinel, was a huge, craggy oak tree with an empty nest in it. He guessed it was either the nest of a fish hawk or an eagle. *Circle around the lake, Chiquito.*

The two travelers glided around the shoreline and saw only ducks and herons and a large eagle circling high over the middle of the lake. Many Wolves had seen these great eagles before, diving into lakes with outreached talons trying to snatch fish at the water's surface. He had watched them steal fish from the smaller fish hawks, which were more accomplished fish catchers, but were unable to hold off the eagle's relentless attacks. Seeing an eagle during his mind-journey would bring him luck, he thought. His grandfather told him that eagles carry one's messages and prayers directly to the Great Spirit. Eagles could soar higher in the sky than any other birds without concern for the sun's scorching rays.

As they watched the eagle sail off towards the falling sun, the images were beginning to fade into a haze. Many Wolves was finding it difficult to focus on what his mind was seeing. He kept flashing back to places he had already been. He tried hard to return to the lake and find the soaring eagle, but the images were scattering.

Suddenly, he opened his eyes and he was back at his camp, sitting cross-legged in the dirt. Cazador was perched on a low-hanging pine limb, but his smallest bird was nowhere to be seen. He stood up and walked around the camp calling

Chiquito's name and blowing his whistle. *Could he still be at the finger lake?* It was not like Chiquito to be out of range of his call. Cazador often wandered and Reina did too, but not the little one.

Many Wolves mounted Elk Dog and rode along the waterway he had viewed from above, periodically stopping to call Chiquito. It excited him to think that if his bird was still flying around or near the finger lake then it meant his vision was real—he had joined with the spirit of his bird.

He weaved between trees, plodding on pine needles and dirt. After some time, he spotted a clearing ahead and then heard Chiquito's familiar cry. He stopped Elk Dog and called to the hawk, holding his fist-perch high in the air. Moments later, Chiquito glided low along the creek, still sounding his raspy shrills, then veered towards Many Wolves and landed on the fist-perch.

Many Wolves laughed. "Chiquito, it's all right!" He spoke gently to try and calm the agitated bird, who kept up his barrage of squawks. "Now, if this lake is up ahead, the one we saw, then I'll know that we were together!"

He prodded his horse forward into a trot, urging him to follow the water's path until Many Wolves saw the lake ahead, with its familiar, still waters. As he rode closer, its surface bounced the glaring rays of the late-afternoon sun into his face. To his left, he saw a big oak tree near the bank: the craggy oak tree with the eagle's nest.

"Chiquito, we have been here before, together! Let's head back to camp. It will soon be dark and I'm starving!"

Many Wolves arrived back at camp at dusk and set up a cooking fire. Suddenly, the silence of twilight was stirred by distant howling. The howls were deep and sustained, unlike the screechy barks and yips of coyotes. *Wolves!* Many Wolves stopped and listened to the sad, moaning howls that often cascaded on top of one another. He counted at least three distinct wolf voices bellowing at the same time. The melancholy sounds chilled him like approaching thunder, and yet, there was a calming sensation, almost like the comforting sounds of his mother's voice. Still, he knew they were the voices of predators. He sat and listened to the beautiful sounds, until finally the howls drifted away with the passing sun, leaving silence and darkness.

Rabbit Hunters

Many Wolves woke up the next morning with the haunting wolf calls still echoing in his mind. The howls had come from the west, past the lake of many fingers, where he had been with Chiquito. He packed up his camp, loaded up Elk Dog, and began his journey westward with the sun warming his back. He enjoyed the damp mornings, seeing the dew glistening on the grass and pine needles, binding the dust to the earth.

The midday sun had consumed all the dew droplets by the time he arrived at the western bank of the lake. The weather was warm and clear, but not scorching as he expected it would be once summer began.

An open spread of grassland expanded out from the lake's western shore. Groves of pines halted the meandering meadow at its north and south boundaries. Many Wolves preferred to have water close at hand, so he decided to set up his camp in the northern stand of trees, which was a stone's throw away from the lake. He also welcomed the protection from the hot sun and from unfriendly eyes.

Once he was settled, he called to his birds who hadn't eaten all day. "Caz, Chiquito, let's go stir up some quail or a rabbit for you to chase." He ventured out with his birds sailing overhead. He made a game out of finding rabbits, challenging his birds to find them before he flushed them out of the grass. Most of the time he won, but every so often one of them would find a sitter first and pounce on the hapless animal before it could scurry away. Those were the quick kills. He felt that his birds preferred these easy catches because they didn't have to work for them.

Suddenly, there was a rustling in the bushes to his left. Both birds dipped into a swoop. Chiquito, with his faster wingbeats, was on top of the rabbit first, but the quarry veered and shifted quickly to avoid his attack. Cazador pulled back to let Chiquito lead the chase and then the rabbit disappeared. The birds stood on the ground looking around, completely baffled by the loss of their meal. Many Wolves laughed out loud. He thought it must seem like some kind of strange magic to them, how an animal could just disappear in a heartbeat. He taunted them, "Where did it go? Where did it go?" and then laughed again.

Most of the rabbits in the high country were of the smaller, white-tailed variety instead of the larger jackrabbits which were much more common in the lowlands. Unlike the jackrabbits who loved to run to safety, their smaller brothers tried to save themselves by diving into the nearest burrow. Cazador and Chiquito had to be especially quick to catch these fleeting animals.

The next rabbit that was flushed underfoot wasn't as lucky. Chiquito was in a perfect position, flying just over it when it bolted. A swift plunge and the victim was entangled in the hunter's sharp claws. Not to be fooled a second time, Chiquito took control and subdued the small animal in his grasp. The rabbit screamed and tried to squirm away, but Many Wolves quickly intervened and broke its neck, silencing it. *Life for life.*

Just then, from the west, echoed the yelps and howls of the wolves. *Had they heard the rabbit's cry?* Many Wolves hurriedly cut open the breast of the dead animal and fed Chiquito the choice organs: the liver and heart. Then he tore off a rear leg and tossed it in the grass next to Cazador. The wolf calls were different this time, not the drawn out, haunting howls that he heard the previous evening, but more like the barks of dogs. He stood up, held his hand over his eyes to shield them from the bright sun, and tried to find the source of the sounds. Scanning the countryside, he thought he spotted some movement in the distance, although it was difficult to see anything in the knee-high grass. Finally, he picked out three of the wolves, all of them looking back at him, and hollering at his presence. One of them was the big red wolf, Rojo.

A Village of Wolves

Each afternoon, Many Wolves set out to find the wolf pack. Some days he could locate them by tracking their footprints, and other days, loud howls and barks led him to them. Still, on other occasions, the pack was too far away to be heard or seen. When he did find them, they seemed tolerant of his presence. Each day he got a little closer, moving slowly not to alarm them. Rojo, the leader, always watched him with a patient eye, his large ears propped to the sky, while the rest of the pack carried on with their normal routines: sleeping, playing, and caring for their young.

On this day, the late-afternoon sun warmed his shirtless back as he watched the wolves. The weather was heating up, though the hint of a chill remained in the air as a reminder that summer had not quite arrived. Alerted by their excited barking, Many Wolves found the pack surrounding a young elk they had just killed. He had hoped to see them bring down an elk or a deer or some other large animal, but he was always too late.

Several crows perched around the carcass, some on the ground and others in the trees nearby. Their raucous cries were full of anticipation. *The buzzards will be here soon, looking for scraps too. They don't miss a meal.* Many Wolves remained concealed in a stand of pines near the wolves and their kill. He sat down next to a tree trunk, motionless, and watched the feast.

Rojo was the first to gorge on the fresh kill, which was a right given to the pack leader. The other six adult wolves stood around guarding the dead elk, anxiously waiting their turn. One of them dashed towards the carcass to try to steal away a quick morsel, but Rojo sprung to his feet and angrily chased the intruder away. Only when he was finished did another pack member approach the kill. Rojo's mate, the black wolf that Many Wolves named Noir, was the only one allowed to approach him.

After Rojo abandoned the elk carcass, he was approached by other members of the pack. He walked with his head and tail held high. The other wolves greeted the leader in a hunched posture, with tails and ears lowered, and licked him gently on the side of the mouth. *This is how they show their respect.* They watched their leader intently, but Rojo only looked at them when he needed to communicate. Many Wolves had seen this "communication with eyes" among his birds and with the people of his village, which made him believe that the wolf pack always sought their leader's approval before acting. Rojo's band seemed very content with his leadership, since there was rarely any fighting, unlike the dogs in his family's village that constantly fought with each other.

Noir, Rojo's mate, walked up to the carcass and began ripping chunks of flesh from the hind leg of the elk. She was smaller in height than most of the other adult wolves. Her sleek black coat covered a stout, muscular body. Noir, like Rojo, was healthier looking, and rounder around the bones, than the other wolves. The rest of the pack were on full alert for any trespassers while the leader rested and his mate consumed her meal. Many Wolves had heard stories that grizzlies often stole food away from wolves, but he had yet to see it happen. The pack continued to watch him with their ears raised high. It was impossible to conceal his human scent when the breeze blew it straight to them.

When Noir was finished, the three pups ran up to her and sniffed her snout, yipping excitedly. She regurgitated a large part of her meal so her young could eat. The pups devoured the moist, pre-chewed meat enthusiastically. One of the pups was also black, like its mother, and was the most aggressive, often chasing the others away from the food.

While Noir ate, one of the other females, which Many Wolves had named Snow Foot, took care of the three pups. She was next to feed. Many Wolves regarded her as the most attractive of the pack. Her fur was a colorful mixture of black, reddish-brown, and smatterings of white on her chest and her left leg. When she lay down to eat or rest, she always crossed her left paw over her right, a vision of contentment. As she feasted, Noir cared for the pups, but it was Snow Foot who watched over them most of the time. Noir rolled on her back, playfully, permitting the pups to climb all over her body. They grabbed her legs with their teeth one moment and then licked her face the next. Even from a distance, Many Wolves could tell that the wolf parents were very gentle and tolerant with their young, who were now about half the size of the adults. It reminded him of the Lipan women of his village and how delicately they cared for their babies.

The last to eat was Shadow Chaser. The flock of relentless crows had expanded and were cawing wildly. The buzzards had arrived and they began to circle overhead. Earlier, Shadow Chaser had tried to steal bites from the carcass, but the other wolves reminded him that it wasn't his turn, so he went back to his favorite game—chasing shadows. Whenever a bird flew over his head he leaped from his lying position and chased after the bird's shadow until it disappeared in the trees. The birds perched on the ground were of no interest to him. He played this game tirelessly with the enthusiasm of a playful coyote. Many Wolves believed that Shadow Chaser was not the smartest of wolves. This lowest-ranking wolf was the lightest-colored of the adult wolves, tawny brown blended with white. He bolted down chunks of meat as quickly as he could as if it were his last meal. Despite his status, the other wolves treated him with affection. He often initiated play with the other adults, approaching them with his front paws on the ground, his rump in the air, and his tongue hanging loosely from his mouth. Many Wolves felt a kindred spirit with the lowest of the wolves. He remembered feeling like the lowest of the boys in his village.

Once the wolves had their share, the crows and buzzards joined in on the feast. The monotonous cawing of the loud birds became squabbling shrieks as they competed for position around the exposed flesh. The pack rested. Only Rojo was standing on guard while the pups played with each other in mock battles. Even though the other wolves were lying down, their ears were pinned to the sky, listening. They were no longer focusing their attention on the familiar human hidden in the trees, but on something else.

Fury

The hissing of arrows split the calm of the moment like thunder. Snow Foot yelped in pain and faltered to the ground with an arrow shaft sticking from her side. Then Noir was hit moments later after more arrows shot from the trees to the right of Many Wolves's hiding spot. Noir tried to run away but the arrow in her leg slowed her to a limp. She was howling until another arrow shot through her chest and laid her down in the tall grass. The rest of the pack barked loudly and scattered away from the source of the slinging arrows.

Many Wolves sat, stunned and helpless, watching the arrows cut down the wolves until two men emerged from the trees into the clearing, both carrying bows and cheering victoriously. "Let me finish the black one," yelled the larger of the two. *They speak in the Northerner language.*

Many Wolves saw that Noir was still alive and struggling to get up and run away. Her anguished cry echoed through the mountains, striking deep into his heart with the force of a warrior's lance. He felt tears envelop his eyes as he thought about how the wolves had become his village, his family. Their companionship had helped ease the burden of loneliness after Ten Arrows had departed. The wolves had accepted him as part of their world and had provided him a safe place, a diversion, away from solitude. Her wailing cries were affecting him in a way he didn't understand.

"The wolf with the white foot is dead," yelled the smaller hunter, who moved closer to inspect the lifeless body of Snow Foot. His voice was younger, not fully adult yet.

Many Wolves was fighting to think clearly as he studied the hunters. They looked more like Ten Arrows than the people of his village and they spoke his friend's language. Their faces were painted red and they wore deerskin leggings with many colorful decorations on them. Neither man wore a shirt. Their chests were colored with many paints: reds, yellows, and blacks. He could barely see the mark of the snake on the younger man's upper left arm. *They are Nokoni!*

Noir stumbled to her feet and tried to run, but she was too weak to move quickly. The larger hunter sprinted after her and grabbed her by the back of the neck. The black wolf yelped helplessly until he knocked her out with one crushing blow of his tomahawk. He raised his weapon to the sky and whooped again. Both men were smiling and laughing.

"Walks On Feathers, your father will be very proud! This kill is yours!" said the larger hunter.

Many Wolves's thoughts were raging out of control. The image of the hunter striking Noir with his tomahawk replayed over and over in his head. Her desperate cries echoed repeatedly in his mind. He felt sorrow and anger at the same time. He had felt the sorrow before when Reina died. But the anger was different, it was new. *The Nokonis have killed my parents and now these wolves, who are my friends.* He did not understand killing for no reason. He had always killed only when he needed food or for protection. *Life for life. But not this! There are plenty of deer and elk to hunt; why kill these beautiful wolves?* The anger was mounting. His head felt like a pot of hot water, simmering with every thought, heating to a boil.

The body of Many Wolves began to move as if someone or something was controlling him—a force he did not understand. He reached into his quiver, extracted an arrow, and stood up. Leaning against the tree that was shielding him, he loaded his bow. He couldn't stop himself even if he tried. He aimed his fully drawn bow at the closer of the two hunters; the one he had learned was named "Walks On Feathers." Without hesitation, he unloaded his bow. The arrow cut through the air and drove itself into the younger man's chest.

The injured Northerner cried out, "Broken Nose!" and then collapsed to the ground.

The older hunter spotted the hidden assailant and sprinted towards him, screaming a battle cry. Many Wolves loaded and released another arrow with trembling hands but it whistled over the head of the enraged Northerner, who was closing in on him quickly. Again, he loaded an arrow, fighting to keep his hands and breathing steady, and shot it at the wolf hunter, hitting him on the right shoulder and nearly knocking him off balance. The Northerner groaned, but continued to charge with angry, bulging eyes and his tomahawk raised above his head. Many Wolves reached for another arrow, but he realized that he didn't have enough time to shoot it. The Northerner was too close. The last thing he remembered were the hateful, dark eyes slicing through him and a pounding thump on the side of his head.

The Cloud Eagle

The brilliant light of the sun burned his eyes and bathed his body in scorching heat. It felt like a hundred suns, not just one. Many Wolves sensed he was floating, moving closer to the heat and the light of the sun. He tried to squint to shield his eyes from the blinding rays, but they still forced their way into his captive mind. He had felt a sensation like this before when he flew with Chiquito. Moments of increased speed were followed by gliding, as they moved straight up towards the dazzling sun. On either side of him, he saw gigantic brown wings—the wings of an eagle—carrying him. *Am I dead? Where is it taking me?*

Eventually, the eagle wings leveled off, turning left, steering away from the sun. He opened his eyes wider to take in the deep blue, cloudless sky. Like staring into a fire and then into the darkness, it took him a while to see clearly again. The eagle carried him in a circling pattern. The land below was tan and green, a familiar desert landscape. He recognized rocky mesas and a large, winding blue river, but details beyond that were impossible to recognize. *Is it the Rio Pecos?* Though he was circling, he felt as if he was drifting in one direction.

He wondered if this was the Cloud Eagle that Ten Arrows spoke of, taking his spirit to another world. *I must have died.* He had no memory of his last moments. He remembered only those things that were jarred from his memory by what he was seeing now: flying with Chiquito, the desert mesas, and the river that looked somewhat familiar. He couldn't hear or smell anything. He could only feel and see.

Suddenly, the Cloud Eagle tucked its wings into a dive. The desert below blurred as he fell from the sky like a lightning bolt. *Where is the Cloud Eagle taking me now?* He had never experienced speed like this before. It was frightening to cut through the cool, rushing air into the spiraling, blurred world below at such a great speed—down, down, down. *Is this how I break through to another spirit world, like an arrow breaking through a thick buffalo hide?* Though it was terrifying, it was also strangely exhilarating. He braced himself for impact with the ground. Then, the Cloud Eagle spread its wings again and balanced itself with the horizon, gradually slowing from the mind-numbing dive.

Many Wolves saw greater detail now that he was closer to the ground: the meandering sage and mesquite, the sandy desert floor, the varied rock formations in the canyons and mesas. The landscape looked very familiar and he felt as if he had been there before during his childhood. He looked ahead and spotted smoke rising from behind the hills. It was not the smoky strand of a single cooking fire, but a large billowing cloud of thick black smoke. The Cloud Eagle was taking him to it.

Once over the hill, he saw bright yellow flames spotting the landscape. The eagle took him lower, below the great smoke cloud, so he could see the flames chewing on the grass-roofed huts he remembered from home. Still, there was no sound. The Cloud Eagle circled lower above the burning village, trapped between the heat of the flames and the sun. Many Wolves spotted bodies of dead people and dogs spread out among the burning huts. Many of the bodies had been thrown into the fires, making them unrecognizable, but others were scattered between the huts in plain view. The great bird took him lower still, so he could see the faces on the unburned bodies. *Why do I have to see this?*

Then, to his horror, he saw the face of his mother, Painted Wings, just as he remembered her when he left the village. The blood was dripping slowly down her cheeks from a wound on her head. His spine chilled in the blazing heat and tears sprinkled from his eyes. He recalled the times she had comforted him when he was hurt and when he had nightmares of the Buffalo People.

The eagle moved further along the path that divided the village homes. Then he saw his father's body with his scalp removed and several arrows protruding from his chest though his bow was still clenched in his fist. Red Arrow was the quiet man who provided food and clothing for Many Wolves and taught him how to make weapons. Lying next to his father was his grandfather, Yellow Feather, who was also bloodied and scalped. The gentle man who told him wonderful stories and taught him everything he knew about animals and tracking. *Are they all dead?* He yelled out, "What happened? Why must I see this!" The storm of tears could not bring them back. The sadness was unbearable. "I don't want to see anymore!"

The Cloud Eagle lifted its wings, pulled him up and away from the burning village, and led him in a straight path. Many Wolves was overwhelmed with sorrow. He didn't understand why the Cloud Eagle took him there. They kept flying away from the village, away from the horrible visions. Up ahead, he spotted another cloud. It was not black from smoke, but brown from dust. The eagle took him closer to the dirty cloud until he saw that it was created by galloping horses. Many Wolves could see fifteen or twenty men riding away from him, most on beautiful, painted horses and carrying bows and lances with scalps hanging from them. Many of them were wearing buffalo headdresses like he remembered from his dream—*The Buffalo People.* Suddenly, the man riding ahead of them turned around and looked straight up at him, revealing his black face. He yelled something out to the men behind him, but Many Wolves could not hear what he said. One by one, each man turned and looked up at him. Most of them had black faces as well, all except the last rider. His face was not painted and his skin and hair were lighter than the others. The last one was him.

Unseen Protector

Many Wolves woke up feeling excruciating pain on the left side of his head. He placed his hands on the blood-soaked headband and felt a large lump on his head. The blood was still flowing from the wound, so he pressed the wrap against it. He sat up slowly and looked around, but the world was blurry. *Where am I?* He tried to stand, but collapsed from the dizziness. He leaned on a tree that was next to him. All he knew was that it was daylight and his head was hurting. He remembered the dream he had with the Cloud Eagle. *Was that real? Would I feel this pain if I was dead?* He was confused, so he closed his eyes, put his head down, and rested.

As he lay under the tree, bits and pieces of his memory started to return. He remembered the wolves, Rojo's pack. He remembered watching them and hearing the arrows hiss through the trees, but nothing else. He couldn't block the pain. He was hungry and thirsty. He drank some water and then poured it on his head to clean off the blood. He found a hunk of dried deer meat in his pouch and sucked the saltiness out of it before taking small bites. He was starting to feel like himself again.

He sat up, looked around, and found the body of a man lying next to him, the broken shaft of an arrow protruding from his shoulder. The large, dark eyes that stared lifelessly into the clear blue sky were strangely familiar. Flashes of this man running towards him played in his mind. *Northerner! But what happened?* He saw the man's mutilated neck and the large pool of blood, now almost completely soaked into the earth. The Northerner still held his large, blood-tipped tomahawk in his right hand. In his other hand, Many Wolves found a clump of reddish hair...animal hair. *Rojo? Why is Rojo's hair here?* He looked at the neck wound again. *A wolf could have done that. Was Rojo protecting me? Did he save my life?*

Many Wolves stood up, using the tree for balance, and looked at the grassy clearing in front of him. There was another man's body and the dead carcass of a large animal that was now being picked apart by buzzards, crows, and ravens. He walked over to the dead man, who was propped up by the animal underneath him. Another Northerner, but this one was younger and smaller. The carcass was a dead wolf with two arrows embedded in it—a colored wolf with a white foot. *Snow Foot.* A recognizable arrow was sticking out from the young man's bloody chest. *My arrow killed him.* There was a snake sign clearly visible on his left arm. *Nokoni.* His deerskin leggings were crafted by skilled hands, decorated with many colored beads and pieces of metal. His hair was straight and neatly braided on both sides. *What have I done? What will happen when the Nokonis find out that two of their people are dead? I need to cover my tracks and leave!* He pulled his arrow out of the young man's chest and grabbed his knife, which had a steel blade like Ten Arrows's, and its sheath. He also took the young hunter's bow, which looked sturdy and well-made, and his arrows.

He walked back over to the larger man's body and took his arrows too. Then he yanked hard to extract the arrow shaft from his lifeless body and found the other half in the grass nearby. His hand trembled as he held it in his hands, his heart pounding. Next to the arrow fragment, Many Wolves found what looked like a blood trail and wolf tracks. *Rojo is injured?* His experience as a tracker told him that the wound was serious from the amount of blood. *If he saved me, then I should help him.*

A Place to Die

Many Wolves tracked the blood path and wolf prints into a forest of aging pines. His head was still throbbing, though the bleeding had stopped and his vision had returned to normal. He felt like he was racing against the long shadows. It would soon be dusk. The pine-needled loam of the forest floor made it easier to follow the path of the injured wolf. He could tell from the flatness and spacing of the footmarks that the wolf was walking, not running, which meant he probably didn't go far. Cazador and Chiquito followed him lazily, flying from tree limb to tree limb.

Then, he spotted the big red wolf lying on his side in a bedding of leaves and pine needles at the base of a large rock. Many Wolves approached him slowly. Rojo was not moving. He came closer and saw the wolf's chest heaving with every breath. *Rojo's alive!* The wolf's hind leg was darker than the rest of his body, soaked in blood. *He's much bigger up-close.* Many Wolves saw a large, deep gash on his leg, as long as the blade of a Northerner's tomahawk. *I should close his wound before he wakes up.*

Many Wolves pulled out a bone needle and some thin, but sturdy, deer sinew from his bag. He carefully washed the wound with water, hoping not to wake the wolf. Then, he tied the sinew to the needle and began suturing the wound like Desert Flower had taught him. Once the wound was sealed, he tucked his sewing tools back in his bag and gently stroked the chest and back of Rojo. His fur was thick like a bear's, but much softer to the touch. Many Wolves noticed there was still blood on the animal's muzzle. *Northerner blood.* He backed away, worried what the wolf would do when he woke up.

Many Wolves huddled against a climbable pine, which was several steps away from the wolf. He wished he had some mint tea to help his aching head, then he realized he didn't have any way to drink it. Instead, he pulled out some mint leaves and chewed on them. As he built a small fire with his fire-making sticks, he thought of Ten Arrows giving him *Noomah* tea after he was attacked by the bear. The flames would give him some light and warmth to chase away the night chill. He looked up and saw Cazador and Chiquito settled in a tree.

One question kept coming to his mind. *Why did this wolf protect me?* Surely, he would have been dead if the wolf had not intervened. Amarillo had given his life to protect him, but his dog was a longtime companion. He was not a friend to the wolf pack, just a stranger who watched from a distance. The only trust they had shown him was by allowing him to approach closer each day. Then a haunting thought occurred to him: *Did the wolves allow the Northerner hunters to get close enough to shoot them because of me?* He closed his eyes as a feeling of guilt washed over him, bringing tears to his eyes and sadness to his heart. He recalled his grandfather's words: "The delicate balance of nature should not be disturbed." He had disturbed that balance and now two of these beautiful animals were dead and another one close to death.

He cried.

Other burning questions entered his head. *Why did I attack the hunters? Is a man's life less than a wolf's?* He had acted on instinct. It was the same instinct that killed Gray Face who would have killed Ten Arrows. He felt there was an inner force that drove him to do these things, which he didn't fully understand, uncovering a bravery he didn't know he had. Attacking Gray Face had led to a friendship with Ten Arrows, but what would killing these Nokonis lead to? He did not want to know the answer. No one must know it was him. *I need to hide our tracks tomorrow.*

Am I interfering again by healing this wolf? The wolf had come here to die and now he was helping him live. *Was Rojo sent by the Great Spirit to protect me?* It didn't matter. He felt compelled to help him, as he would help a friend or a brother. Many Wolves always believed that the Great Spirit had a plan for him. Maybe acting on his instincts was part of this plan.

Suddenly, the wolf stirred. He raised his head to look around and lifted his snout, searching for scents. He tried to stand, but whined in pain, and collapsed. Rojo lay with his head up, panting, looking straight at the young man with his eyes half closed. Many Wolves slowly got up and took a step towards the wolf. Rojo bared his teeth and growled. "So, you have come to this place to die, but you are not ready to give up your life yet, Rojo," he said as he backed up to his original position and sat down.

Many Wolves and Rojo remained in their safe places all night, watching each other with a cautious eye. Many Wolves ate the rest of the dried venison he had in his pouch. He would need to hunt again tomorrow. Every so often, he chewed on mint leaves to alleviate his pain. His injury could have been worse. He felt lucky to be alive. Rojo finally fell asleep. Like his protector, the fatigue overpowered Many Wolves as well.

Peace of Mind

When Many Wolves woke the next morning, both Rojo and the pounding in his head were still there. The wolf was asleep in the same spot. Many Wolves revived the fire to provide some comfort from the morning chill. He gulped down a few swallows of water. *I am low on water and I need some fresh meat.*

He was curious about the bow he found on the younger man's body. He pulled it out of his quiver and examined it. It was made of the same strong, flexible wood as the bow that Ten Arrows gave him, from the Osage orange tree. The surface of the wood was smooth, shaped with great care, and painted black, unlike his bow, which had a natural wood color. A figure of a four-legged animal with horns, like an elk or deer, had been carved into the handle of the bow, above the arrow rest. He loaded the black bow with one of the Northerner's arrows, drew it back, and fired at a pine tree trunk about forty steps in front of him. The force of the arrow cut through the bark and dug into the soft pine. *This bow is easier to draw than my other large bows, but still has power. It will send the squirrels flying off the branches!* He retrieved the arrow and prepared his hunting bag.

"You lazy birds! You have grown fat on the wolf's kill!" he barked in a grinning voice. They seemed content not to lift a feather. With the black bow loaded and ready, he headed back to the dead Northerners to look for squirrels and cover his tracks. The dewy pine needles clung to his moccasins like nettles from the spiny cactus weeds of the desert. The first squirrel he found was a close, clear shot almost directly above him. He launched an arrow at it, but it embedded itself in a limb just below his target. The squirrel escaped and the arrow was too difficult to retrieve, so he left it and kept moving. The next squirrel he found was lower to the ground and less fortunate. A direct shot to its chest knocked it clear off its perch and sent it flailing to the ground. He shoved the dead squirrel in his bag. He could hear the scavengers—the cawing crows and croaking ravens. He was getting closer. His next arrow found its mark as well and added more food to his bag. The gray squirrels were easy to hit as long as he found them standing still, preoccupied with eating or curiously watching him. He believed they didn't know the arrow, like the hawk or the weasel, was a predator until its deadly point pierced their hides.

His keen sense of smell picked up the decaying stench of flesh, and the scavenger sounds assaulted his ears, with fewer trees to shield them. He saw the clearing ahead, so he approached carefully. The ruckus could attract danger that he didn't want to face: mountain lions, grizzlies, even men.

The scene was as chaotic as he expected. A lean, immature mountain lion had claimed the remains of the elk carcass for itself, chasing away any birds that came near. Birds clamored over the other dead bodies or waited their turn to gorge on the exposed meat. *There will be enough to keep the bellies of the scavengers full for many sleeps.*

Many Wolves did not want to linger. He worked diligently to cover up all traces of the injured wolf and himself. He started near the larger Northerner's body and backtracked away from the pandemonium. Hiding their presence was slow, tedious work. There were many of Rojo's blood marks to cover up: on the ground, on pine needles, and on fallen leaves. He worried that rearranging the ground cover to make it look untouched wasn't enough to completely mask his presence. Good trackers like his grandfather could find his mistakes, but he felt he needed to try as best he could. Scavengers would likely trample over any tracks he left around the other bodies, so he didn't bother erasing those, and he had already removed other evidence that could identify him—the arrows from the dead men's bodies.

It took most of the day to retrace his steps back to Rojo's location. The sun was setting on their camp. The air was brisk and a cool breeze whistled through the pines. The red wolf was awake when he arrived, lying with his head and ears propped up. On his way back, Many Wolves had found a small creek, barely wider than his foot, and refilled his water pouch with cool, fresh water. The young tracker was dirty and sweaty from his labor, but he would have to wait to bathe at his lake camp. He expected it would take a half-day's journey to get back there. Elk Dog had never been left alone this long before.

Many Wolves rekindled his fire from hot embers and found a cooking stick for his squirrel meal. He pulled one of the squirrels out of the bag and used the young Northerner's steel-bladed knife to gut it. He was pleased to have a sharp blade that cut so easily through thick squirrel hide and would not dull easily. He poured water over the opened carcass, split it at the chest cavity, and tossed the dead squirrel as close as possible to the red wolf. Rojo flashed his teeth and growled, but did not move. "You'll need to eat, big wolf, if you want to get your strength back."

He gutted and skinned the second squirrel, impaled it on the cooking stick, and began roasting the meat over the fire. It didn't surprise him that the wolf wouldn't eat. He remembered it took some time before his birds accepted food from him. He thought to himself: *If he eats then he wants to live.*

Many Wolves wondered what the rest of the pack was doing. *Have the other adults led the pups away from here, or are they waiting for Rojo's return? Without Rojo or Noir or Snow Foot, who would lead them?* He remembered there was another female, a grayish wolf, in the pack. She would have to feed the pups now. He wondered about Shadow Chaser, the lowest-ranking wolf. *Who would protect him? Would the other wolves drive him away?*

"Rojo, you need to get back to the pack."

Exposed

By the next day, the aching pain in his head felt much better. Many Wolves found Rojo still lying in the same concealed spot, watching him with piercing eyes. All that remained of the squirrel was a few remnants of bone and fur. "I see you have eaten, Rojo. The will to live still burns inside you," he said with a slight smile.

He ventured into the woods to find more squirrels. Hunting would take his mind off the pain. Chiquito and Cazador followed this time—they were ready for a meal. He loaded his black bow with a blunt-tipped arrow and led his birds through the pine forest, in the opposite direction of the decaying bodies and scavengers. His birds followed closely, flying high in the treetops, keeping themselves ready to dive down on unsuspecting prey. The morning air was cool and he embraced the pungent scent of pine. *I will miss this smell when I leave the mountains.* Chiquito chased a mountain jay, but the dark blue bird easily outmaneuvered him. His smallest and quickest hawk loved to chase small birds, but he rarely caught them. Every so often he surprised one on the ground before it could launch itself to safety.

Suddenly, Many Wolves heard the echoing crackle of a branch and looked up to see Cazador pursuing a gray squirrel. The small woodland animal skittered from branch to branch, avoiding the attacks of its chaser until it hid itself behind a thick tree trunk. Cazador flew up to an adjacent tree, at eye level to the squirrel, and the two animals stared at each other. Many Wolves watched as Chiquito circled behind and above the squirrel and dove down from its blind side, knocking it off the tree trunk and on to the forest floor. Within moments, Cazador plummeted straight towards the squirrel and positioned her outstretched talons to encase its head. Its needle-sharp teeth snapped viciously at the bird's feet. Many Wolves ran over to the thrashing squirrel and pressed his hand forcefully against its chest until there was no more air in its lungs. He looked up at the sky and thanked the Great Spirit.

He fed each of his birds pieces of squirrel leg as a reward and carefully hid the remainder in his hunting bag for Rojo. Soon after, he stunned another low-perched squirrel with an arrow, making it easy for Cazador to grab it before it could regain its senses and run away. Just when the sun was halfway to its highest peak, Cazador caught the third squirrel of the day. He divided this one into two portions and let the birds feast on the fresh meat—enough food to last them throughout the day. Satisfied that he had enough food in his bag, he returned to camp.

Rojo was awake and alert when Many Wolves arrived. He circled around the wolf, making sure to keep a safe distance. He grabbed one of the dead squirrels and sliced open its chest to reveal the fresh meat. He hoped the sight would be irresistible to the wolf. He walked carefully towards Rojo, stopping when he saw him bare his teeth and growl. It was the closest he had been to the wolf since the day he mended his leg. He tossed the squirrel and then backed away. The red wolf looked at him and then at the squirrel several times.

"You're tempted, aren't you?"

Then Rojo slowly lumbered to his feet and walked gingerly over to the squirrel. He held his left rear leg up to keep his weight off of it. He placed his front paw on top of the squirrel and lay down in front of it. Cautiously, he picked at the meat with small bites and did not take his eyes off his provider. Using his paws to hold down the meal, he tore bigger and bigger pieces. His powerful jaws and teeth cut through the bones and skull of the squirrel with little difficulty. Eventually, he bolted the rest of the bones and fur down his throat, leaving no trace of the carcass. Then he stood up, slowly hobbled over to his secluded spot in the brush, lay down, and licked the remaining fragments of flesh from his mouth. His eyes stayed fixed on Many Wolves.

The young man watched Rojo with great interest. The wolf seemed to be feeling better than the previous day. He thoroughly licked both of his front paws to clean them. Amarillo used to do the same thing. The red wolf also licked the wound on his rear leg with great care. *This is his medicine.* Whenever Many Wolves moved, Rojo would stop what he was doing and watch him; otherwise the wolf was content to continue his grooming.

Rojo stopped and looked up, past where Many Wolves was sitting. His ears were propped and his head was cocked to one side. "What is it?" He looked back over his shoulder towards the dead Northerners. He stood up and started to walk in that direction. There was no sound or scent on the breeze and his visibility was severely limited by the trees, but he knew something was there, not just scavengers, but something bigger, like a bear or a man. He began to run and then stopped abruptly. He could hear the crows and ravens sounding agitated. The next sound was unmistakable. It was the shouting voice of a man. The words sounded like Northerner words.

Many Wolves returned to his camp, grabbed his bow and quiver, and dashed into the forest. He ran as fast as he could away from the danger. He had no time to think about the signs he left behind. He just needed to get away. Rojo would have to take care of himself now.

He whistled to his birds and signaled with his hands for them to follow. He ran towards the creek that would lead him home to his lake camp. Many Wolves was terrified that his secret had been discovered.

A False Path

M any Wolves arrived late in the afternoon at his lake camp, sweaty and exhausted from running. He was relieved to find Elk Dog standing in the trees nearby, nickering a playful greeting. He crouched down on his knees to rest and slow his heavy breathing. There was no time to conceal his tracks. *If they find my tracks, they will find this place.* It was too tiring to run anymore and riding Elk Dog would leave even more signs of his presence. *I have to try and lead them in the wrong direction.*

His sides ached, but his breathing quickly returned to normal. Elk Dog came up and nipped his face. Many Wolves stroked his horse's nose and mane and spoke softly, "We need to hide you from them." He began cleaning up the camp, packing all his supplies on his mount and removed the stones from around the fire pit, scattering them randomly, then filled it in with dirt and pine needles to make it unnoticeable. He mounted Elk Dog and rode deeper into the forest. "You need to be far enough away so they can't hear you." When he found a location to his liking, he tied the horse's lead to a tree trunk and began the arduous task of covering up the horse's tracks all the way back to the lake camp. Once the hoofprints had been erased, he collected all the horse droppings he could find and buried them.

After covering up his own tracks, Many Wolves created a new path towards the lake and away from his camp and towards the trail that led to where Ten Arrows killed his bear. He climbed a large rock formation and doubled back towards the lake, treading lightly, and covering his tracks again as he crossed the shoreline of the lake, and then dove into the water. The water was freezing, but refreshing. It took a few moments for his body to acclimate to the chill. He swam to the other side of the lake and exited into the trees, hiding his footprints from the lake.

Many Wolves gathered up his food bag and his quiver, where he had hidden them, and climbed a large pine tree that overlooked the northern end of the lake and his camp. *I need to watch these men.* He climbed high and waited. His birds were perched in a nearby tree, at the same eye level as him. His body was tired and his head ached, but now he could relax, eat and drink—and wait.

Sitting silently in the tree concealed by a thick cover of branches and pine needles, it felt good to rest, although the comforts of a tree branch were few. He ate pieces of dried deer meat and some roots collected during the morning's hunt. Chiquito and Cazador seemed content and relaxed with their guts full of squirrel meat.

He waited through the waning, sunny afternoon, expecting to hear the thunder of horses and the voices of men, but the only sounds were from a squawking jay harassing a squirrel, a woodpecker tapping, and the breeze whispering. The silence of the wilderness was both an enemy and a friend—an enemy because it heightened his feeling of solitude and loneliness, and a friend because it brought safety. When the blue jays squawked playfully and the bluebirds sang their sweet, melancholy songs, he knew that there was nothing to fear. There was a rhythm to the sounds of the wilderness, only broken by the presence of a large predator, like Gray Face—or man. No disturbance came.

The light faded into dusk. It was now too dark to track or follow his false path. *Have the men not found Rojo's camp or my path leading away from it? If the men are friends with the dead Northerners then surely they will want to hunt down their killer.* The darkness gave him the opportunity to leave this place and go far away, back to Gray Face's camp.

Many Wolves climbed down from the tree, making every effort to remain in rhythm with the forest silence. He whistled quietly for his birds to follow and then led them to where Elk Dog was tied. He found his horse exactly as he had left him. He poured some of his water into his palms and Elk Dog drank it. "Elk Dog, I need to rest, but before dawn breaks we must head south, back to my home in the foothills."

He grabbed his buffalo-skin blanket and curled up on the ground next to his horse. He was exhausted, so sleep came quickly.

A flock of quacking ducks woke him the next morning, their feet pounding against the surface of the lake to lift off. It was midmorning already. He had planned on leaving much earlier, but sleep had covered him like a storm cloud. *Why are the ducks alarmed?* He got up and quietly made his way towards the lake.

Through the stand of trees, he saw a horse drinking water at the lake's edge. The painted pony was white with patches of brown and black. *A Northerner horse.* It reminded him of the horses the Northerner's rode when they visited his village. He saw a man was crouching down next to the horse, drinking water from his hands. The Northerner was stocky and muscular, dressed only in a loincloth with a single eagle feather hanging down the left side of his head. He appeared to be alone.

Many Wolves approached carefully, staying hidden behind the pines. When the horse was finished drinking, the Northerner caressed its face and mumbled some words. Then the rider mounted his horse and slung a quiver over his shoulder. The horse snorted as he led it along the lake and back to the false path. He rode slowly, scanning the ground for signs until Many Wolves watched him disappear from sight.

So, now they have found signs of my presence and hopefully they won't find Elk Dog's tracks. Many Wolves returned to his horse and packed his buffalo-skin blanket securely, then he whistled for his birds, mounted Elk Dog, and walked carefully through the forest. *When I am far enough away, I will ride faster.* He headed home, back to the Gray Face camp.

A Marked Arrow

"Laughing Crow! Wake up!"

"What is it, Silent Weasel?" Laughing Crow was resting in his lodge after enjoying a hearty meal of roasted buffalo hump, prepared by his wives.

"Walks On Feathers is dead!" blurted out Silent Weasel, breathing heavily.

"What?" The leader stood up and grabbed Silent Weasel with both hands on his shoulders. He hoped it was a bad dream, a nightmare, and he would just wake up. "What happened? Tell me what happened!" he said as he shook his scout's body. His eyes stared intently, secretly hoping that Silent Weasel would start laughing and tell him it was a silly trick. The scout didn't laugh.

"What happened to Broken Nose?" asked the leader.

"They were both killed in the high country."

"What killed them…or who?" asked Laughing Crow, in shock that the news was actually real.

"It was just one man. Your son was killed by his arrow. I think that Broken Nose was mauled by a wolf."

"A wolf?" asked Laughing Crow, puzzled.

"There were two dead wolves next to their bodies, with their arrows in them. Wolf prints were all over the ground and the tracks of just one man. A third wolf killed Broken Nose; his throat was ripped apart. Scavengers or a man couldn't have done that. Little Owl has their bodies on his horse."

Laughing Crow released his friend and felt a rage building up inside. "How do their bodies look? Were they scalped or mutilated?" He needed to know if his son was cursed in the afterlife.

"They weren't scalped, but the scavengers got to them some."

Laughing Crow walked out of his lodge and saw Little Owl leading a horse on foot. He could smell the rancid odor of human decay. The horse was carrying the two bodies, which were completely wrapped in blankets. His son's horse was tied by a lead to the first horse and a third horse followed them. A crowd had followed Little Owl to the leader's lodge. Thorn Bird was there too. His eyes were filled with sorrow.

"We're sorry to bring bad news, *namunewapi*," Little Owl said in a solemn voice.

"Thorn Bird, tell the women and children to return to their lodges," commanded Laughing Crow. Then he looked at his wife, Sun Sparrow, the mother of his dead son. "Do you want to see him?"

She burst into tears, screaming for mercy from the spirits as she looked to the sky. "No! Why have you done this?" Weeping uncontrollably, she fell to the ground.

"Do you want to see him?" repeated Laughing Crow.

She covered her mouth with her hands and then nodded weakly. Broken Nose's mother and father were also there, overcome with grief. They huddled around Sun Sparrow and comforted each other. The other women in the village joined in their lamentation.

"Take them down and unwrap the blankets. I need to see them," said their leader.

The two scouts carefully untied the bodies and placed them gently on the ground. Slowly, they unwrapped the blankets and revealed the corpses. The two mothers screamed at the sight and covered their eyes.

Laughing Crow looked at his son's stiffened, bluish body. Much of the flesh around his chest had been torn away by scavengers, but the deep cut from an arrow was clearly visible. The softer parts of his body, his stomach, and the backside of his legs, had been picked at by larger scavengers, but his face and hair were mostly untouched, which was a relief. *At least he will be able to speak, hear, and see.* Broken Nose's body was similar, except his throat and neck were mostly chewed away. His shoulder was also partially eaten.

"How do you know a wolf killed him?" Laughing Crow asked, pointing at Broken Nose's body.

"I found many large wolf tracks around his body."

"It looks like he was pierced by an arrow in the shoulder," said Laughing Crow.

"I think so too, but the arrows were removed from both bodies before we found them. That wound did not kill him. He was too strong to die from that injury alone," said Silent Weasel. The scout walked over to his horse and pulled two arrows from his saddlebag. "I found these arrows, *namunewapi*. This one was sticking in the ground near the same area they were killed." He handed the arrow to Laughing Crow and continued. "This other one I found stuck high in a tree in a forested area a short distance away from the bodies. It looks like one of your son's arrows."

"It is his arrow," said Laughing Crow, remembering when he gave him the Wichita-made bow from Smoke Cloud. "Do you think it was shot from his bow?"

"I think the man who shot this arrow was the one who killed him. The footprints around the tree where I found it matched the ones I found near the bodies. Whoever he was, he took your son's weapons and Broken Nose's arrows. He was also very careful about covering up his tracks. I followed his footprints to a lake a half-day's ride away, but lost him there."

"This other arrow then…is his killer's arrow?" asked Laughing Crow.

"Yes. It's not a *Noomah* arrow. The shaft is made from the white plum bush and it has three buzzard feathers. The point is made from obsidian. It's *Navoonah*-made," said Silent Weasel. He gave the second arrow to his leader.

Laughing Crow felt a deep-rooted hatred stir inside. *A Navoonah has killed my son!* "Mescalero?" He studied the arrow from different angles as he spoke.

"No, Lipan. The white plum bush grows in the desert lowlands and obsidian is abundant there along the rivers and streams."

"Why was this man so far from his home?"

"I don't know, but I'm certain that he was alone."

"How did you find their bodies in the mountains?" Laughing Crow could feel how the news was sapping his energy. He wanted to know everything that happened to the smallest detail, but he also wanted to be alone to think.

"Little Owl and I found their horses while we were hunting. Their footprints led us west to the bodies."

Silent Weasel again walked over to his horse and untied a fur hide he had rolled up on his saddle. He unrolled it and presented it to Laughing Crow. "This is the hide of the wolf that your son killed. You should be proud that he died as a hunter."

Laughing Crow accepted the hide from his scout. It was patterned in black, white, and brown colors. "Silent Weasel, from this moment on we must honor my son and his friend by not speaking their names. Prepare their bodies for the burial ceremony tonight. I need some time to be alone."

"Yes, *namunewapi*," said his favorite scout, then he left.

"Thorn Bird!" yelled Laughing Crow.

"Yes, *Ahpu*?"

Thorn Bird approached his father and together they walked inside the lodge.

"We will need more men. Ride out to the Penatekas and to the Wichitas and tell them we will make war with our common enemy, the Lipans. Tell them they must honor the white man Fontaine's agreement. I will prepare our men so they will be ready to ride in two sleeps. We will meet you at the Salt Flats then, my son."

"I will leave in the morning, *Ahpu.*"

"Good. And there's one more thing. This is the wolf that your brother killed." Laughing Crow handed him the skin. "Tell Sun Sparrow to make it into a quiver for me so I can take it with me. That is all."

Thorn Bird left Laughing Crow alone with his grief and his thoughts. His favorite son was dead—the one he had hoped would be his successor as Nokoni leader. His pure-blood son, killed by the hands of a *Navoonah*. A fire of hatred was burning in his head. He picked up a clay water pot that sat next to his bed and hurled it at his fire pit, shattering it to pieces. Then, he stood motionless, gritting his teeth, and yelled in anguish, "*Mawumeru Lipanos!*" *We will make the Lipans suffer.*

Requiem for the Lost

"*A*hpu, the bodies are ready."

"Take me to them, Thorn Bird."

Thorn Bird led his father to the lodge where the two bodies were being prepared for burial. The setting sun illuminated the scattered clouds, casting a fiery glow over the village. Soon, the rocky mesa to the west would swallow up the day's light.

Laughing Crow and his eldest son found the bodies laid out flat on blankets. Little Owl was waiting to greet them. The leader's heart stirred with sadness when he saw his son's lifeless body. *If I could trade my life for yours, I would.* His child's face was painted in wavy streaks of vermillion, and a single eagle feather hung from his braided hair on the left side. His eyes were covered with reddish clay. His body and hair were clean and scented heavily with bathing herbs. Both men were dressed in their finest clothing: buckskin leggings, shirts, and moccasins adorned with many colorful beads and rawhide fringes.

Little Owl pulled up Walks On Feather's shirt to reveal a drawing of a wolf with an arrow through its chest, which he had painted black. It was his tribute to the young man's last hunt. Laughing Crow nodded his approval and was pleased to see his son was properly prepared for a warrior's burial. Broken Nose lay by his side with a black raven emblazoned over his heart, and his disfigured neck was wrapped in beaded leather to cover the wound.

"Little Owl, you honor us and your village with your painting skill." Laughing Crow then squeezed Little Owl's arm affectionately.

"I am honored you would let me prepare your son and his friend for their journey to the next world, *namunewapi*."

"Are the graves prepared?" asked the Nokoni leader, looking at Thorn Bird.

"The burial site has been prepared on the top of the hill to the east, as you requested, *Ahpu*. The people have carried many large stones and left them near the open graves."

"Good. Load each of their bodies on a pole-drag, so their horses can carry them one last time to their final resting place. Snake Tooth will lead the families. Thorn Bird, I want you to walk your brother's horse. Make sure to bring the rest of his possessions and our family's gifts with you."

"Thank you, *Ahpu*. I will take care of it."

As light was fading into darkness, the people of the village gathered for the procession. The families of the deceased and the Blood Riders were invited to the burial site. Any woman who wished to mourn with the families was also welcome, as well as two young men with drums. Snake Tooth led the burial walk, carrying a torch and his gnarled snake staff, followed by Thorn Bird and Long Eyes, Broken Nose's father, who led the horses. The families followed in a single line behind their lost loved ones. The mourning women and the drummers came next, and the Blood Riders were last, riding on horseback.

The burial site was just beyond the village and next to a large oak tree on top of the hill. As he stood at the hill's crest, Laughing Crow saw open prairie in all directions. *It is a good resting place.*

Two stacks of dried firewood and buffalo dung were arranged near the burial site; the smaller, tipi-shaped pile was set up in a shallow pit as wide as a horse and ringed with large stones—the funeral bonfire. Two large holes, just deep enough to hold a man's body, had been excavated. A mound of large stones and two buffalo robes had been placed between the two graves.

Snake Tooth lowered his torch with an unsteady hand and lit the bonfire, tossing the torch into the flames once it was burning steadily. He directed the families and mourners to seat themselves in a half circle around the fire facing the graves.

The leader sat in the front and center of the gathering, with his wives and children to his right. Sun Sparrow, the mother of Walks On Feathers, and Thorn Bird were closest to Laughing Crow. Broken Nose's family and the other mourners sat behind them.

Thorn Bird and Long Eyes unhitched the two pole-drags and laid them next to the graves. The women were dressed in ordinary buckskin outfits while the men wore breechcloths with very little painting on their bodies and faces—not the typical ceremonial clothing that was reserved for happier occasions. The Blood Riders carried their lances and shields and stood behind the rest of the family members and mourners. The drummers stood on either side of Snake Tooth.

The old shaman continued the ritual with four puffs from his ceremonial pipe, blowing smoke in each of the four directions. Then, he motioned for the drummers to start a slow, solemn beat. The darkness and the cries of the mourners accentuated the gravity of the moment. Raising his arms to the night sky, Snake Tooth bellowed out his prayers. "Great Spirit! Come to this dark place and see the brave men who lie before you. They have died a warrior's death. Guide them to the next world where the buffalo and deer live in great numbers and where men live without pain and suffering as a reward for their brave deeds in this world!"

As Snake Tooth spoke, Laughing Crow visualized his son riding a painted horse across endless plains, the sun pouring down on his back and the wind caressing his hair. He could see his son's smile and hear his laughter. *There is a better place for the brave.*

Snake Tooth's voice shook him out of his reverie. "Now, we must lay our lost brothers down in their final resting place and offer them gifts for the afterlife." The shaman signaled the drummers to stop.

Thorn Bird and Long Eyes rose and walked over to the bodies. They laid the buffalo robes across each grave, spread open, and then placed the bodies on top with the men's heads facing the mountains where the sun rises. Then they grabbed a large bundle from each of the horses and carefully unrolled them on the ground next to the graves.

After the two men had rejoined the group, Laughing Crow and his family stood up and walked over to his son's grave. Sun Sparrow was crying harder now, clutching her husband for support. Thorn Bird selected several objects from the un-wrapped bundle and laid them next to his brother's body: an Osage orange bow, a quiver of arrows, and a steel-bladed knife in its sheath. In a similar way, each of Laughing Crow's wives presented Walks On Feathers with gifts, like cooking tools and clothing, which he could use in the next world.

Sun Sparrow, who was the last of them, fell down on her only child's body and kissed his forehead. Her tears blanket-ed his stoic, lifeless face. The other wives helped her get on her feet and then led her back to her seat.

Laughing Crow was left alone with his son. He reached down, pulled his knife from its leg sheath, and began cut-ting off his own hair. The hair on the left side of his head was removed until it was only as long as an arrow point. He gath-ered up the cuttings that had fallen to the ground and placed all of them on his son's chest and then placed the boy's hand on top. "You will not be forgotten, my son." Laughing Crow walked back to his family.

After Broken Nose's family offered their gifts for the afterlife, Snake Tooth invited four of the Blood Riders to approach the graves. "Horses have been bred into our way of life. They are as sacred to us as the buffalo that feed us, the sun that warms us, and the water that quenches our thirst. Without horses, our people would perish. As warriors, our fallen sons shall not be denied this sacred animal in the afterlife."

Snake Tooth raised his staff to the sky and shook the dangling snake rattles, mumbling a prayer to the Great Spirit. Two of the Blood Riders stood by one horse and two by the other. They carefully removed the bridles and saddles and placed them beside each grave. The men caressed the horses to calm them. While one man captured the horse's attention, the other drove a lance swiftly through each animal's chest. The screams of the horses echoed through the still night as they fell with a thud. One was still alive, choking and wailing in pain, but was quickly silenced by another thrust of a lance.

Snake Tooth walked over to the bodies and, in turn, cut a small clump of hair from their heads. "Cover them up now."

The Riders carefully wrapped each body with a buffalo robe, lowered it into the hole, and covered the grave with dirt. They heaped stones on each grave to keep the bodies safe from scavengers. Then the Riders picked up what remained of the two men's possessions and threw them into the bonfire. *I wish Malone was here to do this.*

"Your sons have what they need from this world. Let their souls rise above the clouds to the next world!" Snake Tooth tossed the clumps of hair into the swirling flames. Then, he walked away into the darkness.

"Laughing Crow, Valencia wishes to sing for you—an old funeral song she learned from her mother," said Lupe, one of his Mexican wives. Valencia was the tall, big-shouldered Mexican woman he had taken as his slave. Time had not softened her to his sexual advances, and he desperately wanted her to bear him a mixed-blood son. He believed her unwillingness had cursed his hopes. He was curious about this unusual offer from her, so he nodded his approval and motioned for her to sing.

Valencia stood up and spoke briefly with Lupe, who in turn whispered words to the drummers who began playing a slow, steady beat. It was a familiar beat the drummers had learned from the Mexican pony-slaves. Laughing Crow preferred the music of his own people. The Mexican women often sang as they worked, but he had not paid much attention to them.

Valencia's voice surprised him, as he had never heard her sing before. It was deeper than he expected and full of feeling. Her words were languid and steady. She sang, looking into his eyes only. They were not the eyes of a scratching cat that had shown him fear and hate, but the eyes of a tender woman who reached into his soul. Though her long body was shadowed by the bonfire behind her, he saw her curves swaying seductively with the deliberate beat of the drums. He did not fully understand the Spanish words she sang, but he felt their power reach out to him. This song, her song, felt different than others he'd heard. It was the first intimate moment they shared together.

He closed his eyes and thought of his son as she sang and danced for him. Walks On Feathers was different than his other son and not just because he was his only full-blooded *Noomah* son. Everyone loved him and respected him. He could make his father laugh with a funny face or a silly imitation of a person or an animal. He could reach his heart like no one else. *Malone*. If only Malone was here. He would have been proud of Walks On Feathers, proud of his warrior's burial. It was good to escape the hard world for this one soft moment with this one beautiful song.

Laughing Crow opened his eyes again. A single tear fell from his eyes as he looked at his dancing slave. He quickly brushed it aside, but he knew that she saw it. He smiled at her and she smiled back at him, bringing a pleasurable sensation to his loins. He knew that things would be different between them. She would bear his son.

Valencia finished her soulful song and returned to where she was sitting.

Suddenly, Laughing Crow realized that Sun Sparrow was slumped over in his lap. He felt a tickling sensation on his leg, like a warm liquid. Touching it, he found his fingers covered in his wife's blood. She had a knife in her right hand and blood was gushing from a self-inflicted wound on her left arm. She had passed out. He knew this was her way of dealing with her overwhelming grief.

The soft moment was over. His son was buried—the son he had hoped would lead his village someday. His *Noomah* wife had lost her only child and had born no more children. Like a scavenger hoping to tear away the last bits of happiness, deep sadness would follow her now. He felt like his world had been ripped apart. Again, he looked at the blood on his hand and leg. He swore to himself that *Navoonah* blood would spill. *I will cover my body with it.*

Tracked

The pleasant memories of times Many Wolves spent with Ten Arrows still lingered in this place, the Gray Face camp, but now he was alone. The camp was just as he had left it—the fire pit, his cooking tools, the blanket he made out of Gray Face's skin—all of it was there, except for Ten Arrows. A part of him imagined that his friend would be here when he arrived, but it was just a dream, misplaced hope.

His trip back from the lake camp went quickly, as he spent no time searching for bear tracks. Stopping only to hunt and rest, it took him two sleeps to get to the Gray Face camp. Whenever possible, he used rocky paths and shallow, fast-moving creeks to cover his tracks as he traveled. He was sure that the Nokoni tracker had followed his false path by the lake. Hopefully, this camp in the foothills would remain a secret he shared only with Ten Arrows.

As he carefully separated skin and flesh from the large jackrabbit Cazador had just killed, his thoughts wandered back to when he first arrived here. He was a boy who hunted rabbits and squirrels, but now he was a man who killed grizzlies and men. He no longer lived in a boy's world. His mind wrestled with the fact that he killed two Northerners. Was he wrong? After all, they hadn't attacked him and he couldn't be certain if they were from Laughing Crow's band. His conscience would rest easier if he knew with certainty that they were his enemy. Now, the Northerners were hunting him.

He was no longer a shadow in the wilderness, but flesh and blood that left signs for his enemies to find.

Suddenly, he heard birds flushing out of the trees near his camp. He looked into the forest and, in the distance, saw an animal looking back at him. It was a coyote or a wolf. He reached for his quiver and loaded his black bow, keeping an eye on the intruder. It walked around him, watching him. The silhouetted animal was bigger than a coyote.

The animal cautiously approached. Through the filtered light, he saw flashes of color—a reddish color. *Rojo? Is it Rojo?* He saw that the wolf was walking with a slight limp. *Rojo could barely walk when I left him.* The wolf walked closer into a patch of sunshine. His posture was more like the lowest member of the pack, Shadow Chaser, because he was cowered, with his head and tail held low, but the reddish patterns on his fur were unmistakable. It was Rojo.

Many Wolves slowly put down his bow. Rojo lay down about ten steps away from him, panting. Rojo had never come this close before. He did not understand why the red wolf had not returned to his pack, and beyond that, why he would track a human over such a great distance. *Did the pack cast him out because of his injury?*

"You must be tired and hungry." He cut off a piece of jackrabbit and hurled it across his camp. Rojo walked slowly over to the meat, sniffed it, and then grabbed it with his teeth and carried it back to where he had been lying down. He cut into the flesh with his large canine teeth and watched Many Wolves, without flinching, as he inhaled each mouthful, hardly chewing at all. "You have a home here, Rojo, if you wish to stay."

Many Wolves fed the rest of the jackrabbit to the hungry wolf and grabbed some dried deer meat for himself. "Eat up, red wolf. You need to get your strength back." Rojo had lost some of his bulk, but at least his leg looked like it was healing.

He hoped that wolves, like grizzlies, had a magical way of healing their wounds.

He had never expected to see Rojo, or any of the other wolves again, and now it seemed as if they were bound together, like he was bound to Ten Arrows. "Neither of us would be alive if not for the other, Rojo. Neither of us can go home. The Great Spirit must want us to be friends."

A Message of Woe

Many Wolves woke in the dead of the night hearing Rojo's growls. "What is it, Rojo?" The red wolf had not growled, even once, since his arrival at the camp three sleeps ago. Whatever he heard or smelled had chased him into the safety of the trees.

The young tracker put his head to the ground and sensed the faint rumble of beating hooves, which sounded like they came from a single horse. Instantly, he grabbed his quiver and climbed up a tree to the rocky ledge overlooking his camp. *Have they found me already?*

The thundering horse approached, closer and closer. It was too late to ride away or run, so he used the overhang to protect himself as he had done with Gray Face. He slumped back into a nook on the ledge and waited.

"Many Wolves!" a voice shouted.

It was the voice of Ten Arrows. He sighed a deep breath of relief and smiled. "Ten Arrows! I'm up here!" He crawled out, ran to the edge of the overhang, and quickly climbed down the tree.

Ten Arrows rode into his camp on Cloud, his brilliant white horse, and dismounted. Many Wolves embraced his friend. "You came back, like you said you would!"

"It's good to see you, Wild Man," said Ten Arrows, out of breath. Many Wolves sensed a hint of sadness in his friend's voice. "You must return to your village."

"Why? What's happened?"

"Laughing Crow's son is dead and Laughing Crow believes that a Lipan killed him. He is gathering a war party of men from different villages. Laughing Crow's oldest son, Thorn Bird, came to my village asking for our warriors to join him in his war against the Lipans, to avenge his brother's death."

Many Wolves was stunned. *Did I kill Laughing Crow's son?* "What was the name of his son…the one that was killed?"

"They called him Walks On Feathers."

Many Wolves felt heat rushing to his head and a nauseous feeling in his stomach. "Walks on Feathers" was the name he heard the older Northerner call the younger one. He fell to his knees, shocked, and threw his face into his cupped hands.

"My heart is heavy in bringing these words to you, Wild Man."

What have I done? Many Wolves thought to himself. "How did they know it was my people who killed him?" He looked up at Ten Arrows, afraid of the answer.

"They found an arrow. It was made with *Navoonah* hands."

I recovered all my arrows. How could they have found one? He didn't want to tell his friend that it was his arrow that killed the Nokoni leader's son. He didn't want to tell anybody. He wanted to bury the truth far, far into the earth and ride away as fast as he could. This was a nightmare far worse than the ones he had as a child.

Ten Arrows seemed to sense that something else was troubling his friend, so he knelt down next to him. "What's wrong? Are you all right?"

"I'm not all right, Ten Arrows. I killed Laughing Crow's son. It was my arrow that they found." His voice trembled as he blurted out his confession. It was done. The truth was out, but maybe there was a way that Ten Arrows could help him.

"How did this happen?" asked Ten Arrows.

Many Wolves took a deep, quivering breath. "I was watching Rojo's pack, the wolf pack that we found, when Laughing Crow's son and another Northerner began to attack them with arrows. I knew they were Nokoni because they had the snake mark on their arms. They injured two of the wolves and then beat them down with their tomahawks. The anguished cries of the wolves were too much for me to take, Ten Arrows. My only thought was to protect them. I shot an arrow at the younger one, Laughing Crow's son, and killed him. The older Northerner charged me with his whirling tomahawk and war screams. I shot him too, but he kept coming at me. The last thing I remembered was feeling a jolting pain in my head and then the world went black." Many Wolves felt like he was burning inside and his hands were shaking. He couldn't settle them even if he wanted to.

"Then I remember having a horrible dream that my village was destroyed, until finally I woke up with blood all over my head and hands. The older Northerner was lying there dead in front of me. It looked like his throat had been ripped apart by an animal. It was Rojo, the lead wolf that killed him. I don't know why he helped me."

"You are very fortunate, Wild Man. The wolf must have felt a friendship with you...he protected you."

"I followed Rojo's trail of footprints and blood and found him nearly dead. I mended the wound on his leg from the Northerner's tomahawk and left him food."

"There were no other Nokonis there?" asked Ten Arrows.

"No, but others came a few sleeps later. I ran back to my camp by the lake to find Elk Dog and then rode here, covering my tracks as best I could. Rojo followed me here. If you look over there you can see him through the trees." Many Wolves stood up and pointed at the wolf who was watching them in the darkness.

"It looks like you have a new member of your pack, Wild Man," Ten Arrows said with a soft laugh. He stood up and walked around the camp, lost in his thoughts.

"What am I going to do?" asked Many Wolves.

"You need to warn your people before Laughing Crow finds them. I will help you, but I am an enemy of your people. Laughing Crow will kill until he is satisfied that his son's death has been avenged. We must leave now. We will stop only to hunt and rest the horses. Let us hope we can ride with the wind at our backs."

One Hundred Warriors

Laughing Crow rode out at sunrise to meet Thorn Bird at the Salt Flats. Fifteen of his best warriors rode with him. He hoped his son had found many more warriors, perhaps thirty or forty, from the Penateka and Wichita bands. He wasn't sure if the other villages would honor the white man's agreement. Like him, perhaps they did not trust the words of a white man, even one as respected as Fontaine.

The Nokoni men had painted and decorated their favorite war horses and brought extra mounts along so their best horses would not tire from the long journey. Spare horses could also be eaten so that no time was wasted on hunting. Laughing Crow, unlike the other men, refused to eat the pemmican that his warriors brought along, unless he was faced with starvation.

The Nokonis arrived at the Salt Flats by midafternoon. A horde of small, pestering insects and a large flock of shorebirds wading in the shallow lake greeted them. The land was barren and flat in all directions. Where the water had receded, sandy shoreline surrounded the lake.

His village often traveled here to gather salt, which they used for their daily meals and for preserving meat and animal hides. It was a well-known landmark for the people of the Llano Estacado.

"We will rest here and wait for Thorn Bird," he ordered his men.

His warriors dismounted and fetched water for themselves and their horses. Mocking Bird gave the men bear grease to protect their skin from the annoying insects. Some played games with sticks and bones while others rested in what shade there was in the mesquite.

"Little Owl, ride south and find a nice spot with trees and running water for us to stay the night," said Laughing Crow. He knew his scout could be depended on to find a camp that would meet their needs. The nagging insects and rotting smell of the salt lake were too much to endure.

They waited until the sun had almost fallen to the horizon, and still there was no sign of Thorn Bird. Little Owl had returned to tell his leader that he had found a comfortable camp.

"Let us move to the camp that Little Owl has found to the south away from these nasty insects," said Laughing Crow. "I have swallowed too many of them already." His words were met with nods of approval from his men. "We will send patrols back here to check for Thorn Bird."

After a short journey, the Nokoni men arrived at the new camp south of the Salt Flats. They watered their horses and quenched their parched lips with river water. With darkness upon them, the men built several fires and dug out a larger fire pit to roast one of the spare horses.

Laughing Crow rested on his buffalo-skin blanket and stared at the hundreds of stars in the night sky. His thoughts drifted to his home and to Valencia, and to the beautiful, sad song she sang for him. Every time the song came to his mind, so did his son. The two were forever entwined. He coupled with her the night of his son's funeral and several nights after that. She no longer resisted him and he felt that these moments were the most pleasurable he had ever felt with a woman. Soon, he hoped she would be carrying his son. Strangely, he felt that this newborn would share the spirit of his dead son, as if he was reborn into the world. If Valencia did have a boy, he would name him Walks On Feathers.

Laughing Crow felt the low rumble of a horse herd.

One of his men ran over to him. "Laughing Crow, Thorn Bird has come. He has come with many men!"

The leader stood up, untied his horse's lead, and mounted Cheval-Sang in anticipation of their arrival. He wanted to greet them on the back of his war horse—the way of his people. Thorn Bird was the first rider to appear from out of the darkness. Laughing Crow could see the moonlit silhouettes of men behind him.

"I have returned, *Ahpu*, with your war party." Thorn Bird reached his hand out and Laughing Crow greeted him with a nod of approval and a forearm grasp. Laughing Crow summoned Mocking Bird to ride by his side.

As the throng of men grew closer, he saw that their eyes were ringed in black, Raccoon-Eyes, and their bodies were heavily tattooed. It was the Wichitas, not his *Noomah* brothers, the Penatekas. Leading the men was Smoke Cloud, the Wichita leader Laughing Crow met with Fontaine. Smoke Cloud ordered his men to stop and he rode forward alone to greet Laughing Crow.

"I am pleased to see you again, Laughing Crow, and I am honored to ride with you into war. I have brought with me a hundred of my best warriors." Mocking Bird translated the words back and forth between the two leaders.

"It is good you are here. You honor me and you honor my fallen son. The white man's words do carry some weight on the plains," said Laughing Crow, reaching out to grasp the forearm of the Wichita leader.

"It wasn't Fontaine's agreement that brought us here, but the agreement between you and me as leaders. As you can see, the white man's agreement did not bring the Penatekas or the Osage to your side."

"They are not coming?"

"No. They do not feel it is a war they need to fight."

"It does not surprise me that the white man's words have sunk into the dust of the earth," said Laughing Crow.

Smoke Cloud signaled for one of his riders to come forward. "I have brought these bows for you, made from the Osage orange tree. There are two for every one that I promised."

Laughing Crow nodded his thanks. "I see your men are using the long guns. I hope they are well supplied with powder and balls."

"They are well-prepared, Laughing Crow, and honored to ride with a great war leader. They hope to be remembered in stories, as you and your Blood Riders will be remembered."

The Nokoni leader stared into Smoke Cloud's eyes, demanding his full attention. "Now, listen carefully. I will send out my scouts at sunrise to ride southeast along the path of the Rio Pecos. I expect we will find Lipan villages there. Once we find them, we will attack when the moon is high. Do not spare the lives of the women and children. Try to keep some of the men alive so we can ask them if they know who made this arrow." Laughing Crow pulled the death arrow from his quiver and showed it to the Wichita leader, then continued. "If they resist or answer with silence, kill them. The killing will not end until I find the one who took my son's life. Tell them they must follow my orders and mine alone. My men must not die because of their mistakes!" Again, Laughing Crow looked deeply into the eyes of the Wichita leader. "Tonight, we will rest and seal our agreement with the smoke from our pipes."

A River of Blood

Laughing Crow watched as the men of his war party set fire to the grassy dwellings of the third Lipan encampment they had pillaged in five sleeps. The sounds of crackling bonfires and whooping warriors and the smell of charred human flesh ruled the night. The moans of a few Lipans, whose flesh had not yet been cast into the hungry flames, brought a smile to the leader's face. A river of blood now flowed from one Lipan village to the next.

"Are any of their men still alive?" asked the Nokoni headman, looking down at his warriors from his mounted vantage point. Their painted black faces were illuminated by the flickering fire.

"Two of them are alive," answered Silent Weasel.

"Take me to them," said Laughing Crow. "Mocking Bird, come with us."

Laughing Crow and Mocking Bird rode behind Silent Weasel who led them on foot through the path of burning huts. The screams of the Lipan women and children were squelched one after the other by a Nokoni lance or a Wichita knife.

"Over here." Silent Weasel pointed to a Lipan warrior sprawled out on the ground, an arrow stuck in his bloodied stomach. He was moaning in pain, blood trickling from his mouth. He looked up at the three Nokonis with fearful eyes. The scout grabbed one of the arrows from the man's quiver, inspected it, and then handed it to his leader.

Laughing Crow removed the arrow that killed his son from his saddle and compared the two. The arrow points were both made from obsidian and the same size. The flight feathers also seemed similar, both taken from a buzzard, but the markings on the arrows were different. He handed the arrow from his bag to Silent Weasel, held the man's arrow out, and looked at Mocking Bird. "Ask him if he knows who made this arrow."

After Mocking Bird spoke, the Lipan answered slowly, between gasps for air. "He says it was made by a warrior in his village named Red Arrow."

"Where is this Red Arrow?" asked Laughing Crow with a firm voice.

The Nokoni translator repeated the question in the *Navoonah* language. The man shook his head. He winced and grabbed his stomach as the translator sat him up. Blood dripped from his mouth. Mocking Bird pointed at the other dead men who were strewn about the burning village. Again, the man just shook his head "No."

"He doesn't see him here, Laughing Crow."

Laughing Crow motioned for Mocking Bird to release him and move away. He pulled an arrow from his quiver and shot it through the man's heart. "Throw him in the fire."

"There's another survivor at the other end of the village, *namunewapi*," said Silent Weasel.

"Take me to him."

Silent Weasel led the two men, this time to the other side of the village where there was another injured warrior. He searched the surrounding sage thicket and found the warrior's quiver. "*Namunewapi*, look at this." Silent Weasel looked up and handed him one of the arrows.

The leader's eyes lit up as he compared the arrow with the one that killed his son. "They are the same. This must be Red Arrow. You know what to ask him."

The warrior had been shot in the chest with a Wichita long gun and was also bleeding from a serious head wound. He looked up with burning defiance as the three Nokonis approached.

Mocking Bird knelt down and spoke to the wounded man, who spit in his face, but said nothing. Laughing Crow handed the death arrow to Mocking Bird. "Ask him if this is his arrow."

The translator showed the man the arrow as he spoke. Red Arrow looked at it, then looked up at Laughing Crow and smiled. Still, he remained silent.

"Why does this Red Arrow smile, Mocking Bird?" asked the leader.

"I don't know. He must know something about the arrow."

"Ask him if he killed my son. Ask him!" the leader yelled.

Red Arrow finally spoke after hearing Mocking Bird's question. His voice was soft and calm. "He said he wishes he did."

"Ask him who did it. Ask him whose mark is on the arrow!" Laughing Crow sprung off his horse and barreled over to the two men.

The defiant *Navoonah* spoke more words and smiled again even more broadly than before.

"What did he say?" hissed Laughing Crow.

"He said that many men use his arrows. If one killed your son, then he is proud of what he crafted," said Mocking Bird. Red Arrow smiled again and laughed, choking on blood for a moment, but said nothing more. Then he spit on Mocking Bird again.

"He's not going to tell us." Laughing Crow drew an arrow and shot the defiant *Navoonah* warrior in the chest, drawing the life from his eyes. Laughing Crow looked up to the sky and yelled in anger. In his rage, he shot two more arrows into the dead body of the Lipan warrior. "Are any of the women or children still alive, Silent Weasel?"

"Yes, *namunewapi*."

"Bring them to me. *Now!*" bellowed Laughing Crow.

Silent Weasel returned shortly after dragging a young woman by the arm. She was screaming at him and thrashing about, her hands bound behind her back, but the muscular scout easily overpowered her. Silent Weasel threw her at Laughing Crow's feet.

"Ask her if she knows whose mark is on the arrow!" demanded the leader.

Silent Weasel unsheathed his giant steel knife and waved it threateningly at her throat as Mocking Bird kneeled down and talked to her, dangling the arrow in front of her face. As tears fell down, she stared at Laughing Crow, but said nothing.

"Make her talk," grunted Laughing Crow.

Silent Weasel grabbed her shirt and sawed through it. Then, he tore it open with his hands, exposing her breasts. He held her down and cut her lightly across the chest with the tip of his knife, drawing blood. He did this several times until finally she screamed out *Navoonah* words. When she was finished speaking, she cried.

"She says it's her sister's son whose mark is on the arrow." Mocking Bird asked her another question and she shook her head "No." "She doesn't know where he is," confirmed Mocking Bird.

"Find out what his name is."

She mumbled some words between her crying and sniffling. Mocking Bird looked up at Laughing Crow. "She says his name is Many Wolves."

Many Wolves. Laughing Crow remembered hearing that name before, but he couldn't recall when or where. He said the name several times to himself, hoping it would jar his memory. Then he remembered the joke about the trade for many horses. "Many Wolves is the white-skinned boy!" he blurted out, excited that the memory had drifted to him. "Ask her if this is true."

Once again, she nodded favorably to Mocking Bird's question. The tears could not hide the terror in her eyes.

"Where is he now?" shouted Laughing Crow with sweat peeling from his forehead. The Nokoni leader knew that this village was Walking Free's home, but he did not see the old man's body among the dead, and he did not see him during the fight.

She spoke more words this time.

"She says that Many Wolves left the village a long time ago and hasn't been seen since."

"We will keep her as a captive. Keep her hands bound and let the pony-slaves take her back to the village so she can feel Rosa's whips against her bare back. She may be useful to us someday."

Silent Weasel cleaned his knife and slid it back into its sheath. Then, he pulled the woman to her feet and dragged her away.

"Silent Weasel, one more thing. Did you see Walking Free among the dead?"

"No. There were three old men, but none of them was Walking Free."

"I want my scouts to look around the area outlying this camp. He might be hiding and the white-skinned boy could be with him."

"Thorn Bird and Little Owl are already looking for runners. I will tell them to keep an eye out for them."

"Good." Laughing Crow was pleased with the knowledge he had gleaned, although it angered him to know that his son had died at the hands of this white-skinned boy. It was hard to imagine this frail-looking boy as a warrior.

Choking Uncertainty

The Nokoni leader rested in the long shadow of a large cottonwood not far from Walking Free's smoldering village. It was good to be away from the scorching flames and the stench of burning human flesh. After a moonlight raid, he usually enjoyed a late-afternoon rest to soothe his body and mind, but after discovering who killed his son, his mind could not settle.

His moment of peace was interrupted by the arrival of his scouts with Thorn Bird, who dismounted and approached him. "*Ahpu*, there is no sign of Walking Free or the white-skinned boy."

Why is Walking Free not with his people? His best guess was that the Lipan leader was either dead or on a journey. Even as an old man, Walking Free, the man he once knew as Chasing Coyote, still eluded him as he did many summers ago. *He is a man of much puha. He has the luck of a coyote and the cunning of a cat.* "Walking Free has disappeared like a scent in wind, Thorn Bird."

"The white-skin might still be in the mountains, *Ahpu*."

Laughing Crow had wondered about this too. He was hoping that his son's killer would return to the flatlands to brag to the villagers about his brave deeds. How else could he be recognized as a warrior? But Laughing Crow also realized that this murderer might choose to stay hidden in the safety of the high country. To find him there would be an arduous task, and he knew his men would become bored if there was no killing to occupy their minds. Last night had revived their spirits and eased his pain. Finding his son's killer was most important, but for now he needed to spill more blood to wash away the grief. He knew he could find more villages in the lowland desert, although he knew well that Many Wolves might be far away.

Breaking away from his thoughts, Laughing Crow finally answered Thorn Bird. "He might be in the mountains, but at least we know who he is and that he has no village to go home to."

"Should we go to the high country to look for him?"

"No. If he is there, he will be much harder to find. He still might be here in the lowlands with one of the other villages. There are more rocks to overturn in this harsh wasteland— rocks with Lipans crawling underneath, begging for us to bury our arrows and lances into their bellies."

"Smoke Cloud wishes to ride north, Laughing Crow. His men are tired and most of their long guns have been emptied," said Mocking Bird. The Wichita leader was standing nearby listening to Mocking Bird translate the conversation.

His eyes squinting to hold back his anger, Laughing Crow turned to Smoke Cloud. He had already sensed that the Wichitas were weakening. The scorching sun was melting away their enthusiasm and the dusty air was choking their strength. The Raccoon-Eyes were not hardened warriors like his men. They could not ride great distances without frequent rests and they relied on the white man's weapons, not the traditional weapons of his people.

"Our path ends when I say it ends. Your men have knives and bows. They can still fight without their *taibo* weapons."

"We have lost many men already, Laughing Crow. We have fought side by side with the Nokonis as brothers, but my men have had enough of this killing. They wish to return to their homes and their wives and children," he said wearily. Loose strands of long gray hair fell into his eyes as he spoke.

"We are close to finding my son's murderer. He may be hiding in the next village," Laughing Crow pressed on, twisting the truth. He knew he could not continue the raid without Smoke Cloud's men. Village after village, his war party enjoyed superior numbers and the sweet taste of success. Only the most careless of Smoke Cloud's men had lost their lives, while his men remained unharmed. Without great numbers, however, the task at hand would be difficult. "My scouts tell me there is a camp a day's ride from here to the east. It has plenty of trees for wood and shade and a clear, running creek. We will rest there while my scouts look for the next village," Laughing Crow said, calmly. "Send two of your warriors back to your village to retrieve more long gun supplies for your men. In three sleeps, we will be ready to ride again into war."

Smoke Cloud nodded, his usual cheerfulness scuffed, and muttered a message to one of his men before walking off.

They are weak, but I need them to fight.

Laughing Crow wanted to be left alone with his thoughts.

Ashes to Dust

Buzzards. The first thing Many Wolves saw were the buzzards. Hundreds of them were circling overhead in the blue midday sky. He didn't know what they had found. The rolling hills of mesquite and sage hid their prize. He and Ten Arrows rode closer. Perhaps it was a large buffalo or an elk that was too weak or injured to make it to water and had been ravaged by a predator. But there were too many buzzards for just one animal.

A trickling black spire rose to the sky. It was just a single strand of smoke, not a prairie fire that choked the sky with charcoal fumes and casts its ashes into the breeze to be carried away to distant lands. But now, the air carried the raspy squawks of ravens and the cawing of crows. As the two men approached the last hill that blocked their view of death, the breeze slung a stench in the face of Many Wolves. It was the odor of decaying flesh laced with a familiar, nauseous pungency. Heat rushed to his head. He realized the smell was not buffalo or elk, but human.

The grisly scene was revealed to them as they reached the top of the hill. Several large piles of smoldering debris lay before them, one still ablaze. Dead horses and the bodies of men, women, and children were scattered around the ground. A throng of scavenger birds and a few coyotes cleared a path for Many Wolves and Ten Arrows as they rode closer. Many

Wolves did not recognize this place from his childhood. The large rock formations that surrounded him were unfamiliar.

Both trackers dismounted for a closer look. Many Wolves walked over to the nearest body, which was nestled in a bed of sage and had three arrows buried in it. With the suddenness of a thundershower, his thoughts were flooded in sadness when he recognized the familiar leg sheath of his father, Red Arrow. He ran over to him and fell to his knees. He was in shock as he looked over the lifeless body. He began to weep, and then screamed, "This is my village! These are my people!" Then, he burst into tears, pounding his fist to the ground. Ten Arrows embraced and comforted him. "He's dead because of me! They're all dead because of me!" Many Wolves yelled.

Many Wolves staggered over the closest pile of smoldering debris. *How many more have I killed?* He saw bodies with charred flesh and bones, gutted by fire and mixed in with shattered clay pots, bone tools, shriveled pieces of leather, and other remnants of his village. The size and shape of the bones and the condition of the teeth were the only identifying marks left. The smell of burnt flesh was overwhelming. On the ground next to his foot, he found what remained of the rabbit-ear belt that he once gave to his grandfather. What was left of Yellow Feather was lying in front of him. They were all dead. He didn't want to see anymore. He just wanted to get away from this place.

"These are Laughing Crow's arrows in your father's body," said the Northerner, still kneeling next to Red Arrow's body. "Laughing Crow left these here so anyone who found this body would know that he was your father's killer."

Many Wolves wasn't surprised to hear this. It didn't matter to him who killed his family, only that they were all dead and it was because of him. He stepped away from the burnt remains and watched as the breeze lifted the ashes and then, like falling leaves, gently lowered them to the dust. His village was fading away—into the earth.

Ten Arrows reached into the dirt and pulled out the broken shaft of an arrow. "This is a Wichita arrow and many of the tracks around here are from Wichita moccasins. Laughing Crow commands the Wichitas as well as his own men. His war party is large, as large as it was before he was banished."

There was a break in the commotion as the ravens and crows fell silent, for a moment, letting one sound fall from the sky like a floating feather.

It was the sound of chanting.

A Thousand Prayers

Many Wolves recognized the voice immediately. It receded into the background as the scavenger birds resumed their clamor. He ran towards the sound, which led him to several large rock formations. The voice was coming from the top of a large mesa in front of him—a mesa as long as forty horses and as wide as twenty. It looked impossible to climb with its smooth sides, but he knew that there must be a way up.

He ran around it until he found a thin ledge leading up the backside of the giant rock. He climbed the narrow passageway until it ended, then scaled a steep face to reach the highest point. The top of the mesa was flat, as if a knife had sliced off the upper half of it.

Walking Free was sitting near the edge of the plateau with his legs crossed and his arms and head directed skyward. His back faced the boy he once named. Many Wolves ran towards him, then stopped, remembering that a shaman must never be disturbed while he was praying. He wanted to jump on his old friend and hug him like when he was a boy, but he wasn't a boy anymore, and this wasn't a joyous homecoming. There was no village left to come home to. He approached cautiously and sat down a few steps away from the chanting medicine man.

Though his face was more haggard and wrinkled and his body leaner and more flaccid, Walking Free looked about the same as Many Wolves remembered. He was wearing only a breechcloth and red band around his head and his medicine bag lay next to him, along with his pipe, which had left a hint of tobacco in the air.

The chanting continued, uninterrupted by the visitor's presence. Many Wolves enjoyed hearing his people's words again and the prayers helped to lift, at least for the moment, the heavy burden he felt. He closed his eyes and concentrated on his old friend's words.

Each prayer was a dedication to a member of his village. Many Wolves did not fully understand all of the words since some of them were from the ancient language. From what he could tell, Walking Free was recounting experiences, moments of charity and selflessness, from the person's life and then offering them up with these words: "Great Spirit, build from this goodness a shelter of protection." Over and over, Walking Free offered up events from the person's life and then asked the Great Spirit for protection.

Then, all Many Wolves heard was the wind whistling around him.

"Many Wolves, it is good to see you."

Many Wolves opened his eyes and his elderly friend was looking at him, smiling, although there was a deep sadness in his eyes.

"Walking Free, I didn't want to…"

"I know. Thank you for letting me finish. Now, stand up and give this old man a hug."

Many Wolves was pleased to hear the cheerfulness in his voice. They stood and Many Wolves embraced him, returning the smile. It was strange to be looking down on his friend, but now he realized how much taller he was than when he was a boy.

Walking Free felt the muscles of his arms and chest and stroked his face. "You look strong, Many Wolves, like the trunks of oak trees. The years have carved your body into a man's body. Your eyes, they were brown like the buffalo and now they are green like the grass. And I see that the wild spirits obey your call." Walking Free pointed through him, at Chiquito and Cazador who were perched on the smooth, rocky floor behind him.

Many Wolves turned around and called to Chiquito, holding his left hand up. The smaller of the two hawks flew to him immediately and landed on his bare fist. Chiquito's claw dug into his skin slightly as the bird balanced himself in the wind. "This is Chiquito, 'The Little One,' and over there is Cazador, 'The Hunter,' and they're part of my family."

Walking Free stared closely at Chiquito. "I've never seen a wolf hawk this close before. Its eyes are intelligent as if it understands my words. It's as tame as the tamest village dog."

"I have survived this long because of them." Many Wolves began stroking Chiquito's chest with his finger. "They hunt rabbits and squirrels and birds with me. We all share in the kill, just like a hunting party, just like a family. You should watch them hunt, the way they dance with the wind; it's the most beautiful thing I've ever seen."

Walking Free smiled as if trying to picture it in his mind and then his good mood passed, replaced with a tone of concern. "Is the Northerner down there part of your family?"

Many Wolves was stunned by the abrupt change in the medicine man's voice.

"Ten Arrows is my friend, or more like my brother. I saved his life once from a great bear and he did the same for me. We wear these necklaces as a reminder of what we have done for each other." Many Wolves released Chiquito to the sky. The hawk flew off and landed on a protruding rock. Then he pulled the bear-claw necklace away from his neck to show Walking Free.

"How can you call him a friend when he is a Northerner? Look what your *friends* have done to our village?" Walking

Free's eyes sharpened and bore into him like knives. The shaman's suspicion did not surprise the young man. Many Wolves felt a sickness in his heart thinking about all that Walking Free had lost because of him.

"Ten Arrows is Penateka, not Nokoni. He is not a friend of Laughing Crow or the men he rides with." Many Wolves paused, lowering his head before continuing. "What has happened to our village was because of me. It was my fault!"

Many Wolves looked back up at Walking Free and to his surprise the anger in the old man's eyes had relented.

"Laughing Crow killed our people because I killed his son," continued Many Wolves, as his eyes filled with water. There was a quiver in his voice as he spoke to his friend, the leader of their village. "His son was killing wolves in the mountains and I had to protect them. I didn't know who he was. I didn't want to see the wolves die! Laughing Crow found one of my arrows, one that my father made, and he has come here looking for his son's killer. Ten Arrows tracked me to the foothills so I could warn you, but I am too late to help." Many Wolves was expecting the eyes of his friend to turn to knives again and cut his heart open. Instead, his look was soft.

"Many Wolves, you cannot blame yourself for all of this. It is too much of a burden for you to carry. I am as much to blame as you." Walking Free looked at his young friend with eyes full of tenderness and understanding. "I was away from the village when the Nokonis came. I was not here to protect our people. My body should be burning with the others. I have been praying to the Great Spirit for an answer to my question: 'Why was I spared?' The Great Spirit, who watches over all, has told me that I must pray a thousand prayers, day and night, for every person in the village, to help them find their way to the next world. That's why I am here."

"But it wasn't your fault that they died, it was my fault!" said Many Wolves. The tears streamed down his face.

"Many Wolves, you cannot stop Laughing Crow from his path of hatred and death, just as you cannot stop fires from devouring the prairie grass or the winds from uprooting the trees. Only the Great Spirit has power over these things and even he cannot reach into the dark heart of Laughing Crow."

Walking Free held out his hands and invited Many Wolves to join him. "Sit down with me. I have a story to tell you."

The Black Wasp

Ringed by the unending desert, Walking Free and Many Wolves sat down and faced each other. The medicine man spoke to him in his old, crackling voice, which had the warmth of fire.

"This is an old story of the black wasp and the hairy spider. When she is ready to start her family, the black wasp will search the desert floor for the hairy spider, the largest one she can find. Her buzzing red wings will carry her from one burrow to the next looking for the perfect prey. Once she finds one she likes, she attacks it quickly, avoiding its shiny black fangs. She wrestles the much larger spider onto its back and then thrusts her long stinger into its exposed belly. The poison from her sting cripples the spider quickly, but does not kill it. The spider is still very much alive, but it cannot run or fight. She drags the defenseless creature back into its burrow and there she lays her egg on its overturned body. She covers the entrance to the underground nest to protect her egg and then she flies away. Several suns rise and set until her egg hatches and the young wasp begins to devour the helpless spider, sucking the life spirit from it. The young wasp grows strong from its first meal and soon, like its mother, begins a lifelong pursuit of hairy spiders."

Walking Free took a moment to release his breath, but did not release his hold on the young man's eyes. "Many Wolves, the black wasp lives in the heart of the Northerners. They control the horses, which gives them control over the buffalo and the land that we share with them. They crippled us long ago when they took our horses and now we wait like the helpless spider for their children to feed on the blood of our people. It has become the way of the Staked Plains."

"Why didn't our village move far away when we had the chance?" asked Many Wolves.

"The spider can try to hide or hope that the black wasp finds another victim, but it cannot fly away from the winged predator. There was a time when we had horses and we were the wasps, but that time has passed, and someday it will pass for the Northerners as well and another black wasp will come to feed on them."

It was painful to think that the Nokonis had this kind of power over his people, but Many Wolves had seen the blackened corpses and the burnt remains of his village. He knew that Walking Free spoke the truth. *Is there an enemy more powerful than the Northerner?* It was too difficult to imagine what would happen in the days to come. He wasn't a shaman or a visionary, but he needed to know his purpose. "What do I do now, Walking Free?"

"You must ride south to other Lipan villages and tell them what you have seen here. Tell them that Laughing Crow searches for you, the one who killed his son. They will protect you, but you must help them fight. You are a warrior now, Many Wolves. You must shed blood, not tears. Remember the faces of your family, they will give you purpose. But be careful, the Nokonis have many eyes in the desert."

"What are you going to do?"

"I must stay here and pray a thousand prayers. I serve only the Great Spirit now." Walking Free stood up and directed Many Wolves to do the same. The two men embraced once more, perhaps for the last time, Many Wolves thought.

"Go now, Many Wolves, and stop the black wasp before she stings again."

A Vigilant Spirit

The long day was coming to a close for Many Wolves and Ten Arrows. They were sitting by a small cooking pit, roasting a jackrabbit that Cazador had plucked from the desert floor. The half-day's ride and the physical exertion from digging his father's grave in the draining heat had exhausted Many Wolves. His body wanted to sleep, but the sweet aroma of cooked rabbit meat kept his mind alert.

Many Wolves found it difficult to release the gruesome images of the violent demise of his village from his head. The Cloud Eagle had taken him to this forsaken place once in a dream, but now it was real. Any hope of seeing his family again had been snuffed out by the man who had poisoned his dreams for most of his life. He had been running his whole life in fear of this brutal man, but now he was tired and needed it to end. He wanted the poisonous fear cut out of his body, even if it meant escaping it with death.

"Wild Man, I cannot go with you where Walking Free wants you to go," said his friend. "We are reaching the edge of *Noomah* lands and it won't be safe for me further south in the land of your people. This is a battle that you must fight without me."

"Where will you go?" Many Wolves felt a familiar sadness fall on his heart. *I will be alone again.*

"It is time for me to return to my village. I have done what I set out to do—to warn you and deliver you to your homelands—but now I must go. I will ride when the red rays of sun welcome the day."

As they were talking, a coyote was yipping and howling in the distance. For Many Wolves, it was the sound of home. Then, a much closer sound filled the evening air, also familiar to him. It was the deep, mournful howl of Rojo. The red wolf had followed him yet again.

Ten Arrows laughed. "The red wolf has followed the Spirit Walker to his home like a lonesome dog. You have a protector, Wild Man, a vigilant spirit to watch over you. I am glad that you will have this *puha*."

Many Wolves recalled that on several occasions at the Gray Face camp, Rojo had howled like this, always at dusk. He suspected the wolf was trying to talk to his pack, but now that they were far from the high country, perhaps his sad melodies were motivated by loneliness. Rojo's song calmed him. He knew that this wolf, like his dog Amarillo, would warn him of danger. It was hard to imagine there was so much hate and death in a world with beautiful orange sunsets and haunting wolf songs.

"I guess we are brothers now, Rojo and I. He pulls himself further and further away from his pack and draws closer to me. A few nights ago he slept next to me just out of arm's reach. He doesn't come close now because of your unfamiliar scent. I'm glad that he is still wary of strangers. Where I am going, he will need to be cautious."

"Did Walking Free tell you exactly where to go?"

"He told me to travel south past the Giant Hoop Rock and look for the edge of a large canyon to the west. He says to follow the canyon until a gap opens leading to the southwest. Big Sky's village will be there. He says that Big Sky's people will remember me from the summer gatherings."

Many Wolves was satisfied that the rabbit was cooked to his liking, so he set it aside to cool. He was thankful that the

Great Spirit provided enough food for them. The past few days of traveling had been difficult and there was little time for hunting. Hunger drove his birds to hunt small animals on their own, while he and Ten Arrows ate mostly dried meat and nuts. Rojo's weight looked healthy and so Many Wolves didn't worry too much about him. The wolf could easily find an abandoned carcass or hunt on his own.

"You need to be careful, Many Wolves. Laughing Crow has many scouts and they will be looking for you."

"Walking Free says that there are many buttes and mesas along the way. If I ride in their shadows, they will hide me." Many Wolves tore off one of the rear legs of the rabbit, leaving the other for Ten Arrows. "I have been hiding all my life."

As he ate the meat, Many Wolves felt some of his strength returning. He looked around at the mesquite and yucca bushes outlined by the moonlight and then he stared at the stars, wondering what tomorrow would bring. None of his family had survived, apart from his birds and the stray wolf. Laughing Crow had now torn him from his family twice. His village was gone as was the life they had given him. Like Walking Free, he knew he had to do something for the lives that were lost, but he didn't know what it was yet. He was certain he would find out soon.

The warm meat in his stomach soothed him as he sat with Ten Arrows by the dying fire. His friend was hunched over, repairing one of his arrows, using what was left of the firelight. Many Wolves yawned. Sleep was close now. The horses were asleep nearby, lost in their dream world. The birds were perched with buried heads in a large mesquite behind them. The desert air was cool, still, and quiet—except for the chirping of insects and the screeching nighthawks. Rojo was lying a stone's throw away from him, his ears raised towards the night sky.

Many Wolves reached into his hunting bag, pulled out a chunk of rabbit meat, and hurled it towards the red wolf. He had saved a small portion of the uncooked carcass for Rojo, who liked to eat his meal alone in the dark. "Watch over us, Rojo."

The Giant Hoop Rock

The morning sun blasted its brightness into Many Wolves's eyes. He had hoped to rise with the sun, but his body was tired and sore from the previous day. He sat up, looked around, and saw that Ten Arrows was gone. At his feet were several freshly carved and painted arrows, a gift from his friend. Many Wolves was mad at himself for not waking up earlier to say goodbye to his good friend and get an early start on his day's journey, but he also knew his body needed the rest. His birds were nearby, grooming their feathers. *Preparing for hunting and travel.* Rojo was also close, watching him. Rojo always watched him. It reminded him of how the other wolves used to watch Rojo.

He rolled up his buffalo robe and tied it to Elk Dog, who was chewing on a sprig of sagebrush. He walked with his horse over to a gurgling creek and washed the sticky dust off his face and hands. Then he drank several gulps of the silty water, and filled his water pouch. Elk Dog drank alongside him. Many Wolves stroked his mane. "We'll find plenty of the cactus fruits that you like on our path, my friend. There may not be much water where we are going."

He set out south, directing Elk Dog to move in a slow canter. The surrounding landscape of sagebrush, mesquite, and yucca brought back fond memories of his youth. A big-headed lizard, disturbed by his presence, skittered away from the warm rock it was basking on. It had been a long time since he had seen his favorite lizard. The lizard that "ran like a man" still made him laugh. Chiquito watched it with a tilted, curious head, but did not pursue it. "You've never eaten one of those, little brother, and I hope you don't start now. Stick with the furry and feathery ones. Their meat sticks better to your bones!"

Rojo was also following them, but keeping a safe distance—always watching. Many Wolves felt comforted by the thought that the wolf was guarding him.

The sun rose higher and brought with it intense heat. He saw nothing but flat land, no rock formations near him, but there was enough tall brush to cover his movements. He had taken paths like this before when his village traveled south to the summer gatherings.   The Giant Hoop Rock was barely visible on the horizon. He often wondered as a boy how hard it would be to climb that strange rock. He remembered hearing stories of older boys climbing it during their journeys into manhood, leaving an arrow or a necklace or some other object at the top as proof of their bravery. But he never knew anyone who had actually done it.

As he ventured further into the desert chaparral, he spotted another of his childhood favorites, a running bird, with a large snake hanging from its beak. The bird scampered along a parallel path, still clinging to his meal as if to say: "Look at me, the great hunter of snakes. See my prize!" In a harsh, barren world where food and water were scarce, it was strange to see an animal flaunt such abundance.

Many Wolves reached the edge of the large canyon that ran south through the desert, just as Walking Free had described it. Soon, the sun would be falling behind the ridge, leaving a shadow at the base of the rocky hills. It would be a good place to hunt and rest his horse. He dismounted and led Elk Dog to a small patch of sagebrush. "I will get you some desert fruits while we hunt."

The young man slung his quiver around his shoulder and whistled for his birds. They were hungry. He knew both would be sharp on the chase. The shade was refreshing and that meant the rabbits would be more active as the day melted away. It didn't take long for Chiquito to spot the first jackrabbit, which bolted from the sagebrush in a blur. It was a long chase, both birds deeply in pursuit, taking turns trying to pin the quarry to the ground. After the third attempt, Cazador finally subdued the rabbit, whose cries for mercy echoed through the canyon. Many Wolves ran over and quickly killed it with his knife.

Cazador and Chiquito enjoyed their meal at the kill spot and Many Wolves packed the remains in his bag to eat later. As he approached within sight of Elk Dog, he froze. Five men on horses were riding towards him. One of them had tied Elk Dog to a lead on his large black horse. There was nowhere to run or hide. He had to face them. As they rode closer, he saw their headbands. *Lipans!* He breathed a sigh of relief. The men stopped a short distance in front of him and stared as their horses neighed and grunted.

The one in the middle riding the gray horse spoke first. "Can you understand me?"

"Yes, I speak the language of the Lipans." Many Wolves guessed that all five of the men were about his age, perhaps a little older. They were bare-chested and each carried either a bow or a lance. The largest man was the one riding the black horse and he had the most anger in his face. *His face, his angry eyes, are familiar.*

"What do they call you?" asked the biggest one.

"Many Wolves."

Upon hearing this, the largest man leaned over to the one on the gray horse and whispered. When he was finished, the other one nodded and then spoke.

"You once lived with Kicking Bull in Walking Free's village. Is that right?"

Kicking Bull? He knew the angry one was familiar. How could he forget the tormenter of his youth. *If Kicking Bull is alive, perhaps others from my village had survived.* "Yes. It is true. I left my village over five summers ago. I remember Kicking Bull." Many Wolves looked over at Kicking Bull who glared back at him, not offering any acknowledgment or friendship.

"I am Little Sky," said the one on the gray horse. "Why have you come here?"

"Walking Free asked me to come…to find Big Sky. I wish to speak with him and with him alone."

"Walking Free is alive?" demanded Kicking Bull, the anger leaving his face for a moment. His voice was much deeper now—a strong voice to match a strong body.

"Yes, he's alive. He was praying for the dead when I found him."

"We must find him and bring him back!" said Kicking Bull, looking at Little Sky.

"He does not want to leave those who died. He believes he must pray a thousand prayers for the souls of the dead to preserve them in the next world," said Many Wolves.

"Walking Free does not want to be found, Kicking Bull," said Little Sky. "His prayers are needed to guide his people to their next hunting ground. We must not disturb him."

"He will die out there," snapped Kicking Bull.

"That is his choice," said the oldest of the warriors, positioned on the other side of Little Sky. "We will find him if he wants to be found."

"Follow us to our village, Many Wolves," Little Sky said with kindness in his eyes. He motioned for the traveler to mount Elk Dog. "My father will want to meet one who is friends with the wild birds and wolves. You can tell your story to him."

Big Sky

Little Sky and his men led Many Wolves through a narrow gap between two large rock palisades. "These are the walls that protect us," Little Sky said, pointing at the cliffs that loomed high in the sky—steep and rugged. "Our enemies must pass through here to get to our village. The only other way in is through a path far to the west."

The cliffs form a nearly impassable barrier, Many Wolves thought, looking up.

As the horses trotted further down the path, the walls opened up into a wider valley and Many Wolves saw a large group of tipis. *Big Sky's village.* He felt as if he was heading to his home. Then, he remembered the burnt remains of his village, and his heart sank once more.

Many Wolves pulled on Elk Dog to stop. "I wish to stop here and wait for Big Sky," he said. He knew his birds and Rojo were following him and he didn't know how they would react to a village full of strange people and noise. His birds seemed scared of Little Sky and the others. Rojo was nowhere to be seen.

Little Sky spoke to one of the riders, "Go and tell my father that Many Wolves wishes to speak with him. Kicking Bull and I will stay here." The other two Lipans rode off into the village, leaving the three of them behind.

"How did you learn the language of the wild birds and the wolf?" asked Little Sky, with great curiosity. His legs were short and muscular and his face was wide like the moon. There was gentleness in him, in stark contrast to the burning black eyes of Kicking Bull who was still glaring at Many Wolves.

"They know more of my language than I know of theirs. They seem to recognize commands I give with my voice or signals with my hands because I repeat them over and over again. I know the birds are hungry when they squawk at me and their eyes are looking around for prey. I know they are content when they fluff up their feathers and stand on one leg. We learn these things by watching each other."

"If they learn by watching you then why haven't I seen other birds learn this from people?" asked Little Sky. "I believe that the Great Spirit has given you this…magic."

"There is no magic!" interrupted Kicking Bull in anger. "The Great Spirit would not give such a great gift to a white man and not give it to one of our people. It is a trick! The Great Spirit does not give gifts to the weak—to those who are less than Lipan!"

Many Wolves looked at Kicking Bull. He had the same hateful eyes as when they were boys. Still, Many Wolves felt the same cowering silence grip him. Time had changed nothing.

"Kicking Bull! Control your emotions. My father is here," said Little Sky.

Big Sky rode up to him on a gray and white stallion. Many Wolves recognized him from the village gatherings as the old man with the limp. He was small and moon-faced like his son. The sun and wind had aged his sagging skin considerably. His hair was now completely gray and it dangled far down his chest and back. He wore a blue Mexican bandanna around his head and his neck was dressed with the claws of a mountain lion.

"Many Wolves, Walking Free always said that you would come back. I remember you as a boy, but you have returned a man." Big Sky's voice was raspy and crackled with age. Though his body was worn, his eyes were clear and wise like Walking Free's. "You have returned a master of animals, Many Wolves. Walking Free was right about that too."

"He is master of nothing, Father!" said Kicking Bull, waving his arms in disgust. "He has returned and now my village is dead! It's all gone—burnt to the ground! Death walks with him. He is bad luck!"

Big Sky is Kicking Bull's father?

"Death walks with Laughing Crow and the Nokonis, not with him." Big Sky's voice was firm and controlled—the even tones of a wizened leader. "Your vision is clouded, Kicking Bull. Do you not see the marks of the Great Mountain Bear on his leg and the necklace he wears? There is not a warrior in our village who has fought the Great Mountain Bear, a beast who is as strong and courageous as ten men. Kicking Bull, you disgrace me with your outbursts. Take my horse back to the village and leave me alone with Many Wolves."

Big Sky got off his horse and handed the lead to Kicking Bull. "Shall I have the women bring you food and water?" asked Big Sky.

Kicking Bull growled and looked back at Many Wolves, leading the horse away.

"No, I have water and am not hungry, although I will need to cook the rest of this rabbit soon." Many Wolves stepped to the ground and led Elk Dog towards the Lipan elder. He was amazed that the old headman had dismounted so easily without any help. Little Sky looked too young to be his son. He seemed more like a grandson.

"Give the rabbit to Little Sky. He will have the women cook it for you."

Many Wolves broke off a piece of the rabbit carcass to save for Rojo and handed over the rest. Little Sky rode off, leaving the two of them alone.

"Let us talk under the shade of the cottonwoods." Big Sky motioned for the young man to follow. "Walk with me."

"Why does Kicking Bull call you 'Father'?"

"He has taken my daughter as his wife and lives with my family. I am his father through marriage," said Big Sky, calmly.

As the two walked together, Many Wolves was surprised that he was so much taller than Big Sky. It felt strange to see that he was taller than most grown men. His birds followed closely now that the other men were gone. He still didn't see Rojo, but he felt his eyes cover him like a comforting breeze.

"Many Wolves, do not be concerned with Kicking Bull's words. He is young and walks with the sun in his eyes and the wind at his back. It is hard for him to see and smell and hear the truth that walks like a great buffalo before him. Some day he will find the buffalo and on that day he will also find wisdom. He is a good hunter and provider for my daughter. He still grieves very deeply for his family as I'm sure you grieve for yours."

He had not wanted to admit it in front of his tormenter. "There is truth in Kicking Bull's words. It was because of me that my village was killed by the Nokonis," Many Wolves confessed. "Laughing Crow killed them because I killed his son. I came back to try to warn my village, but I was too late."

"What did Walking Free say when you told him this?" sad Big Sky, without hesitation.

"He said that it wasn't my fault and that, in time, Laughing Crow would have killed my village anyway. He also said that it was his fault, too, for not being there when the Nokonis came."

Big Sky motioned for Many Wolves to sit with him, and the younger man accommodated his wish.

"Do you agree with his words?"

"Yes, I suppose so, but I feel that there is more that I should do. I do not have the powers of a shaman to pray as Walking Free does. What can I do?"

Big Sky sat awhile in silence, preoccupied with his thoughts. A soft breeze shifted a strand of his gray hair against his cheek with the rhythm of a drumbeat.

"Laughing Crow will not stop killing until he has found you. This much I know. So, you have two choices. You can hide from him, or you can fight with us."

"What if I surrender to him? Would that stop the killing?"

"You have suffered enough, Many Wolves, why would you want more suffering? A man does not willingly walk into fire," said Big Sky, his eyes filled with sympathy. "My people are not afraid to fight him. He will not surprise our village like he surprised the others. These great canyons around us add to our strength. He has killed my friends and my family too. He is not the only one who thirsts for vengeance."

In that moment, Many Wolves caught a brief glimpse of a fearless warrior, of a great leader, buried within the wrinkled skin of this man with the kind eyes. It was a spiritual gift awarded for a lifetime of bravery. It was a confidence gained by years of experience. *Walking Free has this presence too.*

"Many Wolves," said Big Sky. "We have a great advantage in this fight against Laughing Crow. We have the sweetest nectar that will draw in the hungriest of bees. We have you."

Eyes

Two women from Big Sky's village brought the cooked rabbit to Many Wolves just before sundown, but he decided not to eat it right away. He sat quietly at his secluded spot away from the village, but still within the protective canyon walls. His birds were perched in a nearby cottonwood tree, soaking in what was left of the day's sun. Rojo was laying low within sight of his camp. Many Wolves was reflecting on what he could do to help Big Sky and his people in their inevitable fight against the Nokonis. He had a plan in mind and it meant he would have to prepare by fasting.

As he waited for the peyote–white flower–mint tea mixture to boil, Many Wolves envisioned the journey he would take with Chiquito. His best guess was that Laughing Crow and his men were camped somewhere east of where he was and far enough away to be out of range of Big Sky's scouts. If it was possible to find them, it would be through Chiquito's eyes.

Many Wolves called Chiquito to his fist-perch and then drank the tea quickly as soon as it was cool enough not to burn his tongue. He winced from its bitter taste, as he always did, but he didn't vomit. He closed his eyes and became Chiquito.

Rising above the canyon walls and the valley below, he flew eastward past the narrow path he had taken earlier. He loved the exhilarating sensation of fast-flowing air on his face and the rhythmic pumping of Chiquito's wings on either side of him. He scanned the ground ahead of him to the east, looking for any kind of movement. He spotted rabbits, coyotes, and a wild pig. He also spotted four scouts on horseback from Big Sky's village. They were resting in the shade of the canyon enjoying a meal together.

He soared above the flatlands further east through desert landscapes and sporadic rock formations. He saw objects at great distances on either side of him as if they were close enough to touch. There was no sign of horses or other humans anywhere, only the movements of desert animals. The sun was falling slowly behind him. *I must find the Nokonis while there is still enough light.*

Further ahead, he spotted a river flowing from north to south. *If there are men with horses, they will need water.* He changed his direction to follow the windy river southward, and spotted plumes of smoke and horses grazing on the west side of the river. He moved closer to them, rising and falling on the wind currents. He could see men now, most of them resting in the shade of the trees that lined the riverbank. He estimated there were more than a hundred men gathered at the camp and over a hundred horses.

He circled above the camp to get a better look. Many of the horses were painted mustangs—the favored horses of the Nokonis. He spotted many men with black spots colored around their eyes and tattooed bodies. The men without black eyes were dressed well in deerskin with many fringes and beads, much like the two Northerners he had killed. As he studied them more carefully, he saw the same snake-like marking that Laughing Crow's son had on his body—some had it on their arms, others on their legs, and still others on their chest. It was the mark of the Nokonis. He wondered which one was Laughing Crow.

Two of the men were larger and more muscular than the others and they had very similar body shapes, distinct from the other men, but one was much younger—closer to his age. They looked like father and son. The older of the two men had many decorated markings on his powerful body. His black hair hung straight and low on his back and he had a braid on one side of his head. The hair on the other side of his head was cut short. He was standing under a tree by himself, grooming one of the painted horses, and next to him was a shield with a large black bird on it. *Laughing Crow. Chiquito, we must get back to the village and tell Big Sky.*

He pulled out of his circling pattern and directed Chiquito to fly westward back to the village. He sensed that Chiquito was still flying strong and had plenty of stamina left. The flight back would be quick and direct, now that he had accomplished what he set out to do. *The wind is behind us. We must get back before the light is gone.* He flew into the setting sun.

The heat of the day was passing. It was the most active time for the animals of the desert. Plant-eating animals were either searching for or devouring their last meal before the night forced them into their hideaways. Predators seized this opportunity to fill their guts with fresh meat to ensure a comfortable sleep, uninterrupted by the pangs of hunger. The hunting animals of the night were just waking from their daylight slumber, hungry, ready to search for prey. Many Wolves was intrigued by the world of predators and prey that thrived in the darkness. When the eagles and hawks finished hunting for the day, the owls took over for the night. There wasn't a single moment when prey was safe.

Chiquito, go to the right! Many Wolves spotted a horse hidden in the rocks of the canyon that had somehow avoided his earlier search. *A painted horse!* He directed Chiquito to fly closer and then he saw the men. There were two of them, talking to each other. Chiquito landed on a boulder above them, close enough to hear their conversation, but still hidden from plain sight. *They speak Northerner words.*

"I will need to rest if we are riding by the light of the moon," said the one on the left. When he moved his arm, Many Wolves could see the mark of the snake. "I should get back to my horse when it is dark enough. He will be thirsty."

"Where is your horse?"

"He's hidden in the canyons on the other side of the pass."

"I will signal you with the call of the coyote when it is time to return to the river camp," said the other. "Laughing Crow will be pleased to hear that the white-skin is here with the Lipans."

The one on the left laughed. "He may offer us his favorite wife for finding the white-skin!"

"...Or perhaps one of his favorite horses!" the other added, laughing.

"He would rather part with a wife!"

Both men laughed even louder at that, and the muscular one on the left grabbed the other's shoulder, affectionately. "So, let me guess. You've already eaten all your pemmican!"

"You know me well, Silent Weasel."

"Let me cut some pieces for you, so we can share a meal and a smoke before I leave."

Silent Weasel pulled out some strips of pemmican from a bag around his waist.

Then he walked over to a large, flat rock, slid a big steel knife from his leg sheath, and cut the pemmican into equal portions. Many Wolves was amazed by the size of his blade. He had never seen such a huge, shiny knife before. *That is a knife for killing men, not animals.*

Chiquito, you should get back to camp. Go southwest through that narrow path. I will see you when you return.

He opened his eyes. The empty drinking-shell was lying at his feet and the smell of cooked rabbit filled the air.

Heightened Senses

Many Wolves was starved from his mind-journey with Chiquito. He took a few bites of the cooked rabbit, which the women had seasoned with sage and salt—something his mother used to do. Usually after his mind-journeys, he ate ravenously, but this time it was different. He didn't want to gorge himself without knowing what he was going to do next.

Silent Weasel and the other Nokoni scout were going to ride back to Laughing Crow when the moon was high. They were going to tell him they had found his son's killer. They were going to tell him the location of Big Sky's camp and how many fighting men were there so Laughing Crow could plan his attack.

Many Wolves could not let that happen. He had to make sure the scouts did not make it back to Laughing Crow at all, but dusk was approaching and darkness would soon follow, like buzzards who follow the death-scent.

His thoughts scattered in many directions like a wind-blown hailstorm. *Should I tell Big Sky about the scouts and where they are? Would he believe me? How can I tell them that I saw these men and heard their words through the eyes and ears of a hawk? It would be more believable if I had some proof, like that big, shiny knife, but how do I climb those rocks without his horse sensing me? I know where one Northerner is, but where is Silent Weasel?*

Then a strange thought entered his mind. Rojo could find Silent Weasel in the dark. Rojo could sneak close enough to steal his knife or something else. He stopped eating. *Can I mind-journey with a wolf?*

As he thought about it more, he worried that Rojo was not yet his friend, one of his brothers, like Chiquito. Rojo had slept next to him on some nights and had even allowed him to stroke his thick, soft fur. But there was still a wildness in the red wolf. A part of Many Wolves did not want Rojo to lose this wildness, to be completely tame like Amarillo. He hoped someday Rojo would return to his pack, to his home in the high country. But that didn't matter now. He had to try the mind-journey with him. He had nothing to lose. Many Wolves filled his drinking-shell with water and set it in the low-flaming fire.

He pulled out the leftover, uncooked rabbit that he had saved for Rojo and cut off a sizable chunk with his knife. He whistled and tossed the meat towards Rojo who was watching him from a distance. The wolf's ears perked up and his head tilted sideways. Then he ambled over to the meat. He sniffed it and then grabbed it with his teeth, chewing only for a moment before bolting it down. He licked his mouth, and gave Many Wolves the look that said "mealtime." Many Wolves cut another piece and slung it about half the distance to where Rojo stood. "There you go, Rojo, eat up. We have a journey to take…together."

Many Wolves offered the wolf portions of meat until it was all gone and Rojo was standing next to him. He gently rubbed Rojo's fur and scratched his backside. "You love having your rump scratched, my wolf brother. Amarillo used to love it too." Rojo leaned his big, muscular body against his companion and then lay down beside him. Many Wolves added the peyote and the white lion's paw flower to the drinking-shell and waited for the steam to rise, all the while enjoying the warm company of his wolf brother.

When the tea was ready, Many Wolves drank it down quickly and felt the same cloud of nausea in his stomach. He rested his left arm on Rojo's back and closed his eyes. Colors, like blossoms of the dandelion, floated into his mind and then disappeared as if blown away by a strong breeze. More colors came and went and his mind seemed locked into this vision. He called Rojo's name, hoping, as with Chiquito, the colors would fade and he would see the world through the wolf's eyes. But nothing happened; he saw only more dizzying colors.

He breathed deeply, trying to relax. He focused on the sound of the wind blowing across his ears. The air seemed to rush in and out of his mind as if swirling inside a cave. The whistling sound was almost human, like a whisper, but the words were garbled. He called to Rojo again, but there was still nothing— only the whispering wind and the vibrant colors in his mind.

Many Wolves noticed the smells first. They grew stronger. The smells of the cooked rabbit, then the pungent aroma of sage and mesquite, then the odors from his body and Rojo's, all rushed at his senses. The smells of sage and mesquite were much more pronounced, whereas the subtle differences between Rojo's scent and his own were now in stark contrast to each other—as different as black and white. He could not recall such powerful smells in his mind-journey before.

Sounds were different too. He no longer focused on the whispering. Now, he could hear the cry of nighthawks and the hooting of owls, as if they were sitting next to him. He could hear the laughter of children and the voices of old men talking in Big Sky's village—a distance away.

In his mind, he called to Rojo a third time. The colors faded away and the world appeared around him. He saw the embers of his fire, the emptied cup, and himself sitting with his eyes closed. It was dark, but he saw details in the distance as if it were still daylight. "Rojo, we must find the Northerner scout, Silent Weasel."

Many Wolves walked with Rojo's legs. He heard the flight of a large horned owl before it flew past him. He had never heard their wingbeats before, only their gruff hooting calls. Though he was some distance from his camp, he still heard the popping embers of his dying fire.

His thoughts guided Rojo through the familiar passage between the two canyon walls, leaving the valley of Big Sky's village behind. Once past it, he turned right and ran northward along the edge of the canyon in the direction where he believed Silent Weasel was hiding. Sometimes, he stopped, awed by the intense clarity of the smells and sounds. The silence was blemished by crickets chirping in unison and the occasional rustling of a bush, an owl screeching, or a raccoon chittering. *Rojo, I understand why the Great Spirit has blessed you with these gifts of smell and hearing, so you can hunt and survive.*

Rojo ran to the north until he picked up a new scent. *A horse. We are getting close.* The horse left a scent trail in the air as clear and easy to follow as a plume of smoke from a cooking fire. The half-moonlight and Rojo's vision brought the feeling of dusk turning into nightfall. As the scent became stronger, Many Wolves slowed Rojo to a walk, looking for more clues of the Nokoni's presence. Up ahead, he saw a clump of large boulders stacked into a strange rock formation lying at the base of the canyon wall. Hidden among the small oak and mesquite that covered the lower rocks he spotted a painted horse standing motionless, asleep. *Not too close, Rojo.*

The red wolf walked the perimeter of the boulders and detected the unmistakable scent of human. He stalked slowly closer to the source—close enough to hear breathing. Rojo's padded feet were silent; no stone was rolled or branch broken. *There's the Northerner!* He saw the scout's feet; a clump of mesquite hid his body. Rojo circled to get a view of the man's face. Silent Weasel's eyes were closed. There was a small fire pit and a drinking cup lying next to him. The flames of the fire were scarcely higher than the burnt mesquite that fed them. Rojo looked around the camp, but he could not find the knife. *Silent Weasel must be wearing it.*

Suddenly, Silent Weasel leaped to his feet, his eyes wide open and blazing furiously, as he yelled a warrior's scream: "Yee-ahh!" In his right hand he brandished his large steel knife, which gleamed in the moonlight. Rojo's eyes narrowed, glued to the Northerner, and he growled continuously, refusing to back down or run away. *Be careful, Rojo. Watch the knife!*

"Get away, devil wolf, or I'll cut you to pieces!" threatened Silent Weasel, circling around Rojo with his legs spread and his knees bent for balance. He lunged at the wolf, trying to cut Rojo with the tip of the blade. *Back!* Rojo jumped back away from the whirring attack. The scout backed away too, retracting his blade, then started circling again.

Many Wolves weighed his options. Running away now would mean the scout would ride straight back to Laughing Crow. *We have to get the knife out of his hand, Rojo. After he thrusts his arm, we have to try to grab it before he can pull it back.*

Rojo uttered a low, steady growl as he stayed focused on the man's eyes and on the knife. Silent Weasel lunged at him and missed. Rojo watched the movement of the man's arm. Again the scout lunged and missed. Again, the wolf's sharp eyes studied the movement.

"Why do you attack me, red wolf? Run away before I hurt you," yelled Silent Weasel. "You don't run because you are cursed! You're a devil wolf!" He lunged again, but this time his attack was slower and weaker. Rojo charged at him after the blade flashed past him, and bit down hard on the man's right arm. Many Wolves heard the bone in Silent Weasel's arm snap. He yelled out in pain, dropped the knife, and punched

Rojo hard in the head with his left fist. Many Wolves could taste the blood.

Go for the throat, Rojo! Now! The powerful wolf leaped on the scout, his front paws digging into the man's chest. Silent Weasel fell back into the dirt, trying in vain to push the animal away. Frantically, he looked for the knife, but it was out of reach. Rojo's teeth tore at his unprotected throat, his jaws locked into the soft flesh. The scout shoved hard with his unbroken arm, but Rojo didn't budge. The ferocious wolf ripped the flesh from the Northerner's neck, unleashing a gush of blood that sprayed all over Rojo's face. Silent Weasel's dark eyes stared helplessly into Rojo's as he choked on his own blood and his body went limp. The blood oozed from his mouth, as the Nokoni scout took his final breath.

Many Wolves was stunned, not fully realizing what had just happened. He tasted the warm blood of the dead man and felt the heaving of Rojo's strained breathing. *Rojo, let's get back to camp!*

The wolf didn't move. He stood there, frozen, panting for a few moments. *What is it, Rojo?* Many Wolves didn't understand. It felt like the mind-journey medicine was wearing off. *It should last much longer than this!*

Suddenly, Rojo sprinted away, heading in the opposite direction from where he came. The plants, the trees, and the ground were all a blur as Rojo ran—faster than the full gallop of a horse. *Rojo, turn around!* The wolf kept running, not responding to the thoughts of his human brother. Many Wolves felt the cold chill of air rushing past his face and heard the panting breaths of the panicked wolf. He tried to calm the wolf, to make him stop, but Rojo just kept running further and further away. Finally, Many Wolves opened his eyes and everything was still and quiet.

Rojo was gone.

Gouge Out the Eyes

Many Wolves sat in his camp, sweat dripping down his face and hunger pangs jabbing at his stomach. *What happened to Rojo?* One moment the wolf was his spirit friend, and the next, a frightened stranger running away from him. Chiquito had never reacted that way. His spirit was always calm and responsive. *Is it because I forced him too quickly into a mind-journey, or because I asked him to kill?* Perhaps their bond of trust was not hardened yet and Rojo was still too wild and independent. He felt emptiness drift over his heart like a dark cloud covering the sun. His wolf was gone and it would be impossible to find him in the darkness.

His thoughts returned to the Northerner scouts. One of them was dead, unless of course his mind-journey with Rojo was just a dream. Although he didn't steal the knife as he had planned, the proof he needed was lying lifeless on the desert floor. The other scout, however, was still alive and would be signaling for his friend when the moon was high and bright.

Many Wolves pulled out some dried deer meat and began ripping it into bite-sized pieces. *I must tell Big Sky about the scouts and Laughing Crow's camp.* Soon, the moonlight would be at its fullest.

Many Wolves finished off his light meal, then rose to his feet and ran towards Big Sky's village. The dogs charged out of the village, barking. He slowed to a walk, not wanting to provoke their anger any further. Two warriors with lances ran towards him. He raised his hands high to show he had no weapons. "I am a friend of your village, and your leader, Big Sky. I need to speak with him."

"You are the white-skin that we heard about. Follow me, I will take you to him," said the larger one, who bore the tattoo of a tree on his chest. The dogs were barking wildly, watching the stranger's every move.

The two men led him through the village to a large tipi in the center. Several elders were gathered around a large fire in front of what he guessed was Big Sky's lodge.

"Wait here," instructed the larger warrior, motioning for Many Wolves to stop. Then, the warrior disappeared in the tipi and came back out with both Big Sky, and the leader's son, Little Sky.

"Many Wolves, what brings you to my lodge?" asked Big Sky; his drooping eyes made it appear as though he had just woken up. His body was wrapped in a beautiful buffalo robe, painted yellow and red with several decorative animal symbols.

"Laughing Crow and his men are not far from here, just over a half-day's ride to the east. There's a river there. He and his men are camped at it," said Many Wolves hurriedly, struggling to say the words between his heaving breaths.

"It is the Rio Colorado that you speak of," said Big Sky, his expression more alert now. "How do you know this?"

"I can't explain it right now. My bird has seen them and I have seen them. He is there. I saw his painted horse, his war shield, and the mark of the Nokonis on his skin. He is with many men, about a hundred of them, and many of them have dark eyes, like a raccoon or a badger."

"The Raccoon-Eyed men are the Wichitas. They regard us as their common enemy."

"Also, I have seen two of their scouts, not far from here, just outside your canyon walls. One of them is dead. He is

425

short and muscular and carries a large steel knife. His name is Silent Weasel."

"The one you speak of is one of Laughing Crow's finest scouts and one of his Blood Riders. We have heard many stories about this warrior who walks with the silence of the stalking mountain lion and carries a big knife. We call him 'Long Knife.' How do you know Long Knife is dead?"

The other elders gathered around them as Many Wolves and Big Sky spoke.

"Rojo, my wolf, killed him. His camp is along the canyon wall to the north in a little alcove made from piles of large boulders."

"I know of this place," interjected Little Sky. "It is called the Shelter of Stones. I used to hide there when I was a boy."

Many Wolves felt relieved to hear that he described a real place. Little Sky's memory of the place added truth to his words. "You will find his body there...and his painted horse."

"Little Sky, take four men and ride to the Shelter of Stones. Bring back what you find there," commanded their leader. Little Sky immediately ran off to find men to ride with him.

"There is another Nokoni scout," said Many Wolves. "You will find him south along the canyon wall, hidden in the rocks. I don't know his name, but he is taller and thinner than Silent Weasel. They seem to be friends." Other men from the village gathered around him as he spoke. Many Wolves recognized Kicking Bull among the men in the crowd and he was shaking his head as Many Wolves spoke, as if to say he doubted any of his words were true.

"That must be the one called 'Little Owl,'" said Big Sky. "He is also a Blood Rider and the scouting brother of Silent Weasel. I have heard stories of him as well."

"I heard these scouts talking about their plan to ride back to Laughing Crow's camp tonight by the light of the moon," said Many Wolves, still rushing with his words. "They have seen your village. We must stop him before he gets back to Laughing Crow!"

"How could *he* possibly have learned all of this in one night's time?" interrupted Kicking Bull. "How could he have discovered this ahead of our scouts?"

Big Sky turned to look at Kicking Bull. "There are few things that you understand about the mystical world, Kicking Bull. You only know what you can see with your eyes and feel with your hands. Beyond that, there is only silence, darkness, and mystery for you. In time, you will learn these things." Many of the other elders nodded their heads in agreement. Kicking Bull lowered his head from the embarrassment.

Big Sky looked at the large warrior who brought Many Wolves to him. "Falling Tree, take Kicking Bull and several other men and ride south along the outside canyon wall and search for this Nokoni scout. When you find him, kill him, and bring me back his scalp. Bury his body there after you cut his eyes out. Darkness is all he will see in the next world."

After the hunting party had left, Big Sky invited Many Wolves to sit by the newly revived fire with the elders.

"Many Wolves, we would like to hear your story while we wait for our men to return," said the village leader. "It is not often that a white-skinned stranger comes to our village, especially one who commands the birds and beasts of the desert."

Many Wolves told them how Laughing Crow had killed his white-skinned parents and how he was forced to run away from his village and his family. He described how he raised the three wolf hawks and taught them to hunt with him, and how one of them had died in the blizzard. He told the story of his fight with the great bear, Gray Face. He was careful with his words, however. He did not share the secrets of the white lion's paw flower and his mind-journeys. He also did not tell them about his friendship with Ten Arrows. *What would they think if they know I am friends with a Northerner?* He felt these things were better left unsaid.

The elders watched him with fascinated eyes. They did not interrupt to ask questions, but instead, urged him to continue. They wanted to hear everything about his life. The gathering reminded Many Wolves of the times he sat with his grandfather and Walking Free around his family's fire listening to their stories. He never imagined that he would have stories like theirs to tell, but here he was telling them as if he was an elder too.

Finally, Many Wolves told them about Rojo. He explained how he had watched Rojo's pack from a distance, and had killed Laughing Crow's son to protect them, and he had forged a friendship with the red wolf. He talked about how this was the first time he had killed men, and he didn't fully understand why he did it.

"Why did you leave the mountains?" asked Big Sky, at last.

Many Wolves did not answer immediately. He did not want to tell them that Ten Arrows had warned him. He had to invent an answer, a lie. "I was scared and I wanted to get away from that place where I killed the Northerners. I wanted to go far away, so I decided to come back home. That's when I found my family, all of them dead, and the village destroyed. The only one left alive was Walking Free."

As he was describing his visit with Walking Free, dogs began to bark. Followed closed behind were the whoops of men and the drumming of their horses hooves.

"Little Sky has returned," announced Big Sky.

Five men, led by Little Sky, arrived at Big Sky's lodge with a sixth horse following them. It looked like a body was draped over its back. Little Sky dismounted, carrying a lance with a scalp hung on the end of it.

"We have found Long Knife, Father. He is dead," said Little Sky, breathing hard. "His throat was ripped apart by a large animal. I believe it was a wolf, just as Many Wolves said. Everything was just as he said it would be."

"I had no doubt what you would find, my son," said Big Sky, looking at Many Wolves with a smile and a nod.

Little Sky pulled something out of his saddlebag and handed it to Many Wolves, who recognized it immediately as Silent Weasel's knife, now returned to its sheath. "Take this, Many Wolves. You killed Long Knife, so his prized weapon belongs to you." Many Wolves took the weapon and then Little Sky grabbed his arm affectionately and squeezed it as the other warriors cheered from atop their horses. *This really belongs to you, Rojo.*

Then, Little Sky pulled the scalp off his lance and offered it to Many Wolves. "This is yours also."

"I do not want his scalp," said Many Wolves. "It does not carry the same meaning for me as it does for you and your people." He thought for a moment at what he had said. He had always wanted to be Lipan, in every way, but at this moment he felt like he was not. He felt his beliefs were somehow different than theirs. He remembered stories from his father and grandfather telling about the taking of scalps. Their words seemed so distant now.

"I will keep it for you, Many Wolves. In my eyes and in the eyes of everyone here, it is your scalp and not mine," said Little Sky, as he stuck the scalp back on his lance.

"To have the scalp of Long Knife hanging from one of our lances is a great victory for our village and to all those who are the enemies of the Nokonis," said Big Sky, raising his voice to the men who had gathered around. "Long Knife has killed many men and for years he has been the eyes and ears of Laughing Crow. To have gouged out the eyes of the Nokonis is a great blow to them."

"We should attack them now, Father. We know where their camp is and they won't be expecting us," said Little Sky, looking around for agreement from the others.

"We will wait for Falling Tree to return with the scalp of the other Nokoni scout. Then we will make our war plans," said the old leader. "Attacking them near the Rio Colorado, where most of the land is flat and open, will be very difficult and it requires careful planning."

"What if you could attack him here, surrounded by these walls?" said Many Wolves, an idea blossoming in his mind. "Your horses would be rested and you would be fighting on lands that are familiar to you."

"Why would they come here, Many Wolves? They don't know this is our home," said Little Sky.

"Big Sky, you once said I was the nectar that could draw in the Nokonis," said Many Wolves, looking into the leader's wise eyes. "I have a plan that will lure Laughing Crow and his men to your village, but I will need your help and I will need Silent Weasel's scalp."

The Cursed Messenger

"*Ahpu*, come look at this," said Thorn Bird, urging Laughing Crow to follow him as he pointed to the sky.

His father rested beneath a weeping willow, trying to find shade from the late-morning sun. A refreshing mist from the Rio Colorado was spraying on his back. The Nokoni leader stood up and saw a large bird circling above him in the pale blue sky, surrounded by a few scattered clouds. The bird grasped something hairy and black in its talons.

"It just keeps circling, as if it's waiting for something," said Thorn Bird. "I do not understand why it does not land in a tree and eat its meal."

The hawk circled lower. It was watching them. Laughing Crow had never seen such boldness in a hawk before. Usually they kept clear of people. It was acting more like a crow than a hawk. It was close enough now that he could see the blood-red coloration on its shoulders and the white patch on the base of its tail. He had seen these birds before. Most times they were sitting with their own kind on the tops of trees or cacti. The two Nokonis just stood and watched with their hands raised to their eyes to shield against the glaring sun.

Laughing Crow looked closer at the object it was carrying. It was a mass of black hair, which didn't look like any animal he had ever seen. It glistened with the reddish color of flesh.

As the hawk circled even closer, he spotted flashes of brighter colors entwined within the hair that looked like small red, yellow, and green stones. Two thicker clumps of hair dangled from the object.

Then the bird screeched a raspy cry and dropped the object right at the feet of the two men. Laughing Crow instantly saw that the small, colored stones were beads and the dangling clumps of hair were braids. It was a scalp—a *Noomah* scalp—the scalp of his finest scout. A tingling fear rushed through his body. *Silent Weasel is dead.*

"No!" he yelled from the deepest pit of his stomach. He shouted up at the bird, which was still circling, rising above him. "What is this magic? What is this cursed messenger that carries death in its feet?" He picked up the crumpled scalp and ran his hands through the tangled strands of hair, bound together with dried blood, and then he raised it to the sky. "Who has done this? Kill that bird!"

The men hesitated and before any of the men could raise a bow or a gun, the bird was gone. It disappeared over the towering mesa west of the camp. *They are afraid to kill this devil bird.*

"Thorn Bird, bring Smoke Cloud to me… *Now!*" barked Laughing Crow. *Have the Navoonah found Silent Weasel and killed him? Where is Little Owl? Is he still alive?* He covered his eyes with his bloodstained hands as the unforgiving sun beat down on him. If he could kill this reality, he would stab it a thousand times with his lance and bury it deep in the desert sand. He had to avenge his friend's death. He had to find Silent Weasel's killer.

Suddenly, a voice echoed over the camp. "Laughing Crow!"

The Nokoni leader looked around his camp as if hearing a gunshot. It was a voice unfamiliar to him. He heard it again.

"Laughing Crow! Follow the bird's path and you will see me!"

The Nokoni headman looked up towards the rocky cliffs where the bird had disappeared and saw a man sitting on a horse at the edge of them. *Who is this man who can turn himself into a bird?*

"I am the one who killed your son and your scout, just as you killed my village!" shouted the crackling voice. "My name is Many Wolves! I am the one you want! Come and get me!"

Laughing Crow watched as the one who killed his son, the one he had been searching for in vain, disappeared behind the bluffs.

"Laughing Crow, what is it?" said Smoke Cloud, approaching him from behind. Mocking Bird translated the Wichita leader's question.

"Did you see him? The man who was shouting from that cliff?" Agitated, Laughing Crow pointed to the spot where his tormenter had called to him.

"I heard him, but did not see him."

"He is the one we want. We kill him and this war is over!" said Laughing Crow, gritting his teeth. "Instruct your men that we will ride now and follow his path! Tell them that the one who brings this killer to me will be rewarded with ten of my best horses!"

"But, we must wait for our supplies," Smoke Cloud said, hesitating. "My men will be returning with metal balls and black powder for our long guns. They will be here after we sleep tonight."

"Do you see this?" Laughing Crow showed the scalp to the Wichita leader. "This is the scalp of my finest scout and one of my bravest warriors. This…Many Wolves…has killed him too!" Laughing Crow spat in disgust and then grabbed Smoke Cloud by a braid of hair and pulled his face to his. "We will leave, now!" Laughing Crow turned to his translator. "Make sure he understands every word!"

The angered headman pushed Smoke Cloud aside and yelled to his men, "Nokoni warriors! Gather your weapons and your horses. We will follow the trail of this white-skinned dog until we find him. I want him alive. He must feel a thousand pains before he dies!" Then, he turned to his son and said, "Thorn Bird, we have lost one of our best. I need you to ride out ahead of us and find this dog's tracks. Go now!"

Thorn Bird grabbed his weapons and mounted his horse. "His scent will not escape me, *Ahpu*."

Sweet Nectar

L aughing Crow pulled his horse out of a full gallop just in front of Thorn Bird who was waiting at the bank of a creek. Ahead of the rest of the party, Thorn Bird had found the tracks of Many Wolves's horse and followed them to this first water crossing. Now, Laughing Crow and the others were arriving from a hard ride in the morning sun.

"He crossed the stream just south of here. He's not far ahead of us," said Thorn Bird, pointing to a spot on the other side of the rippling water. The creek was as wide as six horses, and at its deepest point, as high as a man's chest. It wouldn't be difficult for the horses to cross. "I will continue to chase him. The distance between us is closing fast and he will not outrun me with a tired horse between his legs." Thorn Bird's manner was confident and determined.

"Good. He was foolish to show himself. His magic will not save his white skin," said Laughing Crow, catching his breath. He dismounted and led Cheval-Sang to the creek's edge for water.

"We wish to ride with Thorn Bird," said one of the Raccoon-Eyed warriors who had just arrived with two others from his band. He spoke the *Noomah* words with much more skill than most of the other Wichitas. "We want an equal chance to capture the white-skin. Our horses will only need a short rest."

"Take them with you, Thorn Bird," said Laughing Crow.

"They can come, but I will not wait for them if they fall behind."

"It is safer if you take them in case this white-skin has more tricks for us," said Laughing Crow.

"Your wish to spare his life, *Ahpu*, is the only thing that will keep my knife from his throat," said Thorn Bird, staring into his father's eyes, before riding away with six warriors following close behind, three of them Wichitas.

Soon after, Smoke Cloud joined Laughing Crow with the rest of his men.

The Nokoni leader spoke to Mocking Bird. "Tell Smoke Cloud we will rest and water the horses here for a short time. Thorn Bird and three of his men will find this white-skinned dog." He turned and led his horse to the shade of a nearby cottonwood tree.

Laughing Crow felt confident that Thorn Bird would find and capture the one who had killed his full-blooded son and his scout. He looked forward to looking into the eyes of this white-skinned coward. To kill his son was one thing, but to taunt him in front of his men was unforgivable. In a daydream once, he had imagined presenting the still-beating heart of this coward to Sun Sparrow as medicine to ease her misery. He felt he was getting closer to making this dream real.

It was wise to rest the horses, so the men would be ready for any surprises they might find in the desert badlands, thought Laughing Crow. These were *Navoonah* lands, and the presence of his large war party may have been noticed by more than just this white-skin. There were risks to this hasty, unprepared pursuit, but the rewards were worth it. To kill the largest buffalo on the plains or to rip the scalp from the greatest *Navoonah* leader could not compare to the joy of watching this Many Wolves suffer. Though Laughing Crow's blood was boiling, he still felt confident. *Soon, it will be over.*

After he rested, he rose to his feet and shouted to his men, "Nokoni warriors, we will ride now! Mocking Bird, tell Smoke Cloud there is no more time to waste. Tell him they can ride with us if their horses are rested." Then he rode off, following the distant dust cloud left by his son and the men with him.

Laughing Crow pushed his war horse hard through the barren landscape until he caught up to Thorn Bird who was waiting for him on the eastern slope of a rolling hill. All seven men were standing near their horses.

"I see him down there. He's resting under a large shrub oak tree." Thorn Bird motioned for his father to get off his horse and follow him to the crest of the hill. "Do you see him?"

"No."

"Do you see that large rock? Move your eyes to the left and look for the oak."

"Yes, I see him, but he's still far away. How long do you think he's been there?"

"I don't think the dust from his horse has had long to settle."

Three more Nokoni riders joined their group as the Nokoni headman pondered the situation.

He wondered why the white-skin had stopped and why he had not chosen a better place to hide. Perhaps he was too tired or hungry to go on or perhaps he thought they wouldn't find him so quickly. Either way, it was a deadly mistake. *He will not be able to escape us.*

"Thorn Bird, are you ready to seize our prize?" said the father, smiling at his oldest son.

Thorn Bird nodded with a big grin, his white teeth a sharp contrast to the dark skin of his dirty, sweaty face.

Father and son hoisted themselves onto their war horses and led the other men off the crest of the hill. The horses grunted and snorted, preparing themselves for the sprint they knew was coming. The moment had come.

"Remember, ten horses for his capture. I want him alive!" snapped Laughing Crow.

Led by the screams of their leader, the riders charged down the hill, whooping with excitement. The heavy hooves of their horses dug into the earth, spraying clouds of spattered dirt and loose brush behind them. The scattered sage of the desert floor quickly blurred under the feet of his swift mustang. Laughing Crow made sure to stay in front, keeping the dust of the other men's horses from obscuring his vision. He wanted nothing to cut between his eyes and his most precious target.

Seeing the oncoming rush, Many Wolves leaped to his horse and dashed from his resting place like a startled rabbit. Laughing Crow yelled and pointed at the flushed quarry to signal the men that there was a change in his heading. He was surprised that a white-skin could ride so well. But, still, they were closing in with every stride.

Ahead of his target, Laughing Crow saw two towering rock formations with a wide path between them. *So, you think you will be safe there.*

Though he knew that Cheval-Sang was tired, his horse gave him everything he had—every last bit of his strength—as if sensing the urgency. In moments like these, Laughing Crow believed that he and his horse were one spirit. The blood from his thoughts ran through the powerful legs of his stallion.

The eight men followed their prey through the gap between the towering rocks. Laughing Crow, followed closely by Thorn Bird, was now within weapon range, but he did not want to shoot, knowing it would be safer to separate the white-skin from his horse with the butt of his axe. He was so close now that the dust between them had no time to rest.

Suddenly, from behind Laughing Crow's right ear, came the wheezing sound of an arrow as it carved through the thick desert air. It struck Many Wolves squarely on the upper

PUHA

right leg. He screamed in pain and fell off his horse. His body crashed to the earth and rolled through the dust as his horse continued to gallop away without him.

Laughing Crow pulled Cheval-Sang up to the motionless body. He feared that the rewards of torture had been stolen from him. Thorn Bird leaped from his slowed horse for a closer look at the white-skin, feeling his chest for signs of life. "He's alive, *Ahpu.*" The other riders were now gathered around.

Relieved, Laughing Crow looked at his men and bellowed, "Who shot the arrow?"

"It was me." The voice came from the Raccoon-Eyed warrior who spoke the *Noomah* words.

"Why? If I wanted to put an arrow in him, I would have done it myself!" the Nokoni headman blurted out as he rode over to face the Wichita warrior.

"Our horses were tiring and I did not want him to escape," said the warrior, pleading for the leader's acceptance.

"You could see my horse was not tiring! It was your greed that fired the arrow. You could have easily put an arrow through his chest!" With his right hand, Laughing Crow grabbed his war axe by the neck and swung the handle at the man's head, knocking him off his horse. Laughing Crow yelled down at his betrayer, "If he dies, then you will suffer his torture." Turning to his son, he asked, "How bad is the wound on his leg?"

"The arrow did not cut deep."

"Good. Pull it out and wrap the wound. He must be well enough to travel. Tie him tightly to his own horse."

Thorn Bird removed the quiver from Many Wolves's back and unstrapped his leg sheath, then handed them to his father. "This is Silent Weasel's knife."

The war party leader pulled the knife out of its casing and examined it. "I have not seen many others like it." He strapped it to his left leg so that he had one on either side.

Then he looked at the bows inside the quiver, pulled out a familiar black bow, and handed it to Thorn Bird. "Take your brother's bow. I'll keep the rest with me."

Laughing Crow looked down at Many Wolves and breathed a sigh of relief. His long journey was nearly at an end. He could return home now with his son's killer. He ran his hand through his shortened hair and muttered to himself. "My son, this white-skinned dog will spend the rest of this life and the next begging for mercy."

Grim Totems

The rest of the war party arrived at the scene and greeted Laughing Crow with cries of celebration when they saw his prize.

Many Wolves was slumped over backwards on a horse, tied securely to it, with his hands and feet bound with braided horsehair. He was awake now, but appeared disoriented from the fall. Smoke Cloud rode up closer to inspect the captive. "He doesn't look like much of a warrior—more like a half-starved coyote." Looking up, Smoke Cloud added, "See how the buzzards are already circling him."

"Those are not buzzards," interrupted Thorn Bird, after hearing Mocking Bird's translation. "They are blood-winged hawks—his magic birds—and they follow him now like buzzards hoping to gorge on his carcass and pick his bones clean." Thorn Bird laughed and the rest of the Nokoni men joined in.

Laughing Crow grinned. The thought of feeding the white-skin to the magic birds was very agreeable to him.

The lightness of the moment was lost when one of the Raccoon-Eyed men returned hastily from scouting the surrounding area. Laughing Crow watched him speak to Mocking Bird with raised tones and hand gestures. He sensed it was something important, so he rode over. "What does he say, Mocking Bird?"

"He says there are two bodies tied to yucca trees just west of here. You can't see them from here because of the sun," said Mocking Bird. The sun was low on the horizon, making it hard to see anything in that direction. "He thinks they are our scouts, Silent Weasel and Little Owl, but he isn't sure."

"Mocking Bird, bring the white-skin and tell Smoke Cloud to follow." Laughing Crow rode off and motioned for Thorn Bird and the rest of the Nokonis to follow him.

The war party rode into the blinding sun. The high rocky ridges on either side of them funneled the sun's rays even more intensely. The scattered cactus trees, caught in a brilliant haze, were stripped of all detail apart from their outlines. Eventually, Laughing Crow spotted the two trees and approached the one on the left.

The leader found Little Owl's body tied to its trunk, the yucca palms stripped away from it, leaving it bare. His dead scout wore only a breechcloth and his body was covered in dried blood. His eyes and his scalp had been plucked and there were small knife-sized cuts all over his body. *His death was a slow, painful one.* "*Navoonah* dogs! You will pay for this! Your white brother will suffer a thousand pains greater than this!"

He rode a short distance to the other tree and found Silent Weasel's body. His eyes and scalp were also cut out, but he was not tortured with knives. Laughing Crow saw that his throat was torn, not cut by a knife or any other weapon. Pointing, he asked Thorn Bird, "What do you think did this?"

"It looks like he was bitten by a large dog or wolf. I don't see any other wounds on his body. It is similar to the wound that killed my brother's friend."

"It is strange that two of our men died this way, Thorn Bird. Wolves are not killers of men—they are more like scavengers—and I've never seen a dog this big. And how did this white-skin collect his scalp? Was he dead already?" Laughing Crow was trying to make sense of things that seemed impossible.

"I do not know, *Ahpu*. If it was a large wolf, it was much bigger than the wolves and coyotes that roam the desert."

Looking over at Many Wolves, Laughing Crow snarled, "The blade of my knife will cut the truth out of him."

Thorn Bird nodded.

"Laughing Crow, we are being watched," said Mocking Bird, pointing his lance to the west. "Look!"

The leader looked to see the silhouettes of eight riders appear from out of the haze, watching them, just outside the range of their arrows. *Navoonah.*

"Is it a trap?" asked Mocking Bird.

"I don't know. We have ten riders to their one, though it is difficult to see if there are more men behind them. I do not like riding into war with the sun scorching my eyes, even if the numbers weigh heavily in our favor, especially against an enemy with skilled warriors. Maybe they wanted to see our reaction and are ready to run from us like frightened rabbits."

"We could send Smoke Cloud's men as the first line. Promise them the spoils of war and a reward for every scalp," said Thorn Bird.

Laughing Crow considered the idea. He didn't like their position, and he didn't like being surrounded by steep cliffs in every direction. The only escape was the narrow passage where they had entered. He looked carefully all around him, but there were no other signs of life and there were very few places where men on horseback could hide. He sensed there was little fight left in Smoke Cloud and the Wichitas—they were low on supplies and ready to go home. He would have to motivate them to continue this war and he couldn't prolong the effort into the night or the next day without risking their retreat. It gnawed at him, however, that the *Navoonah* dogs were so close, nearly in range of his weapons, and that they were taunting him with grim totems made from the bodies of his scouts.

"Mocking Bird, tell Smoke Cloud that I will offer his men a horse for every *Navoonah* scalp they take. He knows that my words do not bend like the wind. We will lead the charge, and his men will follow in a wide line behind us."

Mocking Bird rode over to Smoke Cloud, carrying Laughing Crow's offer on his tongue. As he waited for a response, the Nokoni leader watched the enemy riders, who had not moved. *What are they waiting for?* He grew even more suspicious that it was a trick of some kind.

The messenger rode back and said, "Smoke Cloud has agreed to your offer, but he wants *his* men to lead the charge. He wants them to have the reward of leading the attack—not us—and, of course, the reward of horses."

This was the same plan that Thorn Bird proposed, and the more Laughing Crow thought about, the more he liked it. Let the Raccoon-Eyed warriors shield his men from the *Navoonah* arrows this time. If there are only eight scalps taken, he could spare the eight horses. The lives of his men were far more precious. "Tell him that we agree to his terms. We will follow his lead and the first wave of attacks will be from the Raccoon-Eyes. Mocking Bird, I will need you to stay back and watch the white-skin. Keep your horse tied to his and make sure you keep him out of danger."

Smoke Cloud ordered his men to spread out in a line, and then sent a small group of riders to the far right and another to the far left. Once all the men were in position, they began to walk their mounts towards the enemy. Smoke Cloud's voice was the only one heard as they moved forward. A line of fourteen Nokonis, with Laughing Crow and Thorn Bird at the center, fell in behind them. Seeing the Raccoon-Eyes, the *Navoonah* riders began to recede. Laughing Crow expected them to bolt at any moment, but they continued to retreat, slowly. This deliberate pursuit continued for several moments until Smoke Cloud broke his horse into a gallop, leading his men in the charge. Their movements were immediately mimicked by the enemy.

After reaching full stride, one of the *Navoonah* riders yelled a command and the others turned to face the Wichitas, uttering their cries of war. Hearing the call of their leader, other *Navoonah* warriors rose from the dusty earth where they had buried themselves like horned toads, while still others appeared from behind bushes or boulders. Like a throng of ants awakened by the floodwaters of a thunderstorm, they poured out in every direction from their hiding places, screaming for blood. The ones with bows fired on the Wichitas, knocking down many of their horses so others with tomahawks and lances could finish off their riders. The Raccoon-Eyed warriors returned fire with booming blasts from their long guns or whistling arrows. Without a quick reload, the men with long guns tried to retreat from the swarms of *Navoonah*, but many were shot or thrown from injured, screaming horses.

Through a cloud of flailing dirt and spattering blood, Laughing Crow unleashed a chain of arrows at the dust-covered attackers, knocking down three and trampling a fourth with the hooves of his horse. He grabbed a handful of arrows for his next foray when he saw another group of *Navoonah* riders come into view, led by the long shadows of their horses. He realized that many of Smoke Cloud's men had fallen and some had begun to retreat. *We are badly outnumbered.*

Doubts dug into Laughing Crow's mind like thorns. A better leader would have sensed the trap. A better leader would not have led his warriors into a strange land—the death-pit of his enemy—without war paint to protect their faces and the hides of their horses. A better leader would not have let himself be blinded by the sun and by revenge. All that didn't matter now. He had to save himself and hope that his men could do the same.

Laughing Crow raised his eagle whistle to his mouth and blew loudly, then he yelled, "Nokonis! Follow me!" He guided Cheval-Sang to a swift turnaround and headed off, his back to the enemy and the treacherous sun. As he looked to either side, he saw Thorn Bird and the other Nokoni men riding for their lives as the arrows whistled past them. The world seemed slower now, sensing his vulnerability, and Laughing Crow felt like he was riding into a numbing headwind. For added protection, he slipped his shield over his back and let it hang over his quiver. To his left, an arrow ripped through the back of one of his men, severing the grip he had on his horse and throwing him to the ground, leaving him like a crippled grasshopper to be engulfed by the horde of stinging ants.

Ahead Laughing Crow spotted Mocking Bird waiting, still holding the lead of the horse, as he was told. The leader slowed his horse and spoke, "Mocking Bird, let me take him. We need to get out of here. Your chances will be better without having to bear this burden. Ride east to the Rio Colorado. Go!"

Laughing Crow looked back to see that his pursuers had stopped momentarily as one of them directed who should stay and who should follow the Nokonis. A smaller group, which didn't include the leader, rekindled the pursuit, but the reprieve provided Laughing Crow and his men a margin of safety. He beckoned his horse to a gallop then directed the six other surviving Nokonis to follow Mocking Bird out of the valley and east towards their camp at the Rio Colorado. It would be difficult to outrun his chasers, whose horses were more rested, or to hide in this barren terrain, which was their home. He had to figure out a plan to fight them—a plan that secured the survival of his men.

The Water's Edge

Laughing Crow, still bearing the load of his white-skinned captive, caught up to Mocking Bird and the rest of his men at the same creek they had stopped at on their westward journey. Seven Nokoni had survived the *Navoonah* ambush. Their horses had labored hard to bring them to this point and now they needed rest and water. The *Navoonah* war party still followed them, but had relented some from their earlier pursuit. *Perhaps they thought we would be easy to catch.* Laughing Crow knew that the painted horses of the Nokoni were bred not only for endurance, but for the ability to survive on a meager amount of food and water. "Don't let them drink too much of it! We will need to ride them again soon."

As his men and horses continued to drink, their leader quickly dismounted and walked towards the middle of the creek. After several steps, he was engulfed in slow-moving, waist-high water. His moccasins sunk deep into the sludgy bottom, the mud swallowing every step. He looked up at the sloping banks on either side. The leader called to Thorn Bird, who was still sitting on his horse. "Cross the creek."

As his son trudged through the water, Laughing Crow watched closely, calculating how many heartbeats it took for him to reach the other side. This was the edge he was looking for. He walked back to Cheval-Sang and remounted, then summoned his men to follow Thorn Bird to the east side of the creek.

Dusk crept into the landscape like a silent, slithering snake. Laughing Crow knew he couldn't wait for nightfall because then the *Navoonah*, who knew these lands, would have the advantage. He looked at the faces of his men, painted with dust and sweat, who were gathered around him at the edge of the creek. Though they were tired, he knew they were the bravest warriors on the plains and he had every confidence in their abilities, even without his two scouts. He promised himself that he would not make another mistake that would barter their lives so cheaply.

"Mocking Bird, take the white-skin away from here," said the leader. The lean warrior did as he was instructed and rode off eastward with the captive and his horse while the rest of the men remained.

"Nokoni warriors, I am tired of running from these *Navoonah* dogs," said Laughing Crow, his voice strong and confident. "This creek will be their grave. We will lure them into it and then bury them with our arrows from higher ground. The mud will cripple their horses and make them easy targets. When we are done, this creek will flow red with *Navoonah* blood and the blood of our fallen brothers will be repaid. Stay low and wait for my signal." Laughing Crow saw the flicker of fire in their eyes as he revealed his plan. They nodded and banged their shields with their hands to acknowledge his command.

Laughing Crow rode up the incline of the creek bank and stopped where it leveled off. He cast his eyes west towards the red sun, which had been sliced in half by the earth. He spotted his pursuers and estimated that their numbers were almost twice as strong as his. Their ghostly outlines rode at a steady canter. When they saw him, they yelped with excitement and urged their horses to press harder. He felt his heart pump faster and the strength of the Thunder-Bird rising up inside him.

The Nokoni leader motioned to his men. They mounted and bolted past him while he watched the incoming invasion. Several moments passed, then he signaled Cheval-Sang to retreat and follow his men. He grabbed the shield from his back and slipped its leather strap over his left forearm, then pulled five arrows from his quiver. He loaded one, and held the others in his right hand. He looked back over his shoulder. He saw his pursuers drawing closer and closer to the crossing, to the water's edge, to the trap.

The blast of his eagle whistle rang through the desert air like a lone coyote's call in a vacant canyon. He halted his war horse and spun around to face his attackers, and his men followed his lead. He guided Cheval-Sang to sprint towards his chasers and heard the chorus of friendly hooves trailing him, closing the distance. He saw several of his enemies lower themselves into the watery trench. His men were nipping at his tail now, their bows drawn. Each man knew where his lethal range began and waited for it.

Laughing Crow and Thorn Bird launched the first assault, aiming at targets that had not yet reached the water. Laughing Crow's arrow dug into the shield of his enemy while his son's arrow cut into the leg of another rider. Thorn Bird's target bent down to check his wound, momentarily lowering his shield and leaving his chest exposed long enough for Thorn Bird's fatal arrow to strike. Laughing Crow then whistled an arrow directly into the throat of his target's horse, slamming them both to the ground just shy of the water. The *Navoonah* warrior lay helplessly trapped by the weight of his horse as blood from its mouth spilled over the man's chest. Laughing Crow launched another arrow across the creek, past the screaming horse, and into the stomach of the fallen warrior.

The Nokonis advanced the assault with a volley of whizzing arrows. They found their mark on many of the half-submerged riders, whose panicked horses were hobbled by the sludgy ditch. The *Navoonah* struggled to balance on their thrashing horses and were scarcely able to mount an effective counter-attack. Like crippled buffalo, they were easy prey for the merciless men who hunted them from above. The sounds of splashing, wailing horses and dying men lit the silence of twilight like a bonfire. One after another, the *Navoonah* men succumbed to the bruising kicks of their frantic horses and the numerous *Noomah* arrows, which tore through their bare-chested bodies. Some of the horses that survived gained their footing, pulled their wet, dripping hides out of the water, and left the dead or dying to stain the silty waters red with blood.

Once the fighting had stopped, the victorious Nokoni lifted their war-whoops to the sky. Only Thunder Voice was injured in the skirmish. He nodded to his leader to indicate his injury was not serious. The other four, besides Thunder Voice and Laughing Crow, climbed down from their horses, knives in hand, ready to silence the injured and claim the scalps they had earned. Laughing Crow had killed at least four himself and Thorn Bird three.

Suddenly, from the bloodied, corpse-filled water rose the largest of the *Navoonah* warriors. He aimed his dripping bow at Laughing Crow and released. The arrow missed the leader but struck Cheval-Sang in the leg. The horse cried out and bucked, but Laughing Crow held his balance. Frustrated, the warrior hurled his bow into the water and pulled his knife from his sheath, yelling threatening words at Laughing Crow.

Thorn Bird loaded his bow, but his father stopped him. "No! He has challenged me. I will let him have his dying wish."

Laughing Crow carefully got off his distraught horse and drew Silent Weasel's knife from his leg sheath. *It will feel good to kill him with this.* He placed his bow in his quiver and strapped it, along with his war shield, on Cheval-Sang, then walked towards his challenger.

The *Navoonah* warrior was as big as him and very powerfully built. His dripping body was mapped with muscle and his chest was marked with a tattoo of a tree. He waded to the middle of the creek and waited for Laughing Crow to come to him, still taunting him with his words.

The light was being pushed slowly down by darkness as the Nokoni leader entered the water, stained by the blood of his enemies. His gaze swung between his opponent's eyes and the knife the warrior brandished in his right hand. *The man's eyes are not tainted by fear.*

The waist-high water stole any hope of quickness for either fighter. They were just over an arm's length apart as they began to circle each other. The *Navoonah* swiped his blade at Laughing Crow's chest several times and then quickly retracted it as the Nokoni backed away, avoiding each thrust. He did not retaliate, but waited for just the right moment to strike. His enemy drew his knife above Laughing Crow's head and lunged downward at his left shoulder, but Laughing Crow was able to slow the attack by grabbing the *Navoonah's* forearm. For several heartbeats, the two men teetered, matched in strength. Then Laughing Crow bore down on the man's arm with his knife and stabbed him squarely on the inner elbow. The *Navoonah* couldn't stop the attack with his free hand and he yelled as he watched in disbelief as the blood spurted from his arm. Laughing Crow withdrew his weapon, shook the knife from his opponent's weakened hand, and watched it tumble to the bottom of the creek.

Knowing he had the advantage he was looking for, Laughing Crow slid his scout's knife back into his leg sheath. Each man reached for the other man's neck with their left hand, but Laughing Crow was able to deaden the *Navoonah's* choke hold by grabbing his wrist with his right hand. His assailant's injured right arm hung uselessly at his side and he could not fight off the Nokoni's death grip. The *Navoonah* warrior's attempts to kick Laughing Crow were muted by the water and the thick, muddy creek bottom.

With his opponent in an unbreakable hold, Laughing Crow threw the man off his feet and leaned down towards his bulging eyes. "This is your last breath, tree warrior!" Then he lowered the *Navoonah*'s head into the water. The man thrashed about like a fish without water, trying in vain to kick or pull himself free, but Laughing Crow held his grip steady as the water splashed in his face. The man's kicks were powerful enough to jolt him, but not enough to shake his foothold. He held on and waited for the struggle to float out of the man's body. The Nokoni leader watched as the *Navoonah*'s mouth gasped for the life-giving air that only his left hand could reach. The last flicker of life drained from the tree warrior's eyes and then it was gone. *Another warrior soul taken.*

Laughing Crow grabbed his victim by the hair and sliced off his scalp with his friend's knife. He lifted the soaking scalp to the darkening sky, feeling his enemy's warm blood run down his arm and yelled "Aaa-hey" to claim his victory.

"*Ahpu*, you have shown once again that no man can kill you," said Thorn Bird, grabbing the head of a dead *Navoonah* and severing his scalp. "Aaa-hey!"

The *Noomah* warriors screamed in unison to hail their leader and to celebrate a great victory over their hated enemy. Scalps were taken and raised to the sky to proclaim bravery, and honor the warriors who had fallen. Laughing Crow held four scalps, two in each hand. *Silent Weasel and Little Owl, your brave deeds will never be forgotten. Live strong in the next world, my friends, my Invisible Ones, my Blood Riders.*

When he was finished gathering his scalps, the Nokoni headman walked over to his horse to inspect the leg wound. Cheval-Sang was holding his rear leg off the ground. He yelled to Mocking Bird who had returned to the party and was still guarding Many Wolves. "How is our captive?"

"He's weak and drifting in and out of awareness. He will mend."

"Good. I need you to take care of Cheval-Sang."

When Mocking Bird had his medicines ready, Laughing Crow quickly wrenched the arrow out of his horse's bleeding leg, causing it to gush. The horse stirred and cried out in pain as Mocking Bird cleaned the wound and then slowed the bleeding with a strip of rawhide. "The wound isn't deep. With rest, he should heal fully in a few sleeps."

Laughing Crow was relieved. The fight went well and Cheval-Sang was spared. He thanked the Thunder-Bird Spirit for their good fortune. The men had gathered the *Navoonah* scalps, weapons, and seven of their horses. "Thorn Bird, have one of the men kill that injured *Navoonah* pony and butcher some of its meat for your journey."

Thorn Bird gave one of the men this task. "What do we do now, *Ahpu*?"

"Take the men and the spare horses to the river camp. If you meet Smoke Cloud there, offer him the *Navoonah* horses for any scalps his men claimed. I must keep my promise. Then you need to take the men home. Our fighting is over."

"Aren't you coming with us?"

"No, I must stay with Cheval-Sang until he is well enough to ride. I will take the white-skin and his horse with me and stay hidden upstream from here. We still have a sleep or two before the *Navoonah* find their men in this creek. They will follow your tracks, not mine. I should be safe if I remain hidden. Be careful and do not stay long at the river camp. I will bring the white-skin home when Cheval-Sang is ready."

"Do I have time to cut up their bodies?" asked Thorn Bird, with a devilish smile.

"There is always time for that," said Laughing Crow, grinning. He handed the scout's knife to Thorn Bird. "Here, use Silent Weasel's knife. He would have wanted it that way. We will bury his knife when we get home, so he will have it in the next world. I hate leaving the bodies of our friends there, but we can't risk going back. They died bravely. There is comfort in that."

Laughing Crow tied Cheval-Sang to the white-skin's horse and then he mounted it, sitting back-to-back with his captured prize, who was half-awake and moaning. He turned his head backwards and growled, "You will not leave my sight until I bury you."

Face to Face

Many Wolves woke from a restless sleep into darkness. The flickering flames from a small fire pit fought off the blackness and illuminated just a small area around it. He saw the blurred form of a man sitting on the other side of the fire, biting into a thick piece of meat. As the man came into focus, his face glowed, revealing the blood dripping around his mouth and chin. The large man ate as if this was the first meal he had eaten in days and Many Wolves felt his stomach ache as he watched him.

Many Wolves's mouth was so dry that he couldn't spit if he wanted to and he winced at the searing pain in his leg. He continued to watch the man take gaping bites, grunting with pleasure after each mouthful. He didn't look up—not even once. *Laughing Crow. It must be Laughing Crow.*

Many Wolves felt the coarse rope burning his chafed hands and feet. He was a captive, Laughing Crow's captive. He was sitting against a tree with his arms bound around its trunk; and his bear-claw necklace was gone. He tried to piece together how he had been captured, how he ended up here with the Black Wasp. He remembered being chased by Laughing Crow and his men, and feeling a sharp pain in his leg. He remembered falling off his horse, and hearing loud, popping sounds like sharp thunder. He remembered riding on a horse with his hands and feet tied, his neck and back whipped with every stride, which explained why his body ached all over. He remembered hearing the screams of horses and men and splashing water, followed by cheers and celebration. But that was all he remembered.

As much as his body hurt, it was his despair that brought him the most pain. *What is Laughing Crow going to do with me? Why aren't I dead already?* He felt helpless, living in a nightmare, with the worst pain yet to come. He fought to keep his eyes dry.

Laughing Crow continued to gorge. He pulled his long black hair on one side of his face away from his food continuously. The hair on the other side of his head was cut short, like Many Wolves remembered through Chiquito's eyes. He recalled that the men of his village also cut their hair to respect a dead loved one. *He did this for his son.*

Laughing Crow finished his meal and then looked over at him, trapping his gaze. "So, the green-eyed devil is awake." He wiped the blood from his face and walked over to Many Wolves, whose mind cowered like a dog about to be beaten.

Tattoos decorated his muscular body—one was a picture of a great bird—and he had many scars as well. *How many wars has he fought to earn those marks?* Many Wolves smelled the pungent body odor of the big Northerner as he bent down and untied one of his hands. The smell lingered even after his captor went back to the fire and picked something up off the ground.

"Here. Drink and eat." Laughing Crow tossed his prisoner's water and food pouches near enough for Many Wolves to grab with his freed hand. "I don't want you dying on me yet." He returned to his sitting place next to the fire.

Many Wolves stretched out his stiff hand, grabbed the water pouch, and drank several gulps. It was refreshing, but he was careful not to drink too much. Then, he grabbed a piece of dried meat from his food pouch and bit into it. He was so famished that he would eat anything.

"Why do you want to keep me alive? Why don't you just kill me?" Many Wolves blurted out.

Laughing Crow grinned and then spoke in anger. "Do you know how hard it is for me not to take a knife to your throat? That would be easy for both of us. But that does nothing for my family and their sadness. My wife cries without end over the loss of her son and bleeds herself to fight the demons in her head. Many others weep and mourn for him. There is nothing I can say to heal their pain. If I bring you to them and make you suffer before their eyes, it will bring them relief and healing."

Many Wolves worst fears were confirmed. *I don't want to die that way.* He gritted his teeth in anger and pulled to free himself from his bindings, but his leg surged with pain, bringing him almost to tears again. He tried to untie his legs with his free hand, but it was too tight. The knots were unlike any he had ever seen. He just wanted to get out and run away, anywhere, even if it meant a slow death with no water or food and no robe to keep him warm at night. Any death would be better than the one Laughing Crow had just unleashed in his mind.

He closed his eyes for a moment and then felt his body jerk as Laughing Crow gripped his free arm with the force of a giant talon and pulled it behind him again. He felt the rope cut into his wrist as if it were woven with the vines of a thorny thistle.

Many Wolves laid his head back against the tree and stared into the flickering stars. He felt a weariness slam into him like a gust of wind. He just wanted to sleep and then pray to the Great Spirit that somehow he would wake up in the morning to a sunrise that offered him his life back. He didn't want to look at the flame-lit face of a man who wanted him to die a slow, suffering death. His mind grew tired and soon he drifted off to sleep, soothed by the howls of distant coyotes.

An Unsavory Meal

Many Wolves's dream the night before gave him little comfort. He remembered being carried down the swift currents of the Rio Pecos, powerless to fight its downward pull, and drifting further and further away from his family who watched him from an unreachable spot upstream. The salty water burned his eyes to near blindness and choked the air from his lungs. The harder he fought, the less he could see and breathe. When the dream finally released him, he woke encased in sweat and surrounded by the orange glaze of sunrise. The throbbing pain in his leg and the hot, itchy burns on his restrained hands and feet reminded him that he was in the same place as he had been the night before.

There were several large oak trees surrounding him, including the one that held him. He heard the airy hiss of running water nearby, but the scrub and mesquite kept it from his sight. He heard the sweet song of a sparrow and a chittering wren rustling around in the brush looking for its first meal. He heard the familiar squawks of Chiquito and Cazador, who must have just noticed he was awake. They were both perched high in one of the oak trees. Many Wolves looked down and saw Laughing Crow wrapped up in a robe near the ashes of the fire pit. He wanted to yell to his birds to fly far away from this place, but he didn't want to wake his enemy. He worried their noise would wake him and wished he could silence his birds—just this once.

Many Wolves heard the bushes crackle and a familiar snort behind him. Elk Dog was crunching on a sage bush, his legs hobbled with rope. It was good to see his brown horse again. Ahead of him, he spotted what he guessed was Laughing Crow's stallion—a brilliantly marked brown and white pinto. The pony was sleek and muscular, but he noticed that it was holding its leg up as it ate, not wanting to put weight on it. Then he saw the bloody puncture in its upper leg. The horse looked up at him briefly and then continued eating.

Laughing Crow woke up suddenly, clearly disturbed. "Those birds just won't stop yelling!" He lumbered to his feet with the robe still wrapped around his shoulders and looked up at the birds. "They're the noisiest buzzards I ever heard!"

"They're not buzzards," replied Many Wolves, softly.

"What?"

"They're not buzzards." This time, he said it louder. "They're wolf hawks."

"Whatever they are, they should know to let a man sleep!" Laughing Crow said in a grumpy voice. He walked away from the camp and towards the water. Many Wolves heard him splashing water over himself. When he walked back, his hair and face were dripping wet. He stopped briefly to stroke his horse and whisper words to it, then he pulled a quiver from the horse's back, got out his bow, and loaded it with an arrow. "So these are your buzzards...your magic birds!"

Many Wolves froze, his eyes glued to Laughing Crow who was loading his bow and looking at the tree where the birds were perched. He yelled to them, "Fly away, Chiquito! Cazador, go! Please go!"

Instead of flying away, Cazador flew to a lower branch, closer to his leader's voice, closer to the deadly bow. *Don't come closer, Cazador.* Many Wolves remained silent, fearing that his voice would lure his birds even closer. He felt completely helpless as he watched Laughing Crow draw his bow back. *Please fly away.*

Laughing Crow released the arrow and it struck Cazador in the chest. Instantly, both birds were silent. Cazador's body tumbled, crashing into a branch before falling to the ground. Chiquito flew away.

Terrified, Many Wolves yelled in Lipan, "Go, Chiquito. Fly far away!" He didn't know if Chiquito understood what was happening. Many Wolves had spent all of his bird's life teaching him to trust humans and now he had watched one of them kill his sister. *Don't come back, Chiquito. Please don't come back.*

Many Wolves felt light-headed and shaken by what just happened. He tried to pull himself free of his bondage, as he watched Cazador flop around helplessly on the ground. The arrow point had passed through to the other side of her feathery body. Her gaping mouth uttered a shrilly, panting cry as she labored for each breath—a cry which reached out to him like a long arm that choked his heart to the brink of tears. Laughing Crow walked over to the wounded bird and severed her head with a single, firm stroke of his knife. Many Wolves watched her beautiful wing flap for several moments before it settled for the last time. It seemed as if every living thing around them, the sparrow, the wren, the horses, all stopped to witness this cold, brutal killing.

"So much for your magic bird, white-skin!" Laughing Crow picked up the bird's head and threw it into the desert. "Your magic couldn't protect it from death and it won't protect it from the maggots and the worms of the earth!"

The fear that had gripped Many Wolves was replaced with anger and hate—a loathing hate that seethed through pores like sweat. He tried again to free his hands, but he was too weak. He remembered the grief he felt when Reina died, but this time he would fight back the tears. He wouldn't give his enemy the satisfaction of seeing his weakness.

Laughing Crow picked up the dead bird by the legs and carried it over to the fire pit. "It would be a shame to let this magic buzzard meat go to waste. Don't you think, white-skin?" He laughed out loud, dropped the carcass on the ground, and then foraged around for pieces of mesquite. He broke two of them so that they forked on one side, and stuck them into the ground on either side of the fire with the forked end sticking up. Then he gathered some dried sage and started a fire. He collected more mesquite from around the camp and piled it next to his fire pit, throwing several pieces in the blossoming fire. He sat down and began to pluck the feathers off the dead hawk, smiling as he worked.

Laughing Crow looked up at Many Wolves, holding a feather in his hand. "These feathers will make arrows that fly straight through the heart of your people." Then, he laughed and returned to his task, clearly pleased with himself.

After most of the feathers were removed, the Nokoni paused and looked at his captive. "How did this bird know how to carry a scalp to me? Tell me of this magic."

Many Wolves refused to answer.

"Now your tongue is silent! Not the same tongue that taunted me from atop that ridge! You don't need to tell me. Your bird is gone from this world, white-skin, and so is its magic."

Laughing Crow impaled the plucked and skinned meat on a third stick and hung it across the other two to roast slowly over the fire. Then, he walked over to Many Wolves and crouched down in front of him.

Many Wolves felt the piercing black eyes of the Black Wasp penetrate his mind.

"Tell me of this magic, white-skin. Tell me of this magic that commands birds to do things that birds don't do—this magic that commands wolves to kill for you. I want to know how it works." Laughing Crow's words were calm and even in tone. His eyes were unrelenting, and sharp as obsidian. They gnawed at Many Wolves's hatred, like a dog gnaws on a bone trying in vain to get at the marrow. The captive did not want to give in to his captor nor did he want to provoke his anger, so he remained silent.

Laughing Crow reached for his throat and gripped it tightly. "Tell me of this magic!" he bellowed, his anger boiling from his eyes and mouth. The smell of Laughing Crow's body slammed into him once again.

"There is no magic, only friendship between us," said Many Wolves in a strained whisper. Laughing Crow released his neck now that he was willing to talk.

"Friendship? Men and wild animals are not friends! They are hunter and prey. You cannot tame them like you can tame a horse or a dog! Not without magic!"

"It isn't magic. It is trust between two living things. It is providing food and protection and then having it provided for you. It is survival in a harsh world that would be too hard to survive alone."

"How can you know this? How can you know things that the wisest of men do not know?"

Many Wolves saw the frustration in Laughing Crow's eyes. Although his young body was pained and his life was controlled like a fly caught in a spider's web, he felt a great satisfaction, a victory. Laughing Crow would never fully understand his "magic"—the wisdom he held over his tormenter. Finally, Many Wolves said with the hint of a smile, "These are things you will never know."

Laughing Crow balled his hand into a fist and struck Many Wolves across the face. The stinging pain shot through the young man's face. Blood poured from his mouth and nose. The blow had forced the tears from his eyes—at last.

"So tell me, white-skin, where is this wolf now?" Laughing Crow stood up and looked down at him. His cold, dark eyes cut through his mind and reminded Many Wolves of the heartless eyes of Gray Face.

"He ran away after…" Many Wolves paused, sucking in the words he was about to say. It hurt to talk. He didn't want to provoke another attack.

"After what?"

Many Wolves spit a pool of blood out of his mouth. "…After he killed your scout, Silent Weasel."

Laughing Crow struck him again on the side of the face, this time with the back of his hand. He leaned down towards his captive and hissed, "This is only the beginning of your pain." Then he walked back to his fire to rotate the meat he had been roasting. He took several gulps of water and sat down again. He seemed calmer now.

"How do you know *Noomah* words?"

Many Wolves spit out more blood. Common sense told him not to reveal the name of his friend, Ten Arrows. It could endanger his life, so he lied. "I learned it when I was younger from an elder in my village."

"I can't believe you would speak Penateka as well as you do after learning it so long ago. But, it doesn't matter now, I suppose. All men scream in the same language." Laughing Crow looked at him with a crooked smile.

The Nokoni warrior pulled the cooking stick off its forked holders to let it cool, apparently satisfied that it was roasted to his liking. All that was left of Cazador was this shriveled hunk of charred meat, her wings and legs barely recognizable anymore.

Many Wolves closed his eyes. He couldn't watch anymore.

"This is not bad," he heard Laughing Crow say. "A little bony, but it tastes good, a lot like prairie chicken." Many Wolves kept his eyes closed, trying to shove the image out of his mind. "Do you want to try some, white-skin?" Then he heard Laughing Crow laugh loudly as he chewed with his mouth open.

After a while, Laughing Crow said, "When your other little animal friends come back, they will provide my fire pit with more fresh meat!"

Then he laughed again and continued gorging himself.

Intervention

Laughing Crow had finished eating his morning meal and had slept awhile in the shade, relaxed by his full stomach and trying to stay cool from the scorching afternoon sun. After he awoke, he walked around the area looking for treats for his horse. He found several prickly pears and red flower stalks from the ocotillo cactus.

His prisoner was fading in and out of sleep. *He is weak. I should make him eat.* Laughing Crow now believed that there was nothing magical about this Many Wolves. Somehow, he had figured out how to make the birds his friends. He had heard stories of people befriending wolves also, but they were old stories and these people never lived during his lifetime. *Can a wolf be trained to kill?* Wolves were like dogs and he knew of some dogs that were so vicious they would attack a man. But most dogs were afraid of men and he couldn't imagine any dog killing a great warrior like Silent Weasel, not without a man's help. There were still certain things he couldn't understand and the white-skin was probably not going to tell him.

He offered a prickly pear to Cheval-Sang as he deliberated. He stroked the horse's mane and face and spoke to him gently, "Your leg is better today. In two more sleeps, we can go home." He ran his hand across the bare arch of the horse's back and along his powerful thighs. The horse nickered, as if speaking back to him. "There isn't a horse that could ever replace you, Cheval-Sang."

"Laughing Crow!"

The Nokoni leader spun around and scanned the landscape. A man on a white horse was watching him from the top of a low-sloping hill. He scrambled to grab his axe and shield. "Who are you and what do you want?" he yelled back.

"I am Ten Arrows of the Penateka. I have come for your white captive."

"What interest do the Penateka have with him?"

Ten Arrows trotted down the hill then commanded his horse to walk closer towards Laughing Crow. He stopped near enough for Laughing Crow to see his eyes and face clearly. He held a bow in his right hand and a quiver of arrows slung around his shoulder. Laughing Crow also saw a steel-bladed tomahawk hanging from either side of the man's saddle and a knife sheath strapped to his leg. *This Penateka has many fine weapons.* His horse was decorated in yellow and red paint and wore several eagle feathers on its mane. His deerskin leggings and shirt were of the finest quality, decorated with beads and shells. *There is wealth in his village and family.*

"The Penateka have no interest in him, but I do. He is my life brother and I have come to take him home."

Laughing Crow laughed mockingly. "What *Noomah* would claim a white-skinned *Navoonah* dog as a brother? It is not the same *Noomah* blood that flows through our veins, Penateka!"

Ten Arrows's horse moved nervously back and forth, snorting and neighing. "Many Wolves and I are bound as brothers by the great grizzlies of the mountains just as you are bound to the warriors you fight with. I'm sure you saw the bear-claw scars on his leg. I have the same marks on my back. Would you not claim a man who saved your life as your life brother, Laughing Crow?"

"This *boy* saved your life? I look at his scrawny, weak body and I can't believe he has the heart of a warrior. He has killed men much greater than himself and he has saved your life? Now you tell me he has killed grizzlies? Tell me how he does this!" Laughing Crow demanded.

"You underestimate him, Laughing Crow. From where I sit, he could put an arrow through your heart!"

Laughing Crow pointed at his listless captive. "He has killed my son with a bow, but the others were killed by a wolf! He uses this demon wolf to do his killing. I have not seen any sign of it, though I have seen his bird friends and their flesh is no different than the chickens that roam the prairie. There is no magic in them."

Ten Arrows laughed. "This wolf is no more of a demon than the dogs of your village! Many Wolves has a special bond with wild creatures. The hawks catch him food and the wolves befriend him. I do not understand how this bond works, but the Great Spirit has blessed him with it and he has learned to use it to survive. He has killed your son and you have taken his white parents and his village from him. There has been enough blood spilled. Let me take him home."

Laughing Crow stepped closer to Ten Arrows and spoke through gritted teeth. "Can you bring my son back to life, Penateka? Can you restore the flesh that the scavengers have taken so he will not suffer in the afterlife? Can you?"

"Laughing Crow, you ask me to do what no shaman can do. I can offer you ten good horses for your captive. My people can help to restore your shattered village. My people can offer protection to the son you still have. This battle today has weakened you and your village. I have seen your scouts decaying in the sun, the birds picking at their mutilated bodies. I have seen the bodies of your men lying in the dust with the Raccoon-Eyes who have fallen beside them. Who will protect your village from the next Pawnee or Lipan attack? Your village will be like an open sore for the scavengers to pick at!"

Laughing Crow felt rage building up inside. *I do not need this Penateka to throw me scraps like a dog.* Nothing this man could offer could bring back his son, his warriors. Making this white-skinned boy suffer and die in this life and the next was foremost on his mind. *I will not give him up so easily. If this Penateka wants to intervene, then he can share in his brother's fate.* "Is the white-skin worth fighting for, Penateka? Would you risk your life for your brother?"

"We are life brothers. I owe my life to him," repeated Ten Arrows, in a firm voice.

Laughing Crow saw that there was no fear in his eyes.

The Nokoni leader knew he was at a disadvantage without his bow and without a healthy war horse. A skilled, mounted *Noomah* warrior would be hard to kill on foot. He knew his limits. He needed to barter for more time. "So, where are these ten horses you wish to offer, Ten Arrows?"

"I can bring them to your village…and you can bring Many Wolves."

"Bring them to Thorn Bird, my son. Then ride here with him so he can tell me that the horses are safe in my village, and I will release the boy to you." Laughing Crow had no intention of giving up Many Wolves, not for ten horses, not for fifty horses.

"Why can't you ride to your village and meet me there?"

"My horse needs to rest." He did not want to reveal to the Penateka that his horse was injured. He had turned Cheval-Sang to try to hide the injured leg from him.

"Your horse needs mending, Laughing Crow. I know his leg is hurt. I could see it in his tracks."

"So, how did you find me, Penateka?"

"I found the creek painted with blood and then saw the dead *Navoonah*. I saw the tracks that your men left going one way and the tracks of my former horse going another. I would recognize Elk Dog's tracks anywhere. They led me to you."

If this Penateka could find him, so could others. *I will have to be more careful.* "I will await your return with Thorn Bird," said Laughing Crow, his eyes squinting in the bright sun.

Ten Arrows nodded, glanced back at Many Wolves, and then rode off, northward to *Noomah* lands.

The Warmth of Blood

The fading hooves of Ten Arrows's horse stopped for just a moment and then started back up again. Laughing Crow sensed the change in sound. He had turned his back on the warrior, expecting the sound of his horse to disappear, but now it was growing louder. He whipped around to see Ten Arrows charging towards him in a full gallop. Still holding his axe and shield, Laughing Crow moved away from Cheval-Sang and towards his attacker. His attempt to rid himself of this threat had failed. He would have to face the Penateka, without his bow, and without his horse. *I will have to draw him close.*

Laughing Crow walked closer to the surging rider, unafraid, and willing to face whatever attack his enemy unleashed. The midday sun cast a stingy shadow on the ground and forced its intense heat on his head and shoulders. Ten Arrows yelled an echoing war-whoop before he sailed two whispering arrows at him, one of which embedded itself deeply into Laughing Crow's thick shield and the other flew past the right side of his head. He raised his shield higher, leaving only his legs, eyes, and forehead exposed to his attacker.

Ten Arrows swung his horse to Laughing Crow's right and sent two more arrows at his shield, tearing through it. One of the arrow's points broke the skin on Laughing Crow's chest, but he quickly pulled it free with a sharp tug on his shield. Blood oozed from the shallow wound. *He shoots with strength and from his left side.*

Ten Arrows spun his horse around and rode from right to left, pulling several more arrows from his quiver with his left hand as he held his bow with his right. Then he turned his horse around again and bellowed another war cry as he galloped to full speed, attacking from the same side of his horse as before. Two more arrows whirred past Laughing Crow's head with barely a heartbeat of time between them and two more found the reinforced buffalo hide of his shield. *My shield isn't going to hold up much longer.*

His attacker circled back again, reloading and preparing for his next assault. Ten Arrows turned his horse to face Laughing Crow, but this time he stopped and yelled. "Your shield has served you well, Laughing Crow, but soon it will be no protection at all! You will fall to my arrows like the great bears of the high country!"

"Get off your horse and fight like a true warrior of the *Noomah*! You dishonor me and your people with your cowardly arrows!"

"It is how I was taught to fight, as I'm sure you were. You call me a coward because you know that the odds weigh in my favor. Would you not attack your enemy with the same advantage?" Ten Arrows's snowy white horse was kicking up the dust below him, hovering at a spot on Laughing Crow's left.

"Well then, show me that you can kill me from the safety of your war pony. When you run out of arrows, will you flee like a dog with its tail between its legs? Or will you face me up-close? Let us mix sweat with sweat, and blood with blood, my *Noomah* brother!"

Ten Arrows yelled and launched his next attack from his speeding horse. The arrows lifted the dirt around Laughing Crow's feet, except for one, which impaled itself in his right thigh. The pain burned through him like a prairie fire in heavy winds. He yelled in rage, then snapped the shaft of the arrow with his right hand. He took several deep breaths with his teeth gritted to compose himself. His face and body glistened in sweat from the intense heat.

To Laughing Crow's surprise, Ten Arrows dismounted his horse and hung his bow and quiver on his horse, even though he had several arrows left. He pulled out the two tomahawks that were laced to his saddle pad, their shiny blades reflecting in the sunlight. With one in each hand, he dashed towards Laughing Crow, bellowing a shrill battle cry. When the Penateka was about halfway to him, the running warrior swung his left arm behind him and arched his back in a throwing motion, releasing the twirling tomahawk. The steel blade ripped through Laughing Crow's weakened shield and sliced open his left forearm. In disgust, the Nokoni hurled the now useless shield to the ground and braced himself for his rushing attacker.

Ten Arrows raised his other weapon high above his head with his left hand and sprinted towards Laughing Crow again. Although he was in great pain, Laughing Crow lifted his battle-axe into position and bent his knees to steady himself. His left arm and right leg were bleeding badly now. He knew that both would start to falter on him. *I have to fight through it!* He screamed to the Thunder-Bird for more strength to help him bury the pain.

The wooden handles of their two weapons clapped down on each other as Laughing Crow deflected the incoming blow. Ten Arrows regained his balance, his chest heaving with each breath. He circled the Nokoni leader carefully, measuring his opponent. He attacked from many different angles, but none of his movements could break Laughing Crow's defenses. The Nokoni's skill and experience were a great advantage—even though his enemy was younger and quicker. The Nokoni warrior anticipated every one of the

Penateka's assaults and sensed that Ten Arrows was growing frustrated with each failed swing. Laughing Crow felt a flash of relief knowing that the advantage was shifting in his favor. Finally, he saw an opening and swung his axe with a backhanded motion at his attacker. The butt end of the steel blade struck Ten Arrows in the side of the head. His body slammed to the ground, convulsing, quivering, and soon he lost consciousness.

Fatigued and dizzy from blood loss, Laughing Crow dropped his axe and fell to one knee, holding himself up with his uninjured right arm. Exhaustion rained down on him with the suddenness of a thunderstorm. He looked over at Ten Arrows and saw that he was still breathing, but motionless, and watched the blood seep into his black hair. Laughing Crow considered him a worthy adversary. He had earned the fearless *Noomah*'s soul, so he rested now, preparing to take it.

Laughing Crow drew his knife from his leg sheath and stood up slowly, staggering with his good leg to keep the weight off his injured one. Suddenly, he heard footsteps and a faint growl. He looked over his shoulder and saw a dust cloud from behind the patches of mesquite. *Is it an animal?* Then, as if rising from the earth, a wolf leaped onto his shoulders, knocking him down. The force of the attack knocked the knife out of his hand. He hesitated for a moment, not knowing how to fight without a weapon. In that instant, the wolf bore down on his neck with its sharp fangs and bit into it deeply. He felt his blood flow over him and he could taste its warmth in his mouth. What was left of his strength was rapidly slipping away. He tried to lift his arms and legs, but they seemed pinned down by the weight of a thousand stones. For the first time in his life, he felt helpless.

The red wolf stared down at him with blood dripping from its jowls. *So this is the magic blood wolf.* As he stared back at the animal, the lifeless eyes of the men he had killed flashed in his mind, one after the other. Their cold eyes chilled his sweaty body. *This isn't how I was supposed to die.* He had always imagined he would die the same way he had taken a soul, face to face, with the thrust of a lance or the slash of a knife. Here he was looking into the yellow eyes of a wolf— not a man. In his chilling pain, the only warmth came from his own blood. Even the sun felt cold to him.

He began to choke on his blood and the pain left his body in these final moments, replaced by a peaceful calm. In his heart, he knew it was better to die this way than shrivel away one winter after the next, like the old buzzards of his village. This brought a smile to his face. He looked again at the wolf and it cocked its head sideways as if it understood his thoughts. "Why are you staring at me, magic blood wolf?" He coughed out some of the blood that was filling his mouth and strangling his last breaths.

In his final moment, Laughing Crow muttered, "There are worse ways to die, magic blood wolf."

The Nokoni headman no longer wondered about the afterlife. It was now an open lodge waiting for him to enter.

Life Brothers

Many Wolves was yanked out of his slumber by a warm, wet tongue on his face. He opened his eyes to see his red wolf staring at him, scratching his cheeks with stiff whiskers, covering his face with saliva, and sniffing his smells with his cold nose. Rojo's muzzle was red. *Blood?*

"Rojo, you came back. Is that blood on your nose?" His words were weak as they came from his sore mouth. He was ecstatic to see that his companion had returned.

Many Wolves realized that he was lying down on his side and that his hands and feet were no longer tethered to a tree, though he felt the lingering burns from the rope. *Why aren't my hands and feet tied?* He sat up and instantly felt the jarring pain in his swollen leg. *Where is Laughing Crow?*

Then, he heard laughter—loud, chest-heaving laughter. *Ten Arrows!*

His friend was sitting near Laughing Crow's fire pit, but he was alone and his enemy was gone. Rojo continued to lick his face until he reached out to pet him and then his hand became the wolf's new target. Ten Arrows just kept laughing as he watched the two of them. "Are you really here, Ten Arrows, or am I dreaming?"

"Yes, I'm here, Wild Man. Things are different than when you left this world for sleep." Ten Arrows's smile filled his face as he spoke. He was heating two cups in the weak flames.

They both laughed together now. Even though it hurt to laugh, Many Wolves was so relieved and glad to see his friend that he didn't care. He was hungry and thirsty, but at least he was alive and Ten Arrows and Rojo were both with him. It was still more like a dream than a reality.

"Why is that bloody bandage around your head?" said Many Wolves.

"It's just a mild head wound, nothing more. It's not as bad as it looks," said Ten Arrows, feeling his head and adjusting the bandage. "It took a while for the dizziness to go away and now I have a headache the size of a boulder. I'm making us some tea for our pain."

"What happened? I don't remember anything."

"Your life brother has repaid you," said Ten Arrows, pouring water into each cup.

"What do you mean? You repaid me?"

"Rojo killed Laughing Crow."

"Laughing Crow is dead?" The instant the words left his tongue, Many Wolves saw flashes of his enemy's face in his mind. Laughing Crow was dying, breathing his final breaths. *Did I dream this or was this real?*

"Yes, his body is over there, wrapped in his buffalo robe." Ten Arrows pointed to a shady spot on the ground behind him.

Many Wolves looked over where his friend directed him and saw what looked like a body wrapped in a buffalo robe lying on the ground. "Rojo killed him?" It seemed unbelievable to Many Wolves that Rojo could kill a man that men could not kill. *Did I help Rojo kill him?*

"He had some help from me, but without him, my scalp would be hanging from a tree instead of Laughing Crow's. I guess I am Rojo's life brother too." Ten Arrows flashed a big smile and laughed again, his head dipping upwards to the sky as his body rocked.

Many Wolves spotted Laughing Crow's scalp dangling from a mesquite branch. He looked at the wrapped body and then back at the scalp. *Laughing Crow is dead.* He had to say this to himself several times to force it into his mind. He had lived in a tormented world for so long now, ever since Ten Arrows had called him back to the lowlands. It was a world of grief and death. Now, he felt the cooling breeze against his face again for what seemed like the first time in a very long time. Rojo's tongue was licking the punctured skin on his swollen leg. It was good medicine.

"He licks you like a female wolf licks one of her pups."

"He's never done this before. I was afraid he had run away from me."

"You're his family, his pack now. He's happy to see you!"

Though Ten Arrows was in a good mood, Many Wolves saw that he winced every time he moved. His friend never complained about pain, even when Gray Face almost killed him. *Laughing Crow almost killed him.* "Is there mint in that tea?"

"Of course, Wild Man, do I make it any other way?" Ten Arrows reached down and pulled the cups out of the pit to let them cool.

"What are you going to do with Laughing Crow? Bury him here?"

"No. He was a great leader for his people. I will return his body to his village so they can bury him properly. He was our enemy but he was also my *Noomah* brother. I owe this to his family and his village. Without him to lead their weakened village, his people might be open to talks of peace with my village."

"Who will lead them now?"

"Most likely Thorn Bird, his son. I've heard he's a lot like his father—more of a warmaker than a peacemaker. His village has been crippled by this fight with your people, so he might need more friends than enemies. He may decide to

477

return to live with Gray Elk's Nokoni, since it was his father who was forced to leave that village, not him."

Ten Arrows looked around at the blue, cloudless sky and the surrounding oak trees. "Where are your birds, Wild Man?"

"All that's left of Cazador is in Laughing Crow's fire pit. Chiquito flew away when he saw his sister's killing." Many Wolves tried to put Cazador's death out of his mind, but it was hard to erase the image of her last, struggling gasps at life. *What has her death done to Chiquito?*

Ten Arrows's face grew solemn. "Your loss is mine, my friend. I know you loved those birds as a parent loves his children. Chiquito will come back, though. You just need to call him."

"My whistle is in my hunting bag over there. Can you get it for me? I don't think I can walk very well." Many Wolves pointed to a spot in the shade where he knew Laughing Crow had stashed his things. Rojo had stopped licking him now and was lying down nearby, watching everything around him.

His Northerner friend stood up, grabbed his bags and quiver, and walked over to him. "Here, I bet you're hungry and thirsty. I filled your pouch with creek water."

Many Wolves drew a few mouthfuls of water and swirled it around his dry mouth before swallowing. Then, he blew his whistle loudly, despite the stiffness in his jaw and cheeks. He looked around at the trees, but the only movement was a breeze caressing their leaves. He spotted several buzzards circling overhead, alerted to the spiraling scent of Laughing Crow's body.

He blew the whistle again and called out his bird's name, but the sounds rose and fell like a stone thrown into the barren desert.

"Just wait, he will come. Let us drink some tea and eat, Wild Man."

"It would hurt too much to eat dried meat, or anything else, with the soreness in my mouth, but I'll have some of that tea."

Ten Arrows brought both cups and sat next to his Lipan friend. After they drank for a moment, he put his cup down and pulled something from his waist pouch—it was Many Wolves's bear-claw necklace. "I found this on the ground near your quiver. Laughing Crow snapped it in half, but I fixed it for you." He slipped the necklace over Many Wolves's head and onto his neck. "Will you ride north with me and stay with my people? At least until your leg is better?"

Many Wolves considered the idea. *How will they accept me, a Lipan? What will Rojo do?* He did not want to face people. He just wanted to go home with Rojo. To him, there was comfort in being alone: moving when and where he wanted, eating only what he foraged and killed, and living on what the Earth Mother and the Great Spirit provided for him. Waking up to the calls of wild birds and falling asleep to the howls of coyotes and wolves. This was the life he knew and the life he wanted. "Your village is not my home, Ten Arrows. I want to go home to the foothills. I want to be far away from the hatred of men." *Though someday I hope I will return here to find Walking Free and visit Big Sky's village again.*

"How will you survive on a bad leg and without your birds to hunt for you?"

"I can still use a horse and a bow. That's all I need. My leg will heal in time."

Ten Arrows smiled. "Someday you will come to meet my family and my village, right?"

"Yes, my brother. Someday I will come, but not now."

"Will you ride north with me until I ride east to my village? I will need to travel slow since Laughing Crow's horse has a weak leg."

479

"I will ride with you, but I don't want to go too deep into the Northerner homelands. Though Laughing Crow is dead, I wish to stay far away from his people."

Ten Arrows laughed. "It's good that you are cautious, my brother. We should get started before the shadows grow any longer. These are *Navoonah* lands and I want to get away from them. Soon, they will be looking for the men who killed their people down river."

Many Wolves stood up slowly. It had been several days since he had been on his feet and his legs were stiff. He hobbled around collecting his things, keeping the weight off his injured leg. He blew the whistle one more time and then packed it in his bag.

Ten Arrows had already packed his buffalo robe on Elk Dog and was now carrying the Nokoni leader's body over his shoulder. He slung it on top of Laughing Crow's stallion and tied the lead to Cloud. "This beautiful horse will have to bear its rider for one more journey until I can get another pack horse from my village."

Many Wolves studied the lines of muscle and the brilliant colors of Laughing Crow's horse. "It certainly is a beautiful animal, Ten Arrows."

"The legend of this horse is as widely known as its rider. His name is Cheval-Sang. He has been Laughing Crow's favorite war pony for as long as I can remember."

"What is 'Cheval-Sang'? I've never heard those *Noomah* words."

"They are white man's words which mean 'Blood Horse,'" Ten Arrows said with a smile. Then he walked over to the mesquite tree and pulled Laughing Crow's scalp off the branch. "Take this, Wild Man, it's your prize."

"But I didn't kill him." *I saw Laughing Crow die in my dream, but I don't think I killed him. It was just a dream. I couldn't kill him without the mind-journey medicine. It was just a dream.*

"Without Rojo, I would be dead. Take it," said the Northerner, insisting.

Reluctantly, Many Wolves took the scalp. The matted black hair and skin were glued together with dried blood. He wasn't quite sure what to do with it. All that mattered was that Laughing Crow was dead, whether he had a part in it or not. He didn't need a scalp to remind him of that. Scalps were prizes in the world that he wanted to escape from. Nonetheless, he placed it in his hunting bag. *I will have to find a place to bury it.*

Many Wolves hoisted his body up on Elk Dog with all the strength he could muster. His leg throbbed in revolt. He looked back at Laughing Crow's camp one more time—hoping it was a place he could soon forget. Then he looked ahead at Ten Arrows, riding Cloud and leading the dead Nokoni leader on his limping horse, and followed.

Many Wolves looked back at Rojo. "Let's go, magic blood wolf."

Puha

Ten Arrows led Many Wolves north along the river, weaving around trees as he carved out a path to their homes. Many Wolves directed Elk Dog to move up alongside his friend so they could talk. Though it hurt his mouth to speak, there were many unanswered questions and worries still lingering in Many Wolves's mind.

"Hadakai once told me that the Nokoni believed Laughing Crow could not be killed because of some special power he had. There was a *Noomah* word for it."

"*Puha*," answered Ten Arrows. "Looks like the Nokoni were wrong about that," he said, looking back briefly at the Nokoni leader's body and grinning slightly. "His people believed this because Laughing Crow survived so many life-taking moments, when a lesser man would have died. When you see a man defy death so frequently, you start to believe that he is invincible, beyond death, and that there is a powerful spirit protecting him."

"It seems like luck plays an important part in surviving this kind of danger. I feel like I was lucky to survive those bear attacks and Laughing Crow's torture."

"Luck is important, Wild Man, but I believe that the Great Spirit grants you luck in these moments. Luck that you have earned throughout your life."

"How do you earn luck?"

"There are many ways that a man earns luck for himself, through hard work like practicing hunting skills, through good deeds, and through helping others who need help. All these are done without expecting anything in return for doing them. But what you receive is luck granted by the Great Spirit when you need it. Earning and receiving this luck is just one part of a man's *puha*. Laughing Crow believed that he earned his luck from killing men."

"My father and grandfather must have earned this luck, but the Great Spirit didn't help them when they died."

"The Great Spirit knows when it's time for a man to go to the next world. It can be hard to understand why these things happen, but you should understand that the Great Spirit has a plan for them and you can't blame yourself for their deaths. All you can do is keep their memories locked in your heart and their spirits will still live in this world when you think about them and remember them in stories. These memories are also a part of your *puha*, your inner strength."

It was hard for Many Wolves to believe that it wasn't his fault that his family was killed. He felt certain that if it weren't for his actions, they would all still be alive. Maybe in time the Great Spirit will reveal his plan to him. It seemed as though Laughing Crow's death was the only good that came out of it.

"Wild Man, when my people hear your story, they will believe that your *puha* was stronger than Laughing Crow's," Ten Arrows said and smiled at him.

Suddenly, Many Wolves heard the distant cry of a hawk. He knew that cry like he knew the sound of his own name. He reached into his hunting bag and pulled out his fist-perch, then slung it on his left hand. He didn't see his bird at first, but knew he was approaching. "Chiquito! Chiquito!" He held his fist-perch up above his head and scanned the mesquite-lined landscape.

Ten Arrows burst out in cheer. "You see, Wild Man! I knew he would come back! I knew it! He wasn't going to let you leave without him!" Ten Arrows stopped and waited for his friend.

Many Wolves's heart almost melted when he finally saw his beautiful little hawk gliding just above the ground towards his outstretched hand. It was the same gut-wrenching feeling he felt when he watched Reina fly to him for the first time. Chiquito landed on his hand and kept screaming excitedly, almost blocking out the roaring laughter of his friend. He lowered his bird to eye level and stroked his breast feathers gently. "It's so good to see you, Little One," he whispered. Tears rolled down his face. He couldn't suppress them any longer. Now, he could cry for Cazador too.

Chiquito looked healthy. His crop was bulging from his chest. "I bet you've been filling up on mice again." The small hawk's squawking was much calmer now, as he swiveled and bobbed his head. Many Wolves couldn't help but smile, tasting the salt of his tears.

"Are we ready to leave now, Spirit Walker?"

"We are certainly ready now, Ten Arrows." He let Chiquito perch on his fist while he rode. He wanted him to stay there so he could be close to his brother for a while. His other brother, Rojo, followed behind them, always looking around and sniffing the air—his ever-vigilant guardian.

Further upriver, Many Wolves spotted the dead carcass of what he thought was a coyote, but he wasn't sure. The buzzards and crows were cleaning out what little flesh was left on its bones. He placed Chiquito on his shoulder and then reached for his bow and an arrow and pulled them from his quiver. He grabbed Laughing Crow's scalp from his saddlebag and tied the clump of hair tightly around the shaft of his arrow. He launched the scalp towards the dead carcass. The birds flinched when they saw the strange arrow land next to them. Most of them resumed their meal, except for two crows who hopped over to the decorated arrow and began tearing at the prize. It reminded him of the scavengers who fought over Gray Face's carcass. Ten Arrows looked back at him and nodded with an approving look.

Life for life.

Many Wolves

Chiquito's chirping squawks woke him at sunrise as they had done so many times before. Many Wolves could not think of a more pleasant sound to rise to. Now that he was back at his Gray Face camp, it seemed somehow different. He was laid out on his buffalo robe as he tried to remember all the details of last night's dream. He closed his eyes and tucked his arms behind his head, enjoying the bliss of this half-awakened moment.

He remembered galloping endlessly through a desert with hills in the distance. Daylight was waning and night brought with it a brilliant full moon, which hovered just over the silhouetted hills. He felt the cool wind brush against his face and whip through his hair. The fresh air seemed to clear the dust from his lungs. He kept riding towards the moon, but it never got closer. The hills never got closer either. He was locked in this endless moment.

What he remembered most about the dream, however, was that he wasn't alone. As the landscape blurred past him, he could see his three wolf hawks keeping pace with him, their wings flapping in a slow, fluid motion. They occasionally turned to look at him as he rode Elk Dog. He looked down, and on the ground were four wolves running alongside him. Rojo was closest to him on the left and next to him was Noir, his mate. On his right were two other pack members, the white-footed Snow Foot and the playful Shadow Chaser.

Their tongues dangled over their chins as they ran and they all looked up at him, ready to follow where his words would take them.

Many Wolves realized that it was similar to the dream that Walking Free had described to him after his naming ceremony. *Is this dream somehow borne out of the medicine man's vision?* He would never know. What he did know was that it was the most beautiful dream he ever had and he wanted it to return. He had not dreamed about Laughing Crow or the Buffalo People since the Nokoni leader's death. He hoped this nightmare was gone forever, eaten away from his mind like his enemy's scalp had been eaten away by the crows and buzzards.

He opened his eyes again and looked at the pine trees that towered above him. He caressed Rojo's fur with his hand as his red wolf slept, laid out beside him. Chiquito was still trying to get him up, but he decided to just lie there basking in the warmth of the dream. He replayed it over and over in his mind, letting it soak in so he would never forget it.

He thought again about the naming ceremony. Walking Free had named him Many Wolves after seeing a dream, a vision like this. Now, he wondered if his name meant something else. *Is it my name, or is it a name for all of us?* He liked the idea that the wolves and birds were somehow a part of him. Though he had lived without a village for a long time, he always felt that he wasn't really alone. It made him believe even more strongly that he belonged in the wilderness with its wild creatures. *Will I ever be able to live in a human village again?*

He looked up at Chiquito and thought of how much his smallest bird had endured. "Little One, you and I were the weak ones, but look how we have survived."

Many Wolves stood up and stretched his arms to the sky. His leg was still sore, but he felt that it was well enough to start hunting again. Rojo woke up and raised his eyes to his.

"Rojo, are you ready to go?" The wolf swung his thick, bushy tail from side to side and stretched his front legs, cutting the dirt with his front paws. Many Wolves drank some water from his pouch, then put on his deerskin leggings and slung his quiver over his shoulder.

"All right, Chiquito, you little beggar, let's find some rabbits."

About the Author

J. Bradley Van Tighem is a graduate of the University of California, Davis, and has worked in the computer industry for over 25 years. He currently lives in Northern California with his sports-loving family. He has a keen interest in Native American History, in particular the Comanche and Apache tribes of Texas. He is an avid naturalist who especially loves to watch and study birds of prey. Puha is the opening novel in the Master of the Wild Series. Visit his Facebook page for more information about the indigenous people and the animals of Texas: www.facebook.com/j.bradley.vantighem.

www.ingramcontent.com/pod-product-compliance
Lightning Source LLC
Chambersburg PA
CBHW030816090426
42737CB00009B/752